American Niceness

American Niceness

A CULTURAL HISTORY

Carrie Tirado Bramen

Harvard University Press

Cambridge, Massachusetts
London, England

2017

Library of Congress Cataloging-in-Publication Data
Names: Bramen, Carrie Tirado, 1964– author.
Title: American niceness : a cultural history / Carrie Tirado Bramen.
Description: Cambridge, Massachusetts : Harvard University Press, 2017. |
Includes bibliographical references and index.
Identifiers: LCCN 2017003004| ISBN 9780674976498 | Subjects: LCSH:
Friendship—United States—History. | Kindness—United
States—History. | National characteristics, American—Public opinion—
History. | Visitors, Foreign—United States—Attitudes—History.
Classification: LCC HM1161 .B73 2017 | DDC 973—dc23
LC record available at https://lccn.loc.gov/2017003004

For my daughters, Lucia and Liliana

To try to please everybody is democratic; to
be indifferent to everybody is aristocratic;
consequently, Americans, men and women,
are the best bred people in the world.

Kate Field, American journalist and actor (1873)

I don't really know what Americans are like.
I've no idea. I know a few things about them.
In my imagination, they have warm peachy
hearts, whereas the English have horrible
spiteful withered hearts.

Sebastian Horsley, British writer, artist,
and self-styled dandy, in *Interview Magazine*
(November 29, 2008)

Contents

American Niceness

Introduction:
American Niceness and the
Democratic Personality

I think everybody should like everybody.

Andy Warhol "What Is Pop Art?" *Art News* (1963)

W HEN I TOLD a British colleague that I was writing a book on American niceness, he said, without missing a beat, "It will certainly be a short book." For many readers, the concept of "American niceness" will be considered an ironic gesture at best, or a bad joke at worst. At a time when the U.S. President epitomizes the bombastic chauvinism of the Ugly American, or the "Ugly Gringo" ("*gringo feo*") to quote the former Mexican president Vicente Fox, skepticism is certainly understandable. But to assume that this skepticism began with the election of Donald Trump would be a mistake. The Ugly American has a longer history and it refers to policy as well as to people. When U.S. weapons routinely kill civilians in the Middle East, for instance, it should come as no surprise that Americans are indelibly associated with violence abroad. This point is reflected in a political cartoon where the caption "Ugly American" describes not a person but a drone.

The Ugly American also refers to violence within the nation, with countries such as France, Germany, Britain and New Zealand warning their citizens about the dangers of traveling in the United States. The Canadian government, for example, released the following statement: "The possession of firearms and the frequency of violent crime are generally more prevalent than in Canada." Although violent crime takes place primarily in "economically disadvantaged areas," the Canadian

1

government cautioned that "robbery and assault can also occur in wealthy residential and commercial districts." In 2016, the government of the Bahamas issued a travel advisory for its citizens visiting the United States, especially young men, who are asked to exercise "extreme caution" in their interactions with the police. "Do not be confrontational and cooperate," advised the Ministry of Foreign Affairs. Perhaps the Ugly American, as the Chicago journalist Joan Beck opined over two decades ago, has now become the Deadly American.[1]

Why begin a book on American niceness by discussing its opposite, namely, the Ugly American? One reason is that political cartoons and travel advisories can be instructive. They have a defamiliarizing effect that allows us to see how national self-perceptions may be challenged domestically as well as internationally. In 1902, a column in William Stead's *Review of Reviews* commented on the pedagogical function of caricatures: "In the caricatures of all nations, we find expressed with brutal candour the salient features of the impression which we produce upon our neighbours. . . . Here we can see ourselves as others see us."[2]

Cartoon by Darren Humphreys and John Schmelzer.
Licensed by CartoonStock Ltd, www.CartoonStock.com.

Introducing American niceness through the figure of the Ugly American also serves another purpose: It underscores how imbricated niceness is with its seeming opposite, nastiness. Polarities structure all nations, according to the nineteenth-century Cuban writer and revolutionary José Martí, in terms of a "permanent duel between constructive unselfishness and iniquitous hate." There are "generous Saxons" and "generous Latins," as well as egotistical examples of both. But the particular form of this duel between generosity and hate, concludes Martí, depends on the "peculiar outcome of the different historical groups."[3] Historical relations, moreover, shape modes of sociability, including affective bonds that give national formations their distinctive inflection. Mark Twain gave this national polarity an embodied form through his conjoined twins, where one brother is belligerent, aggressive, and proslavery, while the other is angelic, amiable, and an abolitionist.[4]

This dualistic portrayal of the United States actually dates back to one of the first British plays about Americans, Richard Peake's *Americans Abroad*, a two-act farce that was performed on the London stage in 1824. Considered to be one of the first antislavery plays, *Americans Abroad* contrasts the nice American, William Delapierre, a well-mannered, wealthy, and dull gentleman settled in London, with his boorish counterpart, Jonathan Doubikins, a flamboyant slaveholder who arrives in Liverpool and is soon thrown out of a hotel for beating his slave. This British depiction of Americans abroad from the early nineteenth century suggests that Americanness is characterized by doubleness—a pairing of the nice with the nasty—which conveys the contradictions at the heart of U.S. democracy as well as British ambivalence toward the nascent republic.[5]

Although the phrase "Ugly American" emerged during the Cold War, its nineteenth-century antecedent was the Vulgar American, a figure based on violence, crass materialism, and braggadocio. Fanny Trollope famously characterized this type in *The Domestic Manners of the Americans* (1832) as a tobacco-chewing, expectorating, patriotic boor with "no grace to their conversation," adding that "thank you [is] an Un-American phrase." But Trollope's churlish figure seems benign when compared to D. H. Lawrence's description of white American masculinity in *Studies in Classic American Literature* (1923): "The essential American soul is hard, isolate, stoic, and a killer. It has never yet melted."[6] These characterizations, ranging from the boorish to the murderous, depict a familiar stereotype of the American as a ruthless and violent aggressor, a national type that developed in the nineteenth century and persists in various forms today.

The predominance of the Ugly American, however, tends to overshadow its lesser-known counterpart, what Henry James and others called the "nice American." In a letter written to his mother in 1869 while traveling in Europe, the twenty-six-year-old James disparagingly commented on the "common traveling Americans" invading Europe and how "[t]heir ignorance—their stingy, defiant, grudging attitude toward everything European" seemed to confirm the Ugly American stereotype. However, three days later, in a revealing postscript in the same letter, James qualified his original assessment of Americans abroad by adding, "I *have* seen some nice Americans and I still love my country" [original emphasis].[7] Why did the young Henry James feel the need to add this postscript?

Perhaps he felt guilty for judging his compatriots so harshly given that his mother had sent her two youngest sons to fight in the Civil War, which had ended just four years earlier, with one son returning physically injured and the other emotionally damaged. Or perhaps this addendum represents James's own snobbery as a member of the Yankee elite toward the new era of mass tourism, a phenomenon that he derides with such terms as "vulgar" and "common." Whatever the reason for this postscript, the letter demonstrates James's ambivalence about identifying as American. But it is also indicative of a more widespread tension in the nineteenth century between two competing figures of national representativeness. Is the nice American the afterthought, the exception to the rule, the well-behaved and quiet anomaly to the outgoing and aggressive norm? Or does it comprise a competing model of Americanness, one that has remained suppressed in the annals of history, confined to a postscript?

By turning to the figure of the nice American and exploring its emergence in the nineteenth century, my objective is to understand how niceness has figured in a national fantasy of American exceptionalism, based not exclusively or even primarily on military might and economic prowess, but on more banal attributes such as friendliness. The distinctiveness of Americans has been largely shaped by the rhetoric of sociality and the importance of likability. Americans are unique because they are nice and friendly. The nation-state as a collective construct requires an affective, interpersonal component of everyday life.[8] In linking the impersonal with the personal, the concept of American niceness allows us to understand how national abstractions find quotidian forms through patterns of sociality.

American niceness is not only a homegrown belief; it has also been produced and perpetuated by non-Americans. Alexis de Tocqueville was among the first to observe that Americans represent a distinct, consolidated type that is selfish yet sympathetic, self-absorbed but compassionate. Their friendliness, he added, made them an ally of the French against the "unfriendly disposition of the English."[9] A century later, the German psychoanalyst Karen Horney took a far more diagnostic approach when she noted in her 1937 study of the neurotic personality that Americans, more than most, place a high premium on being liked since it is tied to the competitive aims of being popular.[10] More recently, the British novelist Geoff Dyer remarked that the "bright secret" about the United States is that "Americans are not just friendly and polite—they are also charming. And the most charming thing of all is that it rarely looks like charm." By contrast, British civil life, he adds, is "predicated on the idea that everyone just about conceals their loathing of everyone else."[11] These examples illustrate how the "nice American" type is as much an international construct as it is a national one, with a longstanding history dating back to the nineteenth century.

American "charm," to borrow Geoff Dyer's term, also has the ability to convert anti-Americanism into affection. In 1889 when Rudyard Kipling arrived in the United States, like Charles Dickens before him, annoyed at U.S. publishers for pirating his books, his initial impressions were not favorable. He described reporters as "rude children," American speech as "a horror," and was disgusted with the ubiquitous male habit of spitting. But he was soon besotted by the self-possession, independence, and charm of American women. ("They are original and regard you between the brows with unabashed eyes.") Toward the end of his book *American Notes* (1891), which consists of articles he wrote for the Indian newspaper *Allahabad Pioneer*, he remarks, "it is perfectly impossible to go to war with these people, whatever they may do. They are much too nice."[12] Kipling's travel narrative depicts the transformative power of American niceness, catalyzed in part by the allure of the American woman. (He would go on to marry an American.)

Although his narrative is full of personal reflections, Kipling was writing within a nineteenth-century transatlantic tradition of travel writing about the nice American that was established earlier in the century by such figures as the Scottish abolitionist Fanny Wright, who observed soon after her arrival in 1818 that Americans are "good-humored," "smiling," "gay-hearted," "lively," "chatty," "kind," and "full of energy." She used the word *cheerful* eleven times in her first eleven letters back home and she especially enjoyed American women's sweetness, liveliness, and gaiety of heart, in contrast to English women's coldness and indifference.[13] Charles Dickens, despite the fact that he could never imagine an Englishman being happy living in the United States, similarly described Americans in the 1840s as "friendly, earnest, hospitable, kind, frank, very often accomplished, far less prejudiced than you would suppose, warm-hearted, fervent and enthusiastic."[14] Although the literal phrase "nice American" was not in common parlance in the nineteenth century, Americans were nonetheless repeatedly described in terms of friendliness and amiability.

Robert Louis Stevenson referred to this quality that I am calling American niceness as the "uncivil kindness of the Americans," which he described as "perhaps their most bewildering character to one newly landed." In his journey to California on an emigrant train where he nearly died from a severe fever, Stevenson explained how he propped open the door of a railcar with his foot to get some air when the newsboy who was selling various items brusquely pushed his foot aside. Alarmed at the boy's rudeness, Stevenson seethed quietly and expected an altercation, when suddenly the same newsboy touched his shoulder and placed a ripe pear in his hand. "For the rest of the journey I was petted like a sick child; he lent me newspapers, thus depriving himself of his legitimate profit on their sale, and came repeatedly to sit by me and cheer me up."[15] This combination of rudeness and compassion is precisely what distinguishes American niceness from Old World civility. Niceness shares with civility the ability to facilitate social exchanges among strangers; it allows us to live a common life with others. But where civility demands a mastery of social form that involves disciplining one's impulses and passions for the sake of manners and decorum, niceness can be rough around the edges. One may not be able to grasp the protocols of politeness, but still have a sense of decency.

The frequent references in nineteenth-century travel writing to American amiability suggest that the nice American is as pervasive as its negative counterpart, but it has been neither studied nor defined as explicitly. This is partly due to the fact that niceness is assumed to be a national default mode, an obvious and superficial gesture not worthy of serious inquiry. Its banality puts it under the radar of cultural analysis. My fundamental claim is that even though it often goes unnamed as a pattern of behavior, niceness pervades the everyday conduct, assumptions, and discourses of and about Americans.

The Legacy of 9/11: Why Do They Hate Us?

My interest in this project began as a way to make sense of the question that one frequently heard in the aftermath of 9/11: "Why do they hate us?" This question, which was so pervasive that President George W. Bush included it in his speech to Congress two weeks after the attack, assumes that Americans are not the ones who hate, but rather are the passive victims of another's wrath.[16] This point is reinforced grammatically, where "us" is the direct object, the recipient of the action, and not the actor, a point that reflects semantically the national response to the crisis, namely that Americans are the innocent targets of Middle Eastern hate. This response illustrates Christopher Bollas's psychoanalytic concept of "violent innocence," which describes how violence is projected onto the other in order to protect oneself from acknowledging one's own capacity to be violent.[17] This act of projection keeps one virtuous and innocent in a Manichean world of good against evil. Americans are the victims of violence but not the agents of violence. It is anathema to a national sensibility based on a fundamental belief in our own capacity for niceness: We can be hated but we cannot be the haters.[18]

The post-9/11 question—"Why do they hate us?"—functions less as a question than a way of making sense of a complex incident by personalizing the political. The global, structural, and historical dimensions of the event are reduced to an interpersonal matter of envy and hatred. It translates a political crisis into a problem of sociability. "Why do they hate us?" is another way of asking "Why don't they like us?" This interrogative response comprehends 9/11 as a failure of likability, and, in particular, a failure of Americans to convert animosity into affection. When it was rumored that one of the hijackers may have lived in Western New York, a bewildered, highly educated neighbor asked how someone could live in our community and still want to kill us. This response, which was all too common in the aftermath of 9/11, assumes the existence of American niceness, along with the belief that Americans can convert even the staunchest anti-American into a friend through a democratic personality that is friendly, amiable, and charming. To know us, the question assumes, is to love us.

The crisis of 9/11 elicited a response that made a certain collective habit of thought perceptible; it triggered a pattern of reactivity that disclosed how firmly rooted Americans' belief in their own niceness is so that it has achieved the status of common sense. American niceness represents less a grand narrative than a sensibility that characterizes the national psyche so profoundly that it does not have to be named. It is a reflex rather than a reasoned response that is as natural as saying "have a nice day."[19]

This book explores how niceness became a way of identifying Americans both at home and abroad. My objective is not to establish whether or not Americans are, in fact, genuinely nice people. I do not think one can make such a claim about any collective, never mind an entire nation. Nor do I want to go to the opposite extreme and say that American niceness is nothing but a lie, a disguise behind which the ugly "truth" about "real" Americans can be found. Instead, I will explore the kinds of cultural work that American niceness has done as a collective behavior that is socially sanctioned as normative. Niceness implies that Americans are fundamentally well-meaning people defined by an essential goodness. Even acts of aggression are framed as passive, reluctant, and defensive acts to protect oneself against the potential aggression of another.

My point is that American niceness assumes that Americans are decent and good-natured people with the best of intentions. Even if they do serious damage in the world, American niceness means that the damage will more than likely be seen as a mistake. This is a version of innocence that Graham Greene described as distinctly American: "innocence ... like a dumb leper who has lost his bell, wandering the world, meaning no harm."[20] It is like having a permanent get-out-of-jail-free card that exempts Americans from acknowledging the consequences of their actions. Political theorist George Shulman defines acknowledgment as the words and actions through which we recognize (or not) the reality of the suffering of others, and the opposite of acknowledgment is disavowal, the willful ignorance of not knowing or what Michael Rogin describes as "motivated forgetting."[21] Such forgetting, as the historian Ernest Renan noted in the nineteenth century, is necessary for nation-building. In the context of American niceness, forgetting depends on repetition, a habit of thought that relies on the reiteration of clichés and banal truisms. Part of the cultural work of clichés is their ability to abet the process of forgetting through their capacity to suppress, conceal, and disavow historical consequences. American niceness is the mechanism through which memory and forgetting play out in the everyday exchanges and social practices that sustain a nation ideologically at home and abroad.

Why Niceness?

Of all the words associated with positive sociality, why focus on niceness? I am drawn to this term because of its ubiquity; its pervasiveness makes it commonplace. It appears to be bankrupt of meaning and especially of any political significance. The word *nice* also has a distinct connection to Americanness in ways that synonyms such as *amiable* and *friendly* do not necessarily have. As Marilyn Monroe noted in 1962, in what would be her last interview, "I was brought up differently from the average American child because the average child is brought up expecting to be happy. 'Have a nice day,' as one might say."[22] Such an expression, as Monroe suggests, is utterly clichéd, but it is also implicated in a class and racial culture—with the affective mandate of cheerfulness—that became representative of normative Americanness. I am interested in how niceness became normative for white middle-class America, and how other, lesser-known appropriations of niceness occurred along the way.

Niceness also has a fascinating etymological history that suggests that seemingly vapid terms are rich with social and historical significance, often possessing contradictory and inconsistent meanings that can be useful for the semiotic archaeologist as well as for the cultural historian. The vacuity of niceness seems to have haunted the term from its very beginning, with its Latin derivation *nescius,* which means "foolish" and "silly." (One does not want to be a philological essentialist, but it does appear that banality was inscribed into the term's etymological DNA.) The word *nice* appears in the first dictionary of the English language, Robert Cawdrey's *A Table Alphabeticall* (1604), where it is defined as "slow and laysie," and its origins are deemed unequivocally French. In the sixteenth and seventeenth centuries, *nice* was also an ambiguous term that could be either an insult or a compliment, referring to someone who was either ostentatiously or elegantly dressed. Not even context in many cases could clarify its intended meaning. By the eighteenth century, the term finally acquired semantic clarity as discerning, delicate, fastidious, and, aptly enough, precise. But the precision of its meaning was short-lived, as the term became a favorite slang expression in the early nineteenth century, when it meant pleasing.

This semantic evolution of *nice* from "precise" to "pleasing" is a distinctly nineteenth-century story that is also transatlantic in scope. The story of *nice* is unusual and surprisingly controversial because it is founded on a paradox, namely, that a word associated with "pleasing" should invoke such displeasure and that the agreeable should be rejected as vulgar. To illustrate the intensity of this (mainly British) disapproval, consider the opening footnote of Thomas De Quincey's essay "English Dictionaries," which is an impassioned tirade against the slang use of *nice* that he describes as "the most shocking of the unscholarlike barbarisms now prevalent." What De Quincey finds most galling is the term's versatility; it could now refer to an object as well as to a person. Loyal to its eighteenth-century meaning, De Quincey insists that "a nice young lady means a fastidious young lady; and a 'nice letter' ought to mean a letter that is delicate in its eating." De Quincey was not alone in his outrage. An 1832 article in the short-lived British journal *Philological Museum* similarly described the popular notion of *nice* as "that stupid modern vulgarism," a term that can now be used indiscriminately to refer to a tragedy as well as a cheesecake.[23] British philologists commonly blamed the degeneration of *nice* on the Americanization of the English language.

In 1898, Brander Matthews, an American playwright and professor of English at Columbia, published a short piece in *Harper's* on the dynamic aspects of language, focusing on the slang use of *nice*. According to Matthews, *nice* as a synonym for the word *pleasing* began as a British "perversion" and was imported to the United States.[24] Its slang usage seems to have originated among British youth, as Matthews notes, but it is important to point out that this slang form of *nice* first became official in the United States, appearing in one of the first editions of Webster's *The American Dictionary of the English Language* (1868), published after the Civil War. For the first time, the respectable, eighteenth-century definition of *nice* as "delicacy" and "exactness" was demoted to a secondary definition, while its slang usage became dominant. In fact, the editors included a note explaining this shift: "Of late a new sense has been introduced, which excludes them [delicacy and exactness], namely, *pleasing;* as a *nice* girl." (British dictionaries continued to list the eighteenth-century meaning of *nice* as its primary definition throughout the late nineteenth century with just a passing reference to its colloquial meaning as "pleasing.") [25]

This semantic coup, whereby the erstwhile colony formally altered Standard English, was the philological equivalent of the spirit of '76. Walt Whitman and Brander Matthews after him hailed this disruptive quality of slang, describing it as a "lawless germinal element," a generative force of culture that was based in common speech. "Certainly philologists," Whitman remarked in "Slang in America," "have not given enough attention to this element and its results."[26] Slang, for Whitman and Matthews, was a democratic form of language, and its usurpation of official speech was not a sign of cultural declension, as De Quincey understood it, but the opposite, cultural vitality.

The Victorian history of *nice* concludes in 1906 when the typically composed lexicographers of the *Oxford English Dictionary* (OED)—in a rare moment of acknowledging their own fallibility—admitted defeat: They could not account for the "semantic development" of the word from its Latin meaning as "foolish" and "silly" to its modern usage as "pleasing." This word, they concluded, "is unparalleled in Latin or in the Romance languages." This admission of bafflement suggests the surprising density of the word *nice.* There is a complexity to the superficial and banal that is worth exploring not in order to reveal its hidden depths but to show how surfaces themselves can be complicated and multivalenced.

On the Versatility of Niceness

To understand the versatility of niceness, Valentin Voloshinov's concept of "multiaccentuality" is especially helpful because it refers to a sign's ability to have different meanings, or what Voloshinov calls "refractions," in different contexts in order to serve a variety of often conflicting ideological positions. The linguistic sign, according to Voloshinov, "becomes an arena of the class struggle" where "various different classes will use one and the same language. As a result, differently oriented accents intersect in every ideological sign." It is precisely through this contested semiotic ground that a sign such as American niceness maintains its "vitality and dynamism and the capacity for further development."[27] But, according to Voloshinov, the vitality and mutability of the sign is always under attack, since the ruling class wants to suppress the contested nature of language and instead strives "to make the sign uniaccentual." Ordinarily, the contradictions lodged in every sign remain suppressed in their dominant usage, and some signs simply become worn out—so utterly banal that they are no longer capable of "serving as arenas for the clash of live social accents."[28] This is why the historian and the philologist are important for Voloshinov, because they can excavate the traces of past contestations, and, in doing so, they can unleash the residual vitality still lingering even within exhausted signs.

In terms of my own project, a cultural history that is especially attentive to the use of linguistic signs can reveal how a banal and over-used word like *nice* can have complex and even violent historical resonances embedded within it, which, when revealed, can demonstrate a clash of social accents that can potentially restore the term's multiaccentuality. The process of philological restoration can recover the forgotten traces of refracted meanings to tell different stories about American niceness, ones that can turn the historical amnesia of disavowal into recognition. Consequently, the traumatic consequences of indigenous genocide and African enslavement—the twinned traumas of the nineteenth century—can in part be acknowledged in banal truisms and clichés.

There is a final aspect of Voloshinov's definition of multiaccentuality that is pertinent to the notion of American niceness: "[E]ach living ideological sign has two faces, like Janus. Any current curse word can become a word of praise, any current truth must inevitably sound to many other people as the greatest lie. This *inner dialectic quality* of the sign comes out fully in the open only in times of social crises or revolutionary change."[29] It is this "inner dialectic quality" that prevents the notion of American niceness from becoming a grand narrative, an abstract ontological category that explains national distinctiveness as *sui generis.* This book will illustrate precisely how the shadow side of niceness—its "inner dialectical quality"—can be made visible by recovering alternative practices of niceness, such as Native American hospitality, to underscore how the making of the United States as a white settler nation can be seen through the contested terrain of sociability.

The cultural work that niceness performed during this period was extensive, contradictory, and long-lasting, and it coincided with the development of the nation from a nascent republic that was largely agricultural at the start of the nineteenth century to an imperial power in the aftermath of the Spanish American War of 1898. Just as the word *nice* underwent a seismic shift in the nineteenth century from its vulgar slang usage as "pleasing" to its official recognition in dictionaries of Standard English, so the United States transformed from an erstwhile colony to an imperial power, moving from the global margins to the center.

This expansion required a tremendous amount of sustained and systematic violence, the highlights of which are as follows: Indian Removal policies that began in the early colonial period and then became far more systematic during the Revolutionary War, with George Washington ordering the destruction of nearly sixty Iroquoian villages in New York State in 1779 by destroying their crops and homes. Such policies continued throughout the nineteenth century, peaking in the 1830s, when the Cherokees were forced off their farms in a nine-month trek westward called the "Trail of Tears," killing over 8,000 men, women, and children.[30] Indian removal was accompanied by white settler violence that destroyed Indian homes, Indian crops, and other forms of Indian sustainability.

The nineteenth century also witnessed the expansion of slavery, which Frederick Douglass described as "this huge system of iniquity." In 1860, there were four million slaves in the United States. But by 1865, the institution had been abolished after a four-year Civil War that cost 750,000 lives, mainly from disease. There were 1.2 million wounded, including 30,000–40,000 amputees among Union troops (there is no equivalent data for Confederate soldiers).[31] Soon after the Civil War, however, slavery reconfigured itself in the form of peonage labor, a point that Mark Twain would continue to make long after many contented themselves with the triumph of the Union. On the eve of the election of 1872, Frederick Douglass similarly warned, "the slave demon still rides the southern gale, and breathes out fire and wrath."[32]

In the Gilded Age, Jim Crow laws and lynching coincided with the passage of the Chinese Exclusion Act that limited Asian immigration to the United States. During this same period, American labor suffered extraordinary violence at the hands of bosses, their lackeys, and the state, leading historians to conclude that "the United States has had the bloodiest and most violent labor history of any industrial nation in the world."[33] Finally, U.S. foreign policy took on a decidedly military cast ranging from the annexation of Texas (1836) and the Mexican American War (1846–1848), where Mexico ceded half of its territory to the United States, to the illegal invasions of Nicaragua and Cuba in the 1850s and the acquisition of its first colonies in the aftermath of the Spanish American War. As the word *nice* underwent a semantic expansion in the nineteenth century to include people as well as objects, so the national borders of the United States experienced a dramatic expansion in the name of manifest destiny. The fact that the semantic expansion was done in the name of pleasing, while the latter was accomplished through the barrel of a gun points to one of the defining contradictions of American niceness: that the concept appeared and expanded during a century of unprecedented bloodshed.

And yet, despite all this violence, W. E. B. Du Bois could reflect on the nineteenth century and declare in *The Souls of Black Folk* (1903) that it was "the first century of human sympathy," when the boundaries of caring expanded to include those who were historically deemed inferior:

> The nineteenth was the first century of human sympathy,—the age when half wonderingly we began to descry in others that transfigured spark of divinity which we call Myself when clodhoppers and peasants, and tramps and thieves, and millionaires and—sometimes— Negroes, became throbbing souls whose warm pulsing life touched us so nearly that we half gasped with surprise. . . .[34]

Du Bois credits the nineteenth century for expanding the bounds of the human. For the first time, the poor and people of color were recognized as possessing a soul. They had an interiority that was considered sacred and contained "that transfigured spark of divinity." This recognition, according to Du Bois, was an ethical innovation; it marked a significant leap in the social evolution of a collective conscience. But Du Bois was certainly not a naïve optimist. Beginning in 1910, he became editor of *The Crisis*, where he published articles, editorials, and statistics on the lynching of black men in the South. How can we account for his observations on racial violence alongside his acknowledgment of human sympathy? What sense can be made of the coexistence of physical devastation and ethical progress? The task of the intellectual, as Du Bois seems to suggest in making this observation, is to try to understand this paradox of modern times, a paradox that the psychoanalytic critic Jacqueline Rose aptly describes as "the human capacity for destruction and the human capacity for improvement," a conflict that has only intensified since the nineteenth century.[35]

This book returns to the nineteenth century—a century of national trauma and nascent humanitarian reckoning—to understand the context in which American niceness as a typological discourse of personality emerged and developed. The multiaccentual forms that niceness took were in part shaped by this century of crisis. It is worth exploring and unpacking the layers of American niceness—who claimed it and why—to discover how the nineteenth century, as an age of unparalleled brutality and compassion, established patterns of behavior that still define Americans today.

On National Types

What figural forms did the nice American take? As a way of characterizing U.S. democracy, niceness played a central role in the formation of a typological discourse that shaped and defined the terms of national visibility in the nineteenth century. The literary critic Amanda Anderson has argued that political practices need to have some sort of human form in order to be understood: "[P]olitical orientations and commitments can never be understood or grasped—or even made manifest in the first place—except through forms of human expression that also reflect, and are routinely taken to reflect, attitudes, dispositions, and characterological elements."[36] As a system of government, democracy is often defined by abstract terms such as consensus and egalitarianism. But democracy is not exclusively about formal reasoning and deliberation; it is also a culture, as the historian Jeffrey Stout has argued, with "enduring attitudes, concerns, dispositions, and patterns of conduct."[37] The personal and the political are combined in our understanding of democracy in a complicated dynamic, where the personalization of the political can be problematically simplistic. But it would be a mistake to dismiss the personal turn entirely, not least because it is the means through which we come to understand political practices as relational forms.

In the nineteenth century, the nice American was largely defined against the haughty Briton as the figural expression of a democratic personality. In 1873, the American journalist and actor Kate Field crystallized this sentiment when she wrote in her travelogue, "To try to please everybody is democratic; to be indifferent to everybody is aristocratic; consequently, Americans, men and women, are the best bred people in the world."[38] Defined against Old World snobbery, the nice American personifies a democratic sensibility, a type of person whose earnest and informal disposition is a refreshing alternative to European aristocratic stuffiness. Yet Field's declamatory words exude a tone of hubris: Americans are not just nice but their niceness is a sign of their exceptionalism; they are, after all, "the best bred people in the world." The rhetoric of American niceness is comparative and competitive. It represents a paradoxical form of democratic arrogance, where Americans are not just friendly but superior in their friendliness. Walt Whitman provides a variation on this theme when he claims that Americans are not only good-hearted, but "the peaceablest and most good-hearted race in the world."[39]

Niceness works in the service of American exceptionalism in setting the groundwork early in the century for what would be understood by the time of the Spanish American War of 1898 as a "democratic empire" or an "imperial republic," committed to what President William McKinley described as "benevolent assimilation." But the ideology of national exceptionalism, as Noam Chomsky has remarked, is not unique to the United States. All world powers have invoked their own specialness to justify their actions. As sociologist Julian Go and historian Anne L. Foster have argued, "The exceptionalist paradigm is possible only through comparison and contrast between the United States and other imperial powers or processes."[40] It is important, in other words, not to exceptionalize American exceptionalism, but rather to interrogate the rhetorical terms and the figural forms of its specialness, and the aggression and injustice that they have enabled. In the U.S. context, this process has involved constructing a democratic personality that is likable and amiable.

For some readers, studying the formation of a national type may seem distinctly old-fashioned and even intellectually dubious. As Theodor Adorno noted in his study of the authoritarian personality, no concept "has been so thoroughly criticized as that of typology."[41] Alongside psychological types, national types have been equally maligned. In *The Protestant Ethic and the "Spirit" of Capitalism*, Max Weber remarked, "Appeals to the 'national character' are . . . a mere confession of *ignorance*," and yet in the same book, he criticizes the greedy Chinese and the shifty Italians, and in doing so exemplifies exactly what he condemns, namely, confessing his own ignorance in making national generalizations.[42] This paradox of national character, which is at once detested and yet still invoked when it suits the purposes of the author, is best described by the historian David Stannard who has observed that "historians take a dim view of any serious attempts to generalize about the 'character' of a nation; on the other hand, most of them constantly do it."[43] Even the term "national identity" suffers from the same dilemma, in the sense that it is a stereotypical concept that can be just as elusive and over-comprehensive as its unfashionable "American character" counterpart. Because of these problems with and concerns about the use of national types, scholars in the humanities have been hesitant to address the persistence of national types and how historical formations, such as nation-states, acquire characterological form internally as well as externally, through domestic and international modes of interpellation.

There is a further dilemma that Fanny Trollope noticed during her extensive stay in the United States, that generalizing about Americans is anathema to most Americans. It goes against the individualist grain. How can anyone generalize about a nation as varied and complex as the United States? While living in Cincinnati for two years, Trollope would share her observations about Americans with her neighbors, but her observations would immediately be met with qualifications. She concluded, "Americans always say that we are too varied; you can't generalize about us."[44] From my experience writing this book, it seems that Americans prefer generalizing about distinct regions rather than the nation as a whole. What about "Iowa nice," "Minnesota nice," or "Carolina nice"? There seem to be as many varieties of niceness as there are states. This suggests that the old debate between federalism and states' rights has an affective dimension, with the legacy of anti-federalism presenting niceness as a local phenomenon, limited to the geographic parameters of state lines, rather than reflecting a national sensibility. Trollope's astute observation from 1832 that Americans prefer to localize their generalities still seems to hold true today. One can generalize about "Iowa nice," for instance, with some degree of confidence but not about the nation as a whole. Although I do explore Southern niceness in the context of slavery in Chapter 2, I do not address the other regional forms of niceness. I will leave that task to others.

Although a study of national types is considered slightly embarrassing for the humanist, such research has garnered federal funding in both the social sciences and health sciences. The National Institute of Health's Biomedical Research Center in Baltimore, Maryland, has set up a Laboratory of Personality and Cognition to establish, in part, a metrics of national character. Robert McCrae, a social psychologist for the U.S. Department of Health and Human Services at the National Institutes of Health, published the results of a national character survey, based on the judgments of five "expert" judges, four of whom were social psychologists who had lived in Japan and the United States. In this survey, Americans scored a high 8.0 for altruism on a scale of 1–10, compared to the Japanese, who received a lukewarm 5.2. In terms of warmth, Americans scored 7.4, whereas the Japanese received another 5.2.[45] McCrae's research confirms American niceness by suggesting through quantitative analysis that Americans are warmer and more altruistic than their Japanese counterparts.

Interestingly, McCrae, whose research is devoted to analyzing the relationship between culture and personality, dismisses national character stereotypes as "groundless." He prefers another concept called "facets of ethos," which describes the "personality profile of the culture itself," unmediated by stereotypical thinking. Although McCrae wants to situate national differences in taxonomies uncontaminated by cultural truisms, his study nonetheless demonstrates the pervasiveness and power of national stereotypes: the disciplined Japanese versus the warmhearted Americans. In contrast to McCrae, who wants to think beyond national stereotypes, I suggest that national stereotypes need to be analyzed, historicized, and defamiliarized because they are anything but "groundless." National clichés are repetitive, predictable, and unoriginal, but they are also ideologically powerful and historically rich. As the nineteenth-century American writer Elizabeth Stuart Phelps once wrote, "Type, not argument, governs men."[46]

Although McCrae's research reluctantly confirms the persistence of stereotypical thinking about national differences, it cannot actually explain how these differences acquired their form. Why are the Japanese associated with discipline and not altruism, while Americans are perceived as tenderhearted? The question of why national cultures take the form they do was addressed by Otto Bauer (whose sister Ida Bauer was "Dora," one of Sigmund Freud's most famous patients). A Jewish intellectual and socialist leader of the Austrian Social Democratic Party in the early twentieth century and author of *The Question of Nationalities and Social Democracy* (1907), Bauer did not assume a national *geist* but instead interrogated it: "Rather than constituting an explanation, the national character itself needs to be explained."[47] Writing on the eve of World War I, Bauer was especially interested in what constitutes Germanness and what establishes the national sense of belonging among Germans. The question of national character fascinated Bauer because he felt that an international solidarity movement needed to acknowledge the national particularities that differentiate the German working class, for instance, from the Italian working class. For Bauer, national cultures have a real historical and material impact on the formation of social movements. Internationalism does not simply transcend the national, but it has to be constituted through diverse iterations of the national.

The questions that guide my own study are influenced by Bauer's analytical approach: How do specific cultural practices become characteristic of a nation? By what authority does the particular become nationally representative? And how does niceness, a term that describes interpersonal sociability, become emblematic of the United States? My goal is not to vindicate national types in order to show that they really are accurate, but rather to interrogate how they are histori-cally constructed and modified over time in order to understand the cultural and political authority that national clichés still wield. Types are both repetitive and differentiated, which is to say that they contain a sameness reproduced over time that is familiar and recognizable, while also being dynamic, with various inflections that demonstrate how types, like Voloshinov's signs, are highly contested.

The pervasiveness of American niceness is therefore significant: Its repetition reinforces the truisms that define national types. As the Dutch critic Joep Leerssen has argued in his study of the semiotic for-mation of national character, "national stereotypes [are] structural ele-ments in a grammar of characterization." He goes on to emphasize the vital role of imitativeness: "National characterizations, like other ste-reotypes, function as commonplaces—utterances that have obtained a ring of familiarity though frequent reiteration. Their strongest rhetor-ical effect lies in this familiarity and recognition value rather than in their empirical truth value."[48] Like the emergent discourse of adver-tising, national types represent a form of branding—a way of acquiring visibility through reiterative practices.

Brother Jonathan as the Nice American

The nineteenth century inherited from the eighteenth century a fascina-tion with classification, epitomized in the *Encyclopédie* of Denis Diderot and Jean le Rond d'Alembert, in which they define national character as a personality trait attributed to each European nation: "[I]t is a sort of proverb to say: airy as a Frenchman, jealous as an Italian, serious as a Spaniard, wicked as an Englishman, proud as a Scot, drunk as a German, lazy as an Irishman, deceitful as a Greek."[49] National types are reductive, simplistic, and, at times, even humorous. They iron out differences in order to give the nation-state an easily readable character so that it is identifiable within a nascent narrative of international relations. It is better to be seen as a wicked Englishman, for instance, than not to be seen at all. For a white settler nation like the United States, its task was to make the New World visible by expanding Diderot's eighteenth-century catalog of European types to include them. How better to contrast a newly sovereign nation against its erstwhile monarch than to claim the opposite of English wickedness? Niceness was the ticket to American visibility and the next step was to give it bodily form.

During the War of 1812, which came to be known as the second war of American independence, the American James Kirke Paulding published a political satire entitled *The Diverting History of John Bull and Brother Jonathan* (1812). Paulding depicts Britain as the cantankerous John Bull, who first appeared in the British popular press a century earlier, and he includes a comparatively new character in his transatlantic political allegory, John Bull's youngest son—and his least favorite—Brother Jonathan, a well-intentioned and inoffensive man who represents the United States.[50] In terms of disposition, father and son are clearly opposites. John Bull, a "cholerick old fellow," lives on Bullock Island and is a quarrelsome and bad-tempered bully with an "overbearing disposition, which was always getting him into some scrape or another." He is rarely seen "without a broken head, a black eye, or a bloody nose."[51] By contrast, Brother Jonathan is a tall, awkward, and simple rustic with a "lively, shrewd look" and the promise of great strength. As an antecedent to Uncle Sam, Brother Jonathan is cast as a "peaceable young fellow," who does not lightly get into a quarrel, and "hated fighting and loved gain."[52] In fact, Paulding underscores Jonathan's patience and reluctance to engage in conflict, in stark contrast with Richard Peake's Jonathan Doubikins, who is thrown out of a Liverpool inn for beating his slave. Unlike the irascible John Bull, Brother Jonathan is long-suffering and "often put up with ill treatment rather than disturb the neighborhood."[53] Brother Jonathan represents the spurned son, a New World revision of the prodigal son, who desires parental love but instead is scorned: "[I]f he had been treated with any sort of fatherly kindness, [he] would have loved him with all his heart." Jonathan's mother, Mrs. Bull, is just as awful, admitting that she has "never much liked the poor fellow."[54] For Paulding, Brother Jonathan embodies the prototypical nice American, who is gentle, kind, and industrious, the innocent victim of parental hostility, preferring to work independently on his farm rather than fight with others.

Thomas Jefferson, Anti-Americanism, and "Why Do [the British] Hate Us?"

John Bull's rejection of Brother Jonathan as the personification of anti-Americanism is one of the founding discourses of and about the United States. The emergence of anti-Americanism coincides with the origin of the nation in the 1770s and 1780s. The OED, that official font of semantic origins, notes that the earliest usage of "anti-Americanism" was in 1773 as a distinctly American term to describe foreign hostility. One sees evidence of it in British humor, as in Samuel Johnson's witty remark from 1778, "I am willing to love all mankind, except an American."[55] French anti-Americanism of the period took a far more humorless form in its "scientific" obsession over nitrate levels in the soil of Pennsylvania and humidity levels in Virginia.[56] And in 1783, the German historian A. L. von Schlözer anticipated a critique that would only intensify in the nineteenth century, specifically, that the United States represents a commercial society that has replaced monarchy and aristocracy with "the nobility of money, which is far more dangerous and tyrannical."[57] Whatever form anti-Americanism took in Europe in the latter half of the eighteenth century to the early nineteenth century, commentators have typically characterized it as an elitist mindset, one shared by aristocrats and the traditional intelligentsia alike.

But Thomas Jefferson, who was an astute observer of anti-Americanism, remarked in a letter from Paris in 1786 that the British contempt for Americans went far beyond the ruling classes. "The spirit of hostility to us has always existed in the mind of the King, but it has now extended itself through the whole mass of the people."[58] Ten years after the signing of the Declaration of Independence, Thomas Jefferson visited Britain as Minister to France, and he was surprised by the extent of anti-Americanism he encountered. In a letter to his close friend John Page, he admits that Britain "hates us, their ministers hate us, and their King more than all other men ... I think their hostility towards us is much more deeply rooted at present than during the war."[59] He found the "impudence" of British anti-Americanism unsettling. When he met King George III at a reception, accompanied by Minister to Britain John Adams in 1786, the king treated them with contempt by literally turning his back upon his American visitors.[60] In his *Autobiography*, Jefferson describes the king as "that mulish being" and notes that "the distance and disinclination which he betrayed in his conversations, the vagueness & evasions of his answers to us, confirmed me in the belief of their aversion to have anything to do with us."[61] In this brief encounter, which really was a non-encounter, the king's behavior was consistent with the way Jefferson characterized him in the Declaration of Independence as "deaf to the voice of justice & of consanguinity." In the Declaration, Jefferson frames the political crisis as a crisis of communication, where the king is blamed for not listening to the "good people." Not surprisingly, Jefferson's *Autobiography* juxtaposes British nastiness with French amiability, and it concludes with effusive praise of French sociality: "A more benevolent people, I have never known, nor greater warmth & devotedness."[62]

What is striking about Jefferson's account of his visit to Britain is the extent to which British anti-Americanism shocks him. I find it curious that the author of the Declaration of Independence, which is, after all, a declaration of war, should be surprised and offended that he is greeted with hostility. He sees himself as the innocent victim of English wrath and the question that begs to be asked but remains unstated is "Why do they hate us?" At points, Jefferson sounds like the rejected son whose father has literally and metaphorically turned his back on him and refuses to acknowledge his existence. This is the son's punishment for challenging paternal authority, committing a political form of patricide, and asserting his autonomy. One of the functions of American niceness then is the persistent enabling of Americans' desire to see themselves as the victims, more sinned against than sinning. From the beginning, whether it was Thomas Jefferson or Brother Jonathan, Americans cast themselves as the innocent victims of English wrath.

With victimhood extolled, American niceness could be read symptomatically as a defensive reaction against anti-Americanism. British anti-Americanism, in particular, often took the form of deflating American sanctimoniousness by showing the absurdity of a democratic republic founded on slavery and Indian expulsion. Perhaps with Jefferson in mind, the English radical Thomas Day wrote in 1776, "If there be an object truly ridiculous in nature, it is an American patriot, signing resolutions of independency with the one hand, and with the other brandishing a whip over his affrighted slaves."[63]

A half century later, Fanny Trollope's anti-Americanism included humorous quips about "republican pigs" and the pervasiveness of spitting, but there was also a serious side to her critique, one that scandalously described Thomas Jefferson as an "unprincipled tyrant" who fathered children "by almost all his numerous gang of female slaves."[64] Living in the United States during the debates on Indian removal,

Trollope also wrote poignantly and powerfully about the injustice of U.S. policy toward its indigenous people:

> But it is impossible for any mind of common honesty not to be revolted by the contradictions in their principles and practice. They inveigh against the governments of Europe, because, as they say, they favour the powerful and oppress the weak . . . you will see them with one hand hoisting the cap of liberty, and with the other flogging their slaves. You will see them one hour lecturing their mob on the indefeasible rights of man, and the next driving from their homes the children of the soil, whom they have bound themselves to protect by the most solemn treaties.[65]

Trollope, who went on to write an abolitionist novel four years later entitled *Jonathan Jefferson Whitlaw*, concludes her travel narrative by declaring, "I do not like [the American people]. I do not like their principles, I do not like their manners, I do not like their opinions."[66] Her critique of the policies and manners of Americans—a critique that was both structural and personal—made her a reviled figure in the United States. To this day, studies of anti-Americanism will quote selectively from Trollope's *Domestic Manners of the Americans*, omitting her more serious criticisms of racial injustice and instead focusing on her remarks about the boorishness of white Americans. This is largely due to the fact that anti-Americanism is often dismissed as an irrational discourse full of petty complaints and invidious sentiments not rooted in legitimate social and political grievances against the United States.

I mention these instances of anti-Americanism to highlight the important strain of American niceness that developed as a homegrown response to foreign hostility, a defense mechanism to deflect anti-Americanism through the rhetoric of amiability and good intentions. In its crudest form, it can be an orchestrated government strategy, as in George W. Bush's "charm offensive" in the aftermath of the U.S. invasion of Iraq when he sent Under Secretary of Public Diplomacy Karen Hughes to the Middle East in 2005 to fight anti-Americanism, equipped with a necklace designed by the Egyptian jeweler Azza Fahmy with the words love, sincerity, and friendship engraved in Arabic.[67] But charm offensives can also work more subtly in the areas of literature and culture to produce a way of being in the world that creates a general impression—an atmosphere of amiability—that converts antipathy into affection.

Each chapter of this book tells the story of the contested uses of American niceness—how mutually exclusive positions claimed to be nice as a distinctive feature of being American. From Native American hospitality, to the (in)decipherability of the slave's smile, to the amiability of Jesus, the uses and abuses of feminine niceness, and ultimately, the fantasy of a democratic empire in the Philippines, *American Niceness: A Cultural History* explores the intersectional formation of American identity through race, gender, class, and religion as seen through the refracted lens of sociality. The contested terrain of American niceness has never been an equal playing field of pluralistic voices. Rather, it is highly asymmetrical and mediated through the uneven distribution of power. For this reason, I spend the remainder of the introduction laying out the dominant formation of American niceness, by telling the story of how whiteness acquired a distinctly amiable inflection in the United States, structured in large part through the niceness (as well as the anger) of subaltern Americans. This dominant version of American niceness is not the whole story, as the following chapters will elaborate, but it provides an important perspective from which to understand alternative versions.

To begin with, Anglo-Americans did not invoke the rhetoric of niceness in consistent or uniform ways. Washington Irving and Lydia Maria Child, for instance, acknowledged the long legacy of white settler violence against indigenous communities that led to nineteenth-century calls of shame. Abolitionists such as Harriet Beecher Stowe called on Southern slaveholders to manumit their slaves. In other words, there was no Anglo-American consensus about who or what the nice American signified. But a hegemonic formation of American niceness nevertheless developed that we can describe by returning to Christopher Bollas's notion of "violent innocence," a concept that refers to the displacement of aggression onto another so as to make oneself seem virtuous. "Violent innocence" describes the psychological mechanism necessary to create a white Christian settler nation, where innocence is regenerative and disavowal represents a habitual mode of thinking. This dominant story is significant precisely because the dialectical quality of American niceness depends on it.

The Hegemonic Story of the Nice American

The hegemonic story of American niceness begins with its founding document, namely, the Declaration of Independence. What stands out about this document, which carefully outlines the reasons for war, is that its authors went to great lengths not to offend the British. This strategy is evident in the opening sentence when independence is declared using the passive voice: "it becomes necessary." The opening scene is bereft of actors as well as action. And yet, in the next paragraph, it calls for the people "to alter or to abolish" a government that no longer represents them. In contrast to Thomas Paine, whose impassioned prose in *Common Sense* actively attacks and vilifies the British crown with such sentences as "the palaces of kings are built upon the ruins of the bowers of paradise," the Declaration rhetorically walks on eggshells. Where Paine wants to break with the Crown ("renounce the alliance"), the Declaration opts to "dissolve the political bands."[68] The Declaration of Independence is a revolutionary text articulated in the politest of terms.

The colonists speak in terms of "facts," using the collective voice of the Enlightenment, of self-controlled, rational, and moderate subjects. For white America, described in the Declaration as "the good people," there is no rage; there is no violence. They already exhibit the exemplary conduct necessary for a democracy, according to the political theorist Jacques Rancière, that is, to be "well-behaved."[69] The Americans were reluctant revolutionaries; their desire was to reestablish harmony between Great Britain and the Colonies right up to 1775. "Reconciliation," according to the historian Pauline Maier, "was still the American dream." Even Thomas Jefferson longed for reunion. Jefferson wrote in a private letter as late as August 15, 1775, "I would rather be in dependence on Great Britain, properly limited, than on any nation on earth, or than on no nation."[70]

Despite his measured tone throughout the Declaration, Jefferson speaks of the separation with Britain in melancholic terms in the penultimate paragraph—a paragraph that the Second Continental Congress wisely deleted: "[T]hese facts [sending mercenaries to fight] have given the last stab to agonizing affection; and manly spirit bids us to renounce forever these unfeeling brethren. We must endeavor to forget our former love for them, . . . we might have been a free & a great people together." By the end, when the British people and not solely the king are addressed, Jefferson describes independence not in the triumphant tones of liberty and sovereignty, but in terms of separation, loss, and mourning. Here, politics takes on a distinctly personal cast, as Jefferson's forlorn words resemble those of a jilted lover, grieving the end of a romantic bond, or perhaps more aptly, given the use of "brethren," the end of a bromance. The parent-child metaphor that characterizes John Bull and Brother Jonathan—and the colonial relationship more generally—is noticeably absent in the Declaration, but the outcome is still the same. Britain, the erstwhile object of affection, has now turned into a backstabbing and unfeeling enemy. Americans are reluctant fighters: Their independence was thrust upon them; it came about as a result of British cruelty. [71]

The founding text of the nation, moreover, can be read as a transatlantic allegory juxtaposing English nastiness against American niceness. In the Declaration, American agency is cast not in terms of aggression or even of assertion, but as a defensive response to the king's tyranny. It describes affect rather than action, hurt feelings rather than defiance. In contrast to Paine, who expressed little nostalgia for the past, Jefferson's version of the Declaration concludes with a wistful evocation of what could have been. It looks longingly to the past instead of defiantly toward the future.

The final way in which the Declaration of Independence represents a sort of urtext for a hegemonic understanding of American niceness is how the king represents the embodiment of evil. He is blamed for all that is wrong in the colonies. Earlier petitions to the British would typically address the "King & Parliament," "the Ministry and Parliament," or the "British Government." After all, the colonies were ruled under parliamentary authority. Protestations against the Stamp Act, for instance, were addressed to Parliament. But the Declaration is unusual in addressing its complaints exclusively to the king. The historian Carl Becker notes in his landmark study of the Declaration that the omission of Parliament seems intentional, due to the fact that the colonists, in announcing their independence, no longer saw themselves as British subjects.[72] Perhaps they also wanted to persuade the English people to support their cause by focusing solely on the king and not British governance. Their rhetorical tactic carefully targeted an individual, not a populace.

Declaring independence from England without offending the British people represents an example of American niceness as a rhetorical strategy, one that was hammered out through committee work and then again through debate in the Continental Congress. Jefferson notes, "those passages which conveyed censures on the people of England were struck out, lest they should give them offence."[73] Jefferson did not entirely approve of this strategy and John Adams found it even more mistaken. For Adams, the exclusive focus on the king overly personalized the colonial critique: "I thought this too personal, for I never believed George to be a tyrant in disposition and in nature . . . I thought the expression too passionate, and too much like scolding, for so grave and solemn a document."[74] Despite the reservations of Jefferson and Adams, who were both on the original drafting committee, the Continental Congress nonetheless decided to place blame exclusively on the king.

Presenting the king as the embodiment of all that was wrong with colonial relations, however, did provide an important function for the nascent nation: It blamed him for slavery and for stirring Indian hostility toward the colonists and, in doing so, absolved white America of any wrongdoing. English nastiness, when figured through the king, had its political uses. The colonists censured the king for fomenting race rebellion in the colonies: "[H]e has excited domestic insurrections amongst us and has endeavored to bring on the inhabitants of our frontiers the merciless Indian savages." And in his famous passage describing slavery as an "execrable commerce," which the Continental Congress deleted, Jefferson accuses the king for "now exciting those very people [slaves] to rise in arms among us, and to purchase that liberty of which he has deprived them." In contrast to the dispassionate "good people" whose affective spectrum goes from bland to forlorn (and never anger), the Indians and slaves are "excited," which is to say, agitated and provoked. Here, passion belongs to the nasty English king and his black and red allies, while white Americans are the innocent victims of brown anger and royal wrath. The Declaration suggests a relationship between race and affect that illustrates the literary critic Julie Ellison's point about the eighteenth century more generally, that "[r]ace becomes a figure for emotion; emotion makes racial distinctions."[75]

The Declaration of Independence illustrates two important aspects of what would become the hegemonic formation of American niceness. First, it personalizes the political, reducing complex structural relations to interpersonal matters by shifting political questions onto a single individual as a way to explain and resolve conflict. The king becomes the personification of all that is wrong with the imperial relationship. He serves a necessary purpose for the crystallization of American niceness: He allows the "good People" of the colonies to disavow their own relationship to Indian dispossession and African enslavement, and, in doing so, he frees white Americans from their own complicity in human rights abuses. As the source of all New World sin, the king liberates the colonists from their own conscience. Second, this dominant formation of American niceness distinguishes niceness from violence: because Americans are nice they cannot be cruel. The two traits are seen as mutually exclusive and take allegorical form through a transatlantic binary. The English are the forbidding aggressors, while the Americans are the reluctant revolutionaries who wished to reconcile with the English but were forced into independence after the English rejected them. This belief carried on into the twentieth century, with the American lawyer and writer Henry Dwight Sedgwick noting in 1908 that the "new American type," which was not particularly new, consisted of "the usual American amiability, domestic kindliness and aversion to cruel sights and cruel sounds."[76] American niceness, in other words, functions precisely to disassociate Americans with acts of violence or even with negative emotions altogether.

John O'Sullivan's Manifest Cheerfulness

Henry Dwight Sedgwick's "new" American type in the early twentieth century bears an uncanny resemblance to John O'Sullivan's description of the American type in the 1830s. Although O'Sullivan is credited for coining the infamous phrase "manifest destiny," he should be given his due for creating another important concept that I will call "manifest cheerfulness." O'Sullivan called for the formation of a national type based on converting democratic principles into such behavioral terms as cheerfulness and optimism. Calvinist pessimism was passé; a new attitude was in order, one based on futurity and happiness. In 1839, O'Sullivan claimed in "The Great Nation of Futurity" that in contrast to European despotism, American democracy represents a "cheerful creed of high hope and universal love."[77] He understood the importance of uniting the country under a single affect because he saw the power of generalization, especially generalizations associated with positive sociality.

In the same essay, O'Sullivan emphasizes the importance of imagining a national *geist* not rooted in the soil: "American patriotism is not of soil; we are not aborigines, nor of ancestry, for we are of all nations."[78] At a time when indigenous populations were being violently excised and uprooted from their land—and their traditions erased from national memory—it is significant that O'Sullivan defined the national *geist* in terms of surfaces rather than depths, a matter of transient and superficial encounters rather than of age-old traditions and customs. In a white settler nation as scattered, divided, and varied as the United States, behavioral conformity became the basis of cohesion. The figure of the nice American is a distinctly modern contribution to the index of national types that foregrounds mobility and impermanence.

Writing in the aftermath of the Panic of 1837, O'Sullivan has as much to say about his alarm at the rise of the "better classes" within the nascent republic as he has about the nation's calling as a beacon of democracy. According to historian Kathleen Smith Kutolski, the Jacksonian period was characterized not by democracy and the dispersal of power, but by the concentration of wealth in the hands of a few.[79] With this anxiety in mind, American niceness played a major role in diffusing class animosity domestically. It had a compensatory function in the early republic as a way to mitigate structural inequalities by behavioral means. The United States may not be egalitarian in an economic sense, but it can still be a social democracy in which citizens treat each other in an egalitarian fashion.

In *Democracy in America*, Alexis de Tocqueville remarks on the democratic sociability of Americans in the form of frequent conversations between the rich and the poor: The wealthy "maintain constant contact with them [the poor], listening to them gladly and talking to them every day. They realize that the rich in democracies always need the poor and that, in democratic times, you attach a poor man to you more by your manner than by benefits conferred." Charm, he adds, can never be resisted and it creates an ease of approach between the classes.

Tocqueville goes on to observe that democratic sociability based on neighborliness is cultivated through minor acts over extended periods of time. "The favor of the people," he writes, "may be won by some brilliant action but the love and respect of your neighbors must be gained by a long series of small services, hidden deeds of goodness, a persistent habit of kindness, and an established reputation for selfless-ness."[80] Tocqueville writes admiringly about the ease with which wealthy Americans are able to cultivate their own likability through small gestures of kindness in order to minimize resentment among the less fortunate. With Tocqueville's observations in mind, it is clear that niceness has a compensatory function in the democratic republic, acting as a behavioral substitute for deep structural inequalities. It replaces economic democracy with social democracy, where friendly gestures—a smile, a handshake, a conversation—compensate for the lack of economic equality. Tocqueville praises U.S. democracy not for its classlessness, but for its ability to handle class divisions through nice behavior.

Catharine Maria Sedgwick and Compensatory Niceness

Published in the same year as the first volume of Tocqueville's *Democracy in America*, Catharine Maria Sedgwick's *The Poor Rich Man, and The Rich Poor Man* (1836) is the literary corollary to Tocqueville's observation that "in democracies, no great benefits are granted but small kindnesses are constantly shown."[81] One of her most popular novels, *The Poor Rich Man* is simultaneously a response to the growing disparities between rich and poor in the early republic and a way of reassuring the reader that the American poor are not really that poor when compared to other parts of the world (i.e., Europe) since they still find plenty of "healthful food." She reminds her American readers, "We must remember that, in our country, there are no fixed classes; the poor family of this generation is the rich family of the next."[82] By displacing fixed class disparities onto Europe, American niceness cultivates the fantasy of American classlessness, or at the very least, the belief that classes in the United States are fluid and flexible. As Hannah Arendt remarked, "America had become the symbol of a society without poverty long before the modern age."[83] In such a society, or so the myth goes, people can develop freely as individuals, each special in their own unique way. American niceness adds an interpersonal layer to an already familiar pattern of U.S. disidentification with Europe: "they" have classes; "we" have free and friendly individuals.

As a New England patrician, Sedgwick believed in a form of trickledown niceness, where class divisions can be mitigated socially through "little kindnesses."[84] In contrast to the rigid class system in Britain, the U.S. version is more fluid and temporary, making it more responsive to social remedies in the form of interpersonal behavior. Sedgwick establishes a narrative of affective conversion that makes the poor behave less bitterly and the wealthy feel less guilty by giving niceness the power to convert sour faces into a "harvest of smiles." A democratic nation is one whose citizens smile together.

Susan May, the good-hearted New England rustic in Sedgwick's novel, epitomizes this philosophy when she says, "when they [neighbors] are kind, it don't seem to me to make much difference whether you are rich or poor."[85] For the wealthy, niceness is compensatory; it provides a way of feeling more comfortable in a social world increasingly comprised of have-nots. For the lower classes, such as Susan, who is a successful seamstress, niceness anticipates the emotional labor demanded of modern-day service workers, whose work depends on taking "pains to fit and please," both in the literal sense of Susan's tailoring and the behavioral sense of pleasing clients: "smiles beget smiles," she advises, "you know—if they are pleased, I am."[86] Niceness is also assimilative, a sign of social mobility or the yearning for such mobility, and, at the very least, it is a way for writers such as Sedgwick to mitigate the threat of working-class animosity. Niceness can convert the angry worker into a complacent one, a transformation that Sedgwick calls "the benevolent principle," a type of alchemy that "converts the lead to gold."[87]

Sedgwick implies in her travel writing that niceness would not work in Britain because British servants—through their obsequious behavior—thinly conceal an undercurrent of contempt for those they serve. They do not show "real deference" but only "real insolence." Sedgwick finds the obsequious British servant unnerving because their deference is performative, a combination of "insolence and abjectness."[88] Sedgwick recounts an exchange with a British porter who is dismayed with the tip she gave him, and he aggressively confronts her and demands more money, even climbing onto the coach and harassing her while the coach moves down a long street. When she gives him a shilling, his demeanor suddenly changes and he becomes sycophantic. "Do you sit quite comfortable, ladies?" he asks. Appalled by his defiant behavior followed by his mock civility, Sedgwick lauds American servants for showing genuine respect and exuding a "quiet kindness."[89] Sedgwick's revealing comparison of the transatlantic class system presents American servants as more genuinely obsequious than their British counterparts, making them the ideal lower-class type.

Although deference is a quality to be praised when speaking about American servants, Sedgwick lauds its absence when describing U.S. manners more generally. She carefully points out that niceness includes good manners but is not reducible to the rules of etiquette. Sedgwick clarifies what she means by good manners: "I do not mean the polished manners of the most highly educated and refined of other countries, nor the deferential subservience of their debased classes— too pleasing to those who prefer the homage to the friendship of their fellow-creatures."[90] By replacing deference with egalitarian friendship, niceness came to dramatize at an interpersonal level the qualities associated with a democratic republic, that is, the promise of access and inclusion.

Harriet Beecher Stowe and Codified Niceness

In many ways, Catharine Maria Sedgwick's reflections on antebellum sociality find their fullest development in the work of Harriet Beecher Stowe, who would become the most important nineteenth-century theorist of niceness because she understood its significance as a social liturgy and a daily ritual of behavior that mollifies conflict and harmonizes everyday dealings. Niceness establishes a form of sociality that arranges mundane encounters into a predictable pattern, a pattern that can be described as an example of what the sociologist Pierre Bourdieu calls "codification." "To codify means to formalize," writes Bourdieu, and codifying refers to a type of symbolic ordering that minimizes ambiguity in particular situations, such as traffic at an intersection.[91] By standardizing trivial exchanges, niceness represents a form of codification that makes daily interactions and communications relatively clear. Codified niceness constructs and maintains social relations and controls potential aggression within these relations. "Democracy does not create strong attachments between men," observes Tocqueville, "but it does make their normal relations easier."[92]

Stowe's understanding of codified niceness is most clearly illustrated in her short sketch called "Home Religion" (1864). Christopher Crowfield, Stowe's pseudonym and narrator, has an amicable disagreement with his son-in-law, Robert Stephens, about what form niceness should take. The earnest Stephens insists that sincerity should guide outward behavior, including the banal exchanges of everyday encounters; otherwise, social niceties become merely superficial. Crowfield, who is Stowe's ventriloquized persona in male drag, challenges Stephens's argument with a defense of superficial niceness:

> The outward expression of social good feeling becomes a mere form; but for that reason must we meet each other like oxen? Not say, 'Good morning,' or 'Good evening,' or 'I am happy to see you'? Must we never use any of the forms of mutual good will, except in those moments when we are excited by a real, present emotion? What would become of society?[93]

Stowe defends niceness not in terms of her famous phrase that appears at the end of *Uncle Tom's Cabin*—to "feel right"—but rather as the absence of emotion. Stowe, the sentimentalist, makes a rather unsentimental case for niceness by arguing that it validates "the forms of mutual good will" that sustain social cohesion. One does not have to feel genuine good will in order to behave in an appropriate manner. Stowe's male persona liberates us from the burden of emotional authenticity and from emotional extremes. To act as the earnest son-in-law recommends (which is similar to Walt Whitman's ideal of democratic sociability based on affection), where every mundane exchange would need to derive from a sincere inner feeling, would be emotionally exhausting.

Stowe's codified niceness as a social form dovetails with the concept's versatility in that sociality in Stowe's sense can turn into its opposite, namely anti-social sociality. This mode of sociality is a way of maintaining distance from others by conforming to everyday rituals or protocols. Stowe liberates niceness from feeling and sincerity, but in doing so, she also creates the possibility of severing ritual from relationality. Niceness can be a means of initiating a superficial social encounter that may develop into something more meaningful, but it can also be a way of warding off contact through social niceties that keep people at bay. Ralph Waldo Emerson articulates a similar understanding of the significance of codification in his essay "Experience": "We live amid surfaces, and the true art of life is to skate well on them." Emerson and Stowe acknowledge the importance of surfaces without having to validate them through an appeal to depths. Surfaces have a surprising density of their own that Emerson describes as a "mixture of power and form."[94] Niceness, for Stowe, is precisely a way to understand this mixture that reconfigures power relations through mundane encounters.

Stowe's understanding of niceness as codification also potentially points to the limits of inclusion through quotidian behaviors that are hateful. Niceness and nastiness are mutually constitutive, and this dynamic dramatizes the politics of inclusion and exclusion within the nation. African American intellectuals of the late nineteenth century wrote about how white supremacy took cataclysmic forms— such as lynching—but also more mundane forms that could be described as micro-moments of hate. In 1897, W. E. B. Du Bois would refer to the "thousand little annoyances and petty insults and disappointments of a caste system."[95] And the African American writer and educator Anna Julia Cooper remarked during the same period that the conductor's hand was never offered to assist her off a train. These observations highlight the fact that racism includes the accrual of minor offenses, the absence of the banal niceties of everyday life, thus reinforcing and making palpable the structural experience of racial inequality. Cooper and others would call for "race etiquette," by which they meant everyday courtesy or codified niceness that is practiced inclusively rather than selectively. The true test of American courtesy, wrote Cooper in 1892, is how white men treat black women: "The man who is courteous to her is so, not because of anything he hopes or fears or sees, but because *he is a gentleman.*"[96] In 1898, the African American activist and writer Frances Harper defined "true politeness" as "perfect sincerity" that constitutes "the social currency of every day life," which is to social life "what oil is to machinery, a thing to oil the ruts and grooves of existence."[97] Both Cooper and Harper recognized that the struggle for civil rights involved both challenging institutional discrimination and transforming everyday social interactions.

Although the journalist Ida B. Wells focused much of her work on antilynching activism and later educational discrimination, she also understood the importance of race etiquette, which she defined in terms of treating black people as "ladies and gentlemen." In her auto-biography, Wells recounts with humor how her return voyage to the United States from Britain in 1893 took a pleasurable turn when fif-teen young, mainly Quaker Englishmen, who were on their way to the Chicago World's Fair, indulged her with the most gentlemanly atten-tion. "They were as courteous and attentive to me as if my skin had been of the fairest. It was indeed a delightful experience. We traveled together practically all the way to Chicago and they seemed to take great pleasure in shocking the onlookers by their courteous and respectful attention to me"[98] The ship had "few if any white Americans on board," a detail that suggests little racial hostility during the trans-atlantic journey. But when she arrived in the United States with her English travel companions, their respectful treatment of her caused alarm among white Americans, which motivated the young men to even greater degrees of attentiveness so as to shock those of their own class and race. When good manners are expanded to include black women, one sees the radical potential of Stowe's codified niceness and Frances Harper's related notion of "true politeness" as "the social cur-rency of every day life." The legacy of this way of thinking about race relations in terms of "true politeness" can be seen in Maya Angelou's definition of paradise in "Preacher, Don't Send Me": "I'd call a place/ pure paradise/where families are loyal/and strangers are nice."[99]

From Stowe's Codified Niceness to
Indigenous Hospitality and the Philippines

This book takes Stowe's trajectory of niceness—with all of its incon-sistencies, contradictions, and limits—and sets it within the diverse context of her contemporaries. *American Niceness: A Cultural History* begins with Native Americans greeting the Puritans in the seven-teenth century, and it concludes with the Filipinos greeting American teachers in the early twentieth century. By starting in Plymouth and ending in the Philippines, a parallel that American politicians and intellectuals noted in the aftermath of the Spanish American War of

1898, this book tells the story of American niceness from its beginnings as an indigenous form of Native American hospitality to the early stages of the United States emergence as an imperial power at the end of the nineteenth century. The dominant story of American niceness depends, in part, on incorporating the niceness of the oppressed—from Indian hospitality to Aunt Jemima's smile—in order to structure white American character. But this study also tells the forgotten history of niceness as an important form of support for the earnest and often fragile calls for justice across the color line that challenged the abuses of manifest destiny, slavery, and imperial expansion.

The first chapter, "Indian Giving and the Dangers of Hospitality," introduces a counter-tradition of American niceness, one that is premised on welcoming rather than fearing the stranger. Indigenous forms of welcoming represent a mode of sociality that prioritizes the common good based on compassion and a concern for the stranger without the expectation of return. This counter-tradition allows us to imagine forms of American niceness that could have evolved if this had become the hegemonic model, but it also encourages us to understand how the shadow side of niceness—one that has been disavowed and buried in the historical archive—has shaped and formed its dominant version today in the context of empire and globalization.

The second chapter, "Southern Niceness and the Slave's Smile," turns to another form of minority niceness, black amiability. The debate on slavery included a debate on black character: Are they kind or treacherous? A friend or a threat? The debate on black character took a figural form that was based on the semiotics of the black face, and particularly on the smile. As a highly contested sign, the smile was not loyal to any side. It could serve the antislavery or the pro-slavery cause. For abolitionists, the smile was a sign of black humanity, but for the apologists of slavery, the slave's smile vindicated the institution because their smiles reflected the kindness of the master. It confirmed the widespread belief at the time that the United States represented a milder form of slavery when compared to other parts of the black Atlantic, such as the Caribbean. By the 1890s, the slave's smile would become iconic through the face of Aunt Jemima as a synonym for Southern hospitality. Like Indian hospitality during this same period, the African American smile became incorporated within a national narrative of American niceness.

Even God was not immune from a character analysis in the nineteenth century. The third chapter, "The Christology of Niceness," discusses God's makeover from the angry God of New England Calvinism, full of fire and brimstone, to a compassionate friend in Jesus. God's authority now derived from his kindness rather than his wrath. No longer associated with terror, Christianity became the religion of niceness in the nineteenth century. What would it mean if God were to exercise his power through love rather than fear? How would this revised notion of authority alter our view not only of religion but also of governance? In addressing God's authority, liberal Christians were raising larger questions about power and the state more generally. By feminizing Jesus, they reimagined the terms of democratic authority.

But where Jesus's niceness was a divine personality trait, feminine niceness had to be continually performed. The fourth chapter, "Feminine Niceness," looks at the fraught relation between femininity and niceness from the writings of Louisa May Alcott, Charlotte Perkins Gilman, and Elizabeth Stuart Phelps to those of Jane Addams and Ida B. Wells. On the one hand, these writers understood niceness in terms of Victorian sociality, as a necessary way to cultivate a sense of belonging and connectedness. On the other hand, their work also presents niceness as an ideological corset that restricts women's behavior and their emotional life. This chapter explores how feminist writers navigated the limits of Victorian society, offering a powerful critique of femininity while at the same time conserving aspects of it.

The final chapter, "The Likable Empire from Plymouth Rock to the Philippines," turns to the era of U.S. imperial conquest, when the Filipino—considered by U.S. generals and politicians as the new Indian—reenacts the primal scene of American niceness. In the debates about the U.S. occupation of the Philippines, niceness was a highly contested term. For some, Americans were simply too nice to be ruthless imperialists, since a democratic sensibility was too firmly rooted in the American psyche to allow for bloodthirsty empire building. Others defended the U.S. occupation on the grounds that it constituted a democratic empire, a kinder and gentler form of imperialism based on a pedagogical model of tutelage as opposed to Old World conquest. According to this point of view, the United States represents a consensual empire, as personified by the likability of the archipelago's first U.S. Civil-Governor William Howard Taft. Mainstream periodicals of the era proclaimed that, thanks to Taft's magnanimous persona, the United States governed through persuasion rather than brute force. This book ends as it began by comparing hegemonic formations of American niceness to indigenous practices, whether it is the Narragansett concept of *wunnégin* or the Filipino idea of *kapwa*. In both, we see the possibility of revitalizing the banality of niceness through an ethics of the nonmarket, where sociality plays a significant role in countering the effects of cruelty and discrimination by imagining social bonds based on sharing rather than profit, on reparative justice rather than exploitation.[100]

The nineteenth-century understanding of niceness was complex, contradictory, and multivalenced: It described interpersonal relations as well as abstract allegiances. It signified a problem as well as a remedy. With the U.S. "Civil" War, a paradoxical phrase if ever there was one, combined with other crises and tragedies, the persuasive power of niceness had found its limit. This limit raises important questions about how much we can expect of nice behavior. How does niceness as a social practice influence social and political change? How and why does it fail? When does it succeed? Although a theory of niceness requires answers to such sweeping questions, the nineteenth century also appreciated niceness in a less dramatic sense as a source of ordinary pleasure and as a way of enjoying the banal exchanges that shape our everyday lives. Ralph Waldo Emerson captures this sensibility when he writes in his essay "Friendship": "From the highest degree of passionate love, to the lowest degree of good will, they make the sweetness of life."[101] This book reflects on various gestures of good will—along with the history of withholding such gestures—to make a case for the importance of niceness found in quotidian exchanges as well as clichéd expressions such as "have a nice day."

1

Indian Giving and
the Dangers of Hospitality

Friday, March 16, 1621

THE PRIMAL SCENE of American niceness occurred three months after the Pilgrims arrived at Patukset (later to be called Plymouth), when an Abenaki named Samoset greeted the strangers in English with the phrase "Welcome, Englishmen." It was the first time that the Pilgrims had directly encountered an Indian, and they were surprised at being greeted in a friendly manner in their own language. Samoset had acquired limited English through his connections with an English fishing camp on Monhegan Island off the coast of Maine, which John Smith, of Pocahontas fame, had set up in 1614. The desperate Puritan Separatists, concerned about their own survival and safety since nearly half of their group had died, were anxious to establish friendly relations with the natives and they showered Samoset with gifts and invited him to return with his friends.

On March 22, Samoset appeared with four companions, including Tisquantum (a.k.a. Squanto), who spoke fluent English, had traversed the Atlantic multiple times (initially as a captive), and had lived in Spain, England, and Newfoundland. They brought with them skins for trade and they entertained the colonists with singing and dancing. They soon returned with their chief sachem, Massasoit, who appeared with sixty warriors on Watson's Hill. By the end of the meeting, the Puritans and Indians had exchanged several gifts and had signed a treaty that would last for fifty years, until the death of Massasoit.[1]

This snapshot of the first Pilgrim-Indian encounter marks the point of national origins. It represents the foundational story of the world's first settler nation, a tale of near tragedy turned into one of triumph, with the Pilgrim's salvation leading to the Indian's demise. The nice Indian features prominently in this origin story of the nation, a story that was reiterated in national and local histories throughout the nineteenth century.[2] The origins of the nation lie in Samoset's friendly salutation of "welcome," in Tisquantum's teaching the Pilgrims how to grow corn and catch eel, and in Massasoit's protection against other tribes who wanted to annihilate the vulnerable colony. The nation, in other words, is founded on Indian giving, in the literal rather than pejorative sense.

Contrast this seventeenth-century encounter with a nineteenth-century one, when George Henry (Maungwudaus), a Chippewa from Canada and a former Methodist missionary, stopped at Plymouth Rock as a tourist in 1848 after his return from Europe, where he had been touring with a dance troupe he organized.

> We went to see Plymouth Rock, where our forefathers first saw the white men; saw the stone first touched by white man's foot; went in the Pilgrim Hall. The Americans have been very kind to us in all places; they are not so fleshy [sic] as the English, but very persevering in all their ways. They pay more respect to their females than the English, and they like to see things belong to others without leave.[3]

George Henry views Plymouth Rock from the perspective of those who were already here. He takes the rhetoric of national inheritance, of "our forefathers," and refers implicitly not to the Pilgrims but to Massasoit and Samoset. He imagines seeing the encounter from their vantage point, where the Pilgrim remains nonparticularized, generic, and at one point even metonymically described in terms of a "white man's foot."

Henry's perspective changes easily from an imagined seventeenth-century historical gaze to a nineteenth-century touristic one, when he describes the kind treatment he received from Americans while traveling in New England: "The Americans have been very kind to us in all places." He juxtaposes the "very kind" Americans against the not-so-nice English, who treat their women with less respect than the Americans. For this cosmopolitan Indian, Plymouth Rock was an opportunity to comment on American niceness, with the American at this point in time being understood as white.

Whether it is the seventeenth-century encounter reflected in Samoset's warm salutation of "welcome," or George Henry's nineteenth-century account of American niceness, Plymouth represents the primal scene where Indian niceness and American niceness converge. The objective of this chapter is to make sense of this convergence and to explore points where it breaks down. What does it mean to acknowledge Indian niceness at a time of mass removals, when Native Americans were systematically uprooted from their lands and forced to move west of the Mississippi, often multiple times? What cultural work did the figure of the hospitable Indian do during such an inhospitable era, when the stereotype of the savage equipped with tomahawk and scalping knife predominated?

Where the introduction outlined the hegemonic form of American niceness that sought to ameliorate economic disparities through amiable behavior, or what could be called "manifest cheerfulness," this chapter turns to an alternative tradition of American niceness during the same period, one that has two inflections: Native American and Anglo-American. First, the native invocation of Indian hospitality in the nineteenth century appears repeatedly in the speeches and writing of Native American leaders and intellectuals from William Apess and Black Elk to Simon Pokagon and Zitkala-Sa. Indian hospitality frames the colonial encounter of the seventeenth century in terms of Anglo betrayal of Indian kindness: Indians generously helped the first settlers to survive, and as soon as they acquired the necessary tools, they killed their indigenous hosts. Native Americans, in other words, translate colonialism into the interpersonal terms of sociality and antisociality, where Indian dispossession is understood in terms of Anglo cruelty and ingratitude. It depicts an indigenous form of shaming that challenges the moral conscience of the white settler.

The second inflection of this alternative form of American niceness concerns Anglo-American invocations of Indian hospitality in order to shame fellow Anglo-Americans about the inhumanity of manifest destiny. This form of American niceness is predicated on turning generational guilt into public shaming by targeting one's forefathers (hence the frequent return to the seventeenth century) and their descendants and exposing the violence committed in the name of nation-building. In the works of Benjamin Franklin, Washington Irving, Lydia Maria Child, Helen Hunt Jackson, and others, this strategy of shaming is based on nonviolent dissent that seeks to convert historical disavowal into acknowledgment. When taken together, Native American and Anglo-American understandings of manifest destiny as the betrayal of Indian kindness constitute an alternative tradition of American niceness based on shaming as a tool of anti-imperial critique that tried to reshape the norms and policies of a white settler nation.[4]

Alongside these dissident invocations of Indian hospitality there emerged a hegemonic variation that inscribes Indian hospitality into the story of national origins, where subaltern niceness structures white U.S. character. This illustrates a form of affective incorporation, where Indian generosity became part of the founding narrative of national exceptionalism. This account of national origins was largely the product of the nineteenth century, a period that combined brutal removal policies with a revisionist glance back to the seventeenth century.

The Nineteenth Century as a Century of Catastrophe

Although W. E. B. Du Bois heralded the nineteenth century as "the first century of human sympathy," Native American writers such as Zitkala-Sa (Gertrude Simmons Bonnin) were more selective in their praise. She focused less on "human sympathy" and more on the "hospitable Indian" as the iconic American. In 1896, just six years after the Wounded Knee Massacre, when U.S. soldiers killed over 200 men, women, and children of the Lakota nation in South Dakota, Zitkala-Sa, a Dakota Sioux, revisited not the site of the massacre but Plymouth Rock, the ur-scene of American niceness. She writes, "Samoset voiced the feeling of his people as he stood among the winter-weary Pilgrims and cried 'Welcome, Englishmen.'"[5] For her, Samoset's friendly greeting was emblematic of Native American hospitality, with its related attributes of fidelity to a treaty, loyalty to a friend, and the willingness to share land with the "paler race." Kindness is not representative of humanity as a whole but is a distinctly Native American attribute. Samoset's greeting was also an invitation to imagine cultural contact in terms other than invasion, bloodshed, and plunder. Zitkala-Sa invokes this seventeenth-century anecdote in the 1890s to rewrite the origins of the nation. By referring to Samoset's warm greeting, she emphasizes the affective dimension of colonialism, casting manifest destiny as a cruel betrayal of native hospitality.

By 1922, Zitkala-Sa would switch her emphasis from Samoset's friendly greeting in the seventeenth century to the catastrophic costs of colonial plunder in the nineteenth and twentieth centuries. Implicitly drawing upon humanity's expulsion from Eden to frame her narrative, she uses the word "catastrophe" to describe metaphorically a post-lapsarian world of crisis: "Catastrophe it was when both the big trees and the ancient race of red men fell under the ax of a nineteenth-century invasion." Genocide is likened to deforestation. The felling of trees and the killing of Indians constitute a human and ecological disaster, with white Americans responsible for the devastation of a living environment. Instead of expansion, that celebrated term that Jacksonian democrats euphemistically referred to as "freedom" and "liberty," Zitkala-Sa uses the more scathing term "invasion." The nineteenth century designated not a century of progress and expansion, but one of destruction and plunder. It is estimated that 55 percent of Cherokees died during the Trail of Tears (1838–1839). The Creeks and Seminoles also lost about half of their populations as a direct result of Indian removal policies.[6] In 1881, Helen Hunt Jackson would describe the nineteenth century as a "century of dishonor," and her lengthy indictment of U.S. civil and military policy toward Native Americans was directed to the Congress of 1880. Over a century later, the Bureau of Indian Affairs issued a formal apology to Native Americans for its long history of "ethnic cleansing" and cultural annihilation.[7]

To put this demographic decline in historical perspective, the population of the Americas when Christopher Columbus arrived in 1492 was over 100 million. Two centuries later, the indigenous population had decreased 90 percent. "In the United States, the native population bottomed out during the 1890s at slightly over 237,000—a 98-percent reduction from its original size," a reduction that Ward Churchill describes as an "extreme demographic catastrophe."[8] The word "catastrophe" here is significant because it is repeated throughout the nineteenth century by native and nonnative writers alike. As early as

1821, an anonymous writer for *The Philanthropist* describes the "extermination" of the Indians as a "catastrophe": "Many powerful tribes are *gone,* and have left nothing but their names & others are rapidly approaching to the same catastrophe" [original emphasis].[9] In Greek drama, catastrophe refers to the change or turning point that produces the conclusion of a dramatic piece, but in its modern usage, it can also denote total disaster, where there is no revelation and no opportunity for escape. When Zitkala-Sa defines the nineteenth century as a catastrophe, she refers neither to a single event nor to punctuated moments of atrocity but to long-term, systematic violence. As she writes in "Side by Side" (1896), "To take the life of a nation during the slow march of centuries seems not a lighter crime than to crush it instantly with one fatal blow."[10] She conceives of the temporality of disaster along the lines of what the historian Fernand Braudel calls the *longue durée,* a diachronic process of extermination that is a slow death.[11]

The history of Indian calamity that Zitkala-Sa describes is precisely what enables a triumphalist narrative of American progress. Catastrophe, in other words, is a necessary ingredient of settler colonialism: The destruction of the indigenous allows for the birth of the white settler. To quote Walter Benjamin, "The concept of progress must be grounded in the idea of catastrophe."[12] National speeches of the nineteenth century did not conceal this fact but made it part of the rhetorical fabric of manifest destiny. Consider Henry Clay's comments as Speaker of the House in 1819 in the aftermath of the War of 1812, a war that secured U.S. hegemony in North America and removed the threat of British-Indian alliances. His oft-cited words illustrate the triumphalist use of Indian devastation for patriotic purposes: "[Initially] we were weak ... and [the Indians] were comparatively strong; ... they were the lords of the soil, and we were seeking ... asylum among them." Now "we are powerful and they are weak." Clay casts the Puritans as asylum seekers and the story of white settlement is not one of invasion but rather of transposition, where the weak become strong, while the native hosts have become weak. Such an inversion is deemed inevitable, and Clay further emphasizes its inevitability through an organic metaphor of "a great wave which has flowed in from the Atlantic ocean to almost the base of the Rocky Mountains, and, overwhelming them in its terrible progress, has left no other remains of hundreds of tribes, now extinct."[13] In naturalizing Indian disaster by comparing ethnic cleansing to a great wave, Clay also naturalizes white settlement as the inevitable result of progress rather than the outcome of long-term, systematic violence.

Manifest Destiny as Hospitality Betrayed

Contrary to Clay, Zitkala-Sa views catastrophe as an assault on nature and part of a man-made policy of extermination. To underscore catastrophe as historically crafted, she invokes the seventeenth century to underscore what is only a minor point in Clay's speech, namely, that Clay's asylum seekers depended on Indian generosity. The theme of hospitality betrayed is an important refrain in Native American writing of the nineteenth century, a refrain that has its origins in the eighteenth century, with Logan's famous speech that Jefferson recounts in *Notes on the State of Virginia*. Logan's speech is a eulogy as he grieves the murder of his wife and children by white settlers in 1774. His lament, which was routinely reprinted in oratory textbooks for American schoolchildren in the nineteenth century, begins by acknowledging Indian hospitality: "I appeal to any white man to say, if ever he entered Logan's cabin hungry, and he gave him not meat; if ever he came cold and naked, and he clothed him not."[14] After the murder of his family, Logan transformed from a hospitable Indian to a grief-stricken and vengeful one: "Who is there to mourn for Logan?— Not one." Logan's speech is precisely about the dangers of hospitality—of letting the stranger inside your home. Indian kindness guarantees neither protection nor safety from white Americans.

Although the authenticity of Logan's brief speech has been contested, its status as an iconic form of Indian censure has not. It was republished extensively in the nineteenth century, including in McGuffey's *Fourth* and *Fifth Reader* in the 1850s and 1860s, when young orators had to commit Logan's words to memory. The oratorical repetition of this speech is itself a metaphor for the way Logan's censorious words were incorporated into a national identity based on collective shame. One schoolbook advises its young readers to listen carefully: Indians "will tell you some truths which you must necessarily hear."[15] The trope of Indian pathos, as Carolyn Eastman has argued, had a pedagogical function; it sought to teach white affect, particularly sympathy and love. Indian suffering, in other words, created nicer white Americans.

Although national shaming could take hegemonic forms as in the McGuffey *Reader*, it was also a rhetorical tactic of native dissent. The Cherokee petition to Congress in November 1829 that opposed forced removal begins by invoking Samoset's greeting: "When your ancestors arrived on our shores, the red man was strong and, although he was ignorant and wild, he welcomed them with kindness."[16] Native American protest writing and speeches often began with the primal scene of Indian giving, when kindness rather than cruelty greeted the European stranger. The fact that Tocqueville included these Cherokee words in *Democracy in America* suggests that he shared their sense of moral outrage, a point that he would make explicit in a rare moment of strong condemnation. In "Two Weeks in the Wilderness," Tocqueville adopts an unusually scornful tone when chastising Anglo-Americans for their cruelty toward Native Americans: "At the heart of this very civilized, prudish, pedantically moral and virtuous society lay a completely insensitive attitude, a kind of cold and relentless self-ishness when it came to the native races of America."[17]

During this same period, Black Elk understood Indian giving as "our mistake" and he blamed Native Americans for being too loving and trusting, while underestimating the white settler's capacity for cruelty:

> The first thing an Indian learns is to love each other and that they should be relative-like to the four-leggeds. The next thing is telling the truth. Whatever they say, they stand by it. Here's where the Indians made their mistake. We should treat all our fellowmen alike—the Great Spirit made men alike. Therefore, we made a mistake when we tried to get along with the whites. We tried to love them as we did ourselves. On account of this we are now in misery.[18]

For Black Elk, Indian niceness failed to humanize the settlers, to incorporate them within indigenous forms of sociality. Black Elk's rebuke blames Indian loving, in part, for Indian destruction—"we tried to love them as we did ourselves"—highlighting how hospitality is an exercise in vulnerability or what Rauna Kuokkanen, a scholar of comparative indigenous cultures, describes as a "fundamental openness to the other."[19] Vulnerability lies at the heart of Indian hospitality, an openness that exposed Native Americans to settler violence.

By the 1890s, Simon Pokagon similarly blamed Native Americans for being too loving. In "Red Man's Rebuke," the title of his 1893 pamphlet printed originally on birch bark to commemorate the 400th anniversary of Columbus's "discovery" of the Americas, Pokagon, a Potawatomi, cites Columbus's impressions of native kindness: "They are a loving, uncovetous people: so docile in all things that I swear to your majesties there is not in the world a better race or a more delightful country. They love their neighbors as themselves, and their talk is ever sweet and gentle, accompanied with smiles, and though they be naked, yet their manners are decorous and praiseworthy."[20] But even though Columbus considered the natives "sweet and gentle," he still pillaged and plundered them. Indian niceness, argues Pokagon, did not protect them from European greed. By inviting the hungry guests inside their homes, literally and metaphorically, Native Americans sowed the seeds of their own demise. "But alas! The pale faces came by chance to our shores, many times very needy and hungry. We nursed and fed them,—fed the ravens that were soon to pluck out our eyes and the eyes of our children."[21] This, according to Pokagon, constitutes "our sad story," a story of hospitality betrayed.

Derrida, Unconditional Giving, and the Dangers of Hospitality

The native understanding of national origins as hospitality betrayed resonates at a linguistic level with the paradoxical origins of the word *hospitality*. Jacques Derrida has shown that the etymology of *hospitality* is derived from the Latin word *hostis*, which is the same root term for the word *hostility*. *Hostis* also means reciprocity and it refers to the guest as well as the host because they are joined by a reciprocal pact. *Hostis*, moreover, is the root term for a series of related antinomies, including hospitality and hostility, host and foreigner, guest and enemy.[22]

There is a fundamental ambiguity, what Derrida aptly describes as a "paradoxical filiation," produced by the fact that these antithetical terms belong to the same etymological family, an ambiguity epitomized in Derrida's hybridized neologism, "hostpitality."[23] The ambiguity of these terms unsettles the relation between host and guest, suggesting that yesterday's host can become today's guest, and vice versa. In the case of the United States, the guest ultimately murders the host. This fact accentuates the dangers of hospitality, since the host does not know if the guest will be friendly or hostile.

Besides Derrida's framing of hospitality as an ambiguous relation that is fundamentally risky, he also understands hospitality as unconditional giving without the expectation of reciprocity. Derrida refers to this form of giving as "absolute hospitality" and "just hospitality," which "requires that I open up my home and that I give not only to the foreigner [. . .], but to the absolute, unknown, anonymous other, and that I *give place* to them, that I let them come, that I let them arrive, and take place in the place I offer them, without asking of them either reciprocity."[24] He contrasts this form of unconditional generosity with the Kantian notion of "the *law* of universal hospitality," as conditional, contractual, limited, based on duty and reciprocity, on the juridico-political laws of hospitality, where the foreigner remains a foreigner. These two forms of hospitality—unconditional and conditional—are "contradictory, antinomic, *and* inseparable," the same semantic trinity that describes the relation between hostility and hospitality, guest and enemy, host and foreigner.[25]

For Derrida, the tensions at the root of hospitality are born out of the term's structuring binaries, such as friendly and unfriendly or conditional and unconditional. This provides a useful way of comprehending the contradictory characterizations of Indian hospitality in the nineteenth century, and its related term, "Indian giving." This phrase—Indian giving—first appeared as "Indian gift" in American English in the mid-eighteenth century (though I suspect it emerged in vernacular speech much earlier). "An Indian Gift," wrote Thomas Hutchinson in 1765 in his history of Massachusetts, is "a proverbial expression, signifying a present for which an equivalent return is expected." An Indian gift implies a model of gift giving based on reciprocity and the mobility of things, when one object is exchanged for another. The emphasis is not on the person who gives but on the act of exchange.

The later phrase, "Indian giver," first appeared in the first half of the nineteenth century, and it foregrounds the identity of the giver, who rejects the gift economy because the giver wants the gift back. An Indian giver is really an antigiver; the phrase is a negation of giving. Bartlett's *Dictionary of Americanisms* (1848) defines "Indian giver" as follows: "When an Indian gives anything, he expects an equivalent in return, or that the same thing may be given back to him. This term is applied by children in New York and the vicinity to a child who, after having given away a thing, wishes to have it back again."[26] That this definition of "Indian giver" appeared in 1848, the year in which Mexico, an Indian nation, was forced to sell over half of its territory to the United States, is bitterly ironic. According to Bartlett's definition, the phrase "Indian giver" associates Indianness with puerile behavior, suggesting that a refusal to take part in an economy of exchange is immature and primitive.

The phrase "Indian giver" can be seen as an example of what Mary Stuckey and John Murphy have called "rhetorical colonialism," a term that describes how language prepares the land for cleansing and the white settler population for violence.[27] But it is important to point out that the Indian in "Indian gift" is not the same as the Indian in "Indian giver." Where one gives, the other refuses to give; where one is based on reciprocity, the other insists on nonreciprocity; where one embraces exchange, the other rejects it. When taken together, the phrases "Indian gift" and "Indian giver" indicate a fundamental contradiction and basic impossibility, which dramatizes the ambiguity of Indian gift giving (and its related notion of Anglo-American receiving). This contradiction plays itself out in white settler anxieties about indebtedness to Indian hospitality, an anxiety provoked by the fact that the triumph of the nation resulted from Native American welfare, a relation of dependency that the United States must disavow by describing the Indian as the antigiver or the conditional giver.

From the Hospitable to the Hostile Indian

It is not surprising that the figure of the hostile savage should flourish in Jacksonian America. White settler colonialism needs the angry Indian to justify ethnic cleansing. In the notorious Indian-hating literature of Robert Montgomery Bird and James Kirke Paulding, for instance, the savage Indian is juxtaposed against the well-intentioned white settler, who typifies the reluctant killer forced to murder Indians in self-defense. In the tradition of Brother Jonathan, Bird's protagonist in *Nick of the Woods* is a Quaker named Nathan Slaughter, who, despite his surname, is a peaceful man who would rather work on his farm than deal with angry neighbors. When the Shawnees approach his homestead, Slaughter shows he wants to live in peace by giving the Shawnee chief his rifle and knife, but the chief rejects the amiable gesture and murders his family instead: "With my own knife he struck down my eldest boy! With my own gun he slew the mother of my children!"[28] Slaughter represents the innocent victim of Shawnee savagery who is transformed into a vengeful murderer only after witnessing the massacre of his family. In the 1850 preface to the novel, Bird admits that the protagonist is based on an obscure legend whose source is long forgotten. But historical veracity is unimportant. Indian anger turns the white settler from an amiable Brother Jonathan to a vigilante firebrand.

In *Regeneration through Violence,* Richard Slotkin argues that violence against Indians played a constitutive role in the formation of a white American identity; in fact, it marks "the first American mythology," beginning with the colonial Puritan, who was the "captive or victim of devilish American savages."[29] The sly and ruthless Indian who collects white settler scalps with the same compulsion as Captain Ahab pursues Moby Dick makes it easier to dehumanize and objectify Indians, which is the ideological precondition for exterminating them. It was, to quote the historian Alden Vaughan, "'open season' on the Indian, friend or foe."[30] White settler violence is displaced onto the Indians so they become the threat, while white settler communities behave defensively, protecting their families from indigenous aggression and making their newly established homesteads secure.

The angry Indian of the frontier has its antecedent in the "merciless Indian savages" of the Declaration of Independence. In that foundational document, the king is blamed for inciting wrath among the natives. White settlers are innocent victims of Indian rage, which the king—and not the American colonists—has stirred up. The English monarch is the repository of New World sin, thus exonerating the white settler from his own guilt since he is never responsible for the consequences of colonialism. This transatlantic disavowal is precisely how, to quote Lorenzo Veracini, "settler colonialism obscures the conditions of its own production."[31]

In 1855, long after Indians were seen as a serious threat to the nation, Harvard physician Oliver Wendell Holmes wrote that Indians were nothing more than a "half-filled outline of humanity" whose extermination was the necessary "solution of the problem of his relation to the white race," and he added that it was only natural for the white man to hate the Indian and to "hunt him down like the wild beasts of the forest."[32] Why does Indian-hating still persist and even intensify long after the threat has diminished? This question preoccupied Herman Melville in the chapter of *The Confidence Man* entitled "The Metaphysics of Indian-hating." Melville's Judge Hall, who is an ironic appropriation of James Hall, the mid-nineteenth century "expert" on Indians and author of *Sketches of History, Life and Manners in the West* (1834–1835), wonders why "the backwoodsman still regards the red man in much the same spirit that a jury does a murderer," when "Indian rapine [has] mostly ceased through regions where it once prevailed."

For Melville, Indian-hating is a projection of fear that each generation repeats as it becomes a habit of mind. "But are not some Indians kind?" "Yes," answers Melville's Indian-hater Colonel Moredock, but "kind Indians may be forced to do unkind biddings. So 'beware the Indian, kind or unkind,' said Daniel Boone.'"[33] Even kind Indians cannot be trusted as it could be an insidious disguise, as the Tsalalians' smiles are in Edgar Allan Poe's *The Narrative of Arthur Gordon Pym of Nantucket*. The savage Indian has a life of its own, as Melville suggests in this brief chapter, as a residual type that continues long after the actual threat has disappeared.

Defending Indian Niceness in the Age of Indian Removal

In this tradition of Indian-hating, Indian kindness was viewed with suspicion, as a subterfuge for "unkind biddings." But this distrustful view was not the only Anglo perspective on Indian niceness. There emerged during the antebellum period another type of Indian—the amiable Indian—who was not a threat to white settlement but a potential friend. Inspired by her friendship with Red Jacket's granddaughter, Minnie Myrtle challenges the pervasive stereotype of the Indian as a bloodthirsty savage in her book *The Iroquois; Or, The Bright Side of Indian Character* (1855): "Almost any portrait which we have of Indians, represents them with tomahawk and scalping knife in hand, as if they possessed no other but a barbarous nature."[34] Myrtle, whose actual name was Anna Cummings Johnson, understood the relationship between stereotype and policy. The "stupid' or "savage" Indian was a necessary type to justify taking indigenous lands. There was, in other words, an instrumental motive to the array of negative types. Conversely, the amiable Indian could counter such stereotypes with a positive alternative that humanized the other and could consequently influence policy.

Just as there was no political consensus over Indian removal, so there was little representational consensus about how to depict the Indian, and particularly the nice Indian. Myrtle writes: "There were not at any time more than a fifteenth part of the whole nation in favor of removal, and the consent of those few was obtained by misrepresentation and bribery."[35] The absence of a dominant consensus in support of Indian removal can also be seen in the divided Congressional vote on the Indian Removal Act, which narrowly passed the House in May 1830 (101 to 97).[36] It is within this highly contested political and representational terrain that Myrtle attempts to depict a positive portrait of Indian character, one based on domestic practices centered on the wigwam. This is largely due to the fact, confesses Myrtle, that the Indian no longer poses a threat: "[T]hey are so utterly wasted away and helpless that we can afford to listen to the truth, and to believe that even our enemies had virtues."[37]

Myrtle's candor is refreshing; only the vanquished Indian can be seen as pleasing. Niceness is a trait that is retroactively attributed to the Indian when they are no longer perceived as a national threat. Indian culture is a dead culture, preserved like an historical artifact, so it is now safe to humanize them. This includes Indian hospitality, a custom framed in the past tense: "Hospitality was one of the Indians' distinguishing virtues, and there was no such thing among them as individual starvation or want."[38] There is more to Myrtle's praise of Indian hospitality than a quaint remark about erstwhile Indian customs. By situating Indian hospitality as a past custom and hailing its virtues—a society with no starvation, hunger, or stealing—Myrtle implicitly censures mid-nineteenth century U.S. society with its rising materialism, greed, and crime. Her praise for indigenous modes of sharing serves as a critique of the growing inequities of her own contemporary culture. The Golden Ageism of Indian hospitality, as a precapitalist society where resources are equitably distributed, is pointed and meaningful.

At the same time as Minnie Myrtle was humanizing the Native American for general readers by presenting their culture of hospitality as an alternative to one organized around private ownership and profit, the anthropologist Lewis Henry Morgan was also dedicating much of his academic scholarship to Native American customs of hospitality. Beginning with his earliest work, *League of the Iroquois* (1851), Morgan describes Indian amiability as "his simple integrity, his generosity, his unbounded hospitality, his love of truth, and, above all, his unshaken fidelity."[39] For Morgan, whose work on Native Americans would influence his contemporaries Karl Marx and Friedrich Engels, Indian hospitality established an equitable society where there was no deprivation. "Hunger and destitution could not exist at one end of an Indian village or in one section of an encampment while plenty prevailed elsewhere in the same village or encampment. It reveals a plan of life among them at the period of European discovery which has not been sufficiently considered."[40] According to Morgan, Indian hospitality is not just a practice associated with preconquest culture; it still continues in a modified form throughout the Americas, from the Iroquois in New York State to the Maya of the Yucatan. Its value is significant, Morgan argues, because Indian niceness is not just a social convention or a behavioral mode for greeting the stranger, but it also signifies a relation to property that is collective and communal. It points to a way of life based on "communistic living in large households," where resources are shared and equitably distributed. Although Morgan indulges in an evolutionary framework that sees Indian communism as designating a less developed stage when compared to private property, the latter is not necessarily an improvement. Morgan suggests that socialist utopianists like Robert Owen and Charles Fourier should "take lessons" from the Maya.[41]

For Morgan, Indian hospitality represents a distinctly noncapitalist social practice that is at odds with private ownership. This is precisely why it posed a threat to a settler nation, where "Indian dispossession," to quote Michael Rogin, "is part of the history of American capitalism."[42] Indian hospitality, and related forms of Indian sociality more generally, needed to be exploited and gradually dismantled in order to facilitate the development of capitalism, a process that Rosa Luxemburg, the socialist thinker and writer, succinctly summarizes: "Since the primitive associations of the natives are the strongest protection for their social organizations and for their material bases of existence, capital must begin by planning for the systematic destruction and annihilation of all non-capitalist social units which obstruct its development."[43] This strategy, which the geographer David Harvey has aptly called "accumulation by dispossession," describes an imperial endeavor that has its U.S. origins in Indian dispossession, a process that absorbed noncapitalist social formations into capitalist accumulation through the forced sale of Indian lands for private ownership.[44]

To acknowledge Indian hospitality is to open the possibility of recognizing alternative forms of organizing society beyond private ownership. The debate over Indian character, in other words, was part of a larger debate that involved the costs and consequences of settler development. Indian stereotypes, as Minnie Myrtle claimed, facilitated and justified a constellation of assumptions and practices that, in part, dictated policy. The recognition of Indian sociality—and Indian character—was a way to humanize the Indian and, in doing so, unsettle the assumptions behind those policies.

Wunnégin/Welcome

The origin of this counter-tradition of the white settler acknowledging and valuing Indian hospitality occurred fifteen years after Samoset greeted the Puritans with "Welcome, Englishmen." In *A Key into the Language of America* (1643), Roger Williams recounts his own warm welcome in what would become Providence, Rhode Island, when upon his exile from the Massachusetts Bay Colony, he arrived on the shores of the Narragansett and he and his family were greeted with "an animating salutation, *Whatcheer, Netop, Watcheer.*" He ironically remarks that while his fellow Puritans banished him from their community, he was warmly received among Native American strangers: "[T]he red men of the forest give them the welcome which their white brothers have refused."[45] It is not surprising that the word for "welcome" in Narragansett—*wunnégin*—should feature in *A Key into the Language of America*. This Narragansett term reflects a general sense of "civility" and "courtesie." The term also refers to a more fundamental value based on sociability: "[T]he sociablenesse of the nature of man appears in the wildest of them, who love societies; families, cohabitation, and consociation of houses and townes together."[46] *Wunnégin* describes the rituals of hospitality, but it also connotes a whole way of life imagined as a web of relationships that establishes the daily rhythms of sociability. It foregrounds belongingness, highlighting the interdependent ways one is interpolated communally.

Although the concept of *wunnégin* refers to concrete acts of hospitality rather than to a social theory, as Scott Pratt points out in *Native Pragmatism*, it nevertheless captures a central feature of Narragansett culture, epitomized through the notion of the open door, namely the general belief in tolerance that constituted a moral principle that helped to frame interactions within the community. *Wunnégin* signifies the ethical core of Indian sociability, which Roger Williams demonstrates etymologically by showing how the same root word, *wun*, also defines *well* and *good*, as in the phrase *"Wunnetu nitta"* ("all goodnesse is first in the heart"). *Wunnégin* reflects an openness, according to Scott Pratt, that expresses a "willingness to share one's resources, ideas, time and affection."[47]

Roger Williams understood this practice of welcoming to be a distinct feature of native culture, a point that he makes in the opening pages of *A Key:* "[T]hey are remarkably free and courteous, to invite all Strangers in; and if any come to them upon any occasion, they request them to *come in*, if they come not of themselves" [original emphasis]. He then lists the various phrases for gratitude and notes that he has seen among them a "heart sensible of kindnesses," far more than what he has witnessed "amongst thousands that call themselves *Christians*."[48] *A Key* also contains Williams's verse, where he adapts the theme of Indian hospitality to poetic form by contrasting Indian niceness with English rudeness:

> The Courteous Pagan shall condemne
> Uncourteous Englishmen,
> Who live like Foxes, Beares and Wolves,
> Or Lyon in his Den . . .
> If Natures sons both wild and tame,
> Humane and Courteous be:
> How ill becomes it Sonnes of God
> To want Humanity?[49]

Roger Williams juxtaposes the "Courteous Pagan" against the "Uncourteous Englishmen," thus anticipating by more than a century the Declaration of Independence and its reliance on English nastiness to define American niceness. New World niceness, whether in its indigenous form (Roger Williams) or its colonial manifestation (Thomas Jefferson), depends on English rudeness, which Williams personally experienced during his exile from the Puritan colony. This firsthand experience led him to identify with Native Americans as fellow outlaws in relation to the nascent Puritan state. Furthermore, Williams establishes an enduring binary that will structure an anti-imperial critique from Benjamin Franklin and Washington Irving to William Apess and Minnie Myrtle. By inverting the discourse of civility, Williams unsettles the ideology of white supremacy that will legitimate Indian extermination. Indian sociability is aligned with their humanity in contrast to the English, who are described as wolves and lions—animals on the prowl—who suffer from "a want of humanity." The Anglo recognition of Indian hospitality marks an emergent human rights discourse, exemplified by James Fenimore Cooper's Deerslayer, who believes that Indians belong inside "the category of human rights."[50]

Roger Williams also understood that Indian hospitality signaled a cultural response to danger, in which the concept of *wunnégin* was at times used to negotiate encounters with the figure of the cannibal, or the guest as ultimate threat, through techniques of tolerance and civility. Such cannibal stories in the Narragansett tradition were called *Mohowaugsuck* stories. As Pratt notes, welcoming strategies were often ways to disarm the stranger by incorporating him into the community. It was a strategy of conversion, whereby Indian niceness could turn the stranger's animosity into affection. It was a dangerous strategy, especially because the host was more than likely a lone woman. In one such story that Pratt relays, a Micmac story transcribed in the late nineteenth century, a woman was chopping wood when she was suddenly surprised by a *Cheenoo*, a cannibal giant who was a combination of man and beast. Rather than respond with fear, the startled woman decided to run up to the stranger and exclaim with feigned joy, "My dear father." "The *Cheenoo* was amazed beyond measure at such a greeting where he expected yells and prayers, and in mute wonder let himself be led into the wigwam."[51] In this story, the woman's feigned kindness disarms the fearful ogre; her embrace of the stranger as "my dear father" is a mode of incorporation, literally and metaphorically. It is a strategy that depends not on concealing one's vulnerability, but on exposing it by welcoming the other inside the home. As Pratt acknowledges, cannibals are dangerous, but the response to them "involves hospitality and kindness instead of violence, a stark contrast to Puritan modes of dealing with similar situations."[52]

These stories illustrate how Indian niceness or *wunnégin* represents a method of self-protection that wards off danger through affection, and it also functions as a therapeutic that converts a monster into a human being through social incorporation. Indian niceness describes a form of diplomacy, a way of dealing with the stranger through invitation rather than banishment, through peace rather than war. But cannibal stories also acknowledge the risks involved in such encounters, when indigenous welcoming strategies fail.

Benjamin Franklin, the Conestoga Massacre, and White Settler Guilt

One historical example of the failure of Indian niceness to convert the white settler (the *Cheenoo* figure) into a cohabiter occurred in Lancaster County, Pennsylvania, in 1763. The origin of this settlement, where a small native population lived alongside white settlers, bears an uncanny resemblance to the Puritans' arrival in Plymouth: "When the English first entered Pennsylvania," writes the novelist and human rights activist Helen Hunt Jackson over a century later, "messengers from the Conestoga Indians met them, bidding them welcome and bringing gifts of corn and venison and skins."[53] And like the peace treaty signed between the Puritans and Massasoit, the Conestoga signed a treaty of friendship with William Penn. Whether it is Plymouth or Pennsylvania, Indian hospitality greets the white settler. This familiar encounter narrative marks the reiterative story of pluralistic origins for the settler nation.

By 1763, there were only a few Conestoga Indians left, and they were "miserably poor" and earned a living making brooms, baskets, and wooden bowls. According to Helen Hunt Jackson, "They were wholly peaceable and unoffending, friendly to their white neighbors and pitifully clinging and affectionate, naming their children after whites who were kind to them." On December 14, 1763, a group of fifty Scotch-Irish settlers brutally murdered six sleeping Native Americans in the small village of Conestoga, sixty miles west of Philadelphia. The victims were hacked to death with tomahawks and scalped. Their homes were set on fire and most were burnt down. The fourteen survivors were taken by the government to Lancaster. However, on December 27, another mob from Paxton broke into the workhouse and killed all of the Native Americans who had sought shelter. The Paxton Boys, as they were called, saw themselves as heroes for their bravery in ridding the frontier of Native Americans. A few days later, a growing mob of over 250 wanted to kill more Native Americans, including a group of Christian Indians who had sought refuge in Philadelphia, when Benjamin Franklin, with six other civic leaders, confronted the mob and persuaded them to stop their pursuit. As historian Susan Kalter noted, "Franklin was instrumental in preventing a planned genocide."[54]

In the days that followed, Benjamin Franklin wrote a pamphlet entitled *A Narrative of the Late Massacres in Lancaster County, of a number of Indians* (1764). It pleads for justice and powerfully expresses moral outrage at what he witnessed. He refers to the series of murders as "massacres" and he anticipates the language of Zitkala-Sa when he describes the violence as an "unfortunate Catastrophe." The massacre represents a catastrophe not only for Native Americans but also for what it says about the perpetrators of the crime, who are described as "white people" and "English" interchangeably. Franklin understands the tragedy in terms that we would today call a racially motivated hate crime: "The only Crime of these poor Wretches seems to have been, that they had a reddish brown Skin, and black Hair."[55] He then goes on to refer to the victims by name, beginning with Shehaes, an elderly man who was "a faithful and affectionate Friend to the English," together with his daughter Peggy, who cared for her father "with filial Duty and Tenderness." By naming the victims and briefly describing them in terms of their relation with others, Franklin humanizes the Native Americans and juxtaposes Indian kindness against "Christian white savages."[56]

Though written before the Revolutionary War, Franklin's *Narrative of the Late Massacres*, which earned him many enemies in Pennsylvania, represents a foundational text of American niceness for how it critiques white violence by emphasizing Indian kindness, betrayed hospitality, and white guilt. Franklin's pamphlet inaugurates a rhetorical practice that will continue well into the nineteenth century, epitomized in Helen Hunt Jackson's article on the Conestoga massacre, where she revisits the Paxton Boys' violence and quotes from Franklin's pamphlet on the eve of another round of settler violence against the "peaceable Utes" of Colorado in 1880.[57] Franklin's pamphlet also sets up the binary between the Ugly American (the "mad men") and the nice American (the "just men"). The "mad men," according to Franklin, are those who perpetrated the crime, and they are described as "white Christian Savages," while the "just men" are those like Franklin who are outraged by white settler violence and feel morally obligated to bear witness to the human rights abuses that will continue to haunt them and their progeny.

Franklin's pamphlet, moreover, is significant for how it articulates white settler guilt as the foundational affect of the nation. The rhetorical form that this guilt takes is betrayed hospitality, where Indian kindness is not reciprocated but instead violently rejected. In his pamphlet, Franklin returns to the seventeenth century and the primal scene of American (i.e., Indian) niceness:

> The poor People have been always our Friends. Their Fathers received ours, when Strangers here, with Kindness and Hospitality. Behold the Return we have made them!—When we grew more numerous and powerful, they put themselves under our *Protection*. See, in the mangled Corpses of the Last Remains of the Tribe, how effectually we have afforded it to them![58]

What sickens Franklin is how the elderly Shehaes mistakenly believed that he would be safe among them. Franklin, a diplomat and Indian treaty negotiator, would go on to write twenty years later in "Remarks Concerning the Savages of North America" (1784) that hospitality is a form of diplomacy that involves safety and respect, where the host offers the guest sanctuary and security.[59] The fact that the guest in this case is not a stranger but those "who were born among us" makes this betrayal all the more morally repugnant.

Franklin then connects white guilt with national shame in refusing to bury Indian bones; instead, he insists on keeping them visible for all to see as "bloody Proofs of their Inhumanity and Cruelty."[60] The bones take on a metaphoric quality in the sense that they remain visible in order to facilitate national reckoning. Franklin understands that guilt and shame can be productive emotions, necessary for galvanizing political and social change. Although he uses these terms interchangeably at points, there are also differences. Where guilt is experienced internally and refers to one's moral conscience, shame is a social emotion that is public and visible, linked to exposure and one's reputation.

To differentiate between guilt and shame, Franklin borrows from the conventions of classical rhetoric, where each term has a different metaphoric relation to the senses. Shame, for instance, is traditionally conveyed through sight and being seen, which Franklin describes through the "mangled Corpses" of the victims and warns that their "spectres" will haunt "your innocent Children!" By contrast, guilt is classically associated with metaphors of hearing, particularly the voice of judgment or the voices of the dead. Franklin expresses this through the "dying Shrieks and Groans of the Murdered, [who] will often [be] found in your Ears."[61] Guilt, described through the aural metaphor of an internal voice of judgment, is private; it is something that festers inside.

By bringing guilt and shame together, Franklin shows how guilt needs to be exposed as shame. It must be externalized onto the body politic as a way to shock the nation into more humane behavior. It is a moral imperative that private guilt be made public as a way to shame white settlers for their complicity in colonial violence. This shame-based model of moral outrage anticipates what Karl Jaspers, in writing about German guilt after the Holocaust, would call "guilt consciousness," a necessary practice of remembering the past—with all of its atrocities and suffering—in order to cultivate humility as a precondition for a new form of "self-consciousness."[62] Franklin's angry words on the Conestoga Massacre would be repeatedly invoked throughout the nineteenth century as an example of ethically motivated remembering. When Helen Hunt Jackson published her colossal account of Native American mistreatment in Century of Dishonor in 1881, she sent a copy to every member of Congress with the following quote from Benjamin Franklin written in red on the cover: "Look upon your hands. They are stained with the blood of your relatives."[63] By quoting Franklin, Helen Hunt Jackson invoked a counter-tradition of American niceness, one that linked a shamed-based model of moral outrage with a call for national humility. She wanted to switch the national rhetoric from one of disavowal to acknowledgment, as a way to recognize the consequences of manifest destiny.

Yet Franklin was also a facilitator of and a believer in manifest destiny, thus illustrating the very tensions embedded in the terms *hospitality* and *hostility*. As Susan Kalter noted, Franklin's stance on Native American issues was highly contradictory, torn between imperial designs and his appreciation of Native American people, ideas, and culture.[64] He could be heroic, as he was with the Paxton Boys, as well as complicit in Indian dispossession through his diplomatic work as a treaty negotiator in Pennsylvania. Consequently, his call to acknowledge shame and guilt was not only national but perhaps also deeply personal.

Washington Irving, Native Americans, and New World Guilt

In referring to the specters of Conestoga and the groans of the dying Indians, Franklin describes generational guilt and ancestral shame, where the deeds of one's ancestors haunt the living. Franklin's words acquired a spectral form that haunted future generations of Americans, who carried on his task of national shaming through a sense of inherited guilt. His most immediate descendant was Washington Irving, who like Franklin spent much of his adult life abroad in Europe, a geographical distance that made him, to quote Wai Chee Dimock, one of the "great un-American authors of the nineteenth century."[65] American critics were uncomfortable with his expatriate status, since it had produced literary works that had, to quote poet and critic Richard Dana, Sr., "lost too many of her home qualities." In 1822, Edward Everett, who was then editor of the *North American Review,* expressed his disappointment that Irving did not put his energy into "topics purely American."[66] Everett objected to the fact that one could read *The Sketch Book* and not know the nationality of its author. But what Everett's reprimand ignores is the power of Irving's essay about Native Americans in *The Sketch Book.* "Traits of Indian Character," which originally appeared in *Analectic Magazine* in 1814, recounts the atrocities committed against Native Americans during King Philip's War in 1675–1676.[67] For the Puritans and their descendants, King Philip's War was a holy war against the forces of barbarism, but Irving broke ranks with this dominant Anglo-American interpretation and described the war as a calamity.

"How wars are remembered," writes historian Jill Lepore, "can be just as important as how they were fought and first described."[68] This was particularly true for nineteenth-century writers, such as Irving, Lydia Maria Child, William Apess (who claimed he was a descendent of Philip), and the playwright John Augustus Stone, who penned *Metamora*, the most popular Indian play of this period, which was largely based on the Philip of Irving's essay. All of these writers were interested in retelling the atrocities of this seventeenth-century war from the native's perspective. This short but brutal war, according to Lepore, "proved to be not only the most fatal war in all of American history but also one of the most merciless." [69] The Puritans declared war against Massasoit's youngest son, Metacom, whom the English called King Philip, for allegedly planning a conspiracy to kill the English. It was, as we would say in today's parlance, a preemptive war. The English went on to destroy numerous Indian villages, while selling captives, including Philip's surviving wife and son, into slavery in the West Indies. After describing the massacre of innocent Indian villagers, including children, whose bodies were cut into pieces, Irving pauses and addresses his reader directly: "Do these records of ancient excesses fill us with disgust and aversion? Let us take heed that we do not suffer ourselves to be hurried into the same iniquities." Irving invokes the seventeenth century to ask his reader why these distant crimes stir more horror than contemporary examples of Indian killing. Today, he says, "we are reconciled to the present perpetration of injustice by all the selfish motives with which interest chills the heart and silences the conscience."[70]

Irving is one of Franklin's "just men." By expressing outrage at the absence of guilt, Irving targets his own class: well-educated individuals in secure homes in cities and in other populous regions, far away from the supposed threat of Indians, who nonetheless speak rationally about "exterminating measures." According to Irving, Indian-hating pervades the country and the city, the educated and the uneducated, the urbanite and the backwoodsman alike. Irving asks his readers to look back in time in order to provide a point of comparison to assess what the U.S. military is doing today, particularly in "the ravaged country of the Creeks to behold a picture of exterminating warfare."[71] Irving was referring to the Creek War of 1813–1814, and specifically to the mass murder of 800 men, women, and children at Horse Shoe Bend, Florida, where General Andrew Jackson supervised the mutilation of corpses, which involved cutting the tip of each dead Indian's nose to count the number of victims and taking long strips of skin from the dead to use as bridle reins.[72] Notably, all references to the Creek War were removed from Irving's essay when it appeared the following year in *The Sketch Book.*

Like Benjamin Franklin before him, Irving invokes guilt and shame through visual and aural metaphors. Irving, for instance, implicitly refers to shame through the image of "mangled corpses," and he invokes guilt aurally through the "cries" of the dying. Resurrecting the past to awaken the same horrific response in the present, Irving ends by looking toward the future: How will future generations look back upon the nineteenth century? Posterity, he writes, "will either turn with horror and incredulity from the tale, or blush with indignation at the inhumanity of their forefathers."[73] Irving does not present the Vanishing American as an elegiac figure whose disappearance is seen as the inevitable price of progress. Like Franklin, Irving is outraged at the policies of extermination and the ideology of Indian-hating, particularly by those of his own race and class. There is nothing inevitable about these crimes; they are preventable. They are, as Zitkala-Sa argued at the end of the nineteenth century, man-made disasters. And this represents the most tragic aspect of the situation for Irving, since it does not need to be this way.

The power of Irving's words cannot be underestimated. They were quoted and his essay reproduced and disseminated throughout the first half of the nineteenth century. Cherokee writer and editor Elias Boudinot, who often reprinted the speeches and words of white supporters in his newspaper *Cherokee Phoenix,* republished Irving's "Indian Character" in its entirety in his book *A Star in the West; or, a Humble Attempt to Discover the Long Lost Ten Tribes of Israel, preparatory to their return to their beloved city, Jerusalem* (1816). Referring to himself in the third person, Boudinot introduces Irving's words as those of a kindred spirit when he writes, "He was rejoiced to know that such despised sufferers, however degraded, had found compassion in other breasts besides his own."[74] He only wishes that the original Europeans had arrived with "disinterested historians" who could have represented the Indians' cause "fully and fairly to posterity." This is one of the reasons why nineteenth-century Americans, native and nonnative, return to the seventeenth century: to rewrite conquest in order to recognize the humanity of the Indian. To underscore Indian humanity, Boudinot refers to Indian hospitality: "frank and candid, but plain and blunt hospitality and kindness . . . that often astonishes white people." The guest is simply asked: "Are you come a friend, in the name of the great spirit!"[75]

In addition to Irving, another kindred spirit whom Boudinot published in the *Cherokee Phoenix* was Lydia Maria Child, whose political activism began in antiremoval politics and then went on to include abolitionism.[76] She, together with Irving, built on this counter-tradition of Anglo-American dissidence by revising the historical narrative of encounter from the seventeenth century. In her 1829 book *The First Settlers of New England*, Child quotes extensively from Irving's second sketch on seventeenth-century history, "Philip, King of Pokanoket," which appeared in 1814 and was published again in *The Sketch Book*. Privately printed but never publicly distributed, Child's *First Settlers* praises Indian hospitality in relation to Puritan hostility and wishes that Puritan society had been influenced by Indian generosity, an influence that would have gradually "improved and softened the stern and morose feelings" of the superstitious Puritans. Written in the voice of a mother to her daughters, Child's mother says that by quoting Irving she wants to show that opposition to Indian removal and the acknowledgment of the historical mistreatment of Indians constitute part of a larger tradition that consists of "many truly worthy and intelligent individuals."[77] Her daughter asks rhetorically whether Washington Irving was related to George Washington, and, in doing so, suggests a counter-lineage of American nationhood, one with both a conscience and self-awareness of the bloodshed involved in nation-building, a counter-lineage that exists alongside the dominant story of triumph that justifies violence in the name of self-defense. Child quotes the most poignant part of Irving's portrait of Philip: "It is painful to perceive even from these partial narratives how the footsteps of civilization may be traced in the blood of the aborigines; how easily the colonists were moved to hostility by the lust of conquest; how merciless and exterminating was their warfare."[78]

Quoting Irving became a standard part of how this counter-lineage was created. Incorporating his words into other texts, whether Cherokee or Anglo-American, established an alternative version of U.S. development. In 1948, the American political theorist E. M. Winslow commented that the nineteenth-century critique of the human costs of westward expansion, epitomized in such figures as Washington Irving, would produce "some of the sharpest anti-imperialist sentiment ever developed in any country."[79] Winslow's view of Irving as an anti-imperialist goes against the critical grain, which more commonly views Irving as an apologist for American progress, one who laments its tragic implications as inevitable.[80] But such a reading overlooks the extent of Irving's moral outrage about contemporary human rights abuses against Native Americans and his strategy of invoking the distant past, particularly the seventeenth century, to shed light on the legacy of Indian-killing in U.S. history. Winslow's most significant observation is that the U.S. critique of imperialism begins as a response to domestic imperialism and Indian dispossession in the first half of the nineteenth century, and not as it is conventionally argued, with the acquisition of overseas territories in the aftermath of the Spanish American War of 1898. The full nineteenth century, and not just its tail end, produced a long-standing tradition of anti-imperial dissent that took the form of public shaming.

O Shame, Where Is Thy Blush?

The word *shame* is etymologically derived, as Charles Darwin notes in a footnote in *The Expression of the Emotions in Man and Animals*, from the idea of shade or concealment (the low German *scheme* for shadow). Since shame needs to be seen, the face became the vehicle for making this particular affect visible. The face in nineteenth-century sentimentalism, as Christopher Castiglia notes, represented a window into one's soul and marked the border between interiority and exteriority, private and public.[81] The ethics of blushing depended on the legibility of one's face, reflecting the belief that bodies do not lie.

It is significant that blushing, which is typically seen at this time as evidence of the maidenly virtue of innocence and modesty, should also refer to the recognition of guilt, corruption, and murder. Blushing, in this context, signifies not a lack of knowledge, but rather one's possession of it. Furthermore, blushing only happens to those who pause and reflect, who take heed of the consequences of violent actions and show their disapproval. In contrast to sentimental aesthetics, where the blush is involuntary, frequently a spontaneous reaction to sexual desire that exceeds the subject's will, Irving and others refer to a different kind of blushing, one that is predicated on reflection and connected to thinking and reasoning. Irving's "Traits of Indian Character" concludes with the theme of posterity, where he imagines future white Americans reacting to the violence of their ancestors by wondering whether they will "blush with indignation at the inhumanity of their forefathers." [82]

For many, blushing was thought to be the exclusive property of white people. According to the historian George Bancroft, Indians have little "transparency of the skin." Instead of blushing, the Indian expresses his passions through "strong contortions or the kindling of the eye, that seems ready to burst from its socket. With rare exceptions, he cannot blush."[83] The capacity to blush was an index of a race's ability to control their emotional impulses. Since one could not readily see blushing on dark skin, many assumed that Indians and blacks were shame-free. "While this made conquest and the slave trade easier to conduct," writes the cultural critic James B. Twitchell, "it was based on mistaking the absence of expression for the absence of affect."[84] Charles Darwin, in his chapter on shame and blushing in *The Expression of the Emotions*, goes against the dominant strain of contemporary race theory by insisting that dark-skinned people can in fact blush, and he cites an eyewitness account: "Mr. Washington Matthews has often seen a blush on the faces of the young squaws belonging to various wild Indian tribes of North America."[85] Darwin counters the race theorists of his day by insisting that blushing signifies our common humanity. It is not the preserve of a single race, nor should it be used as a ploy in defense of white supremacy. Yet in the United States, there are different registers of blushing: Anglo-Americans who have a strong ethical sensibility blush from the guilt they feel for the violence they have collectively and historically committed, whereas for Native Americans, blushing is a sign of their humanity. What unites them is their niceness: Blushing connects the ashamed Anglo-American with the amiable Indian.

The tactic of white shaming and the concomitant defense of blushing as a multiracial affect were not exclusive to Native Americans. In 1879, black nationalist Martin Delany would make a similar case for the capacity of black people to blush in order to show that blushing is not a sign of white superiority but instead reflects our common humanity.[86] Frederick Douglass also understood the power of blushing, primarily as an expression of white shame. In his speeches, he would frequently invoke—as did abolitionist rhetoric more generally—the epithet "our guilty republic" or "our national shame" in order to show how the entire nation was implicated in the system of slavery: "[T]he whole American people," said Douglass, "are responsible for slavery and must share, in its guilt and shame."

In one speech, Douglass describes how abolitionist Wendell Phillips was returning to the United States from Europe in 1842 on a state-of-the-art American ship and was experiencing a feeling of national pride while aboard such a modern vessel, when he realized that it would be used to defend the Atlantic slave trade. Phillips said, "I blushed in utter *shame* for my country."[87] Wendell Phillips's blush is a dramatic moment in Douglass's speech because it illustrates at an individual level what Douglass and others wanted the entire nation to feel: to be ashamed at the injustices committed in the name of the United States. This is the same sort of blushing that Franklin and Irving are asking their readers to experience when considering Indian extermination. For Lydia Maria Child, the recognition of national guilt in terms of Native Americans was connected to the defense of black rights. As she wrote in *An Appeal for the Indians* (1868), "without intermitting our vigilant watch over the rights of black men, it is our duty to arouse the nation to a sense of its guilt concerning the red men."[88] This counter-tradition of American niceness demonstrates how the affective language of guilt and shame played a fundamental role in the nascent movement for human rights that developed domestically in the nineteenth century.

Franklin's legacy, which includes Irving, Lydia Maria Child, and Helen Hunt Jackson, focuses on the human rights abuses of manifest destiny in ways that are truly significant, anti-imperial, and courageous, but they avoid a structural critique, one that would address the systematic violence embedded in settler colonialism that depends on continual Indian dispossession. There are certain questions that cannot be asked, such as: Is it possible to have a mild form of manifest destiny? Could there be nicer modes of settler colonialism? These questions reappear in the subsequent chapters of this book with slightly different inflections depending on the topic: Is it possible to have a moderate form of slavery? And later in the century, after the Pullman Strike of 1894 and the Spanish American War of 1898: Could there be a kinder form of capitalism, where the profit motive was curbed? And what would a democratic empire look like? All of these questions are implicitly interrogating the limits of reform as well as the extent to which violence is always already embedded in economic, political, and social relations. Settler-Indian dealings provide an important urtext for inquiring into the limits of sociability, where hospitality is itself haunted by its etymological shadow side of hostility.

Indian Testimonials and White Shame: The Case of John Heckewelder

To see Indians as amiable rather than knife-wielding scalpers is to recognize their humanity, and that was a risky thing to do at a time of Indian killing. The extent of the opposition to portrayals of Indian amiability can be seen in the strong attack against the ethnographic writing of Moravian missionary Reverend John Heckewelder, who spent three decades living among the Lenape in Pennsylvania and Ohio. He depicted the Lenape as possessing a rich and intricate language (that he spoke fluently), a generous and hospitable demeanor, and well-honed diplomatic skills. Heckewelder was credited for humanizing Native Americans, demonstrating their fondness for metaphor, their passion for oratory, and their ability to resolve conflicts peacefully. When his *History, Manners, and Customs of The Indian Nations* was published in 1818, one reviewer praised the book and called for a change in national policy since Indians deserve "respectful treatment, and to all possible justice at the hands of their white countrymen." In the *North American Review* in 1819, another reviewer similarly commended Heckewelder for inspiring readers to "feel more kindly towards that unfortunate race."[89] Depictions of Indian niceness could cultivate white sympathy, which could then lead to calls for social justice and an end to their mistreatment.

For those who supported Andrew Jackson's Indian policy, and particularly those employed to enforce it, representing Indian amiability was dangerous. Heckewelder received acrimonious comments from leading figures of the age that saw him as an apologist for the Indian, and they discredited his work as being fictitious because he turned Indian defects into virtues. Lewis Cass, the governor and superintendent of Indian affairs for the Michigan territory and Andrew Jackson's chief of Indian removal, wrote several pieces dismissing Heckewelder.

In 1828, Cass sardonically wrote, "The most idle traditions of the Indian, become for him sober history . . . their astonishing improvidence, hospitality." Heckewelder's "sin" consists of the fact that he was too generous in his rendering of Indians. Although the Moravian missionary had died five years earlier in 1823, Cass nonetheless criticized Heckewelder by condescendingly saying that although the Moravian missionary was a sincere and well-meaning man, his work is merely "a collection of anecdotes" and is "little better than a work of the imagination."[90] Concerned about how the prestigious British journal *Quarterly Review* was citing Heckewelder's work to denounce frontier settlers and the U.S. policy of Indian "extermination," Cass was intent on discrediting Heckewelder's work by accusing him of exaggerating Indian intellectual and moral development while considering them superior to frontier settlers.[91] For Cass, the integrity of frontier settlers had to be redeemed at the expense of Indian character and intelligence.

John Heckewelder was one of the first to recognize the significance of listening to Native Americans. Fluent in Lenape, he transcribed Indian speech and included reiterations of a central theme, namely, white settlement as the betrayal of Native American hospitality. In *History, Manners and Customs of Indian Nations*, he describes listening to native retellings of Anglo-Indian encounters based on "European ingratitude and injustice": "Thus these good Indians, with a kind of melancholy pleasure, recite the long history of their sufferings." He then translates their speeches and testimonials as instances of bearing witness to settler-invader violence: "When the white men arrived in the south, we received them as friends; we did the same when they arrived in the east. It was we, it was our forefathers, who made them welcome, and let them sit down by our side . . . we thought they must be a good people. We were mistaken."[92] This Lenape refrain—"we were mistaken"—anticipates Black Elk's notion of the Indian mistake. Listening to these Lenape stories told in their own language, which according to Heckewelder, "our polished idioms cannot imitate," leads him to conclude: "I felt ashamed of being a *white man*."[93] By admitting shame, Heckewelder courageously acknowledges the violence embedded in whiteness, while at the same time recognizing the limits of translation. In doing so, he does not respond defensively to these memories of encounter but instead stays and listens, translating the pain of these oral testimonies to an Anglophone audience.

What Lewis Cass finds most appalling in Heckewelder's book is the fact that he represents Indian speech. "Their language is plain and unornamented free from the labored conceits," Cass defensively argues, "as they themselves are from affectation."[94] Cass finds Heckewelder's depiction of Indian eloquence to be implausible and even staged. According to Cass, who was not fluent in any indigenous language, Indians lack rhetorical skill; they are stoic, simple, and unemotional. Cass's Indians are stereotypes, whereas Heckewelder's are passionate, melancholic, and articulate. By telling the story of westward expansion through the words of its victims—and to quote the Indian extensively—is to ascribe to them an affective dimension that humanizes them as feeling subjects. Just as dangerously, these stories also incite an emotional response in white listeners, making them feel ashamed to be historically complicit in Indian extermination.

Heckewelder's ethnography resensitizes white Americans to the consequences of their own history. This is precisely why Cass felt compelled to discredit Heckewelder's amiable Indian. To *feel* shame is part of a moral compass encapsulated in the words of Heckewelder's contemporary Edmund Burke: "While shame keeps its watch virtue is not wholly extinguished in the heart."[95] For Heckewelder, as well as for Irving and others, the blush of shame is a manifestation of moral conscience.

Natty Bumppo as the Reluctant Indian-killer

Lewis Cass's disparagement of Heckewelder also extended to James Fenimore Cooper. As literary historians have frequently noted, Cooper was highly influenced by Heckewelder's ethnographic writings, and he relied on them to depict his Native American characters. The "nice" Indians in Cooper's Leatherstocking Tales are almost always Heckewelder's Lenapes. The missionary and the novelist, according to Cass, depicted the Indian through rose-colored glasses as the Noble Savage cut off from reality with "no living prototype in our forests." Cass mocked Cooper's Indians relentlessly, concluding that he had "consulted the book of Mr. Heckewelder, instead of the book of nature."[96] Cass wasn't alone in his criticism. The literary reviewer W. H. Gardiner wrote in the *North American Review* that Cooper "relied exclusively upon the narrations of the enthusiastic and visionary Heckewelder." The nineteenth-century consensus on Cooper was that his Indians were implausible because they were too nice. "They are the Indians of Mr. Heckewelder," writes Cass, "and not the fierce and crafty warriors and hunters, that roam through our forests."[97] An anonymous reviewer of *The Prairie*, while praising the novel as a whole, remarks: "Mr. Cooper is not apt to idealize his characters, but he has presented the aborigines of this continent in far too flattering colors ... Mr. Cooper has given us Cato and Coriolanus dressed in blankets and moccasins."[98]

James Fenimore Cooper has been described as the most "original" writer and "the most thoroughly national." Melville referred to Cooper as "our national novelist," and historian Francis Parkman called him "truly American."[99] Cooper's expatriate status did not seem to affect his national credentials in the same way that it did Washington Irving. But for Irving, far more than Cooper, the Indian question involved the issue of responsibility: Who is accountable for the systematic violence against the indigenous population and what retribution should there be? For Irving (like Benjamin Franklin before him), Indian hospitality is a way to talk about human rights. By contrast, Cooper avoids questions of responsibility and justice. Instead, Cooper turns to the personal, preferring the mythological rather than the historical in focusing on the interracial friendship between Natty Bumppo and Chingachgook. This "archetypal relationship," according to Leslie Fiedler, "haunts the American psyche: two lonely men, one dark-skinned, one white, bend together over a carefully guarded fire in the virgin heart of the American wilderness."[100]

Despite Natty Bumppo's insistence that a white man has "white man's gifts" and a red man has "red man's gifts," Cooper's novels depict the frontier as a multilingual site of encounter, where Natty speaks proficient Lenape and understands the cultural mannerisms and rituals of the Delaware, while his lifelong friend Chingachgook speaks fluent English. Their conversations frequently switch from one language to the other or are a combination of both.[101] Furthermore, Indians have taught Natty Bumppo to cultivate greater sympathy, especially for people with disabilities. In *The Deerslayer* (1841), Natty

Bumppo refuses to disparage the "half-witted Hetty": "[H]is education among Indians had taught him to treat those who were thus afflicted by Providence, with more than common tenderness."[102] But even in this intercultural space there are distinct binaries. Not only does Cooper juxtapose the nice Indian and the savage Indian, he also contrasts the nice American (Natty Bumppo) and the ruthless frontiersman (Tom Hutter, Abiram White). The dualism of the nice/vulgar American finds its white and native inflections throughout Cooper's novels.

In contrast to the typical white frontiersman whose conscience hardens through fear and violence, Natty Bumppo becomes more open-minded and compassionate; Indian tenderness changes him and he recognizes the Indian as fully human. This points to another instance when subaltern niceness structures white American character. But where Franklin, who was writing in the context of the massacres of the Conestoga Indians, considered "backwoodsmen" to be murderous whites, Cooper's Natty Bumppo complicates such a type, showing how a backwoodsman can be a gentleman in rawhide. He can be decent, broad-minded, and multilingual, more at home among the Lenape than in New England society or even among other white frontiersmen.

Natty Bumppo's niceness is most apparent in his hesitancy to use violence. In *The Deerslayer*, Bumppo is the reluctant Indian killer, only killing when he is forced to do so. He shoots his first Mingo while defending himself against Indian aggression. It was a situation where it was either he or the Indian; one had to die. Wanting to provide the wounded Indian with as much comfort as possible, Natty gives him water and "took the head of his mortally wounded adversary in his own lap, and endeavored to soothe his anguish, in the best manner he could."[103] Although circumstance forced him to kill the Indian, Natty feels badly for doing so, and he does everything in his power to make sure the dying Indian has a pleasant death (he promises no scalping). Natty Bumppo is the nice American who kills with compassion, recognizing the dignity of his victim.

Leslie Fiedler writes that Cooper tells the same truth about the Indian as Harriet Beecher Stowe tells about the slave: "[I]n each it is guilt that speaks, the guilt of a whole community."[104] But there is a significant difference. Where Stowe's abolitionism wants to eradicate the source of that guilt, Cooper seeks to assuage the guilt, just as Natty

Bumppo soothes the pain of the dying Indian. Natty Bumppo, as the nice white American, attempts to harmonize two irreconcilable desires: to recognize the integrity of Indians and the necessity of westward expansion. Indian dispossession was a capitalist endeavor, and for Cooper, who had investments in the Atlantic cotton trade and western land speculation, the task was to reconcile profit with kindness.[105] Natty Bumppo embodies the contradictions produced by the clash between manifest destiny and liberal guilt. In this sense, Natty Bumppo's niceness is compensatory. It compensates for the brutality of westward expansion through Bumppo's likability as a slightly awkward introvert who is Brother Jonathan in the wilderness.

In fleeing civilization, Natty Bumppo is not only escaping heterosexual marriage and the conventions of society, but he is also, to quote Fiedler, "fleeing from his guilt."[106] By refusing white sociality in the form of pioneer culture or even the company of other backwoodsmen, Natty Bumppo disassociates himself from the collective plunder of white settlement. Despite his comments about "white gifts," he doesn't really bond with white men. By befriending Chingachgook, Bumppo can be loved by the victim in a form of an interracial male love that accentuates Bumppo's innocence and exonerates him from complicity. He is the white exception. In fleeing society, Natty Bumppo acknowledges shame—shame at his whiteness, shame at his culture, shame at his nation—and one wonders to what extent Cooper is making a similar move, taking refuge in his Leatherstocking world, which, to paraphrase Richard Slotkin, provides the possibility of resolving conflicts that could not otherwise find resolution.[107] Cooper depicts the prototypical nice American in the twinned forms of the nice frontiersman and the friendly Indian. Their interracial friendship personalizes the political, cutting their bond off from a larger context through the hermetic world of the wilderness. In contrast to the counter-tradition of American niceness that Irving represents, which depends on Anglo-American shaming, Cooper's version of American niceness operates more as an apology than as a condemnation. It turns a history of colonization into one of red-white amiability, where Indian hospitality is incorporated within a larger narrative of nation-building.

Where Indian hospitality for Franklin and Irving was a way to introduce an alternative mode of diplomacy, a different structure of sociality that could have formed the basis of an alternative trajectory of progress, Cooper turns to interpersonal niceness. The friendship of Bumppo and Chingachgook exists in the transhistorical imaginary world of the wilderness, with camaraderie providing a way to forget the past and escape generational shame. But historical time still permeates the forest so that Natty Bumppo's niceness can also be seen as a form of compensation for the treachery of white settlement; his generosity ameliorates the brutal seizure of land. It is the squatter's way of saying, "I'm sorry."

Metamora and the Making of the Nice American Girl

Several of Cooper's novels were turned into popular dramas, including his novel about King Philip's War, *The Wept of Wish-ton-Wish* (1829). Although the novel was considered a failure at the time, the play became a commercial success on the antebellum stage. But by far the most successful nineteenth-century play that addressed Indians, and particularly the seventeenth-century history of New England removal, was *Metamora; or, the Last of the Wampanoags* (1829), based on Massasoit's second son Metacom. This highly successful play brought King Philip's War to a nineteenth-century audience at the height of Indian removal and it continued to be performed through the 1880s. In 1828, actor Edwin Forrest offered five hundred dollars for "the best tragedy, in five acts, of which the hero, or principal character, shall be an aboriginal of this country." Headed by the poet William Cullen Bryant, the committee selected John Augustus Stone's *Metamora*, a play largely based on Washington Irving's sketch of "Philip of Pokanoket." As Jill Lepore has noted, *Metamora*, like Irving's essay, reverses the Revolutionary-era's version of King Philip's War by championing Metamora as a true American patriot in the vein of Patrick Henry.[108]

The play also shares Irving's sympathetic portrayal of the Native Americans' plight, together with a sense of moral outrage at what the English did in the name of freedom. But critics have been divided as to whether this backward glance is an implicit critique of Indian removal policies in the nineteenth century. Some have argued that the play exonerates white Americans from guilt because it portrays Indians as a tragic race whose demise was inevitable. The play, moreover, gives the Vanishing American a theatrical form. In my view, *Metamora* does not let white Americans off the hook that easily. It participates in a genealogy of national shame, like Irving's sketch, by looking back to the first wave of Indian killing in order to critique the repetition of Indian extermination in the nineteenth century. *Metamora* engages New World guilt, provokes this guilt, meditates on it, and then offers a way to reconcile it. The question to be asked of *Metamora* is not whether it is pro- or anti-Indian removal, but how does it allow a white settler nation to grapple with a guilty conscience?

Metamora shames white America and then offers a way out of that shame by incorporating the Indian into a national narrative of American niceness that combines colonial guilt with Indian hospitality. In contrast to John Brougham's *Metamora; or, The Last of the Pollywogs* (1847), a burlesque parody of Stone's tragedy, where the Indian is reduced to a ridiculous figure not worthy of respect, Stone's drama is serious, earnest, and didactic. Stone draws heavily from the Romantic stereotype of the Noble Savage to depict Metamora as a loyal, brave, and dignified chief, but he also emphasizes Metamora's domesticity: He is a family man who loves his wife, Nahmeokee, and his infant son and is most frequently depicted at home. Although the play tells the story of King Philip's war, which destroyed native New England in the seventeenth century, it tells this story primarily through its impact on the Indian village and particularly the wigwam as the site of Indian hospitality.

The opening scene of the play presents the problem of white guilt and its possible solution by portraying two types of white people—the nasty English aristocrat Mordaunt and his daughter Oceana, the nice American girl. Mordaunt, a regicide, yearns to return home to Britain and he literally faces eastward, looking toward his motherland, anxiously awaiting the arrival of a British ship to take him home. On this ship is Lord Fitzarnold, whom Mordaunt has arranged to marry his daughter Oceana so they can all return to Britain to resume their class position among the English nobility. Oceana, however, has fallen in love with Walter, a local orphan, and despite her name (which she acquired because of her nautical birth), she is firmly rooted in the New World and does not want to go to Britain or marry an English aristocrat. In a sense, Stone is playing with the same duality of whiteness that Franklin inaugurated in his comparison between "just men" and "mad men," but in this case the "just men" consist of the young

American girl and her boyfriend Walter, who are sympathetic toward Metamora and his family. The "mad men" are the English villains, who are, to use Franklin's phrase, "the Christian White Savages." This juxtaposition of two competing types of whiteness—the nice American and the savage Englishman—is important in terms of how each relates to Metamora and Indian hospitality.

In the opening scene, Oceana appears with Walter and Metamora, the latter of whom saved her life the previous day by killing a panther on the beach with a perfectly aimed arrow. Now she finds Metamora injured from a wolf attack and she offers to wrap his wounds with her scarf, and in gratitude, he invites them to his home: "Come to my wigwam." This opening scene presents Indian hospitality in the context of reciprocity, with the nice American girl aiding the injured sachem as a way of thanking him for saving her life. His subsequent lines, when taken together, read like a manifesto of Indian kindness: "Metamora forgives not a wrong and forgets not a kindness," and he adds, "to those that spoke kindly to me in the words of love I have been pliant."[109]

Soon after, Metamora is forced to appear before the English council to determine if he was involved in the death of John Sassamon ("Sassamond" in the play), a Christian Indian who told governor Edward Winslow that Metamora was planning to attack the colony. Before the English colonists, Metamora pauses and recounts the primal scene of American niceness: "The red man took you as a little child and opened the door of his wigwam . . . Your little ones smiled when they heard the loud voice of the storm, for our fires were warm and the Indian was the white man's friend."[110] In the subsequent scene, when he returns to his wigwam, Metamora finishes this speech among the Wampanoag: "When the strangers came from afar off, they were like a little tree; but now they are grown up and their spreading branches threaten to keep the light from you. They ate of your corn and drank of your cup, and now they lift up their arms against you."[111] Metamora repeats the familiar refrain of Indian hospitality betrayed, with the Puritans attacking the very people who once saved them.

The play portrays King Philip's War as an attack on the Indian home, and specifically, the Indian family—father, mother, and infant son. Sentimentalism is applied not to the English but to the Indians, humanizing them through their domestic relations. The English are portrayed as baby-killers, a claim that is visually reinforced when Nahmeokee shows Metamora the corpse of their murdered son. She asks her husband, "Metamora, is our nation dead? Are we alone in the land of our fathers?" Rather than to be sold into slavery, the fate of the actual wife of Metamora, Nahmeokee consents to her murder by the hand of her husband. Soon after he stabs her in the heart, he is found by the English and shot. As he is dying from his wounds, he looks directly at the audience and exclaims, "My curses on you, white men!"[112] Metamora's final words, which are also the final words of the play, shame white America.

Edwin Forrest performed the role with his trademark combination of vitriolic pathos and passion, a style that may have seemed heavy-handed to some highbrow Americans, but nonetheless had a powerful effect on Jacksonian audiences. In January 1830, the same month Jackson proposed the Indian Removal Act, a theater reviewer noted that *Metamora* owes everything to Forrest: "[I]f it had fallen into the hands of any other actor it would no doubt have been short-lived, as the rest of the Indian dramas generally,—a night or two, or a week or two at the most, and then oblivion."[113] But *Metamora* went on to become the most famous play of the nineteenth century, leading even those cynical about Forrest's acting ability, such as the editor of *Harper's Weekly* George William Curtis, to note in 1863 that "there was never a more genuine or permanent success than the acting of Forrest. We may crack our jokes at it. We may call it the muscular school; the brawny art; the biceps aesthetics . . . but what then?" Curtis concedes, however reluctantly, that Forrest's portrayal of Metamora is powerful: "[H]e moves his world nightly."[114]

Reviews of opening night at the Park Theatre in New York City in December 1829 describe the atmosphere as much as the play. Those in attendance comprised "one of the most brilliant audiences that perhaps ever graced the walls of the Park Theatre—and hundreds were obliged to leave the doors, not being able to find standing room." At the end of the play, with "nearly the whole audience standing," the audience broke into "rapturous applause."[115] Audiences continued to pack into the theater night after night as the play traveled from New York to Philadelphia to Boston, and then to Britain. Reviews continued to take as much interest in the audience as in the performance. The *London Times* review describes the audience's response: "rapt

silence, the copious tears, and the all-shaking plaudits of the unprecedented crowds." This same review concludes that the tragedy portrays "the awful sense of right that makes the Indian respected as a
wronged man."[116]

Edwin Forrest's early biographer, Gabriel Harrison, similarly
observed that Forrest expressed "the pathos of Metamora" and was
therefore able "to excite the sympathy of the audience."[117] Harrison
goes on to explain how Forrest cultivated such sympathy through his
gestures, silences, and expressions, precisely those significant details
that cannot be reproduced in printed versions of the script. In the final
scene, for instance, after Metamora is shot, he attempts to crawl to the
bodies of his wife and son so he can die alongside them, but he falters
and stops. A bit earlier in this final scene, when he consensually murders his wife, Harrison describes how Metamora takes his wife in
his arms and embraces her as he also stabs her—as the audience sat in
rapt silence.

Forrest's biographer attributed the power of his performance to his
preparation for the role. As a proto-method actor, Forrest studied carefully the writings of Washington Irving and James Fenimore Cooper
before going to live among Native Americans for several weeks. "He
adopted their habits, shared their food, slept in their huts, mingled
with the chiefs of their tribes, smoked the pipe of peace." Harrison was
expecting to see one of Cooper's Indians, picturesque yet rather flat,
but instead he found a truly powerful and sympathetic figure: "I felt
myself in contact with the red man of the new land, . . . No other actor
or author had ever presented the Indian character in such complete-
ness for the stage before."[118]

Sympathy toward Metamora, however, was contingent upon
region. In Northern cities as well as in London, Metamora received
unqualified praise. But when Forrest performed the same role in
Augusta, Georgia, in 1831—the very region that benefited from
Cherokee expulsion—the audience responded with violence. Actor
James Murdock recounts a performance when, in the final scene,
Metamora scolds the elders for "their unjust and cruel treatment of his
tribe, and denounces war and vengeance upon them until the land they
had stolen from his people should blaze with their burning dwellings
and reek with the blood of their wives and children." Murdock goes on
to describe how the curse elicited "a perfect storm of hisses from the

excited audience." The actors feared that the enraged audience would storm the stage and destroy the scenery. Eventually, order was restored, but the audience still continued to denounce Metamora audibly until the curtain fell.[119]

Georgians took the play's criticism personally, and their rebuke took an equally personal form. The next day, Edwin Forrest was charged with insulting the people of Augusta and condemning their land-claims of the Cherokee. There was a direct connection, in other words, among the character of Metamora, the actor Edwin Forrest, and Indian removal policies. Portraying a seventeenth-century Indian as a beloved leader, a nurturing father, and a loving husband was considered a seditious act. Indian niceness, in this context, was unequivocally subversive. Not surprisingly, Georgians boycotted the remaining performances and the play closed early, showing how white Southerners were highly offended by what they saw as an explicit attack on Indian removal policies.[120]

The conflicting responses toward Metamora reveal the lack of consensus over how to depict Native American character, and by extension, the lack of agreement over Indian removal. While Augustan audiences boycotted the production, a delegation of Penobscots from Maine were traveling to Boston to petition the government to protect their lands from white settlers, and they threatened to establish an independent government to protect their political autonomy. Their request was ignored, but while they were in Boston, they attended a production of Metamora at the Tremont Street Theater. After Metamora's closing curse on white America, according to one nineteenth-century account, the Indian delegation was "so excited by the performance that in the closing scene they rose and chanted a dirge in honor of the death of the great chief."[121] One wonders whether this dirge for the seventeenth century was also an expression of grief for their contemporary trials and the rejection of political sovereignty.

Metamora's final words (which are fictitious) illustrate the native's jeremiad, a public form of exhortation that begins with a litany of current woes and ends with a glimmer of hope; it combines subaltern critique with a hint of optimism. According to Sacvan Bercovitch, the jeremiad represents a ritual "designed to join social criticism to spiritual renewal, public to private identity, the shifting 'signs of the times' to certain traditional metaphors, themes, and symbols."[122] The performative aspects of the play create a space whereby red rage and white guilt can find expression through the native's rebuke. Within this highly sentimental play that narrates the tragic plight of an Indian nuclear family, the nation's original sin, stemming from the seventeenth-century scene of Indian hospitality, is exposed. The native's jeremiad, which concludes with Metamora's dying curse, incites guilt, but it also provides a degree of solace. The theatrical space enables a lamentation of sins and the promise of redemption.

Metamora looks back to the seventeenth century to retell the story of conquest and catastrophe, while also offering Oceana as a figure of possibility: she is the nice American who can heal through kindness. Forrest's early biographer, Gabriel Harrison, recounts the opening act when Metamora first meets Oceana, who offers to wrap his wounded arm: "For several moments he looked at Oceana with a stern and contemptuous expression, as if thinking of the harsh treatment his people were receiving from the white man." But then Forrest's facial expression undergoes a transformation when she begins to wrap his arm with her scarf: His gloomy face "lightened up with a pleasant smile as he gazed upon the girl with the assurance that he was her friend."[123] By recovering the actors' gestures and facial expressions, Harrison's eyewitness account of the play highlights the importance of Metamora's smile. Here, Oceana converts through niceness in changing Metamora's gloomy face into an amiable one. As this opening scene suggests, the objective of *Metamora* is to acknowledge national trauma and then immediately suture this historical wound through the healing power of the nice American girl. The promise of futurity will mend the traumatic past.

This idea of the American girl as the healer of both Indian and national wounds shows how Oceana mends the errors of her father's ways, in part by exchanging her English father for an Indian one. Metamora becomes her adopted father, a man more loving and protective of her than her own English father. Metamora also kills Lord Fitzarnold for kidnapping his wife and child, thus freeing Oceana to marry whomever she wants in the New World. Oceana is also the witness to the crime: She commits race treason by rebuking the English soldiers for taking Metamora and Nahmeokee's baby from them, and she allies with her Indian family by initially taking refuge in their wigwam. With the baby now dead, Oceana is the future American, one who understands the significance of native hospitality, reciprocity, and gratitude.

In addition to Oceana's role as healer, the play also mollifies white guilt by displacing it onto the English. They are the villains in this melodrama, portrayed as a group of militarized men who speak in formal, starched prose with no affect. With little attempt to individualize them, the English seem interchangeable with each other, undifferentiated and cold. They embody the law, while Metamora and his family together with Oceana represent the heart. Jacksonian Anglophobia underwrites the white guilt of *Metamora*, as the original sin of the nation is displaced onto the English and exported back to Britain. White America, by contrast, is able to feel the pain of the Indian, like Natty Bumppo feels the pain of the dying Indian whom he has shot. In contrast to England, white America has a heart; it can tear up at Metamora's suffering as a sign of American redemption. *Metamora* provides a way to incorporate the Indian into a national narrative of white settlement, not by banishing the Indian through the elegiac trope of the Vanishing American, but by showing their centrality in the national narrative of betrayed hospitality.

But even in these progressive attempts to acknowledge white guilt in the process of settlement, there is still a limit. These narratives must rely at some level on forgetting because the guilty conscience, even a collective one, can only bear so much responsibility. One instance of such forgetting is what actually happened to Metacom's corpse (the figure on whom Metamora is based), a detail that cannot be included in either Irving's sketch or Stone's play. After Metacom was killed (by another Indian and not an Englishman as the play depicts), his body was dismembered and his head taken back to Plymouth on a spike where it remained for twenty years. Writing two decades after King Philip's War, Cotton Mather would see this gesture not as a sign of white barbarism but of Christian triumph: "His [Philip's] *head* was carried in triumph to Plymouth, where it arrived on the very day that the church there was keeping a solemn thanksgiving to God. God sent 'em in the head of a leviathan for a thanksgiving-feast." Cotton Mather represents Thanksgiving as a cannibalistic feast, which literary critic John McWilliams describes: "After nearly sixty years, the first Thanksgiving feast with Massassoit [sic] has evolved into the metaphoric devouring of Massassoit's son's head at yet another Plymouth

Thanksgiving feast."[124] This gruesome observation illustrates the ambivalence at the very root of *hostis*, where the guest in this case devours the original host, a gothic inversion of Thanksgiving that the play *Metamora* cannot acknowledge. Why not? Because *Metamora* targets the moral conscience of the largely white audience through public shaming, while yearning, like Oceana, for a harmonious resolution to the conflict through the pluralistic union of the amiable Indian family and the nice young Americans.

William Apess: Why Do They Hate Us?

A contemporary of John Augustus Stone, William Apess, a Methodist minister of mixed Pequod-Anglo heritage who claimed to be a descendent of King Philip, sought to understand the persistence and virulence of Anglo Indian-hating, while at the same time eulogizing King Philip as the founder of the nation. William Apess returned to the seventeenth century, and specifically King Philip's War, to create a counternarrative of the nation based not on George Washington, but on an Indian Founding Father, Metacomet, or King Philip, who was "the greatest man that was ever in America."[125] Writing at a time when *Metamora* was at the peak of its popularity, Apess retells the origins of the nation in order to pose the question: "Why have whites reacted with hatred to those who have saved them?" Apess's *Eulogy on King Philip, as Pronounced at the Odeon, in Federal Street, Boston* (1836) has been praised as one of the most powerful and radical examples of antebellum oratory. His eulogy is founded on the theme of Indian kindness framed as a question posed directly to his white auditors and then immediately answered: "Did you ever know of Indians hurting those who was kind to them? No."

Apess then echoes the refrain of hospitality betrayed by creating a genealogy of Indian kindness beginning with the primal scene of encounter, when the Puritans depended on Indian generosity:

[The Indians] gave them venison and sold them many hogsheads of corn to fill their stores, besides beans. This was in the year 1622. Had it not been for this humane act of the Indians, every white man would have been swept from the New England colonies. In their sickness, too, the Indians were as tender to them as to their own children; and for all this, they were denounced as savages by those who had received all the acts of kindness they possibly could show them. [126]

Delivered in the 1830s during that charged decade of Indian removal, Apess's *Eulogy* recounts the kindness of Squanto and Samoset, who showed "the Pilgrims how to live in their country and find support for their wives and little ones; and for all this, they were receiving the applause of being savages." Instead of gratitude, the "Christians" sought to destroy the Indians "at their first discovery." [127] This pattern would continue throughout the seventeenth century, culminating in King Philip's War; it would then persist in the nineteenth century, Apess anecdotally adds, in the form of racist comments he encountered through mundane conversations with white New Englanders: "These things I mention to show that the doctrines of the Pilgrims has grown up [sic] with the people."[128]

Apess's *Eulogy on King Philip* provides a history of acknowledgment rather than one based on disavowal. Directed to the "sons of Puritans," he carefully describes the events leading up to King Philip's War and the ensuing battle, including its most egregious atrocities, which Stone's *Metamora* could not depict, specifically, the enslavement of Philip's ten-year-old son, who is sent to the Caribbean, and the dismemberment of Philip's corpse. Borrowing from the diary of colonial officer Benjamin Church, Apess writes, "[H]e [Philip] was quartered and hung up upon four trees, his head and one hand given to the Indian who shot him, to carry about to show, at which sight it so overjoyed the Pilgrims that they would give him money for it, and in this way obtained a considerable sum. After which his head was sent to Plymouth and exposed upon a gibbet for twenty years; and his hand to Boston, where it was exhibited in savage triumph."[129] Apess reveals what even sympathetic nineteenth-century accounts had to suppress, namely, how the Puritans displayed Philip's dismembered body as a sign of "savage triumph." By foregrounding this act, Apess inverts the binary of savagery and civility to suggest that the settler-invaders were the true barbarians.

In the vein of Franklin and Irving, Apess exposes the sadistic behavior of the first settlers in order to incite national shame, which his *Eulogy* encodes in terms of blushing: "Let the children of the Pilgrims blush, while the son of the forest drops a tear and groans over the fate of his murdered and departed fathers."[130] Indian tears and Anglo blushes produce a collective conscience that recognizes the grief of settler trauma and tries to overcome it not by forgetting but by acknowledging its irrevocability. In giving voice to the crimes of the Puritans against Philip and his family, Apess exclaims: "I blush at these tales, if you do not, especially when they professed to be a free and humane people."[131]

Like Logan's speech and Metamora's curse, Apess's *Eulogy on King Philip* serves as a form of Indian censure, a rhetorical tactic that criticizes white America for its ingratitude, cruelty, and slanderous treatment of Native Americans.[132] It signifies a lament for the ongoing violence toward Native Americans as whites refuse to live according to their own Christian principles. Interestingly, Apess's rebuke proved to be very popular. He delivered this oration in Boston, and the public demanded an encore performance. How are we to understand the popularity of Apess's castigating words? The Indian's rebuke illustrates an instance of national shaming that the Boston audience embraced. White guilt becomes a constitutive part of liberal configurations of U.S. identity (as opposed to the Jacksonian model of unabashed Indian-hating), an identity that depends in part upon the castigating words of the angry victim, with Indian flagellation becoming a way to exonerate white sin. The Indian's rebuke turns shaming into a therapeutic event.

But what happens beyond shaming? Where Stone imagines Oceana as a healing archetype for the future, Apess grapples with the problem of memory: Do we acknowledge colonial plunder as a mistake or do we forget and become friends? "What, then, shall we do? Shall we cease crying and say it is all wrong, or shall we bury the hatchet and those unjust laws and Plymouth Rock together and become friends?"[133] The fact that Apess presents the solution as a series of questions suggests that he is not entirely convinced that forgetting and friendship can actually happen. Although he admits that he has some "good friends" among whites, he does not fully trust them. "Having been deceived so much by them, how can I help it?"

Apess offers one type of remedy, expressly reciprocal hospitality, where the "Christian [would] take me by the hand and bid me welcome to his cabin, as my fathers did them, before we were born."[134] This model of mutuality would entail the abolition of "unjust laws" and the creation of "one general law" that fully acknowledges the humanity and citizenship of Native Americans. The interpersonal dynamics of hospitality and friendship are both literal and metaphoric; they are invoked to reconfigure a settler state in terms of a democratic union where Indian and settler sit at the same table and are subject to the same laws.

The nation can be modeled on Indian hospitality and interracial friendship only through collective forgetting: "[Y]ou and I have to rejoice that we have not to answer for our fathers' crimes; neither shall we do right to charge them one to another. We can only regret it, and flee from it."[135] The "it" refers to "our fathers' crimes"—an allusion to the past and historical memory. One forgets, he suggests, by fleeing. But "flee" is a loaded term in the Native American context, especially at a time of Indian removal when Native Americans were being forced to flee west. Manifest Destiny depends on Indian flight; it is the very dynamic that sustains settler colonialism and the freeing of land for white settlement.

So what does it mean to flee from memory? And how does one forget? "Really to forget something," as Jacqueline Rose wrote in an essay called "Shame," "you have to forget that you have even forgotten. You have to be 'forgetful of forgetfulness.'"[136] Apess's *Eulogy* remembers in order to forget, which is especially ironic in a eulogy, a genre dedicated to memorializing the past. Yet Apess's *Eulogy* seems to imply that one must go through memory and come out the other side. Forgetting is the ultimate solution for personal as well as national healing, letting go of past injustices in order to forge new intercultural friendships. Forgetting takes the form of wishing, where the hurt from the past transforms into the desire for future attachment. The fact that Apess ends with the call for "peace and righteousness" as "the wish of a poor Indian" suggests that he is eulogizing a life—imagined to be rich with interracial friendships, just laws, and full citizenship rights—that remains unrealized. He yearns for the white hospitable Christian to take him by the hand, but he never arrives. The figure of the wishing Indian haunts Apess's *Eulogy*, whose fantasy of mutual hospitality has the therapeutic effect of making his own difficult life bearable. This gap between the life that Apess wants and the life he actually leads is generative of his political consciousness, where the tension between desire and frustration produces a vision of a just world.[137]

Imagining the First Thanksgiving during the First World War

Nearly a century after Apess's call for citizenship, Zitkala-Sa describes her own fantasy of national reunion. In "Americanize the First Americans" (1921), she recommends that all sit down together at the dinner table, where she imagines a reciprocated form of hospitality. Now the Indian, who is "suffering from malnutrition," can be fed in the literal and metaphoric sense with full legal rights as citizens and with resources to leave the reservation, which she describes as "a system of solitary isolation from the world," where Indians are "virtually prisoners of war in America."[138] Zitkala-Sa consistently links Indian hospitality and the primal scene with changes in policy. Progressive-era reforms need to be framed not as philanthropy but as restitution for national indebtedness to Indian hospitality. This is how the notion of shame—or what she calls the "stain"—can be removed from national consciousness. The United States can be purged from its ancestral guilt through "the gospel of humanitarianism."[139]

American niceness, for Zitkala-Sa, is the recognition of indebtedness to Native Americans for welcoming the persecuted to the New World: "The American people still remember how their early ancestors fled from the autocracy of Europe to the open arms of the Red Man a few centuries ago."[140] As a way to say thank you for this primal scene of Indian giving, together with the service of Native American soldiers in World War I, Zitkala-Sa calls on the U.S. government to turn native wardship into full citizenship rights, a model of belated reciprocity, where the white settler nation would give not charity but justice. In this way, her strategy combines the memory of Indian hospitality with a call for contemporary political reforms.[141]

At the same time as Zitkala-Sa was developing the counter-tradition of national shaming for the twentieth century, inaugurated by Native Americans such as Apess and Anglo-Americans like Franklin and Irving, Indian hospitality became an iconic part of a hegemonic narrative that celebrated Indian generosity as the *sine qua non* of American niceness. One could return to the seventeenth century without a sense of guilt but with a triumphant sense of national pride. Apess's hatchet was certainly buried. Characters such as Natty Bumppo and Oceana allowed Indian niceness and American niceness to become one through the experience of a shared pain. In this way, the inconvenient savagery of actual historical events could be managed or disavowed altogether and converted into something more palatable and flattering to white Americans. By the early twentieth century, the savagery of Mather's Thanksgiving feast had been left behind and replaced by representations that for the first time depicted Indians together with white settlers.

Prior to the early twentieth century, Thanksgiving was portrayed as a holiday centered around the New England home or wintry landscape scenes.[142] It was a holiday marked by contemporary themes rather than historical events, and for this reason, it was also a holiday bereft of Indians. In the early twentieth century, however, artists began to reimagine Thanksgiving as an intercultural holiday based in the seventeenth century and epitomized in such paintings as Jean Leon Gerome Ferris's *The First Thanksgiving at Plymouth, 1621* (circa 1912–1915). Ferris was a popular historical genre painter, or what was referred to at the time as a "painter historian." His paintings and illustrations depicted notable moments in U.S. history, such as when William Penn was greeted by friendly Indians, shown in *The Landing of William Penn—1682* (a scene that Helen Hunt Jackson also recounted in *A Century of Dishonor*). His work was frequently published in *Literary Digest* and *Ladies Home Journal.* His painting *The First Thanksgiving at Plymouth, 1621* appeared on the cover of *The Literary Digest's* Thanksgiving issue in November 1928.[143]

Commissioned during the First World War, Ferris's painting portrays interracial harmony and intercultural feasting, incorporating Indian hospitality into a national version of American niceness. Ferris memorializes this iconic meal by inverting its foundational power dynamics; it turns the Indians into the guests and the Puritans into the hosts, as the ones who possess the food. Incorporating Indian hospitality through the consumption of food is reminiscent of John O'Sullivan's bodily metaphors of manifest destiny as "devouring" and "swallowing."[144] But what is most significant about the painting is that its central figure is a white hostess giving food to Native American men. This figure feminizes the colonial encounter by presenting white American womanhood as the mediating figure between two groups of men—Anglos and Natives. She aestheticizes the settler-Indian relation and, in doing so, removes any tension from it. She is the Oceana

Jean Leon Gerome Ferris, "The First Thanksgiving at Plymouth, 1621" [c. 1912]. Reproduced from *The Pageant of a Nation*, No. 6 (Cleveland, Ohio: The Foundation Press, Inc., 1932). Library of Congress Prints and Photographs Division, Washington, D.C., LC-USZC4–4961.

figure of Ferris's scene, linking Indian hospitality with feminine niceness.[145]

The painting illustrates Stephen Turner's concept of "settlement as forgetting" in that Ferris's historical depiction of the first Thanksgiving of 1621 is paradoxically a disavowal of history.[146] Forgetting here takes the form of several historical inaccuracies. First, at the original Thanksgiving meal in 1621, Indians outnumbered whites two to one.[147] The Puritans, moreover, were a distinct minority at a primarily Native American feast. Second, the New England Indians who attended the first Thanksgiving would not have worn headdresses (which are Sioux). Third, the style of clothes worn by both the Pilgrims and Indians are not historically accurate. In his notes, Ferris explains that he did not want the Puritans to appear drab in "sad colors" but insisted that the Puritans wore "scarlet, bright green [and] orange." He did not want to paint dour Puritans. Based loosely on William Bradford's account (and inflected by W. T. Davis's 1908 editorial comments), Ferris's Puritans are a cheerful lot who wore brightly colored outfits and gave generously to the Wampanoags Indians, who are portrayed with Sioux headdresses. These anachronisms allow Ferris to reconcile the contradictions of colonial encounter by turning to myth. Indians are recognizable through familiar stereotypes like the iconic Indian of cigar boxes, and the brightly colored clothing suggests an atmosphere of merriment. The demographics of 1621 were also significantly inverted to depict a white majority and an Indian minority. Even at the first Thanksgiving, or so this painting claims, Indians were outnumbered.

The absences in Ferris's rendition of Thanksgiving are revealing for what they suggest about ongoing anxieties regarding Indian giving. Edward Winslow's account of the first Thanksgiving refers to Massasoit arriving with ninety warriors who brought five deer after a successful hunt, and the Pilgrims also had several fowl for the three-day feast as well as a bountiful corn harvest. Winslow underscores in his journal *Mourt's Relation*, which is credited with being the first description of the 1621 event, that it was a collaborative and cooperative gathering, not necessarily religious or even monumental. Winslow notes, "[W]e often goe to them, and they come to us."[148] The success of the Pilgrims' colonial venture was not yet secure. During the following winter, several more Pilgrims would die from malnutrition and illness. Yet Ferris's portrayal of this first feast shows the Indians receiving the Pilgrims' food, not the other way around. According to Ferris's own notes that are loosely based on Bradford's text, Massasoit just brought along some popcorn, while the Puritans supplied a full banquet consisting of wild fowl, hasty pudding, clam chowder, cold boiled beef with mustard, along with a bowl of turnips. In fact, one art reviewer in 1924 commented favorably that Ferris's Thanksgiving depicts the "idea of generosity, the only true kind that gives from frugal resources." But whose generosity? The reviewer repeats the menu items that Ferris himself had noted from Bradford and remarks that "more aesthetic Indians" brought popcorn, which "we imagine produced some pop-eyes, for it was unheard of novelty to those who had so recently trod the noble rock."[149] There was no mention of the five deer that Massasoit and his men had brought along. By portraying the Pilgrims as the givers and not the receivers, the painting affirms white sovereignty, independence, and self-sufficiency. The Pilgrims are the figures of abundance, the people of plenty, generously giving to the poor Indians, whose inferior position is reinforced through sitting, while the white men stand around them.

Imagine another version of this painting, where Native Americans would be standing and offering food to the Puritans, who would be sitting. What would such an inversion imply? To show an Indian giving food to the Puritans would be a far more accurate portrayal of the inter-cultural dynamics of 1621, but it would acknowledge something that Ferris's painting actively disavows, namely white dependency on Indian generosity. Or to put it explicitly in gendered terms, white men needed native men and women to survive. This is the source of national shame that cannot be enunciated because to acknowledge it would mean to admit vulnerability and dependency—the antithesis of nor-mative white masculinity. But it would also mean showing gratitude, the second point that this painting must not depict. Because white people are offering food to Indians, they do not need to say thank you. Thanksgiving here is portrayed as Indian gratitude for white gener-osity, playing into a colonial fantasy of cultural inheritance that legit-imates Anglo possession of the land. By being nice to the natives, white America justifies its occupation.

Hospitality, then, was the vehicle by which Indians were incorpo-rated into a white national discourse. European colonizers arrived as guests and became American. The Anglo guests appropriated Indian hospitality as their own, a point that Ferris's painting represents: The white colonizer evolves into the gracious host. This painting illus-trates what Yael Ben-zvi has called "the fantasy of inheritance in which colonial and U.S. culture is nourished by consuming Native American cultures." [150] This process of Indian incorporation describes the shift in nineteenth-century race relations from a tripartite structure—red-white-black (as immortalized in Tocqueville's chapter on "The Three Races in the United States")—to a white-black binary by the early twentieth century, epitomized in W. E. B. Du Bois's famous statement in 1903 that "the problem of the Twentieth-Century is the problem of the color-line." Du Bois's "color-line," as Steven Conn notes, reflects the disappearance of Native Americans from the U.S. racial land-scape.[151] Redness disappears through the demographic catastrophe of the nineteenth century but also figuratively through its incorporation into mainstream notions of American niceness. The reiteration of Indian hospitality in the primal scene of encounter continues throughout the nineteenth century until the reiteration becomes a cliché, a naturalized part of a national mythology of origins.

From Indian Hospitality to National Manners

During the 1920s, the same decade when Native Americans were granted U.S. citizenship while their "extreme poverty" was documented in the Meriam report, Indian hospitality further morphed into mainstream American niceness through etiquette manuals.[152] Lillian Eichler published an etiquette book on modern American manners entitled *The Customs of Mankind* that credited the Indian as the "pioneer of hospitality."[153] Having begun her career in 1919 as an eighteen-year-old copywriter for a New York advertising agency, she soon demonstrated her ability to write in an entertaining and popular style by rewriting Eleanor Holt's Victorian tome *Encyclopedia of Etiquette*, which became the highly successful two-volume *The Book of Etiquette* (1921). This book sold over two million copies at two dollars each and it appealed to a mass audience of first- and second-generation Americans in ways that her competitor Emily Post could not. A Jewish teenager from New York City who became a self-made millionaire, Eichler, according to one historian, was "without a doubt the great forgotten figure of American manners." In contrast to the formal and detached tone of Emily Post, Eichler was, in the critic Edmund Wilson's words, "friendly and accessible."[154]

After publishing another successful book, *Etiquette Mistakes in Pictures*, Eichler embarked on an ambitious study of manners that combined ethnography with modern etiquette, entitled *The Customs of Mankind: With notes on modern etiquette and the Newest Trend in Entertainment* (1924). In this mammoth work, which did not have the commercial success of her earlier endeavors, Eichler praises the sophistication of Indian customs: "North American Indians have always been highly advanced in the art of hospitality."[155] Following a familiar pattern, she turns to the seventeenth century and the original scene of American niceness when the Native Americans gave to the Pilgrims: "Few people were as open-hearted and generous as they. Their unaffected kindness and their willingness to share a last morsel astonished the early white settlers who came into contact with them." Eichler understands this intercultural exchange in terms of borrowing rather than theft: "We have borrowed many things from our Indian brother . . . but nothing more valuable than their custom of generous hospitality. They paved the way for the hospitality which has become so peculiarly associated with this country."[156] The peculiar has now become national, showing the adaptive powers of whiteness as dynamic and flexible, able to assimilate indigenous ways. The guest figuratively ingests the indigenous host—culture and all—so that the guest-as-parasite acquires the same customs of hospitality that once characterized the original host. Indian culture lives on in the everyday habits and mannerisms that define Americans as amiable and generous.

As the daughter of Jewish immigrants, Eichler made etiquette accessible to an immigrant readership, where Indian hospitality greeted them with the same warmth as they greeted the Pilgrims. Eichler's book embraces rather than banishes the Indian by making this figure iconic in the national culture. In doing so, Eichler deflects attention away from the actions and policies of genocide and instead celebrates the afterlife of Indian sociability as the distinctive feature of American niceness. Ferris's painting is the visual corollary of Eichler's thesis: Indian hospitality has come to form the basis of American niceness, with cross-cultural feasting symbolically founding a white settler culture distinct from Englishness.

The twenty-first-century legacy of this dominant narrative of Indian hospitality can be seen in the one-dollar coin issued in 2014, recognizing "how Native American hospitality ensured the success of the Lewis and Clark Expedition."[157] The obverse design (heads side) features Sacagawea, while the reverse side depicts a Native American man offering a pipe and a woman sharing provisions such as corn, fish, and gourds. This commemorative coin renders manifest destiny as a cooperative effort, a joint venture, rather than a process of sustained and systematic violence. The figure of the gift-giving Indian, according to the historian Roxanne Dunbar-Ortiz, feeds into a multicultural narrative that emphasizes "contributions" of distinct minority groups to "the country's assumed greatness."[158] The irony of reconciling Indian hospitality with U.S. coinage would not have been lost on Lewis Henry Morgan, Zitkala-Sa, and many of those cited in this chapter.

If Black Elk called Indian giving the Indian mistake and Zitkala-Sa saw it as the condition for reparative justice, then Charles Eastman understood it as moral strength. In *The Soul of the Indian* (1911), Eastman defends Indian giving as a central part of native culture. The Indian, writes Eastman, "literally gives away all that he has, to relatives, to guests of another tribe or clan, but above all to the poor and

A Native American Dollar Coin issued by the U.S. Mint in 2014.
Author's collection.

the aged, from whom he can hope for no return." The child is taught at an early age to learn "the beauty of generosity" by giving what he prizes most.[159] Such an act is neither a gesture of foolishness nor one of self-destruction but just the opposite: It is an act of courage. Indian giving is a sign of strength, where one is willing to experience the vulnerability of loss in order to be kind.

For Eastman, Indian hospitality represents the foundation of an indigenous ethics, one predicated on interdependency and generosity. It reflects an ethical practice premised on the recognition of our common vulnerability. Rather than an Indian mistake, Indian hospitality is the source of our collective salvation—economically, socially, and environmentally—when giving takes precedence over taking and vulnerability is protected rather than exploited. Indian giving signifies an alternative model of American niceness, which is also an alternative ethical practice based on what Cornel West has described as "non-market values," such as "love for others, loyalty to an ethical ideal and social freedom."[160]

Where niceness in the native context took the form of Indian hospitality, it would have a significantly different inflection when applied to African Americans. The next chapter turns to the question of literary representation and the relation between Southern niceness and black amiability. For white and black abolitionists as well as for pro-slavery advocates, the antebellum debate on slavery included a related debate about black character in the double sense of moral character and literary characterization. Where Indian niceness focused on cultural practices of welcoming the stranger, black amiability in the context of slavery centered on the question of how to represent the black face and specifically the semiotics of the smile: Is it a sign of genuine contentment or a veil of concealed rage?

❧ 2 ❧

Southern Niceness and the Slave's Smile

There ain't nothing wrong with being hated.

Chris Rock

Michael Brown, 18, due to be buried today, was no
angel. . . . At the same time, he regularly flashed a
broad smile that endeared those around him.

John Eligon, *The New York Times* (August 24, 2014)

IN HER REVIEW OF Harriet Beecher Stowe's *Dred; a Tale of the
Great Dismal Swamp* (1856), George Eliot praises the novel for its
"rare genius—rare both in intensity and in range of power." But in the
final paragraph of the review, Eliot raises an objection. She wonders
why Stowe must portray her black characters as fundamentally nice.
"[O]ne of her artistic defects," writes Eliot, is "the absence of any pro-
portionate exhibition of the negro character in its less amiable phases."[1]
By showing blacks as "vastly superior to the mass of whites," Stowe
risks confirming, according to Eliot, the proslavery argument that
slavery is a civilizing force and "Christianizing Institution." Eliot is
disappointed that Stowe alludes to the demoralization of slaves
without actually depicting it, and she concludes by asking, "yet why
should she shrink from this, since she does not shrink from giving us
a full-length portrait of a Legree or a Tom Gordon?" Why are Stowe's
black characters always so good-hearted and kind?

96

Charles Dickens made a similar observation though in a more direct and disapproving tone. In an 1852 letter to Stowe after the publication of *Uncle Tom's Cabin,* he wrote that she had elevated the black man's character "too far and seeks to prove too much." He added, "Slavery had evils enough without trying to make the African race seem to be great!"[2] Dickens took issue with Stowe's romantic racialism, a doctrine embraced by the antislavery movement that, as George Fredrickson explained, was more invested in rendering blacks as symbols than as persons, as "a vehicle for romantic social criticism than as a human being with the normal range of virtues and vices."[3] Like Eliot, Dickens did not believe that Stowe needed to depict an entire race as Christlike in order to reveal the inhumanity of slavery.

Stowe was certainly aware of this dilemma. In *Dred,* the light-skinned slave Harry Gordon, who is also the half-brother of the young mistress of the plantation, echoes Stowe's own sentiments when he expresses his frustrations with the mandate for black niceness: "We are the people that are *never* to do wrong! People may stick pins in us, and stick knives in us, wipe their shoes on us, spit in our face—*we* must be amiable! We must be models of Christian patience!"[4] Where Uncle Tom actually behaves in this self-sacrificing manner, in *Dred* Stowe turns black niceness into an emphatic statement, typographically accented with multiple exclamation points. Gordon's ardent tone suggests anger, frustration, and impatience with the narrow parameters of black characterization.

Connected to the dilemma of black amiability is the related matter of how one represents black rage. How can black characters have the same emotional range as white characters without being reduced to a stereotype or perceived as a threat? Stowe can describe Simon Legree and Tom Gordon as violent and abusive because white characters can be depicted with more range, which is an example of how white privilege manifests itself in literature. Whites do not have to be nice. Legree's sadism does not call into question the humanity of white people. By contrast, black characters carry the burden of representation because of the metonymic relation between the individual and the race. To put it another way, Uncle Tom and Harry Gordon are racially representative, while Legree does not have to be.

But even when Stowe portrays black rage as she does in *Dred,* a novel that was written largely in response to her critics, and particularly her

African American critics who saw in Uncle Tom a figure of black obse-quiousness and domestic passivity, she is careful to combine anger with kindness as she gives black rage a context within the injustices of slavery.[5] Like Uncle Tom, Dred is deeply religious, but he signifies less a New Testament Jesus than an Old Testament prophet. Stowe named her eponymous character after one of Nat Turner's co-conspirators, and like descriptions of Nat Turner, Dred has a mystical charismatic pres-ence, or what she calls "prophetic power." Dred demands vengeance through "insurrection and bloodshed," while also exhibiting a genuine sympathy for the dispossessed and a gentleness that "softens the heart towards children and the inferior animals."[6] Having killed an abusive overseer years earlier, Dred sought refuge in the swamp, where he formed a small fugitive camp resembling an alternative domestic space, which assists runaways, including children seeking sanctuary from a tyrannical system. Stowe describes metaphorically the black revolu-tionary in terms of "what a mother might feel for the abuse of her help-less child, and multiply that by infinity."[7]

Black rage is likened to a mother's vengeance—magnified and intensified—an analogy that translates black affect across the color line through the gendered language of maternity. Where Uncle Tom has been described as a Christ-mother (often in a disparaging tone), Dred can be seen as another type of mother figure, the vengeful mother, who still responds generously to white kindness. Dred's sympathetic nature, for instance, impels him to rescue the life of a kind slave owner (soon to become an abolitionist) who was severely beaten by a malev-olent one. Like Uncle Tom, Stowe's black revolutionary also has a heart of gold.

This chapter begins with Stowe because she understood what was at stake in the representational politics of black characterization. At one level, her insistence on black amiability is deeply cynical because it shows that she did not trust her white readers to accept black char-acters on any other terms. Black characters had to behave like Jesus in order to be seen as human. The fact that Stowe understands and even anticipates Eliot's and Dickens's objections and yet still affirms black amiability suggests three things. First, when it is read symptomati-cally, black niceness is a sign of an intensely racist culture. It is com-pensatory in the sense that blacks have to be rendered superhumanly nice precisely because they are so brutally de-humanized. There is a very narrow affective spectrum within which sympathetic whites can represent blackness in the nineteenth century. To show black rage exclusively, untempered by gestures of kindness, is to play into white fears of black treachery and revenge by conjuring the ghost of Nat Turner. The fact that Eliot and Dickens could object to this fact says as much about their world as it does about Stowe's. Neither Eliot nor Dickens read *Uncle Tom's Cabin* or *Dred* in a slave nation, where the buying, selling, and capturing of (runaway) slaves was ordinary business. Dickens can critique Stowe's racial romanticism and Eliot can entertain the question of black interiority in all of its complexity only from such a distance.

Second, black amiability was part of a nascent human rights rhetoric that combined the conventional understanding of rights in terms of personhood with the generalizing force of racial typologies that foregrounded the geniality of black character. Debates on slavery often centered on the nature of the African race, a generalizing rhetoric that was paradoxically cast in interpersonal terms: Are black people gentle or fierce, good-natured or brutish? Their humanity was determined according to the language of sociability. Black nationalist Martin Delany, who detested the character of Uncle Tom and criticized Stowe for her ignorance of black people, nevertheless defended black amiability by arguing that African sociability can be traced back to the Yoruba, who are the friendliest and most sociable of Africans. The farther inland one goes on the African continent away from the coastal regions, Delany observes in *The Origin of Races and Color* (1879), the nicer are the inhabitants: "Friendly, sociable and benevolent, they are universally the politest of people."[8]

The defense of black amiability as part of a nascent human rights rhetoric dates back to the latter half of the eighteenth century. The early abolitionist pamphlet *A Short Account of that Part of Africa, Inhabited by the Negroes* (1762), written by Benjamin Franklin's friend, the Quaker Anthony Benezet, argues that Africans are, according to a number of European travel narratives, a "civil" and "good-natured people" who are "friendly to Strangers" and a "sincere inoffensive People." Benezet devotes the opening portion of his pamphlet to portraying blacks as likable in order to inscribe them within the category of the human, an inclusion that would make Africans worthy of "that Tenderness and Sympathy for the Sufferings of . . . Fellow Creatures."[9]

Likability is the precondition for white recognition of black humanity, which is to say that nascent human rights rhetoric depends on the visibility of black niceness. By being nice, blacks become worthy of white sympathy and political support in the form of abolitionist activism. Stowe would give this racial type a figural form through the character of Uncle Tom. Seen in this light, niceness is not only an attribute of black character, but it is also part of a rhetorical strategy of persuasion. Benezet's pamphlet, in part, successfully persuaded Benjamin Franklin to lead an abolitionist society in Philadelphia.

Third, Stowe makes an essentialist case for black niceness. She argues that amiability is an inherent part of black character and not in any way attributable to the Christianizing influence of slavery, as pro-slavery advocates such as George Fitzhugh claimed. Stowe presents such traits as friendliness and kindness as innate to black people in order to make the case for their resilience against the degrading forces of slavery. In this sense, George Eliot is absolutely right to say that Stowe sees blacks as "vastly superior to the mass of whites." In her preface to *Uncle Tom's Cabin* (1852), Stowe juxtaposes the "hard and dominant Anglo-Saxon race" with the "gentle, domestic heart" of the African. As the literary critic Ezra Tawil notes, character operates for Stowe as an essential interior property that is transmitted to descendants along with racial inheritance. Stowe represents black culture as the "highest form of the peculiarly *Christian life*"—a natural religiosity—in order to argue for the full humanity of black people.[10] Just as Stowe's insistence on black amiability is compensatory, so is her insistence on black moral superiority to whites. Both are defensive tactics to counter not only slavery but also the ideology of white supremacy that legitimized it.

Minority Niceness: Black Amiability and Indian Hospitality

The debate on black character parallels in many ways the debate about Indians: Are they hospitable or savage? Kind or treacherous? This debate was not solely a matter of defining racial types; it also had repercussions in terms of policy. To fear black and brown people as savages justified the cruelty of African enslavement and indigenous genocide. But what if Indians and African Americans were seen as hospitable and kind, as people not to be feared but to be liked? This chapter builds on the first in terms of outlining the significance of minority forms of niceness in shaping and determining a national notion of American niceness. Indian hospitality and black amiability are attempts to acknowledge the humanity of black and brown people through the language of sociability. This emphasis on the amiable character of the indigenous and the enslaved was part of a nascent human rights rhetoric that marks what W. E. B. Du Bois referred to as the humanitarian turn of the nineteenth century.

There are significant points of intersection between Indian hospitality and black amiability that are important to acknowledge in order to avoid seeing these two forms of minority niceness as completely separate. Black abolitionist writing in particular acknowledges Indian hospitality in a gesture of thankfulness as well as a way to rebuke the ruthlessness of white America. In this tradition, Indian hospitality has a dual purpose of gratitude and reproach. In a speech delivered in 1850 in Rochester, New York, Frederick Douglass exclaimed, "The slave finds more of the milk of human kindness in the bosom of the savage Indian, than in the heart of his *christian* master. He leaves the man of the *bible*, and takes refuge with the man of the *tomahawk*."[11] Here, Douglass rejects the stereotype of the savage Indian and praises Indian kindness as more in the spirit of Christianity than the slave master who carries a bible in one hand, while whipping his slave with the other.

Indian kindness was often a euphemism for sanctuary, for assisting the runaway slave in an indigenous underground railroad. Slave testimony illustrates black appreciation for Indian hospitality, as in Edinbur Randall's account of his escape from Florida on a ship carrying lumber to Massachusetts. When the ship docked near Martha's Vineyard and the captain threatened to call the authorities to return the fugitive, Randall, on the advice of sailors, took refuge among the Gay Head Indians, who spurned the sheriff's bribe, defied the Fugitive Slave Law, and "kindly ministered to my necessities."[12] An Indian woman named Beulah Vanderhoof concealed him in a gown, shawl, and bonnet and took him from the swamp to her grandmother's house. Her elderly grandmother promised him safety and declared that she would have a kettle of boiling water ready to scald the sheriff if he entered her home. Randall's narrative is in many ways an expression of gratitude for the courage of his Native American hosts.

But there are also important differences between these two minority forms of niceness, particularly in their relation to whiteness. The Anglo-American recognition of Indian hospitality is often accompanied by the rhetoric of shame, a sense of inherited guilt that was passed down from the Pilgrim Fathers. The seventeenth century looms large in this nineteenth-century narrative of national rebuke, as a way to apologize for the sins of the white settler nation. The Anglo-American recognition of black amiability is less historical and more phenomenological; it is less about generational guilt and more about the hermeneutics of reading black bodies. It is more intimate, more physical, and more personal.

The debate on black character often took a figural form that depended on the semiotics of the black face, focusing particularly though not exclusively on the smile as a metonymic sign of black niceness. This chapter will trace the multiaccentuality of the black smile through antislavery and proslavery literature to show how its versatility was also a sign of its contested meanings. The abolitionist defense of black niceness centered on the frame of the close-up rather than the panorama, on individual faces rather than on a collective people, where the proslavery use of black amiability was frequently typological and plural—the happy slaves. Equally contested was the decipherability of the black face. Within the context of slavery, the black face represents a veil, a mask of concealment and manipulation within the potentially explosive dynamics between master and slave. But the slave's smile was also coerced, a mandated cheerfulness that women in particular were expected to effect on the auction block to facilitate their own commodification and appeal to prospective buyers.

The slave's smile participates in a larger ideology of Southern niceness in concealing the brutality of the master-slave relationship in order to showcase how the system as a whole exemplifies a "mild" form of slavery. White northerners bought into this myth of Southern niceness as much as white Southerners who insisted on the relative benignity of U.S. slavery. Nathaniel Hawthorne wrote that the southern master and the slave "dwelt together in greater peace and affection . . . than had ever elsewhere existed between the taskmaster and the serf," and Harvard physician Oliver Wendell Holmes commented favorably about "slavery in its best and mildest form."[13]

Anti-Uncle Tom novels in particular contributed to a fantasy of consensual slavery, where the happy slaves want to be enslaved, thus illustrating a distinctly American form of democratic slavery. Happy slaves, according to slavery's apologists, vindicated the institution because their smiles reflected the kindness of the master. The figure of Sambo, the happy-go-lucky house slave who was a staple in minstrel shows and plantation novels, confirmed the benevolence of the "nice massa." As a fantasy of the slavemaster, Sambo signified sheer devotion to the master as a loyal son to a beloved father, preferring to serve and defend than to desire his freedom. "Without Sambo," historian John Blassingame wrote, "it was impossible to prove the essential goodness of Southern society."[14] Southern niceness feeds into a national narrative of American exceptionalism, showing how U.S. slavery represents a kinder and gentler form of slavery, especially when compared to the rest of the Black Atlantic. And yet paradoxically, it was precisely this figure of the happy slave that undermined the Confederacy during the Civil War. Recruited as spies for the Union, southern blacks masterfully imitated the cheerful Sambo-type while infiltrating the everyday spaces of the Confederate leadership.

The chapter turns to two fictional examples of the deceptive power of black amiability in Edgar Allan Poe's *The Narrative of Arthur Gordon Pym of Nantucket* and Herman Melville's *Benito Cereno*. What does the earnest belief in black niceness disclose about white American niceness? What unsettling insights does Captain Delano's gullibility reveal? The chapter concludes with the incorporation of the black smile in terms of Aunt Jemima's pancake mix, which made its debut at the 1893 Chicago World's Fair. While Frederick Douglass and Ida B. Wells protested the exclusion of African American accomplishments from the fair, Nancy Green was hired as the first Aunt Jemima and entertained passersby with childhood stories about the plantation while cooking and serving pancakes. Black niceness is framed within the familiar terms of Southern hospitality, and like Indian hospitality, both minority forms of niceness are incorporated within a larger national narrative of American niceness.

The Racialization of Faces

The face signifies the part of the body that is objectified in the making and remaking of racial typologies. As the rhetorician Ellen Cushman argues, the face is intimately connected to racialization: "[P]eople come to read the face to determine race."[15] In the nineteenth century, the face was a central marker for the typological categorization of racial difference. In Josiah Nott and George Gliddon's *Types of Mankind* (1854), a book that aimed to give "scientific" authority to racial subjugation, the face functions as the determinant of racial classification. In his Introduction to the volume, Josiah Nott cites a British journal to relay the "obviousness" of racial difference through three general types of faces and heads:

> The NEGRO, or African, with his black skin, woolly hair, and compressed elongated skull; the MONGOLIAN of Eastern Asia and America, with his olive complexion, broad and all but beardless face, oblique eyes, and square skull; and the CAUCASIAN of Western Asia and Europe, with his fair skin, oval face, full brow, and rounded skull: such, as every school-boy knows, are the three great types or varieties into which naturalists have divided the inhabitants of our planet.[16]

In the nineteenth century, race scientists overcoded the face and the head in relation to other body parts as the main signifier of race. Racialization, in other words, took the form of facialization, which, according to Gilles Deleuze and Félix Guattari, represents a tactic of normalization that regulates behavior through the overcoding of the face as the locus of meaning, primarily in terms of individuality.[17] But the face can signify individuality as much as uniformity through racial typologies that homogenize difference through standardized forms. Deleuze and Guattari's concept is useful for thinking about how faciality intersects with the uneven reproduction of racial types, where whiteness, for instance, is individuated by subjective agency while others are reduced to a static type. Faciality illustrates a normalizing process that is highly partisan and unequal. In an attempt to justify slavery through faciality, Nott's race science must foreclose the multi-accentuality of the black face, reducing it to a fixed sign of black inferiority.

In addition to the emergent "race science" of the period, the black face was also the iconic trope for one of the most popular forms of entertainment in the antebellum period, minstrelsy, or what was commonly known as "blackface." The black face—as an exaggerated and satirical sign—repeatedly surfaced in the visual culture surrounding minstrelsy from advertisements to songbook covers. As Michelle Ann Stephens notes, "The blackface act highlights the black face as the be-all and end-all signifier of blackness, and this effect only increases as audiences become more sensitive to its racial connotations over time."[18] Like the race science of the day, blackface minstrelsy sought to reduce the multiaccentuality of the black face to a handful of recognizable minstrel types, leading to a situation where facialization paradoxically resulted in facelessness. But the repetition of familiar types was also part of the genre's appeal. It would be a mistake, as Eric Lott argues, to foreclose the multivalence and contradictions of minstrelsy and reduce it to a univocal meaning. Frederick Douglass saw in black minstrelsy, particularly when the performers were themselves African Americans in blackface, a possible way to obliterate racial prejudice. "It is something gained," he wrote in the North Star, "when the colored man in any form can appear before a white audience."[19]

Although Frederick Douglass's remarks on blackface minstrelsy may seem overly sanguine, they illustrate his belief in the indeterminacy of seemingly univocal types. Although racial stereotypes rely on the face, they can be challenged, undermined, and contradicted through the face as a countervailing force of individuation and distinctiveness. The face, moreover, can be a vehicle for typological seeing and objectification, while at the same time possessing an individuating power that compels the recognition of one's full humanity. Although Josiah Nott and other race scientists intended to reduce the black face to a fixed racial type associated with black inferiority, they did not entirely succeed. Racial types promise fixity, stability, and order, but they cannot guarantee such outcomes, since the reading of social signs is always indeterminate. Equally indeterminate was the race science of the nineteenth century, which could invoke the African face to legitimize slavery (as Josiah Nott intended) or challenge the institution as the antislavery Englishman James Cowles Prichard sought to do in The Natural History of Man (1843).

Frederick Douglass recounts his experience of reading Prichard's The Natural History of Man in My Bondage and My Freedom. While perusing its pages, Douglass was taken aback when he saw a sketch of an Egyptian that stirred a vague memory of his mother's face: "the head of a figure—on page 157—the features of which so resemble those of my mother, that I often recur to it with something of the feeling which I suppose others experience when looking upon the pictures of dear departed ones."[20] In contrast to the proslavery bent of Nott's

Fig. **48.**

Head of Rameses.

Etching of Ramses II in James Cowles Prichard,
The Natural History of Man (London: H. Bailliere, 1843), 157.

American School of Ethnology that vilified Egypt, English abolitionist Prichard considered Egypt the cradle of modern civilization, thus using race science to underscore the commonality of the human race.[21] The figure that Douglass refers to in Prichard's ethnographic study is the face of Ramses II, an Egyptian pharaoh whose profile is sketched from a tomb, with features that are deemed characteristic of the royal physiognomy of Egypt. In the etching of the Egyptian king, Douglass recognizes his mother: The profile of Ramses II is reminiscent of the "side view of her [my mother's] face" that is "imaged on my memory." Like the image in Prichard's book, the memory of his mother is mute: "I have no striking words of hers treasured up."[22]

Separated as an infant from his mother, Douglass admits that his memory of her is "very scanty" but "very distinct." His mother, Harriet Bailey, who Douglass only briefly described ten years earlier in his *Narrative of the Life of Frederick Douglass,* is given more form and feeling in his second autobiography. Douglass focuses on her face, her "weary, sad, downcast countenance and mute demeanor—full of heartfelt sorrow."[23] Framing his mother in sentimental terms, Douglass converts a type into an intimate portrait, where an impersonal etching of statuary becomes the poignant memory of a son recalling the face of his late mother.

Frederick Douglass, Madison Washington, and the Problem of Black Amiability

Just as the black face designated a representational battleground upon which the humanity of black people was fought over, so the smile denoted an equally contentious semiotic domain. Douglass was particularly attuned to these matters when they involved his own self-image. Scholars have noted that no other American was photographed as much in the nineteenth century as Douglass, and yet he was highly selective when it came to choosing an image for the frontispiece of his books. Robert Levine points to Douglass's dismay when he saw an engraving of himself with a half-smile that appeared in the first Dublin edition of the *Narrative of the Life of Frederick Douglass, an American Slave.* Despite his protestations against what he considered a dandyish image, it appeared again in a British edition of *A Tribute for the Negro* (1848). In the *North Star,* Douglass explained why he considered this engraving of his smiling face so objectionable: "[It] has a much more kindly and amiable expression, than is generally thought to characterize the face of a fugitive slave." He then lambasted white artists, more generally, for their inability to depict black faces accurately: "It seems to us next to impossible for white men to take likenesses of black men, without most grossly exaggerating their distinctive features."[24] But his objection stems not from the question of likeness and exaggeration, as he claims, but from the belief that a kindly expression is at odds with the "face of a fugitive slave." Douglass's response to the engraving, in other words, betrays his own anxieties about black amiability.

But why should Douglass object to an image of himself slightly smiling? Why is looking "kindly and amiable" so offensive? Several years later in *Life and Times of Frederick Douglass* (1881), he would confess that he does possess a cheerful disposition and that he tends to see "the funny side of things." His sense of humor has allowed him to see the absurdity of racial prejudice and to laugh at its "follies," which others would resent more deeply.[25] Laughter has been his salvation. This aspect of his personality, however, had to be downplayed when he posed for a portrait to be used as the frontispiece for his first autobiography. Even at this early stage of his public career, it is as if Douglass was fully aware of how his facial expression had to personify the heroic fugitive slave outraged at racial injustice. The image that he selected for the American edition is a portrait of him sternly staring into the camera with an expression of self-possession and seriousness. His lips are firmly sealed without the slightest hint of a grin; his eyes peer directly at the viewer. His masculinity shows no signs of effeminacy, his dignity bears no trace of the dandy.

For Harriet Beecher Stowe, amiability was a crucial trait for humanizing black characters, and even her revolutionary character Dred could on occasion manage "a pleased expression, approaching to a smile."[26] For Douglass, however, the smile was not consistent with the face of the fugitive. Yet, the question of black amiability would return a few years later when he wrote his only fictional work, *The Heroic Slave* (1853), a novella based on a slave mutiny aboard the ship *Creole* that left Richmond, Virginia, bound for New Orleans in 1841. It features the leader of the mutiny, Madison Washington, who had escaped slavery years earlier only to be re-enslaved when he returned to Virginia to rescue his wife.

In writing his novella, Douglass was confronted with the dilemma of how to characterize the black leader of a successful slave mutiny who many white Americans considered a murderer. The biggest challenge was the depiction of black anger. Douglass wanted to express Washington's rage at racial injustice without discomfiting white readers who needed to be persuaded to share in his outrage, or at the very least, to understand where it came from. He sought to combine the tactics of moral suasion with the representation of black dissidence.[27] To do this, Douglass understood that he needed to portray the slave mutineer as worthy of respect and as both personable and likable. Black niceness had to be integrated with dignity and even awe. Douglass framed Washington's anger in terms of black male heroism stemming from the same sense of moral outrage that motivated the patriots of the American Revolution after whom he is so aptly named. The final result is a protagonist who is admirable as well as amiable, courageous and kind.

In the opening pages of the novella, Madison Washington is physically described as having a "manly form," which is "tall, symmetrical, round, and strong." The narrative lens then focuses on Washington's face, depicted as "black and comely," citing a verse from Song of Solomon. Like Harriet Beecher Stowe's black fugitive character Dred, who enjoys the company of children, Douglass is quick to reassure his readers that although Washington exhibits "Herculean strength," there is "nothing savage or forbidding in his aspect." A child may "play in his arms, or dance on his shoulders. A giant's strength, but not a giant's heart was in him. His broad mouth and nose spoke only of good nature and kindness." In order not to make Washington appear too avuncular and sentimental, we are told that his voice "could terrify as well as charm." Similar to Metamora's threat to his audience that he can either be a loyal friend or a terrible foe, so Washington is presented as having the potential to be "sought as a friend" or "dreaded as an enemy."[28] Published a year after *Uncle Tom's Cabin*, Douglass's novella characterizes its protagonist more in the vein of the noble Indian chief who is kind but shrewd rather than the Christlike figure of Stowe's eponymous character.

What is significant about *The Heroic Slave* is that Madison Washington is presented to the reader exclusively from the perspective of white characters. First, the story is told through the character of Mr. Listwell, an Ohio traveler who initially encounters Washington in a wooded area in Virginia and overhears the latter's soliloquy on wanting freedom. Mr. Listwell quietly leaves the scene and returns to Ohio, now an abolitionist. Five years later, while sitting by the fireside of his "happy home," Washington turns up on his doorstep asking for shelter and assistance to Canada, which Listwell generously provides upon immediately recognizing him from Virginia. "I know not your name but I have seen your face," he admits, as it has been "daguerreotyped upon my memory." For Listwell, the memory of Washington's face is inextricably connected to his own conversion to abolitionism. The personal and the political are fused together so that the particularity of Washington's face triggers a larger political sensibility that results in Listwell's participation in the Underground Railroad. *The Heroic Slave* is as much about the life of Madison Washington as it is about white kindness and interracial friendship.

Years later, Listwell encounters Washington again but now in Richmond, where the latter has been re-enslaved after being caught trying to free his wife, who was shot dead in their attempt to escape. About to board the slave ship *Creole,* bound for New Orleans, Washington secretly receives from his friend money and strong files with which to remove the iron chains. Although this gift does not appear in other contemporaneous accounts of the slave mutiny, it plays a central role in *The Heroic Slave,* precisely for how it implicates a sympathetic white ally in the slave revolt. Listwell's gesture of kindness, moreover, enabled the mutiny. Douglass seems to be implying that black niceness is not enough. It requires "the powerful and inextricable net-work of human brotherhood."[29] The joining of black amiability with white kindness through the bonds of interracial friendship creates the foundation for abolitionist solidarity.

The second narrative frame, through which the story of the slave ship mutiny is told, centers on a conversation between two white men in a coffeehouse in Richmond: Jack Williams, a slave trader and overseer, and Tom Grant, the first mate, who witnessed the slave mutiny firsthand and returns, like Coleridge's ancient mariner, to tell the tale. While not an abolitionist like Mr. Listwell, Tom Grant, the second white narrator of the novella, finds the slave trade morally objectionable and has decided never to sail aboard another slaver. The staging of this conversation is strategic. Jack Williams is the unsympathetic proslavery Southerner who refers to the mutineers as murderers and blames the sailors for not quelling the revolt, while Tom Grant expresses reluctant admiration for Madison Washington: "The only feeling with which we regarded him was, that he was a powerful, good-disposed negro" with the "utmost propriety." This echoes an observation that Douglass and Stowe made about the leaders of slave rebellions: that the most good-natured and well-behaved black men initiated slave revolts, those who were considered the least suspicious. As Stowe writes in *Dred* regarding Denmark Vesey's foiled plot in Charleston, South Carolina, in 1822: "[T]here was not a man of bad character among them. They had all been *remarkable* for their good character."[30]

Douglass shares with Stowe this insistence on good character in that black mutineers are not murderers but patriots fighting for their freedom in the spirit of '76. Even the name of Madison Washington underscores this genealogical connection to the Founding Fathers. When Washington could have killed Tom Grant but instead preserves his life, Washington says to him that he is not motivated by vengeance but rather by the love of freedom: "You call me a *black murderer.* I am not a murderer. God is my witness that LIBERTY, not *malice,* is the motive for this night's work." To demonstrate these words, Washington saves Tom Grant's life when one of the mutineers attempts to kill Grant with a handspike that Washington intercepts. Douglass goes to great lengths to qualify Washington's anger: his rage is directed at racial injustice not at white people. What motivates the slave mutiny is not malevolence but the love of freedom.

Where Listwell stresses Washington's likability and kindness, Tom Grant underscores his dignity and power. Through these two white narrators, Douglass integrates the traits of niceness with heroism, tempering terror with likability. They bear witness to Washington's good character and thus serve as the white messengers of black amiability. But Douglass's text is also instructive; it teaches the sympathetic white reader (or the potentially sympathetic one) how to read black character primarily through the face, as Mr. Listwell had so perceptively done. From the start of the novella, Douglass invites his readers to understand that Washington's "broad mouth and nose spoke only of good nature and kindness," while his voice, as an index of his soul, could "terrify as well as charm."

The Black Faces of Harriet Beecher Stowe

For Frederick Douglass and Harriet Beecher Stowe, the black face was a sign of personhood that possessed a transparency, where one could witness the soulful longings of black subjectivity. While the smile was complicated for Douglass since it could compromise manliness with suggestions of dandyism and even weakness, for Stowe the black smile signified living proof of black humanity that individuated a population that was rarely particularized through facial expressions. Black characterization, for Stowe, was largely achieved through a prosaic portrait or what she describes in *Uncle Tom's Cabin* as a "daguerreotype." She often began with the popular racial types from minstrelsy and plantation novels. By detailing the black face and giving it an affective dimension such as a wistful look or a nuanced expression, Stowe turned caricatures into characters.[31]

In depicting Uncle Tom, Stowe transformed a minstrel type into a character by adding particular details through a description of his face: "a face whose truly African features were characterized by an expression of grave and steady good sense, united with much kindliness and benevolence. There was something about his whole air self-respecting and dignified, yet united with a confiding and humble simplicity." Stowe combines black amiability with dignity by illustrating how facial features reveal truths about one's inner character. Later, she describes this combination of seriousness and warmth through his distinctive smile: "Tom had a sober, benevolent smile."[32] Stowe resists the minstrel stereotype of the "grinning" Negro and instead uses the smile to individualize her black characters by showing, for instance, how Aunt Milly's direct manner is reflected in her "frank smile."[33]

What distinguishes Stowe and makes her such an insightful thinker on race is that she believed that the black face was decipherable. She applied sentimentalism's earnest belief in the hermeneutics of transparency, that the face reflects one's interiority, to African Americans. In fact, Stowe believed that it was a moral imperative that white people become astute readers of black faces. They had to be able to look into Aunt Milly's eyes and recognize her "wishfulness and longing." In *Uncle Tom's Cabin* and *Dred*, Stowe mediated this face-to-face contact across the color line, repeatedly forcing her predominantly white readers to look black characters in the eye.

Tom's death scene is depicted precisely as his characterization began: through a description of his face. After being brutally beaten by Legree for not betraying the hiding spot of two runaway slaves in a courageous act of passive resistance, Tom lay dying for two days. Upon realizing that his original master's son George Shelby was by his side, Tom's "vacant eye became fixed and brightened, the whole face lighted up, the hard hands clasped, and tears ran down the cheeks." Before "that mysterious and sublime change passed over his face, that told the approach of other worlds," Tom carefully relays to George that he should not tell his wife, Chloe, about the abject state of his beaten body. Tell her instead his "victory." Stowe underscores Tom's own self-consciousness about dying with dignity in describing his face as having the expression of a "conqueror."[34] Like Little Eva, who died with a "glorious smile," so Tom's final expression was a triumphant smile. Through the twinning of their dying faces, Stowe underscores their common humanity.

Stowe's brand of sentimentalism signifies a politics of disclosure, where the abuses of a system can be traced in the scars and expressions of the slave's face. The interpersonal is the lens through which the structural is exposed. Black amiability invites the white reader to look at the slave closely and to witness the pain of an institution engraved through the lines of her face. Stowe's foregrounding of the black face has its antecedent in an earlier generation of antislavery writing, such as the Unitarian theologian William Ellery Channing's *Slavery* (1835), a book that claims how the master's treatment is reflected in the slave's face: "The African is so affectionate, imitative, and docile that in favorable circumstances he catches much that is good; and accordingly the influence of a wise and kind master will be seen in the very countenance of his slaves."[35] Although both underscore black amiability, Channing sees the slave's face as a reflection of the master's treatment, a claim that a number of proslavery writers also made. Channing understands slavery less as a system and more as a personal relation between master and slave, whereas Stowe insists that black amiability is an essential attribute of black character, regardless of the master's behavior. Tom's kindly and benevolent face does not change whether he is owned by the kind Mr. Shelby or the sadistic Simon Legree. As George Boulukos argues, this marks a significant shift in the representation of the grateful slave, in that Stowe revises this eighteenth-century figure so that the slave is faithful to Christ rather than to a specific master.[36]

Harriet Beecher Stowe's Critique of Southern Niceness

Harriet Beecher Stowe understood, as did Frederick Douglass, that humanizing black people through a defense of black amiability would not be enough to challenge slavery. In particular, Stowe used her abolitionist novels to defend black amiability while challenging another form of niceness, one that lay at the heart of the institution, namely, Southern niceness. This ideology legitimized slavery by casting the institution as a benevolent form of paternalism. It claimed that the Southern aristocracy created a form of human enslavement that was mild in comparison to its practice in other parts of the Black Atlantic. Southern niceness was a regional appropriation of American exceptionalism that justified slavery as a kind and gentle institution through the benevolent slave owner, who was not only a Southerner but also a representative American. For the defenders of slavery in the North and South, Southern niceness was cast as a constitutive element of American niceness, in which power was rendered genteel, part of a pastoral landscape of banjo-playing slaves and Southern belles sipping mint juleps under the Spanish moss.

What makes Harriet Beecher Stowe's *Uncle Tom's Cabin* such a powerful critique of slavery is her depiction of slavery at its most benevolent. The novel begins on the Shelby plantation in Kentucky, a state that was reputed to have, in Stowe's words, "the mildest form of the system of slavery." The Shelbys are respectable people described from the start as "good-natured and kindly," with Mr. Shelby referring to himself as a "humane man," while his more modest wife is portrayed in terms of her "natural magnanimity and generosity of mind."[37] Stowe took these stock characters from the proslavery plantation fiction of the 1840s and turned them into figures of critique. As she acknowledged in *A Key to Uncle Tom's Cabin*, published a year after her famous novel, if slavery consisted solely of the Simon Legrees—of the brutal and tyrannical slave owners and overseers—then the institution would have already ended. Stowe understood that it was the kind slave owners who sustained slavery by making it respectable.

Even though Stowe is closely associated with sentimentalism and the ethics of feeling right, she bases her condemnation of slavery on a suspicion of such amiable behavior. According to Stowe, kindness cannot redeem the institution because even when slavery is practiced in its most humane form, it is still fundamentally inhumane. In *A Key to Uncle Tom's Cabin*, she writes that "all the kindest feelings and intentions of the master" do not curtail the "absolute despotism of the slave-law."[38] Slavery cannot be made humane through strict regulations barring torture and other forms of physical abuse; it cannot be reformed internally but must be abolished. As she wrote in the opening chapter of *Uncle Tom's Cabin*, "it is impossible to make anything beautiful or desirable in the best regulated administration of slavery."[39] Stowe refused to countenance slavery in any form, and in doing so, she made an important ethical intervention by distinguishing niceness from justice.

For Stowe, the nice slave owner represents a powerful figure for conveying the paradox of cruelty and kindness. It allows her to show how positive modes of social behavior, such as amiability and generosity, do not necessarily imply ethical behavior. Kind people can do cruel things. They can get into debt, like the Shelbys did, and be forced to sell their beloved slave. To be nice is not necessarily to be just. But Stowe does not believe that niceness can be easily dismissed as a way to disguise cruel intentions through good manners. She seems earnestly invested in Southern niceness. Perhaps this is a feigned earnestness on Stowe's part, a tactic to persuade the South to abandon slavery voluntarily rather than to resort to war. But even if it is, her point is the same: By taking Southern niceness seriously, Stowe illustrates the complexity of this regional characteristic. The paradox of the nice slave owner, in other words, resides precisely in the genuineness of their kindly behavior. The Shelbys sincerely believe in their own goodness.

Consequently, Southern niceness in Stowe's antislavery fiction is both the problem and the cure. It prolongs slavery, and yet, it can also be used strategically to eradicate slavery. On the one hand, Stowe clearly sees that the respectable slave owners are the ones perpetuating the system by giving it credibility. In this sense, Southern niceness enables slavery to continue. But in *Uncle Tom's Cabin* and *Dred*, Stowe refused to alienate her Southern readers by criticizing Southern character; her goal was one of persuasion, to encourage Southern slaveholders to end slavery voluntarily to avoid civil war. She made sure to target her critique at a system and not at individual Southerners. Her goal was to depersonalize slavery by showing it as a structure of power that was truly national rather than exclusively regional. Her rhetorical strategy can itself be described as nice in the sense that she did not want to upset her Southern readers and went to great lengths to depict the slaveholders, to use her own words, as "amiable, generous and just."[40]

One of Stowe's most astute readers, the critic Charles Dudley Warner, understood this strategy when he wrote in 1896 that she aimed "to touch the South by showing that the inevitable wrong of it [slavery] lay in the system rather than in those involved in it." After all, Simon Legree, the cruelest slave owner, is a Northerner from Vermont. Stowe and her circle of friends believed that she had depicted southern slaveholders so favorably that a friend who had many relatives in the South wrote to Stowe, "Your book is going to be the great pacificator; it will unite both North and South."[41] She had expected hostility not from Southerners, but from New England abolitionists, who she thought would denounce the book for being "too mild." But to her surprise, writes Warner, "it was the extreme abolitionists who received, and the entire South who rose up against it."[42]

Southern hostility took many forms from attacks in the Southern press to hate mail that in one instance included a black person's severed ear with an anonymous note criticizing Stowe's defense of the "D—n niggers." Her husband, Calvin Stowe, opened the package and disposed of its contents without letting Stowe see it. Although Stowe insisted on a critique of slavery that was systemic rather than personal, the white Southern response is telling; it shows how the structural and the personal were irrevocably fused together. To expose the cruelty of slavery was to discredit Southern niceness at its ideological core. And yet in 1853, in the midst of ongoing animosity from readers, Stowe still felt the need to defend Southern character. As she wrote to her friend Lord Shaftesbury, she has a "true heart of love for the Southern people."[43]

Stowe invokes Southern niceness as a tactic of persuasion, but she also understands the dialectical potential of the concept. Southern niceness enables slavery, but it can also eradicate it if the scions of the slavocracy were to awaken to the injustice of the system and reject slavery in an act of moral disgust. Southern niceness, when taken to its logical ends, Stowe believes, could result in voluntary manumissions, with all slaveholders following the example of George Shelby, who is persuaded by the kindness of the dying Uncle Tom "never [to] own another slave."[44] Uncle Tom's niceness, in other words, leads to George Shelby's deconversion, where he renounces his class and race privilege by abolishing slavery on his family's estate and hiring the former slaves as wage laborers.

Stowe reiterates the progressive power of Southern niceness in her next novel, Dred, when Virginian patrician Edward Clayton voluntarily manumits his slaves when he realizes there is no way to reform the institution through legal means. There cannot be a humane form of slavery or a gentler and kinder version with tighter regulation. Instead, Clayton decides to establish a settlement of freedmen and women in Canada, which becomes one of the wealthiest parts of the region and whose success entirely wins over the white Canadian settlers who were initially skeptical. In both novels, Southern niceness is cast as the genteel act of bequeathing freedom to one's slaves, with Southern gentility going beyond hospitality and good manners by dismantling the institution altogether in order to enact more humane forms of labor and community. As a way to end slavery and avoid war, Stowe's ideal of Southern niceness is not antithetical to justice but is its fullest expression.

But it is important to add that Stowe is not particularly hopeful about realizing her fantasy of voluntary manumissions. The final paragraph of *Uncle Tom's Cabin*, when she addresses the reader directly and cites Old Testament verse, is full of apocalyptic threats of imminent war. As Kevin Pelletier argues in *Apocalyptic Sentimentalism*, Stowe employs the fire and brimstone rhetoric of fear in a novel otherwise committed to the persuasive power of love.[45] Stowe becomes her father, Lyman Beecher, the Calvinist minister who warns her readers to act with mercy or else God's wrath will come down upon them. In the last instance, she hedges her rhetorical bets: If New Testament niceness doesn't persuade, perhaps Old Testament fear will.

The Scars and Smiles of Runaway Slave Ads

The persona of the New England minister inciting her congregation to act shapes the rhetorical tone of Stowe's nonfictional work *A Key to Uncle Tom's Cabin*. She still imagines a way to end slavery without war by calling on all American churches to oppose slavery. She similarly urges Southern patricians who believe slavery is a sin to have the courage of their convictions through God's love to free their slaves. She explains in prose what her novels enact through plot. But she is bolder in her nonfictional, antislavery book and less cautious about impugning Southern character. Stowe published *A Key to Uncle Tom's Cabin* after the huge success of *Uncle Tom's Cabin* as a supplement that offers her skeptical readers nonfictional proof of slavery's horrors. In *A Key*, Stowe quotes extensively from Theodore Weld's *American Slavery As It Is: Testimony of a Thousand Witnesses* (1839), a book that influenced Stowe so profoundly that she claimed that she "slept with it under her pillow until it crystallized into *Uncle Tom's Cabin*."[46] Weld's abolitionist anthology of testimony was substantially assembled and edited by the Grimké sisters and was widely read and discussed throughout the 1840s. In his Introduction, Weld positions the reader as a "juror" who will listen to eyewitness accounts from those who have visited the South as well as slaveholders and former slaveholders. His objective is to collect facts without commentary and to catalog the inhumane treatment of slaves through the accounts of white people.

For Stowe, writing about slavery is a form of testimony that involves listening to what had for too long remained opaque and concealed. In the final chapter of *Uncle Tom's Cabin*, Stowe speaks directly to the reader to acknowledge "there are living witnesses, all over our land, to testify."[47] One year later, in *A Key to Uncle Tom's Cabin*, Stowe would expand this point by describing slaves as "witnesses" and their stories as a form of "living testimony." Witnessing becomes a form of activism in which human rights abuses are documented, with the evidence carefully cited and then publically disseminated. In this sense, Stowe bears witness to the nation's massive trauma, where the African American face plays a central role, as it did in her abolitionist fiction:

> But we shall be told the slaves are all a lying race, and that these are lies which they tell us. There are some things, however, about these slaves, which cannot lie. Those deep lines of patient sorrow upon the face; that attitude of crouching and humble subjection; that sad, habitual expression of hope deferred in the eye, would tell their story if the slave never spoke.[48]

Stowe speaks of being haunted by such sorrowful faces for weeks after seeing them. Her objective in *A Key to Uncle Tom's Cabin* is to authenticate her critique of slavery, and her most powerful sources are stories of escape, abuse, and violence. But the source that seems to fascinate Stowe the most comes not directly from the slave but from the slave owner: the genre of runaway slave advertisements.

Runaway slave advertisements intrigued Stowe because they came from the slaveholder and yet undermined the fundamental tenets of slavery, namely, Southern niceness and its paternalist myth of the plantation as an extended family of benevolent masters and contented slaves. If slaves are so happy on the plantation, Stowe asks, then why are they running away? In *A Key to Uncle Tom's Cabin*, Stowe performs an against-the-grain reading of runaway slave ads, interpreting them as revealing the lie of U.S. slavery as a "mild" institution. In describing the identifying marks of their runaway slaves in terms of scars, missing limbs, and disfigurements, the slave owner implicitly confesses that torture is part of the daily cruelty that sustains slavery. For Stowe, there was no greater critique of Southern niceness than the slaveholder's own words that appeared in the runaway slave advertisements.

Stowe was not the only one who found this genre a powerful indictment of slavery. Over a decade earlier Charles Dickens had published *American Notes* (1842), which included a controversial chapter on slavery that is almost entirely focused on runaway slave advertisements culled from Theodore Weld's book as well as from Southern newspapers printed during Dickens's extensive tour of the United States. What astonished Dickens in his reading of these advertisements was how open slaveholders were about the physical abuse they inflicted on their slaves' bodies. Their torture was not closeted, which would imply a degree of shame, but rather brandished on the pages of the local paper. For Dickens, the fact that a slave master would announce under his own name in a local newspaper that "I burnt her with a hot iron, on the left side of her face. I tried to make the letter M," suggests that such acts are considered ordinary in the slave states.[49] They are beyond reproach. Consequently, the slave-master mentality has produced a population of white Americans who use violence to solve conflicts among themselves. For Dickens, the violence of the plantation does not stay on the plantation but permeates every aspect of U.S. culture from hotels and bar fights to duels and business deals gone wrong. The slave master's brutal treatment of the slave is emblematic of violence within the nation as a whole, whether in Mississippi or Wisconsin.

Dickens concludes his critique of slavery by invoking Indian niceness as an alternative to the fraudulence of American niceness. In calling for the decolonization of the United States and a return to the Native American village, where wigwams and forests would replace the "stars and stripes," Dickens argues that Indians treat each other better than "the cruelties of Christian men."

Frederick Douglass refers to Dickens's discussion of runaway slave advertisements in a speech he gave in England in 1846. According to Douglass, such advertisements are not anomalous but demonstrate the necessity of cruelty to sustain slavery. Whether it is the whip, thumbscrews, bloodhounds, or starvation, all of these torture tactics are necessary, argues Douglass, in order to *make the slave a slave, and to keep him a slave*" [original italics]. The flagrant descriptions in slave advertisements of branding and mutilation demonstrate how the "bloody paraphernalia of the slave system are indispensably necessary to the relation of master and slave."[50] How can kindness play any role in slavery, asks Douglass, when one is "robbed of wife, of children, of his hard earnings, of home, of friends"? Such an assumption is "most absurd, wicked, and preposterous." If kindness were the rule in the master-slave relationship, argues Douglass, Southern newspapers would not be filled with runaway slave advertisements that describe branding with irons, scarring from whips, and being enchained.[51]

Southern niceness is a mask that conceals the necessary cruelty of the system and Douglass's self-imposed task is to "tear off the mask from this abominable system [and] to expose it to the light of heaven . . . that it may burn and wither it out of existence."[52] Like Dickens, Douglass also references Indian kindness but as a way to juxtapose the genuine kindness of the Indian against "the pretended kindness of slaveholders."[53]

More than even Dickens or Douglass, Stowe turns to slave advertisements for the way they demonstrate the intersection of the structural and the personal, how the character of a cruel system is revealed in the slave master's portrayal of his victims. She reads these advertisements as a writer who sees in these brief lines a slave master's inadvertent attempt to characterize another human being. They are snapshots in prose that attempt to retrieve property but instead become testimonials to the slave's personhood. There is a fundamental paradox that intrigues Stowe. In describing lost property, the slaveholders are forced to acknowledge the humanity of their slaves, the very quality that the master has to suppress.

Black abolitionist Samuel Ringgold Ward made a similar claim about runaway slave advertisements: that they are filled with phrases that describe the face as "intelligent countenances," "had a bold look," and "very intelligent." For Ward as for Stowe, the runaway slave advertisements offer fleeting moments of characterization that demonstrate the superior courage of the fugitive who undertakes the dangerous journey northward. Such individuals represent exemplary models of good character, according to Ward, based on "patience, fortitude, and perseverance."[54]

The word *character* comes from the Greek word *kharakter*, and was originally defined as "a mark engraved or impressed, the impress or stamp on coins and seals" and then extended to include "the mark impressed (as it were) on a person or thing, a distinctive mark, characteristic, character."[55] Within the context of nineteenth-century print culture, character referred to metal types in the production of mass-produced publications. Character, in other words, refers both to the technology of impressing newspapers with typeface to produce the runaway slave advertisements on a massive scale and to the defining traits of the slaves who are the focus of the advertisements.

But there is also another sense in which the word *character* informs these advertisements. Character refers to a "mark" or a "cutting into" that is literally manifested in the scars on the slave's body, a common feature of the genre, according to Stowe's own study. The description of scars as markers of individuality tells a story of abuse at the hands of cruel masters and overseers. But the scar as an identifier of individuality loses its ability to distinguish through the ubiquity of the scar on the slave's body and the massive scale of the advertisements. Each advertisement blurs into another, as each runaway slave collapses into the multitude. The repetitiveness of the genre makes the scar an ineffective marker of a particular person since all slave advertisements include references to scars (and only occasionally to their absence).

And yet, given the uniformity of the genre, Stowe is struck by the glimpse of individuality captured in the brief descriptions of the slave's face. Each advertisement, in other words, tells a story:

> He calls himself DANIEL TURNER; his hair curls without showing black blood, or wool; he has a scar on one cheek, and his left hand has been seriously injured by a pistol-shot, and he was shabbily dressed when last seen.[56]

With Turner's hair showing no sign of black blood, Stowe ironically wonders who his father is. She then quotes an advertisement from Kentucky, a state that has the reputation of practicing the mildest form of slavery: "The girl's name is Julia, and she is of light brown color, short and heavy set, rather good-looking, with a scar upon her forehead." In *A Key to Uncle Tom's Cabin*, Stowe interweaves these fragments of runaway slave advertisements with Henry Wadsworth Longfellow's description of the slave's face:

> A poor old slave, infirm and lame;
> Great scars deformed his face;
> On his forehead he bore the brand of shame,
> And the rags, that hid his mangled frame,
> Were the livery of disgrace.[57]

For Longfellow, the scar deforms the slave's face as well as brands him with shame, but Stowe insists that such violent attacks on the slave's face actually shame the slave owner, and in the case of Julia's scarred forehead, the scar shames even the kindest slave owners from Kentucky.

Intermingled with these advertisements featuring scars, Stowe cites several runaway slave advertisements that focus on the slave's smile, where the face is the locus of personhood, a marker of one's individuality.

> Kosciusko Chronicle, Mississippi: TWENTY DOLLARS REWARD, Will be paid for the delivery of the boy WALKER, aged about 28 years, about 5 feet 8 or 9 inches high, black complexion, loose make, smiles when spoken to, has a mild, sweet voice, and fine teeth. Apply at 25, Tchoupitoulas street, ... Peace be with him!

> Newberry Sentinel, South Carolina: A negro man, by the name of ALLEN, about 23 years old, near six feet high, of dark mulatto colour; no marks, save one, and that caused by the bite of a dog . . . He is quick-spoken, lively, and smiles when in conversation.[58]

The smile is inscribed onto the body like a scar that becomes an identifying marker of a person. Yet scars and smiles seem to be opposing signs. Where scars are permanent markings, smiles can change. They are dynamic, temporary, and situational. But these advertisements describe the two as interchangeable. There is a static quality to the smile that makes the smile a type of scar, a permanent feature of the face. Phrases that often appear are "generally has a smile on his face" or "usually has a smile on her face."[59] Given that slaves were often forced to smile while working or while being auctioned off, it is noteworthy that the smile was even mentioned as an identifying trait.

Within the context of slavery, the smile can represent a type of open wound, a traumatic mark that was often coerced as a sign of a slave's consent to her own enslavement. But it can also be a tactic of negotiation to make the slave's position more comfortable and safe through what former slave Jermain Loguen called "counterfeit smiles."[60] The slave's smile can also be a sign of African American resilience. In an 1850 speech given in Rochester, New York, Douglass makes a case for the black smile beyond coercion and concealment:

> I admit that the slave does sometimes sing, dance, and appear to be merry. But what does this prove? It only proves to my mind, that though slavery is armed with a thousand stings, it is not able entirely to kill the elastic spirit of the bondman. That spirit will rise and walk abroad, despite of whips and chains, . . . his very mirth in such circumstances stands before God as an accusing angel against his enslaver.[61]

Similar to Stowe's defense of Uncle Tom's amiability as a sign of his spirit rather than a reflection of his master's treatment, Douglass makes a case for black pleasure as the expression of the indomitable "elastic spirit" of the slave who can "dance in his chains" in defiance of the slaveholder's whip.[62] It is not a sign of the benevolence of slavery but an example of the slaves' refusal to be broken by its brutality.

Anti-Uncle Tom Novels, Southern Hospitality, and the Power of Persuasion

Just as Stowe challenged slavery at its ideological core in *A Key to Uncle Tom's Cabin* by exposing the fraudulence of Southern niceness, so did Frederick Douglass in declaring that the "slaveholder, were he kind or cruel, was a slaveholder still."[63] Therefore, it should come as no surprise that the defense of slavery should attempt to resuscitate the two major characters of this mythology, the kind slave owner and the happy slave. An important part of the slavery debate over how to represent the South involved the contested site of niceness: Who can lay claim to amiability, and why? Was the slave smiling due to the kindness of the master or in defiance of the master's cruelty? Was the master's kindness a masquerade to placate Northern visitors or a genuine sign of his paternalism? The proslavery performance of Southern niceness was part of a cultural charade, described by the historian David Robertson as a "Magnolia Curtain" and a "Sable Curtain," which provided a form of disavowal for the slave-owning class and subterfuge for the slaves.[64]

Stowe's *Uncle Tom's Cabin* inspired twenty-seven proslavery, anti-Uncle Tom novels written between 1852 and the Civil War. They included novels written by men and women, northerners and southerners, and although they did not attain the commercial success of Stowe's novel, some did go through multiple printings and were widely read in the North. Despite the variety of anti-Uncle Tom novels, there is a certain consistency to the genre that hinges on the intersection of Southern niceness and black amiability, an affective alliance that attempts to legitimize U.S. slavery as a benevolent institution. But where Stowe uses black amiability in the figural form of Uncle Tom to convert George Shelby to the antislavery cause, the anti-Uncle Tom novelists use white Southern niceness combined with black amiability to persuade Northern skeptics that slavery is ultimately benign. The fact that several of the anti-Uncle Tom novelists were Northerners suggests that proslavery sentiments were not exclusive to the South but were part of a national effort to legitimize slavery through the kindness of the master and the smiles of the slave.[65]

Anti-Uncle Tom novelists often dramatize the conversion they want to enact in their readers through their characters. For example, Robert Criswell's anti-Uncle Tom novel *"Uncle Tom's Cabin" Contrasted with Buckingham Hall, The Planter's Home, Or, A Fair View of both sides of the Slavery Question* (1852) is based on converting skeptical Yankees to the Southern cause. Criswell's novel centers on a love story between Eugene Buckingham, the son of South Carolinian planter Colonel Buckingham, who owns several plantations and nearly four hundred slaves, and Miss Julia Tennyson, an aspiring writer in New York City, whose father is a Scottish physician vehemently opposed to slavery.

Where Colonel Buckingham detests Northerners and refuses to send his son Eugene to a Northern university, preferring to have him educated in South Carolina, Dr. Tennyson dislikes Southerners, and when he finds out that the young gentleman visiting his daughter in their Manhattan home is the heir of a Southern planter, he forbids his daughter from seeing him again. The narrative thus establishes a

Romeo-and-Juliet scenario adapted to an American context. Once the respective fathers witness the deleterious effect their animosity has on their children, they decide to meet at Colonel Buckingham's estate in South Carolina.

The latter half of the novel turns into a familiar story of the Northern traveler going South to witness slavery firsthand. This is where the novel turns into a *roman à clef*, in that Robert Criswell, a Northerner, spent several months traveling in the South, during which time he visited nine Southern States. From this experience, he claims in the preface that he is able to write an "impartial" account of slavery. Criswell was a fervent Unionist, and he wanted both sides to compromise on slavery in order to preserve the nation. Criswell's Unionist sentiments appear at the start of the novel with a conflict between the young lovers' families that is then gradually resolved through a process of compromise and accommodation. By the end, the two fathers give their blessings to the motherless young lovers while keeping the Southern plantation intact.

Seduction plays a large role in this conversion narrative not only in terms of the romantic subplot between the young lovers but more significantly between the two fathers, when the wealthy planter persuades the Scottish father that slavery is as benign as the colonel's son. By combining Southern niceness with black amiability, Criswell's novel aims to convert Dr. Tennyson as well as the readers. As in all good seduction novels, Dr. Tennyson initially insists that he cannot be seduced. In a letter to Colonel Buckingham, Dr. Tennyson writes from New York, "I never can consent to suffer *my* daughter to marry a *slaveholder*, a man who engages in that *horrid traffic* of buying and selling *human flesh and blood*, and treating his fellow men as brutes." With kindness and forbearance, Colonel Buckingham responds graciously by inviting Dr. Tennyson to visit his estate in South Carolina to show that "we are not the inhuman monsters the abolitionists represent us to be." For the sake of his daughter, Dr. Tennyson accepts the invitation but insists, "you have not made a *convert* of me *yet*."[66]

Dr. Tennyson's visit to the Buckingham plantation also includes a visit to a jail of field slaves up for sale, a slave auction, and then, in the evening, a discussion about Stowe's *Uncle Tom's Cabin* over a glass of wine with his host. Although featuring various institutional sites of slavery, Criswell's novel reverses Stowe's structural critique of slavery by emphasizing the personal. Stowe insists that the kind slave owner does not make slavery humane because slavery must be understood as a system of power that reduces human beings to property. In Stowe's opinion, the slave owner, whether kind or cruel, is still guilty of this fundamental crime against humanity. By contrast, Criswell personalizes the political. He makes the proslavery case that slavery is not about a system or a structure of exploitation but rather an interpersonal bond between kind planters and happy slaves.

In a gesture that is repeated in several anti-Uncle Tom novels, the proslavery argument concedes that there are bad apples in an otherwise well-functioning institution, and it frequently juxtaposes the bad master with the kind master. Criswell actually names these types, contrasting Hamilton, the benevolent slave owner, with the aptly named Harding, the bad master, who is, not surprisingly, a Northerner like Simon Legree. Southerners make kinder masters and more genteel authority figures compared to their brash and brutal Northern counterparts. But in personalizing slavery's authority in the singular figure of the benevolent master, the proslavery novel fails to address Stowe's concluding point, namely, her fundamental critique of the South's individualist understanding of slavery: "There is, actually, nothing to protect the slave's life, but the *character* of the master."[67] The slave is dependent, in other words, on the whims of the master. Power is completely personalized, and the slave has no recourse to the law, which is to say, an authority beyond the master. Criswell's argument reassures the reader that the master possesses a good character, thus making the law nugatory. The state does not need to intervene when amiable individuals are in charge. The proslavery argument depends on personalizing the political, and the fiction underscores this trend by normalizing the kind slaveholders as the slaveholder *par excellence,* with just a handful of bad apples thrown into the narrative mix to illustrate the exception to the rule.

Southern hospitality succeeds in persuading Dr. Tennyson that slavery, when practiced responsibly and kindly, is not so bad after all. After another glass of wine, Dr. Tennyson admits that from what he has observed personally, the plantations were better than he had assumed. Seeing a "smile of triumph" on the planter's face, Tennyson quickly adds that he still remains opposed to slavery in principle but it "will not interfere with our personal friendship—we have each a right to our different opinions."[68] Slavery is reduced to a difference of opinion, a subject about which Tennyson and Colonel Buckingham can simply agree to disagree. This intersectional bond between the two future fathers-in-law parallels Criswell's Unionist fantasy of reconciling slavery with national unity. This fantasy, however, depends on the attitude that Dr. Tennyson ultimately adopts: It doesn't matter what Colonel Buckingham gets up to below the Mason-Dixon line because he's a decent fellow. In this way, southern likability trumps social justice.

Proslavery Fiction, the Happy Slave, and the Fantasy of Consensual Slavery

Southern niceness depends not only on the kind master but also on the happy slave, whose smile confirms the benign nature of slavery. It was largely assumed that the character of the master was written on the face of the slave. For this reason, proslavery novels depict various forms of black pleasure, whether in the form of banjo playing, dancing, or singing. These depictions renounce the fear and violence that lay at the heart of the system. As South Carolina's Senator James Hammond, owner of more than three hundred slaves, confessed, "We have to rely more and more on the power of fear. We are determined to continue masters, and to do so we have to draw the reign [sic] tighter and tighter day after day to be assured that we hold them in complete check." [69] This sort of confession is what proslavery fiction had to disavow through the reiteration of Southern niceness, which insisted on the respectability of slavery by assuming that cruelty and kindness were mutually exclusive.

Proslavery novels compensate for the despotism of plantation rule by showing how slaves consent to their own enslavement. In this literature, the slave's smile is a mark of consent, a sign that they are having fun in bondage because they are free from the worries of having to supply their own wants in the Northern city. Criswell's novel depicts this fantasy most gratuitously by making it part of a minstrel-style song that the plantation slaves perform for the visiting Northerners:

Darkies dey don't wan'
be free, Case dey happy
as dey be: Massa gibs 'em
plenty meat—Berry apt
to fo'git *de treat.*[70]

With reference to the nice "massa," Criswell's novel depicts black amiability as the affective expression of voluntary servitude. This is to say that the novel recognizes slave agency by, paradoxically, confirming their lack of it.

In addition to showing happy and contented slaves at play, another way in which proslavery fiction enacts the fantasy of consensual slavery is through fugitive slaves who regret running away, going so far as to beg their former masters to re-enslave them. This is the plot of a Northern proslavery novel published in Buffalo, New York, entitled *Life at the South, or "Uncle Tom's Cabin" As It Is,* written by W. L. G. Smith. *Life at the South* is unusual among anti-Uncle Tom novels in that it features a black protagonist. Typically, black characters were relegated to the narrative margins.[71] Dedicated to Henry Clay (like Criswell's novel), *Life at the South* portrays Uncle Tom as regretting his escape from Mr. Erskine's plantation in Kentucky. Once exposed to the hardships of making a living as a boot-black in wintry Buffalo, Uncle Tom begs the benevolent Mr. Erskine, who happens to be touring Niagara Falls, to take him back home. Upon his return, Uncle Tom has "a pleasant smile, and a kind word for all he met." He embraces his children and starts to weep at his good fortune: "He had not language to express his emotions of gratitude, for being permitted again to stand upon his native soil."[72] Unlike Stowe's Uncle Tom, whose amiability is a sign of his love for God rather than the direct reflection of any bond with a master, Smith's Uncle Tom smiles at his own enslavement, and in doing so, personifies the grateful slave who appreciates his good fortune in having a kind master in a congenial climate.[73]

Smith's *Life at the South* is a reminder that Northerners sympathetic to slavery bought into the myth of Southern niceness as much as their Southern counterparts. Within this context, Stowe as an antislavery Northerner writing about the plantation was in the minority. The vast majority of Northern writers who wrote about the Southern plantation endorsed slavery by defending it along the lines of Southern gentility.

The final example of how proslavery fiction portrayed the slave's consent to their own enslavement is slave testimonials, which were presented as the "authentic" words of the "genuine" slave. This move to include slave testimonials was in large part a response to the abolitionists' use of testimonial accounts in Theodore Weld's popular collection *American Slavery As It Is*, Stowe's *A Key to Uncle Tom's Cabin*, and Douglass's *Narrative*. Caroline Lee Hentz employs this technique in her highly successful novel *The Planter's Northern Bride* (1854), which begins with a prefatory account of her several years' residence in the South as an "indwelling guest." The opening paragraphs address Southern niceness in terms of the personal relationship between the kindness of the master and the happiness of the slave. Hentz invokes her first-person testimony to claim, "during our residence in the South, we have never *witnessed* one scene of cruelty or oppression, never beheld a chain or a manacle, or the infliction of a punishment more severe than parental authority would be justified in applying to filial disobedience or transgression." Born in New England, Hentz eventually moved with her family to Cincinnati, where she became acquainted with Stowe as a fellow member of the Semi-Colon Club. Like Harriet Beecher Stowe, Hentz employs the same motif of "witnessing" as a way to authenticate her point of view. But where Stowe's nonfictional account turns to the "facts" of slavery as they were inadvertently revealed in Southern newspapers, Hentz bases her authentic appeals on her own personal impressions.

Once she establishes that slavery illustrates an exercise in authority no more terrifying than "parental authority," Hentz then turns to the other half of the equation, the contented slaves. "We have been especially struck with the cheerfulness and contentment of the slaves, and their usually elastic and buoyant spirits." The happy slave is further proof of the master's kindness, a point that Hentz underscores in an informal interview with a slave who spoke lovingly of her former masters, who had died many years before: "'Oh!' said she, her eyes swimming with tears, and her voice choking with emotion, 'I loved my master and mistress like my own soul.'"[74] Hentz's native informant is a stereotype of the mammy who prefers her master's family to her own and who assures the white interviewer that she would never leave her master even if manumitted. As George Boulukos notes, no more backstory is needed since the mammy "legitimates the idea of slavery as a familial and as a mutual emotional bond."[75] The mammy stereotype has an explanatory power that can simply be invoked; her genuineness can be taken at face value. In this regard, it is important to note how Hentz describes the black face as rich with emotion when speaking of a black woman's love for her former masters. Her tears are sentimental proof of her masters' kindness as well as evidence of her own sympathetic nature.

Hentz concludes that slaves are not only happy in the South, but that they are "the happiest *labouring class* on the face of the globe."[76] According to this logic, the happy slave is not only the happiest worker in the United States, but in the world. Here, we see how Southern niceness gives American exceptionalism a regional inflection. For Hentz and other proslavery writers, U.S. slavery represents a kinder and gentler form of slavery when compared to other parts of the black Atlantic. Consequently, proslavery literature nationalized Southern niceness, thus making the kind slaveholder the nice American *par excellence.*[77]

Transparency and Disguise

The slave's face was at the center of the representational debate about slavery. Proslavery fiction depicts the slave's smile as the voluntary expression of the slave's contentment and, by extension, a validation of American slavery's benevolence. Testimonials from former slaves, however, tell another story about how the slave's face was under the control of the master. Part of the micromanagement of slavery was to shape and determine the parameters of black expressivity. John O'Sullivan's description of U.S. democracy as a "cheerful creed," or what I refer to in the Introduction as "manifest cheerfulness," takes on a far more disturbing valence in the context of slavery as mandated cheerfulness.[78] The master could demand cheerfulness from his slaves as a way to disavow the misery of the system. In this sense, a sorrowful countenance could be a silent form of dissent, a way to register one's unhappiness by striking an affect of critique that the master sought to banish.

Elizabeth Keckley, who later became the seamstress to Mary Todd Lincoln, recounts her days as a slave and tells of one master who "never liked to see one of his slaves wear a sorrowful face, and those who offended in this particular way were always punished." Henry Watson similarly remarks how "the slaveholder watches every move of the slave, and if he is downcast or sad,—in fact, if they are in any mood but laughing and singing, and manifesting symptoms of perfect content at heart,—they are said to have the devil in them."[79] Especially for those who had to work in daily contact with their master or mistress, such as house servants, they had to personify the contented slave whose docility and contentment allayed white anxieties of black revolt and perhaps, on a subconscious level, also appeased white guilt.

In a collection of testimonials from former slaves in South Carolina, one woman recalls how her master forced her to smile while witnessing her brother receive 450 lashes:

> "you mus' smile when Massah see you, else you get just same; and when eber you whipped, you untied, you must look right up in Massah's face and smile; and when white men come roun' you must smile and say, 'You happy!' and 'Massah so good,' else you get whipt so awful, so awful!"[80]

No part of the slave's body was outside the domain of the slave master's authority. Even the face must serve the master through the policing of slave affect. The black face operated at the impersonal and personal levels, as a generalized stereotype as well as through more intimate forms of direct, interpersonal control. Black niceness was mandated behavior, another way in which the slave master exercised his authority, where the happy slave was produced through fear and the threat of punishment.

Slaves were also forced to smile on the auction block as a marketing tactic to facilitate their own sale. All three parties involved in the exchange—the trader, the slave, and the slave buyer—understood the artifice involved. William Wells Brown recounts how he was hired out as a slave working with a slave trader to prepare the older men for auction by shaving their faces, plucking gray hairs, and dyeing their hair black when necessary. Artifice was involved not just in the physical preparation of the slave's body for auction but also in terms of behavior and disposition. This convergence of the physical and the behavioral can be seen in the frequent use of the word *likely* in slave advertisements of the period. On the one hand, *likely* referred strictly to one's physical appearance as healthy and handsome, a meaning

consistent with its British usage. But in the U.S., there was an additional meaning that included both the physical and the behavioral. In
the context of slavery, *likely* referred to a slave who was pleasant as
well as healthy and handsome. Within the slave auction, the smile was
a sign of a likely manner, which is to say, a slave who would have a
pleasing temperament.

In his detailed description of a New Orleans slave pen, former slave
John Brown describes how "a man or woman may be well made, and
physically faultless in every respect, yet their value be impaired by a
sour look, or dull, vacant stare, or a general dullness of demeanor. For
this reason the poor wretches who are about to be sold, are instructed
to look 'spry and smart': to hold themselves up, and put on a smiling,
cheerful countenance." Performing the part of the happy slave is evidence of slavery's terror. In addition to answering questions quickly
and "with a smile on their lips," slaves were also ordered to do as they
were told in order to show themselves off: "dance, jump, walk, leap,
squat, tumble, and twist about, that the buyer may see they have no
stiff joints, or other physical defect."[81]

But coerced smiles could not always conceal the pain of the auction
block. British artist Eyre Crowe, who accompanied the novelist
William Makepeace Thackeray on his 1852 tour of North America as
his secretary, wrote of one woman he witnessed at a Richmond slave
auction: "While the sale of her was going on," he said, "I saw the big
tears slowly & as if imperceptibly to her trickling down her cheeks."[82]
In *A Key to Uncle Tom's Cabin,* Stowe recounts a similar story told to
her by Milly Edmondson, a former slave who asked the Stowes for help
to manumit her daughter Emily, who was auctioned off in New
Orleans. Stowe relays the mother's description of Emily's experience
at the sale: "Emily soon began to cry, upon which an overseer stepped
up and struck her on the chin, and bade her 'stop crying, or he would
give her something to cry about.' Then pointing, he told her 'there was
the calaboose, where they whipped those who did not behave themselves.'"[83] As soon as he turned away, a slave woman came and told her
to look cheerful, if she possibly could, as it would be far better for her.

In *Uncle Tom's Cabin,* Stowe describes the slave warehouse in similar terms, emphasizing the fact that a refusal to be merry is considered
dangerous and risks punishment. "Briskness, alertness, and cheerfulness of appearance, especially before observers, are constantly enforced

upon them, both by the hope of thereby getting a good master, and the fear of all that the driver may bring upon them, if they prove unsalable."[84] The slave's forced smile at the auction softens the power inequity at both ends of the spectrum; it makes domination appear less blatant and the slave's suffering less extreme. It participates in the slave master's fantasy of consensual slavery, where the slave is made to smile as a sign of their consent to their own sale.

In this context, black amiability can also be seen as a self-protective form of behavior, a type of masking that Joel Dinerstein calls the "Uncle Tom-mask," which refers less to the actual character and more to the "set of gestures involved in the survival technique of masking." This mask of black amiability assured the white South that blacks consented to their own inferiority. "What was under attack was the *lived embodiment of deference* marked by the mask in the public sphere . . . as a marker read by whites of African American acceptance of national racial ideology." All slaves wear masks, according to Orlando Patterson, as a survival technique before those who "parasitize" them.[85]

Although Frederick Douglass argues for the decipherability of the black face in his novella *The Heroic Slave,* his speeches and autobiographies disclose the role of facial concealment. To maneuver within a system of everyday terror, the slave had to master the art of facial disguise. This was an exercise in self-control whose goal was to make "counterfeit smiles" seem genuine and ignorance appear authentic. According to Douglass, "[just] as the master studies to keep the slave ignorant, the slave is cunning enough to make the master think he succeeds." When the slave master's authority extended to the micromanagement of black expressivity, Frederick Douglass and other black writers would underscore the importance of indecipherability and of concealing one's thoughts, feelings, and plans from others. Douglass writes in *My Bondage and My Freedom,* "I hated the secrecy, but where slavery is powerful, and liberty is weak, the latter is driven to concealment or to destruction."[86]

As Douglass implies, slaves had to learn the art of performance and facial self-control, but they were also skilled readers in their ability to interpret the face of the master. Along with the mask, this semiotic skill was another survival strategy to accommodate their behavior to the master's moods. John Brown, an ex-slave from Alabama, wrote that as a slave he "had been forced to watch the changes of my master's physiognomy, as well as those of the parties he associated with, so as to frame my conduct in according with what I had reason to believe was their prevailing mood at the time." When Jermain Loguen returned to his brutal master after being hired out for several months, he "went through the servile bows and counterfeit smiles to his master and mistress and other false expressions of gladness." Niceness in this context was ritualized behavior that could conceal the slave's hatred of the master through "counterfeit smiles," while assuring the master of his/her benevolence, thus sustaining the fantasy of Southern paternalism. As historian John Blassingame noted, slaves were highly literate readers of white men's moods and actions, while at the same time able to conceal their own: "The docility of the slave was a sham, a mask to hide his true feelings and personality traits."[87]

The slave's mastery of such concealment can be seen in the letters and diaries of Southern slave owners about their inability to read the black faces around them. In contrast to the self-assured tone in pro-slavery fiction of the master's ability to understand their slaves, there were instances of bafflement in actual life. On a number of occasions, the master admitted defeat: the slave's face was utterly inscrutable. In 1842, a Georgia planter remarked, "Persons live and die in the midst of Negroes and know comparatively little of their real character . . . The Negroes are a distant class in community, and keep very much to *themselves*. They are one thing before the whites, and another before their own color."[88] Proximity does not necessarily lead to understanding.

Anxieties surrounding the slaveholder's inability to interpret the black face intensified during the Civil War. In *A Diary from Dixie*, Mary Boykin Chesnut, the wife of a South Carolinian politician and slave owner who had close ties to the Confederate leadership, recounts how the faces of their slaves were increasingly indecipherable: "I am always studying these creatures. They are to me inscrutable in their ways, and past finding out." As the war progressed, the slaves' facial inscrutability became increasingly unnerving to Chesnut: "They go about in their black masks, not a ripple or an emotion showing; and yet on all other subjects except the War they are the most excitable of all races. Now Dick (a slave) might make a very respectable Egyptian Sphinx, so inscrutably silent is he."[89] During the final year of the Civil War, the silence of the slaves became even more unsettling: "I have excellent servants, no matter for their shortcomings behind my back. They save me all thought as to household matters, and they are so kind and attentive and quiet . . . But these sphinxes give no sign, unless it be increased diligence, and absolute silence. They are as certain in their actions and as noiseless as a law of nature— when they are in the house!" Where the metaphor of the sphinx referred to a single slave in 1862, it now refers to the slaves as a collective, an indecipherable mass seemingly made of stone. In the aftermath of Appomattox, Chesnut notes that the "Negroes seem unchanged." She adds, "They are more circumspect, politer, quieter; but that's all."[90]

Chesnut's diary marks the different stages of the Civil War through the unchanging faces of her slaves, which attests to the masterful self-control slaves exercised over their facial expressions and Chesnut's failed attempts to decipher them. The black face continued to be impermeable to the scrutinizing gaze of the white slave owner, suggesting that estrangement characterized the domestic intimacy of the slaveholding household. By the war's end, Chesnut realized, along with many of her class, that the people she encountered on a daily basis remained complete strangers to her.

Although the impenetrability of the black face during the Civil War was a source of anxiety for white Southerners, it could be a great advantage when blacks served as spies for the Union. "The chief source of information to the enemy," General Robert E. Lee acknowledged in May 1863, "is through our negroes." The Uncle Tom mask that served as a self-protective shield during slavery could also be a useful disguise within the Confederacy to gather military secrets in an elaborate network of Union espionage. In his autobiography, Allan Pinkerton, head of the Union Intelligence Service at the start of the Civil War, described his recruitment of black spies: "I have found the negroes of invaluable assistance and I never hesitated to employ them when after investigation I found them to be intelligent and trustworthy." He recounted the tactics of Mississippi slave John Scobell, who was a "good-headed, vigilant detective" who easily fooled the Confederates around him by assuming "the character of the light-hearted, happy darkey."[91] Slaves' ability to assume racial stereotypes provided the necessary subterfuge to infiltrate Confederate households and extract valuable papers and other information. Another highly successful spy for the Union was

Mary Bowser (née Mary Jane Richards), who was the manumitted slave of the liberal Virginian Elizabeth Van Lews, who became an important spymaster for General Ulysses S. Grant in Richmond. (He later awarded Van Lews the postmaster appointment of Richmond after the Civil War.)

During the Civil War, Mary Bowser became Van Lews's most trusted informant, renamed "Ellen Bond," a slow-thinking but competent servant whose dim-witted persona concealed her photographic memory. She began assisting Jefferson Davis's wife at formal functions as a servant and was eventually hired full-time in the Davis household, cleaning and serving meals. Benefiting from the invisibility of black labor, she acquired a tremendous amount of information through her daily tasks. Mary would convey her information to the local baker, Thomas McNiven, who was Richmond's main spymaster. When he came to the Davis household with the daily delivery, Mary would greet him without suspicion, and they exchanged information encoded in the banal terms of domestic supplies. According to some sources, the Davises became aware that there was a leak in their household, and Mary Bowser quickly disappeared in January 1865. After the war, the federal government destroyed the records of spy activities to protect Southern spies from retribution, and the Bowser family inadvertently destroyed her Civil War journal in 1952.[92]

Whether it is the black spy in the Confederate South during the Civil War or the sphinxlike faces of the slaves in the plantation household during the collapse of the Confederacy, African Americans understood that conforming to racial stereotypes could be an important form of disguise that masked dissent. This strategic use of stereotypes illustrates what I call the politics of nonrecognition, where social invisibility was produced through the racial stereotypes of hypervisibility. Black faciality provided a mode of facelessness that protected and concealed individuals through their conformity to a generic type. In other words, racial stereotypes offered a form of social camouflage. Racial stereotypes could be brutally dehumanizing, but they could also be strategically enabling, as the success of black spies during the Civil War demonstrates. The very personae that whites attributed to black people provided the means by which African Americans undermined the Confederacy.

The Black Smiles of Edgar Allan Poe's Tsalalians

Where proslavery fiction disavowed the impenetrability of the black face by making it easily readable and knowable, Edgar Allan Poe gave white Southern anxieties about black inscrutability a fictional form. In doing so, he employs the trope of black amiability not as an earnest invocation of good character but as a duplicitous strategy that conceals black rage. In *The Narrative of Arthur Gordon Pym of Nantucket* (1838), no one's face—black, red, or white—can be taken at face value. Southern niceness turns into a nightmare, where black aboriginal niceness is not a sign of contentment but a terrifying omen, epitomized in the natives' black smiles, which are literally black in that their teeth are also black. According to Leslie Fiedler in *Love and Death in the American Novel*, the utterly black Tsalalians are a gothic projection of white Southern fears and anxieties. The Island of Tsalal represents the black belt, where Pym, as one of the last surviving whites, is "overwhelmed by a sense of isolation and peril."[93] The novel, Fiedler argues, is about slavery, and it anticipates how the South would one day destroy itself in defending the institution. But the novel can also be read, whether Poe intended it or not, as a way to depict black agency, where the duplicity of black amiability comprises part of a collective strategy of anticolonial struggle, in which the black inhabitants of a distant island use niceness as a ruse to oust Euro-American commercial settlements. The novel is not just about white anxieties about black rage but also how black rage can take the form of amiability as a tactic of resistance. In successfully ridding their island of white traders, the Tsalalians enact exactly the ideal that David Walker articulates in his *Appeal:* a call for black solidarity to overthrow slavery through armed struggle.[94] This fact reminds us that one person's gothic nightmare may be another person's liberation fantasy.

In *The Narrative of Arthur Gordon Pym*, Poe fuses together the two racial specters that haunt white America in the nineteenth century—Indians and Blacks. He combines Indian hospitality with black amiability in characterizing the aborigines of Tsalal. In this fictional travel account, the New England protagonist Arthur Gordon Pym describes the blackness of the natives: "jet black, with thick and long wooly hair." Their friendliness is initially seen as a gesture of hospitality, but it also signifies a source of uneasiness for the suspicious Pym. "Throughout the whole of their visit they evinced the most friendly manner. There were, however, some points in their demeanour [sic] which we found it impossible to understand."[95]

Pym is unsure whether Tsalalian hospitality is genuine or a ruse, but the ambiguity surrounding aboriginal niceness is resolved as the plot develops. Realizing that the sea is rich with *bêche de mer*, a type of seaworm that is a delicacy in Chinese cuisine, Captain Guy decides to turn the island into a trading outpost for the export of *bêche de mer*. The crew establishes an amicable agreement with Chief Too-wit that the islanders and the sailors will construct buildings to prepare the product for export. The Tsalalians will comprise the local workforce in exchange for beads, knives, and red cloth, objects that the natives showed great joy in receiving. By the end of the month, the crew of the *Jane Guy* plans to return to the West, leaving three or four men to oversee the nascent factory, but Too-Wit insists on a farewell ceremony. Given that the natives had shown such cooperation and kindness, Captain Guy and his crew agree to attend the ceremony. The natives' hospitality, however, is a subterfuge to kill the Euro-Americans to prevent the further colonization of their island: "[T]his apparent kindness of disposition was only the result of a deeply-laid plan for our destruction, and that the islanders for whom we entertained such inordinate feelings of esteem were among the most barbarous, subtle, and bloodthirsty wretches that ever contaminated the face of the globe."[96] The friendly Tsalalians lead the unsuspecting sailors along a long path to the center of the island when suddenly they set off an enormous booby trap that triggers an avalanche that buries all the sailors except for Pym, Dirk Peters, and their crewmate Allen.

Pym's suspicions are confirmed. The black smile turns out to be a sign of murderous intent. But to Poe's credit, he refuses to write off the black face as simply an immovable veil that conceals emotion. The Tsalalian face contrives emotion; it deceives through affect. There is a semiotic complexity to the black smile that Poe refuses to either patronize and domesticate or make transparent. Instead, the inscrutability of the black smile is a powerful trope of duplicity and terror. This duplicity can be interpreted as confirming racist assumptions of black treachery and monstrosity, but it can also be read as a challenge to the earnestness of Stowe's romantic racialism and her defense of an amiable black character. Here, Poe is doing exactly what George Eliot recommends: portraying black nastiness, or what Eliot calls "the Nemesis lurking in the vices of the oppressed."[97] But in *Pym*, vice is contingent on subject position. For the Tsalalians, the smile operates as a strategy of anticolonial struggle. The contrived landslide can be read as a successful mutiny against the commodification of *bêche de mer* and, by extension, their own commodification in the East-West networks of global trade. Friendliness proves to be an effective anti-imperial weapon. The same point that Madison Washington makes in Frederick Douglass's *The Heroic Slave* in defending the slave mutiny also applies to the Tsalalians: They are not murderers but patriots fighting for their liberation. Native niceness represents a shrewd strategy of self-determination, one that destroys an outpost of empire at its incipience. Thanks to the indecipherability of the black smile, this cunning scheme to protect native sovereignty succeeds.

Melville's *Benito Cereno* and the Monstrosity of the Nice American

Where Arthur Gordon Pym is saved by his suspicious nature, Captain Amasa Delano is protected by his credulity. Whether the setting is a distant fictional island or a slave ship in the harbor of an uninhabited island off the coast of Chile, both novellas foreground race relations in terms of how whites interpret black niceness. Do they take it at face value? Or are they skeptical? Far away from the shores of the United States, the fate of the white American protagonist depends on either his accurate reading or his misreading of black amiability. As Melville will go on to elaborate in *Benito Cereno*, being a facile reader of faces can actually save your life. It pays to misread your environment.

Proud to be from liberal Massachusetts, Captain Delano is a firm believer in black amiability, never once questioning its veracity when he is aboard the *San Dominick*. In terms of the ship's Spanish captain, Benito Cereno, Delano observes his aristocratic bearing, his gentlemanly reserve, and his expensive clothes ("dressed with singular richness"). He assumes that the African Babo, who has an expressive "rude face" where "sorrow and affection were equally blended," is Cereno's loyal slave.[98] Delano is impressed with the nurturing care that Babo offers his ailing captain, always "keeping his eye fixed on his face, as if to watch for the first sign of complete restoration, or relapse." What

Delano mistakenly interprets as the nurturing gaze of a devoted slave is actually the threatening stare of the lead mutineer, silently enforcing the master-slave tableau for the gullible American who naively exclaims, "Don Benito, I envy you such a friend; slave I cannot call him."[99]

Through Delano, Melville reflects on the blinding power of typological seeing. Social types translate unfamiliar and potentially confusing situations and make them familiar and decipherable. The aftermath of a bloody slave mutiny aboard the *San Dominick* is concealed through the ship's conformity to racial stereotypes that confirm the master-slave relationship: Babo is the happy, devoted slave tending to his ill master. Delano fails to see through Babo's façade of black amiability because he is too invested in understanding individual black people as racial types. He suddenly shifts from describing Babo's "intelligent smile" to general statements about black people: "Most negroes are natural valets and hair-dressers; taking to the comb and brush congenially as to castinets." They have the "great gift of good humor," not just in terms of "grinning and laughing," but also in a "certain easy cheerfulness, harmonious in every glance and gesture."[100] Melville here reiterates the clichés of plantation fiction and minstrelsy with the Sambo stereotypes of grinning faces. Melville is also mimicking the romantic racialism found in Stowe's sentimentalism by portraying a world of benign and good-hearted black people, a world that frustrates otherwise sympathetic readers such as George Eliot.

Delano, as a good sentimentalist, believes in the transparency of the face, because it reassuringly confirms that we live in a decipherable world. Melville offers a sobering antidote to this worldview by presenting a gothic world of deceit, duplicity, and melancholia that lies just below the surface of Babo's servility. It is not that Delano is always a bad reader, for as Peter Coviello notes, he does pick up on subtle signs, recognizing, for example, that the parched lips of those on the *San Dominick* show that they are thirsty.[101] But what ultimately blinds Delano is his abiding faith in black geniality.

In this respect, it is important to understand that Melville presents Delano's faith in black amiability as a reflection of Delano's investment in his own niceness. In other words, Delano's belief in black amiability echoes his own "benign" nature and "benevolent" mind.[102] The narrative is littered with references to Delano's generosity, and the legal deposition at the end includes the epithet "the generous

Captain Amasa Delano." There are also multiple references to Delano's "charitable" nature, such as when he is described as "the American in charity." We are told at the start of the tale that Delano has a "singularly undistrustful good nature" and a "benevolent heart."[103] His belief in black amiability is less a reflection of the actual people on the *San Dominick* and more a sign of Delano's generous gaze. To put it more critically, Delano's misreading of the scene before him is a symptom of his credulity, itself a sign of his own magnanimity.

Leslie Fiedler describes Delano as the "good American," and I would add that he is also the nice American who sees in the black smile confirmation of his own (white) amiability.[104] The use of the word *nice* to describe Delano is especially appropriate because the etymological origins of the word *nice* come from the Latin word *nescius,* which means "foolish" and "stupid." By underestimating the shrewdness of Babo and others, Delano misreads the entire scene on the *San Dominick,* thus betraying his own foolishness.[105] But he cannot relinquish his faith in black amiability, no matter how deceiving it is, because it confirms a worldview that lies at the core of American niceness: that the world is ultimately benign and good. Suspicion is un-American and Delano is quick to feel remorseful when he begins to question the motives of those around him.

Interestingly, Delano's magnanimity is accompanied by its opposite, pettiness. Delano becomes increasingly preoccupied, for example, with Cereno's "discourtesy." Cereno apparently refuses to recognize proper etiquette, but Delano insists on taking the higher ground: "unwilling to appear uncivil even to incivility itself."[106] At first, Delano, who is, after all, a generous reader of others, gives Cereno the benefit of the doubt and rationalizes his inconsiderate behavior as a sign of his reserved Spanish manner. But this rationalization soon wears thin. "Well, thought Captain Delano, if he has little breeding, the more need to show mine." Delano becomes increasingly petty, keeping track of Cereno's breaches of decorum. He then makes sense of such incivility by appealing to national stereotypes: "[T]he very word Spaniard has a curious, conspirator, Guy-Fawkish twang to it."[107] He then insists that Spaniards are still on the whole "good folks" so as not to jeopardize his belief in a friendly and well-intentioned world. But he increasingly suspects Cereno is a "horrible Spaniard" conspiring to kill him and planning to take over his ship. Where Babo represents the nice Negro, the loyal and docile slave who tends to the needs of the master with affection, the Spaniard acquires the same negative attributes as the "bad nigger": ungrateful, cunning, violent, and dishonest. These traits also describe the Spaniard of the Black Legend or *la leyenda negra*, which is a story based on Spain's imperial past and its cruel treatment of the indigenous populations of the Americas, where the Spaniard becomes synonymous with tyranny, violence, and backwardness. This legend, as María DeGuzmán argues in *Spain's Long Shadow*, has played a constitutive role in making Anglo-American identity representative of Americanness[108]

Melville uses Delano's pettiness to juxtapose national types—Americans versus Spaniards. The Black Legend is invoked here to fuse together, at least in Delano's mind, white American benevolence with black amiability, as opposed to Spanish malevolence. Here we see how American niceness enables the comparative discourse of American exceptionalism, with American magnanimity being advanced at the expense of Spanish arrogance. The democratic personality of the American is contrasted with the aristocratic Old World reserve of Cereno, with his opulent clothing and aloof demeanor. But in the end, all is revealed. Babo's "intelligent smile" suddenly vanishes, and he turns into the black monster whose face is "lividly vindictive" as he tries to stab Cereno.

With black amiability revealed as a subterfuge for black aggression and Spanish "discourtesy" exposed as a symptom of distress, the nice American and the European can now try to bond. Once Babo is exposed as a treacherous avenging African, then the Spaniard can become as nice as his white American counterpart. But this attempt at Anglo-European bonding fails due to their diametrically opposed worldviews. Traumatized by what he has experienced, Cereno retires to a monastery in Lima and dies six months later, thus ignoring Delano's cheerful advice: "But the past is passed; why moralize upon it? Forget it. See, yon bright sun has forgotten it all, and the blue sea, and the blue sky; these have turned new leaves."[109] Melville's novella updates the Black Legend and gives it a sardonic twist with Cereno trapped in the past, representing an empire in decline, while Delano epitomizes American enterprise and an unfailing belief in the future.

Delano exemplifies what I am calling manifest cheerfulness, and *Benito Cereno* can be read as a sustained spoof of this national affect, with the resilient American dispensing unsolicited advice to the traumatized Spaniard: Forget about the past and move on. In the context of a slave mutiny and the traumatic aftermath of its violent suppression, Melville implies that American cheerfulness offers a therapeutic way of forgetting that is based on evading reality rather than grappling with it. During the mutiny, Delano, as the cheerful American, is preoccupied with trivial slights stemming from Cereno's "discourtesies." The nice American's preoccupation with the Spaniard's rudeness substitutes for what Delano cannot acknowledge, namely, the black struggle for liberation.

Here, we arrive at an interesting point of contrast between Poe and Melville. Whereas Pym is saved by his suspicion of the Tsalalians, Delano is protected by his faith in American niceness, which takes the form of both his own magnanimity and that of the happy slave. His ingrained ability to see and not-see saves Delano in two ways. First, his "smiling and chatting" on board the *San Dominick*, as Cereno acknowledges at the end, is a sign of his charmed life. Delano's niceness is a form of protection that does not ignite the wrath of Babo and the others. Although Delano credits Providence for his survival, Delano's belief in black amiability is actually what saves him. Second, Delano is saved psychologically because he is able to forget what he has witnessed, a habit of disavowal that cannot acknowledge the violence that devastates Cereno.

What does this difference between Pym and Delano suggest about the racial politics of niceness? For Poe, black amiability successfully inverts power relations, enabling the Tsalalians to overtake the crew of the *Jane Guy* in a triumphant act of aboriginal resistance. But for Melville, black amiability destroys both the master and the slave, while the white American blithely stares into the Peruvian sunset rejoicing in his own good luck. In the end, Babo becomes simply "the black." He is beheaded in Lima, and his head, "that hive of subtlety," is displayed on a pole in the plaza, becoming the grotesque object of "the gaze of whites." Like Metacom's head, which was displayed on a pole in Plymouth (not far from Delano's home of Duxbury) over a century earlier, the overcoded black face becomes an instrument of terror. Despite this difference, both Poe and Melville see black amiability as a disguise, a form of concealment that depends on context. By contrast, white American niceness, personified in the figure of Delano, is always transparent, unwavering, and consistent. To be seen as transparent is to be seen as fully human; it is a sign of free self-expression that has no need for subterfuge, duplicity, or masquerade. Where black amiability is complex and overdetermined, white American amiability is steadfast and true.

But from Melville's perspective, there is something deeply disturbing about Delano's earnestness. His unwillingness to respond to the horror that he witnesses, together with his advice to forget the incident and instead appreciate the beauty of nature, is far more monstrous than Babo's final facial expression. Captain Delano's cheerful disavowal is not only impossible but also inhumane for Benito Cereno. The bright sun and the blue sea, argues Cereno in his final words to Delano, have no memory because "they are not human."[110] To be human, Cereno implies, is to have the burden of memory. If Harriet Beecher Stowe is the century's finest theorist of American niceness— of its possibilities to humanize the ostracized—then Herman Melville reveals the shadow side of niceness, its capacity to blind white Americans to the consequences of their own actions through an abiding faith in their magnanimity and optimism. *Benito Cereno* is ultimately a critique of the dissociative violence that American niceness enables.

The Incorporation of the Black Smile:
Aunt Jemima and the Legacy of Southern Niceness

Delano's recovery from the violent incident aboard the *San Dominick* hinges on his capacity to see and not-see, being both unable and unwilling to acknowledge the horror that he had witnessed. In this sense, Delano's advice to the traumatized Spaniard—"But the past is passed; why moralize upon it? Forget it"—becomes the implicit mantra of the United States in the aftermath of Reconstruction's failure in the late nineteenth century. In the context of the post–Civil War era, forgetting takes the form of remembering the past, but a past that is sanitized, filled with smiles and good old-fashioned Southern hospitality. In this nostalgic appropriation of antebellum culture, the slave's smile reigns supreme as the iconic emblem of American cheerfulness, where slavery is depicted without terror and the plantation is free of whips, guns, and bloodhounds. One form that this postbellum nostalgia took was the plantation novels of Thomas Nelson Page, whose fiction found a national readership and a profitable home in New York publishing houses. As civil rights attorney and novelist Albion Tourgée noted in 1888, American literature had become confederized. The North may have won the military battles, but the South had won the culture war.[111]

The confederization of American literature could be expanded to describe the United States in general, including the mass consumer culture of advertising. Similar to the proslavery novels that incorporated Southern niceness into a national narrative of American niceness, corporations in the late nineteenth century fused Southernness with Americanness through the ubiquity of the slave's smile. The relationship between advertising and the slave's smile has a long history, as Stowe's work on runaway slave advertisements attests. But what Stowe cound not have predicted was the afterlife of the slave's smile long after the Civil War. The slave's smile was precisely the image that would link the antebellum south with the modern corporation during a period that cultural historian Alan Trachtenberg has called "the age of incorporation." Literally and figuratively, the slave's smile was incorporated into the national culture as the iconic image of the nation's first ready-made pancake mix.

The inventor of this mix, Chris Rutt from St. Joseph, Missouri, needed a symbol for his new product in 1889, an image that would make the pancake mix recognizable nationally. He attended a blackface minstrel show by the comedians Baker and Farrell, and the high point of their show included a New Orleans–style cakewalk performed to a tune called "Aunt Jemima," one of the most popular songs of the day. The song was written by Billy Kersands, a highly successful black minstrel performer and comedian, whose long career began as an underground black entertainer in the antebellum South and ended as a nationally and internationally regarded vaudeville star who gave a command performance before Queen Victoria.[112] Kersands performed this song more than three thousand times, including this version from 1875:

> My old missus promise me
> Old Aunt Jemima, oh, oh, oh
>
> When she died she'd set me
> free Old Aunt Jemima,
> oh, oh, oh

> She lived so long her head
> got bald Old Aunt Jemima,
> oh, oh, oh
>
> She swore she would not die
> at all Old Aunt Jemima,
> oh, oh, oh.[113]

In this song, the old mammy Aunt Jemima patiently waits for her mistress to die so that she can be freed, but her irascible mistress refuses to die, which is the source of the song's humor as well as pathos. Performed on that autumn night in Missouri in 1889 by the white minstrel singers who were dressed as mammies with aprons and red bandannas, "Old Aunt Jemima" was exactly the figure that Chris Rutt was looking for. Although he did not have the funds to advertise his new product, Rutt sold it to another Missouri mill, R. T. Davis Mill and Manufacturing, in 1890, and they hired Nancy Green, who became the first Aunt Jemima.

Nancy Green was born a slave in Montgomery, Kentucky, in 1834 and she moved to Chicago, where she cooked for a local judge. When R. T. Davis met Green, he knew he had found that perfect combination of a friendly personality with culinary talent: "She was a magnificent cook, an attractive woman of outgoing nature and friendly personality, gregarious to the extreme."[114] With little money left for advertising, R. T. Davis risked the business's fortune on a promotional exhibition at the 1893 World's Columbian Exposition in Chicago, where Green cooked pancakes, told stories about her days on the old Kentucky plantation, and chatted with the various visitors. At the same World's Fair where Green was charming her audience with good food and Southern stories, Frederick Douglass and Ida B. Wells, among others, distributed a pamphlet entitled "The Reason Why the Colored American is not in the World's Columbian Exhibition," criticizing the Fair's organizers for not including African Americans on the planning committee and not highlighting African American accomplishments. But African Americans did participate in the fair as employees, performers, exhibitors, and fair goers. Not surprisingly, the most popular African American at the fair was Nancy Green, the "Pancake Queen," whose visibility was procured by conforming to type, namely that of the black mammy as the personification of Southern hospitality.

Nancy Green's booth at the World's Fair was an enormous success and led to a national advertising campaign spearheaded by James Webb Young, the *wunderkind* of the J. Walter Thompson Advertising firm. His task was to invent a backstory for Aunt Jemima, one that would link the consumer with the image of the smiling mammy on the box. Young, who grew up in Covington, Kentucky, created an antebellum story where Aunt Jemima was a slave on Colonel Higbee's vast plantation on the Mississippi River, and she and her master became synonymous with Southern hospitality: "Her pancakes, cooked from a secret recipe, made her the envy of many Southern cooks." Kentucky-style slavery, which ever since Stowe's day had claimed to be a kinder and gentler form of slavery, became the way plantation culture was packaged, distributed, and remembered as an iconic image of American niceness.

James Webb Young decided to present Aunt Jemima's backstory in the form of verse, which appeared in magazine advertising for the pancake mix. Notice how he incorporates the quintessential signs of

Aunt Jemima at the 1893 World's Fair, an advertisement in the *Ladies Home Journal* (Philadelphia: The Curtis Publishing Company, March 1921): 86. Schlesinger Library, Radcliffe Institute, Harvard University.

Southern pastoralism—magnolias and cotton—into the mass-produced packaging of the pancake mix.

> The story of Aunt Jemima, whom we know as Pancake Queen,
>   Starts on an Old Plantation, in a charming Southern scene.
> Here folks grew sweet magnolias and cotton in the sun,
> And life was filled with happiness and old-time Southern fun.
> The owner, Colonel Higbee, a most kind and gracious host,
> Served his guests fine dishes, though they liked his pancakes
>   most.[115]

Illustrated by artist N. C. Wyeth in 1919, the Aunt Jemima legend centered on nostalgia for the Old South's two iconic figures—the kind slaveholder and the happy slave. This promotional advertising strategy links the proslavery mythology of Dixie with corporate America in the form of Southern charm. But the face of Southern niceness was not the Southern belle with her blond curls and crinoline dress but instead the black mammy with her dark skin, broad smile, and red bandanna. Her iconic face represents the "mammification of the nation," according to historian Kimberly Wallace-Sanders, where she belongs not just to the Southern home but to the "national household."[116] She was part of a post-Reconstruction fantasy of reunification in which her recipes signified gifts of reconciliation, while her face became emblematic of the nation.

Although the Aunt Jemima icon contains all the signs of a repetition of proslavery ideology, with its combination of the pastoralism of Dixie and the benevolence of the "mild" institution, there is one important difference. Young's advertising campaign features the black woman as the singular representative of Southern hospitality, with Higbee, the kind master, as a minor figure who eventually disappears from the story. This marks a significant contrast with contemporaneous literary depictions of the Old South, which, like their proslavery antecedents, focused on the kind slaveholders, with blacks as minor figures peopling the pastoral landscape. The disappearance of Colonel Higbee combined with the exclusive focus on Aunt Jemima demonstrates how the twentieth-century version of Southern niceness tells a story of national reunification, with white America now reunited through the feminized icon of the black smile.

With the figure of Aunt Jemima in mind, one cannot help but note an interesting parallel between the respective fates of Native American hospitality and black Southern hospitality in the 1920s. Both became assimilated into a national narrative of American niceness through customs, etiquette, and food. Similar to Lillian Eichler's *The Customs of Mankind* (1924), which thanked Native Americans for "pav[ing] the way for the hospitality which has become so peculiarly associated with this country," the multimillion dollar advertising campaign around Aunt Jemima, purchased by Quaker Oats in 1926, thanked Aunt Jemima for her "free" recipe. Minority hospitality becomes mythically incorporated into a national narrative of American niceness, a narrative that depends in part on historical forgetting. Just as Captain Delano recommends to Benito Cereno the therapeutic power of moving on, so the incorporation of Native American and African American niceness into a uniform brand of American niceness implies the desirability of forgetting inconvenient truths about genocide and slavery, or at most revising those truths in such a way that they are remembered in a highly selective manner.

As the nineteenth century progressed into the twentieth, American niceness increasingly became part of an American religion, a faith in which red, white, and black smiles melded into a national affect of manifest cheerfulness directed toward a harmonious future rather than being mired in the past. The next chapter will turn to the role of Christianity in the making of this national religion. From a Calvinist God ready to smite and punish in the early decades of the nineteenth century to the calm and loving Jesus as eternal friend after the Civil War, the nineteenth century witnessed a Christian makeover. In transforming the deity from an impersonal figure of authority to a highly intimate one, Christianity experienced an affective turn from fear to love. Theological debates were trumped by interpersonal concerns, and consequently, an alternative model of authority based on the banality of niceness emerged.

 3

The Christology of Niceness

"We choke on a Victorian Jesus, a caricature that has turned men into mice."

Paul Coughlin, *No More Christian Nice Guy* (2005)

I T IS TAKEN FOR granted today that niceness is one of Jesus's defining traits, but not everyone is happy about this fact. Paul Coughlin recollects in his self-help book, *No More Christian Nice Guy* (2005), how he grew up with the iconic image of "Jesus [as] the Supreme Nice Guy," an image that he blames for creating passive and spineless Christian men. "We choke on a Victorian Jesus, a caricature that has turned men into mice." Instead, he calls for a dissident Jesus, one who loves a "good fight."[1] This dismissal of niceness is not unique to the evangelical Christian press. Literary critic Terry Eagleton, in his introduction to the Verso edition of *The Gospels*, insists that Jesus is "no mild-eyed plaster saint but a relentless, fiercely uncompromising activist," who "is interested in what people do, not in what they feel."[2] Where Eagleton and Coughlin want a more virile Jesus, one more invested in action than feeling, the Pauline turn in recent continental theory finds Jesus a rather pathetic figure, not worthy of serious analysis. Giorgio Agamben, for instance, begins his study of Paul's Letter to the Romans by quoting the philosopher Jacob Taubes's wry observation that "Hebrew literature on Jesus presents him in benevolent terms—as a 'nice guy.'"[3] For evangelical Christians, literary theorists, and continental philosophers, Jesus's reputation as a "nice guy" counts against him, either making him too emotionally mushy to fight the good fight or lacking Paul's complexity as a messianic thinker.

I want to situate the banality of the nice Jesus and its historical origins in the nineteenth century in the context of the rise of liberal Christianity. The historical narrative about how the perception of God's authority changed from the wrath of a Calvinist God to the gentle benevolence of a Liberal Christian God is a familiar one. Whether it is Ann Douglas bemoaning the decline of Calvinism and the rise of vacuous sentimentalism, or religious historians' comprehensive overviews of American Christianity, or recent studies of the American Jesus, the claim that the nineteenth century witnessed a significant transformation of religious authority has become something of a historiographic cliché. Not only is the nice Jesus banal, but so is the historical narrative that underwrites him.

My objective is to take banality seriously by describing the formation of this cliché as well as unpacking it. Banality tends to be overlooked as an analytic term precisely because it appears to be so obvious. Working against this tendency, however, several thinkers have attempted to give depth to their explorations of the banal. "Banality?" asks Henri Lefebvre, "Why should the study of the banal itself be banal?" Maurice Blanchot similarly recognizes that "the everyday is platitude, but this banality is also what is most important, if it brings us back to existence in its very spontaneity and as it is lived—in the moment when, lived, it escapes every speculative formulation, perhaps all coherence, all regularity."[4] This romantic understanding of the everyday, where boredom and repetition can yield unusual and unexpected results, justifies the study of banality by showing its capacity for what Lefebvre describes as "the surreal, the extraordinary, the surprising."

But what about the banality of the everyday that remains resolutely ordinary, defying all attempts to redeem it through spectacular variations? This banal form of banality, which lacks the dimension of the magical or the mysterious, is more complex than it appears at first glance, and this complexity emerges more clearly when we study the similarities between banality and two closely related concepts: niceness and triviality. Within a social sphere, banality and niceness infuse everyday encounters and associations with a habitual ease so as to minimize conflict and awkwardness. Moreover, both concepts are deemed to be little more than clichés, hackneyed formations not worthy of serious study. Not surprisingly, there is a close relation between banality and niceness on the one hand, and triviality on the other, a term that is treated in a similarly dismissive fashion.

Significantly, the dictionary definition of *nice* is intimately related to the trivial. The synonymic relation between *nice* and *trivial* first appeared during the Renaissance, and it remained in British usage throughout the nineteenth century. Although "trivial" becomes an increasingly minor definition of *nice* in the United States after the Civil War, I nonetheless want to argue that the trinity of banality, niceness, and triviality continued to feature prominently in religious writing in a most unexpected form, namely, in representations of Jesus. But exactly how do these undervalued concepts of the everyday underwrite such a sacred figure? How, in other words, is the banality of niceness effectively incarnated in the nineteenth-century American Jesus?

This chapter explores the transformation of religious authority from the "Christology of the sublime," to borrow David Morgan's phrase that describes a highly masculine God who inspires awe, to what I refer to as a "Christology of niceness," where Jesus is fundamentally social, amiable, and kind.[5] This emphasis on a humane Jesus is epitomized in Harriet Beecher Stowe's distinction between an impersonal Christ who represents the "law" and a personal Jesus who is a "soul-friend." For Stowe, Jesus is a "lovable" teacher who "came to love us, to teach us, to save us . . . in the kindest and gentlest way."[6] Over thirty years later, Washington Gladden, a liberal Congregational pastor and leader of the Social Gospel movement, similarly declared, "religion is nothing but friendship" and described Jesus as "the Great Companion."[7] This new relationship was based on a personal and intimate bond with Jesus, who became less divine and more human. This personalization of God as friend, epitomized in the popular mid-century hymn "What a Friend We Have in Jesus" (1855), became a religious type as Christianity changed from a religion based on doctrine and theology to one focused on the personality of Jesus.

The Christology of niceness, I argue, played a major role in the democratization of U.S. Christianity in the nineteenth century, when religious leaders used "democratic persuasions," to quote historian Nathan Hatch, "to reconstruct the foundations of religious authority."[8]

What would a democratic God look like? Can one be both nice and mighty? For the Calvinists who believed in an angry God full of fire and brimstone, niceness was not an issue. For Jonathan Edwards, Christ (he rarely, if ever, spoke of Jesus) loved from a distance, but he hated passionately and fiercely, smiting those who met with his disapproval without a hint of guilt. Christ's authority was sublime, inspiring awe and devotion at the same time. His wrath forced men to obey, respect, and submit to His authority in the name of righteousness. The Calvinist God of New England combined the intellectualism of theology with the forcefulness of machismo. But by the mid-nineteenth century, God's wrath was running out of steam. Women, who comprised the overwhelming majority of the churchgoing population, were getting tired of being afraid of God's temper. They wanted a mellower God, a more personable and ordinary deity who they could call a friend, a confidante, and a good listener. They also wanted a God whose shoulder they could cry on to mourn their Civil War dead. Harriet Beecher Stowe, the daughter of a Calvinist minister and the mother of two sons who fought in the Civil War and returned home emotionally destroyed and physically injured, understood the religious needs of the era, particularly those of its women.

Harriet Beecher Stowe was an important architect of the nice Jesus—the Victorian Jesus that Paul Coughlin rejects. For Stowe, and for liberal Christianity more generally, the banality of niceness is a social liturgy comprised of the seemingly insignificant rituals of association, where the sacred and the ordinary meet to give form to the everyday. By appreciating the significance of the trivial, Stowe can be read as a religious modernist who understands the potential of literature to revitalize Christian platitudes. She makes Christianity new again not by shocking the reader into an epiphany but through a more gentle approach that awakens the reader's religious sensibilities by exploring through literary form seemingly trivial details that highlight characterization and social relationships. Stowe explains this technique in her preface to *Uncle Tom's Cabin:* "The poet, the painter, and the artist, now seek out and embellish the common and gentler humanities of life, and, under the allurements of fiction, breathe a humanizing and subduing influence, favorable to the development of the great principles of Christian brotherhood."[9] Although *Uncle Tom's Cabin,* with its portrayal of the tragic violence of slavery, seems like the antithesis of the trivial, Stowe's understanding of the sacred and the tragic derives, in part, from an appreciation of the power of banality.

For Stowe, niceness integrates three key aspects of religious modernism. First, niceness is an expression of Christian sociability, or what was described in the nineteenth-century Christian press as a "social democracy," which is the belief that "man reaches fullness of life not alone but in relations."[10] Second, religious liberalism assumes a liberal subject who is generous and open-hearted. For an evangelical writer like Stowe, the liberal subject is the evangelical's fantasy—a subject always open to persuasion. Compared to the rigidity of orthodoxy, the liberal character is largely defined by flexibility and open-mindedness. "The charm of polite society," writes Stowe in a sketch called "Repression," is when each member of a circle is "pliable to the influences of the others." Being pliable is a requisite for a democracy since consensus relies on persuasion, and persuasion depends on people being willing to change their minds. Third, to convey niceness in aesthetic terms, Stowe employs the novel, a genre that is designed "primarily to please," to quote *The Methodist Review* in 1860.[11]

Stowe brings together Christianity, liberalism, and literature based on what they have in common; all three depend on pleasing, whether it is the potential convert or the reader-as-consumer. The nice Jesus is the literal incarnation of pleasing as a form of persuasion. Like the nineteenth-century French historian Ernest Renan, who describes Jesus's voice in *The Life of Jesus* (1863) as "sweet," Stowe's Jesus also possesses a "sweet voice" and "graceful manner." As the political scientist Bryan Garsten argues in *Saving Persuasion* (2003), "the word 'persuade' arises etymologically from the same root as the words 'suave' and 'sweet,' which reminds us that democratic persuasion requires insinuating oneself into the good graces of one's audience."[12]

This chapter builds on the previous ones by highlighting the multi-accentuality of niceness within a variety of contexts ranging from Native American hospitality to slavery and now religion. As with Native American hospitality, Stowe understands the dangers of niceness. The story of Jesus is precisely how the act of giving could result in betrayal. Kindness imperils rather than protects, much like the Native American experience with the first Europeans. At the heart of niceness is a politics of vulnerability that Stowe finds both terrifying and inspiring. But unlike Native American hospitality, where the Native American is the marginal figure within a national history of conquest, Stowe explores the relationship between vulnerability and power. Stowe's brand of Christian feminism engages directly with questions of authority and ruling institutions by taking the conventionally feminine traits of niceness and sociability to democratize Christian authority far beyond the personality of Jesus to include the state. Through the figure of Jesus, Stowe redefines democratic governance based on an ethics of care.

The legacy of Stowe's nice Jesus as a figural form of democratic authority carries into the late nineteenth and early twentieth centuries through Elizabeth Stuart Phelps's biography of Jesus and W. E. B. Du Bois's short stories on the Black Jesus. Both combine the feminization of power with the politics of vulnerability. For Phelps, this takes the form of moving inward rather than outward by exploring Jesus's psyche: How does a sensitive introvert with depressive tendencies grapple with being perceived as a messiah? Phelps's *fin-de-siècle* Jesus is also anxious about his masculinity in ways that Stowe's Jesus was not. Vulnerability within this context centers on the problem of nice masculinity at a time when masculinity was becoming increasingly described in martial terms.

For Du Bois, Black Christianity already had a language of racial injury with which to understand the vulnerability of a gentle Jesus. Within the context of lynching, vulnerability signaled a particular legacy of oppression and not a universal human condition. Du Bois's Black Jesus recognizes the inextricability of vulnerability and violence, leading him to rethink the violence of John Brown: What does it mean to kill out of kindness rather than rage? The chapter concludes by turning to Du Bois's work as the editor of *The Crisis* and the publication of articles on Jewish niceness that explore the origin of Jesus's niceness and its significance for the twentieth century as either a strategy of Jewish integration into Gentile society or a source of anxiety about assimilation. By including these articles in *The Crisis*, Du Bois acknowledges a connection between Jewish vulnerability in a Christian nation and black vulnerability in a white nation. In both cases, a minority position is articulated through the politics of vulnerability that relies, in part, on the affective language of niceness.

Characterizing the Lovable Jesus

Harriet Beecher Stowe's most important contribution to liberal Christianity was to translate the doctrine of love into a characterization of a lovable Jesus. According to Francis Greenwood Peabody, professor at Harvard's Divinity School, the teaching of Jesus was primarily a teaching of character. In *Jesus Christ and the Christian Character* (1905), Peabody points out that the gospels are "an artless and incidental summary of an oral tradition" in the nineteenth century, he adds, "we need to add dimension to his character."[13] Liberal Christians, beginning with Unitarian minister William Ellery Channing, attempted to elaborate on the character of Jesus but not initially in a way that emphasized his similarity to ordinary people. Channing wrote in 1821 that "His character has in it nothing local or temporary," and that he is a "solitary being" who lived as if he were from another world.[14]

Horace Bushnell was similarly uncomfortable with historicizing Jesus, preferring instead to emphasize his difference from the human. In his *The Character of Jesus* (1861), tellingly subtitled "Forbidding His Possible Classification With Men," Bushnell is, at least to some extent, torn about how to characterize Jesus: Does one insist on his divinity or his humanity? On the one hand, we are told that Jesus had a "superhuman or celestial childhood," while on the other hand he is described in rather banal terms, as someone who stays calm in the midst of "petty vexations." To produce a few more markers delineating Jesus's character, Bushnell awkwardly turns to Jesus's sense of humor. It is never reported, Bushnell claims, that Jesus ever laughed. That does not mean, however, that Jesus was unhappy or sad; he was, in fact, filled with "sacred joy."[15] The tensions in Bushnell's account of Jesus reveal that characterization, especially when it involves the divine, requires a degree of banal detail that Bushnell can only give reluctantly because he believes that too many such details detract from Jesus's divinity.

It is only with Stowe's younger brother, Henry Ward Beecher, that we get a sense of a sociable and affable Jesus that comes closest to his sister's depiction.[16] Beecher, a Congregationalist minister in Brooklyn who became the most famous liberal Christian of the period, published his hagiography *The Life of Jesus, The Christ* (1871), which calls for the life of Christ to be "rewritten for each and every age." The personality of Jesus, he warns, cannot be lost in "sublime abstraction," but must be captured in terms of his "personal tenderness and generous love." Appearing just six years before Stowe's book *Footsteps of the Master*, Beecher's *The Life of Jesus, The Christ* depicts a Jesus who is "genial and cheerful," thoroughly enjoying the company of others: "He loved wayside conversations with all sorts of men and women," and actively took part in "social festivity."[17]

In portraying a more sociable and festive Jesus, ministers such as Beecher all too often fall short because their characterizations are ultimately too prescriptive and not adequately descriptive. We are told, for instance, that Jesus enjoys conversation but there are no scenes of dialogue. Their Jesus remains too wooden and flat. What philosopher and theologian Albert Schweitzer said about David Friedrich Strauss's *The Life of Jesus* (1864) also applies to Beecher's work and that of his predecessors, that is, they do not write "like an imaginative novelist, with a constant eye to effect."[18] Stowe, better than anyone else of her generation, brings to her characterization of Jesus the skills of the "imaginative novelist" who translates the moral notion of character, derived from the ethical value we place on our relations to others, into a palpable and sympathetic figure. In other words, she blends the concept of moral character with the novelistic techniques of characterization.

Biography and Victorian Sociability

In 1905, Selden Lincoln Whitcomb wrote in *The Study of a Novel* that the novelistic method is "cumulative," by which he means that "a discovery of character [occurs] by the gradually increasing momentum of items often trivial enough if taken separately."[19] This cumulative strategy of creating character through trivial details is precisely Stowe's technique, a strategy that she adapts from the novel form to what were known in the nineteenth century as "spiritual biographies" or "divine biographies." Biographies were a popular and even pervasive genre in the nineteenth century. For Thomas Carlyle, the popularity of biographies attests to the innate sociality of human beings. "Man's sociality of nature evinces itself," writes Carlyle in 1832, in "the unspeakable delight he takes in Biography."[20] Literary historian Scott Casper has explained the popularity of this genre in terms of its power to allow readers to "learn about public figures and peer into the lives of strangers." More than satiating curiosity, biographies possess the cultural power to "shape individuals' lives and character and to help define America's national character."[21]

Footsteps of the Master is a Victorian rewriting of the Gospels that combines biography with the novel, creating a hybrid genre that also includes poems and hymns from well-known writers of the day such as Alfred Lord Tennyson and Elizabeth Barrett Browning. Although widely read and advertised as an ideal Christmas gift in 1877, this book was seen by reviewers of the time as not up to the same literary standard as *Uncle Tom's Cabin*. It was, however, a book that Stowe thoroughly enjoyed writing. In a letter to her son Charles in 1876, she wrote, "I would much rather have written another such a book as *Footsteps of the Master*, but all, even the religious papers, are gone mad on serials."[22] In her obituary in *Current Literature* in 1896, *Footsteps* is mentioned, alongside *Uncle Tom's Cabin* and *Dred*, as one of her most memorable works.[23]

Stowe inscribes Jesus within a tradition of sentimental realism, portraying him not as a miracle worker but as an ordinary person, as a living presence rather than as an action hero or an iconic figure on the cross. In highlighting Jesus's ordinariness by representing him as a social being with friends and family, Stowe weds two seemingly antithetical discourses: the banal and the sacred. The exceptional story of Jesus can be told within the rhythms of the everyday, characterized by such things as dinner engagements, feasts, and a tidy home. Stowe seeks to revitalize Christianity not by turning to the exceptional but by using the excessively familiar as a way to defamiliarize Jesus and make him worthy of notice again.

Stowe's biographical account of a domesticated Jesus can be seen as part of a larger generic trend dating back to the eighteenth century, when "biographical exemplarity underwent a revolution that replaced the illustrious by the domestic example."[24] Stowe inherits this model of biographical exemplarity in foregrounding the mundane details of Jesus's character as the source of his exceptionalism. Exemplarity is an ethical notion, one that is fused with the Victorian ideal of good character, which for Stowe is a way to translate divine authority from the sublime to the just. This emphasis on good character would resonate strongly with her Victorian readers as a pedagogical tool of moral instruction. Exemplarity is inscribed in Stowe's very title, where "footsteps of the master" refers to the importance of imitation as a way to model public action.[25]

It would be a mistake, however, to understand Stowe's characterization of Jesus as a secularizing gesture. She fuses exemplarity with the sacred in order to revitalize Christianity through a counterintuitive strategy, one that resists the spectacular and instead portrays the excessively familiar. The biographical novel is an ideal vehicle for conveying an ordinary Jesus because the genre is wedded to the common life, and the source of its aesthetic vitality is derived from the particular details that create a referential world that authenticates Jesus's corporeality. "Romance is full of marvels," writes Terry Eagleton, "whereas the modern novel is mundane . . . It is wary of the abstract and eternal and believes in what it can touch, taste and handle."[26] But the mundanity that characterizes the novel is not used by Stowe to construct a secular reaction against eternal values; rather, she uses it as a way to demonstrate the pervasiveness of the eternal in the material practices that give shape to our daily lives. Domestic description renders Jesus fully human, representing a form of aesthetic incarnation whereby the prosaic revitalizes the sacred.

Just as *Uncle Tom's Cabin* describes the inside of Tom's home as a way to introduce her protagonist to the reader, so Stowe depicts Jesus's interior surroundings, whether it be his home or his tomb, by using techniques associated with literary characterization. Stowe's Jesus is the *exemplum fidei* of Catharine Beecher's ideal housekeeper. He has "careful domestic habits. He was in all things methodical and frugal. The miraculous power he possessed never was used to surround him with any profusion." Even in death, Jesus remains tidy. In describing Jesus's resurrection, Stowe departs from convention by concentrating not on the transcendence of the soul but rather on the meticulous state of his tomb: "There is a touch of homelike minuteness in the description of the grave as they found it—no discovery of haste, no sign of confusion, but all in order: the linen grave-clothes lying in one place; the napkin that was about his head not lying with them, but folded together in a place by itself; indicating the perfect calmness and composure with which their Lord had risen."[27] Jesus's things—his folded clothes and napkin—are metonymic expressions of his steadfast and calm temperament. Jesus, in other words, is the anti-hysteric, one who provides a behavioral map for grappling with the demands of everyday life with a degree of peaceful joy. The mundane prevails in Stowe's religious narrative, structuring even her account of the Ascension.

Just as realist details give Stowe an appropriate way to emphasize the mundane, domestic fiction also underscores the importance of friendship for Christianity because it is devoted to depicting the complex web of associations that constitutes a community. "Victorian fiction, like fiction in general, has a single pervasive theme," writes J. Hillis Miller, "interpersonal relations."[28] In this sense, *Footsteps of the Master* is a typical Victorian novel, not necessarily in a formal sense with its eclectic combination of poetry, hymns, and narrative, but rather in its thematic emphasis on sociability. After all, Jesus has few opportunities to be nice when alone in the desert. Jesus's niceness, in other words, is a social practice that can only be made visible through its effect on others: "everywhere warming, melting, cheering; inspiring joy in the sorrowful and hope in the despairing; giving peace to the perplexed."[29] In converting sorrow and despair into joy and hope, niceness transforms through interpersonal contact. This social contact is precisely what makes Stowe one of "the most profound of the sentimental apologists," since she believes, to quote the literary scholar Joanne Dobson, that "human connection is the genesis, in this life, of the divine."[30]

Stowe's emphasis on sociability challenges Ian Watt's understanding of the relation between Christianity and the novel. For Watt, Christianity influences the novel primarily through the inward movement or introspection of Puritanism, in the process creating a fictional character's depth that leads to identification for the reader. Stowe, by contrast, believes that Christianity influences the novel most when characters cultivate social bonds of connection and affection; in other words, when they move outward, not inward, to form relationships of various types.[31] Unlike introspection, which is a trait that exists independently of others, niceness, amiability, and kindness are fundamentally social, in that they are primarily perceptual attributes rather than intrinsic qualities.

Stowe's Jesus embodies the liberal Christian ethos, reflected in Henry James Senior's advice to his children: "[W]e need never fear not to be good enough if we were only social enough."[32] Similarly, Stowe's Jesus is rarely portrayed alone, but primarily in relation to others, the epitome of a social democrat who receives invitations from people of all classes:

"Jesus was often invited to feasts in the houses of both rich and poor, and cheerfully accepted these invitations even on the Sabbath day."

Although Stowe illustrates more profound levels of intimacy such as the "soul-love" he has for his mother, what is remarkable is the frequency of his ordinary social encounters. "They [rich and poor] crowded round him and he welcomed them; they invited him to their houses and he went; he sat with them at the table; he held their little ones in his arms; he *gave Himself* to them."[33] By situating Jesus within the home as a domesticated figure surrounded by children, Stowe replicates through prose one of the most influential visual representations of the nice Jesus, epitomized in Bernhard Plockhorst's *Christ Blessing the Children* (1885). In this iconic image, Jesus sits with an infant on his lap, surrounded by animated children vying for his attention, with their doting mothers beside them. Rather than peering upward into the heavens appearing aloof, Jesus gazes into the faces of the cherubic children, fully engaged in the social scene before him. The Victorian Jesus, whether in the form of Stowe's prose or Plockhorst's iconography, is the embodiment of maternal love.

The Sexual Politics of the Nice Jesus

Although Jesus's niceness, reflected in his popularity, seems like a rather inconsequential trait, it has significant implications that involve questions of power. Niceness is not an awe-inspiring category. It is too banal to be sublime. The niceness of Jesus and the divinity of Jesus have a difficult time coexisting. The authority of Jesus could easily be compromised through his humanization, which is to say, through his embodiment in a realist narrative of everyday details and social encounters. Stowe's depiction of the nice Jesus requires a radical rethinking of divine authority that involves the question of gender. In 1852, Unitarian minister Theodore Parker acknowledged the gendered language of niceness in a sermon on the death of Daniel Webster: "Bulk is bearded and masculine; niceness is of women's gendering."[34] Not only is niceness gendered female but so are the quotidian spaces where this niceness is performed: primarily within people's homes. Niceness, together with the trivial and the everyday, is a feminized concept that represents an alternative form of authority, one that counters the fiery rhetoric of Calvinist catastrophe.

Bernhard Plockhorst, *Christ Blessing the Children* (1885).
Reproduced from Abram P. T. Elder and E. H. Elder, eds., *The Light of the
World; or, Our Saviour in Art* (Chicago: The Elder Co., 1896):
pl. 99. Courtesy of David Morgan, Duke University.

Susan Bordo reminds us of how the "'definition and shaping' of the
[gendered] body is 'the focal point for struggles over the shape of
power.'"[35] Religious historians have been reluctant to take on the consequences of liberal Christianity's humanization of Jesus at the level of
gender and sexuality. Cultural historian Richard Wightman Fox in
Jesus in America (2004) insists that liberal Protestant love, embodied
in the character of Jesus, was not reducible to "feminized domestic

virtue" but was "androgynous," a love that transported both men and women out of social conventions.[36] Androgyny suggests a symmetrical fusion of male and female in equal measure to produce a synthesis that combines both. In relation to Stowe, I want to suggest that the gendering of Jesus was far more contentious and uneven. Rather than blurring the binary of masculine and feminine into a gender-neutral third term, her portrayal of Jesus actually maintains the binary. Specifically, Stowe's Jesus is a decidedly feminized figure, a form of asymmetrical union that favors the feminine in rather unapologetic and uncompromising ways. Stowe's Jesus does not transcend social conventions, but rather exploits the conventions of feminine niceness, and specifically motherly love, as an exemplary model of democratic power.

For Stowe, Jesus signifies a "new style of manhood" based not on "force" but on love: "His mode was more that of a mother than a father. He strove to infuse Himself into them [his friends and followers] by an embracing, tender, brooding love; ardent, self-forgetful, delicate, refined."[37] Stowe further feminizes Jesus by coupling his domestic and sentimental niceness with a biological explanation that implies a proto-genetic argument. In other words, she buttresses her behavioral account of Jesus's love with an essentialist one: "All that was human in him was her [Mary's] nature; it was the union of the Divine nature with the nature of a pure woman. Hence there was in Jesus more of the pure feminine element than in any other man. It was the feminine element exalted and taken in union with divinity."[38] Jesus's incarnation is not a symmetrical blending of God and Mary, where the divine and human each contribute half; instead, Jesus's nature is emphatically asymmetrical, in that the human parent Mary is the determining force. As a result, woman becomes the universal standard by which the human is defined.

By emphasizing Mary's role in the biological making of Jesus, Stowe emphasizes the importance not only of women but also of Jewishness to any understanding of Jesus. Stowe anticipates what Friedrich Nietzsche would later acknowledge, namely that Jesus and Saul were "the two most Jewish Jews perhaps who ever lived."[39] Early in *Footsteps of the Master*, Stowe writes, "To study the life of Christ without the Hebrew Scriptures is to study a flower without studying the plant from which it sprung, the root and leaves which nourished it. He continually spoke of himself as a Being destined to fulfill what had gone before."[40] Stowe's Jesus is decidedly Jewish, and Jewish men are "*affectionate men.*"[41] In *Woman in Sacred History* (1873), written four years before *Footsteps of the Master*, Stowe argues that one of the most important lessons of the Old Testament is that Jewish men are highly loyal and domestic: "[W]e find no pictures of love in family life more delicate and tender than are given in these patriarchal stories."[42] Jews have a "sacredness and respect" for family life, which actually encourages Jewish women to have multiple roles that include wife and mother as well as "leader, inspirer, prophetess." This romantic view of biblical Jewish life as a proto-feminist religion is reminiscent of her brother Henry Ward Beecher's *Life of Jesus, The Christ* when he writes that "[a]mong the Jews, more perhaps than in any other Oriental nation, woman was permitted to develop naturally, and liberty was accorded her to participate in things which other people reserved with zealous seclusion for men."[43] Both brother and sister idealize biblical Jews to the extent that Jewishness becomes an exemplary model for Christian sociability that combines the sacred with the mundane, affection with respect, and domesticated men with powerful women.

In contrast to Stowe's contemporaries, such as Octavius Brooks Frothingham, who sought to revitalize Christianity by imagining a transcendent Jesus of metaphysical Spirit, Stowe's narrative involves a retroactive dynamic, where modern Christian sociability is based on ancient Jewish materiality.[44] As the embodiment of Jewish materialism, the demonstrative parent becomes the evangelizing force that revitalizes Christian belief. As the literary critic Thomas Loebel argues in his discussion of Stowe's theology, Stowe is a "good Jewish mother" who strives for a "certain recovery of Jewish materiality as necessary for Christian efficacy in transforming the world."[45] In *Footsteps of the Master*, Mary nearly steals the show from her son, since the most suitable image for depicting the Master, according to Stowe, is through "one of those loving, saintly mothers, who, in leading along their little flock, follow nearest in the footsteps of Jesus."[46] Jesus's love is equivalent to motherly love, a strategy that Leslie Fiedler spots in *Uncle Tom's Cabin* when he describes Tom as "a white mother like his author, despite his blackface and drag," representing "the Blessed Male Mother of a virgin Female Christ."[47] This symbiotic relation between the Virgin and a maternal Christ is at the heart of Stowe's Marianism, a relation that feminizes liberal Christianity by adapting Catholicism's adoration of the Madonna.[48] By grafting Marianism onto Christology, Stowe explores what Julia Kristeva in *The Feminine and the Sacred* calls "the feminine of man," whereby the feminine becomes a new universal that operates as an "open invitation to man's femininity."[49]

The Christology of niceness as an invitation to man's femininity recasts authority in terms of love, as a force of attraction that inspires an intense personal affection. In describing the authority of Jesus, Stowe writes "he governed personally," which is to say that he asked "not only for love, but for intimacy—he asked for the whole heart."[50] In "The Authority of Jesus" (1830), Ralph Waldo Emerson conceives of Jesus's power in similar terms, as representing a new model of authority based not on the ability to make men "cower" but on the power of exemplarity: to inspire others through love to "embark in the same cause by word and by act."[51] Jesus persuades organically through truth, according to Emerson, rather than supernaturally through miracles. As Emerson wrote in 1843, "There is nothing in history to parallel the influence of Jesus Christ."[52] This word, influence, is absolutely central in Stowe's theory of power as an alternative to force, as a way to legitimize love as a potent social force of suasion. In *Little Foxes*, aptly subtitled, "Or, The Insignificant little habits which mar domestic happiness" (1866), she writes, "*Influence* is a slower acting force than authority. It seems weaker, but in the long run it often effects more. It always does better than mere force and authority without its gentle modifying power."[53] Influence, for Stowe, indicates a slow transformation that is ultimately more effective and longer-lasting than sudden change.

Understanding Jesus's power in terms of influence is vital for Stowe because she is not interested in portraying Jesus's niceness as an end in itself but rather as a strategy of conversion. As she writes, "[T]he influence of Jesus was no mere sentimental attraction, but a vital, spiritual force."[54] Stowe, in other words, does not reject power but recasts it in terms of gentle persuasion. "Christianity is a system of persuasion," Stowe's sister Catharine Beecher wrote in 1837, "tending, by kind and gentle influences, to make men willing to leave off their sins."[55] Stowe's Jesus is the embodiment of her sister's understanding of the power of "gentle influences," which Stowe colorfully conveys through various examples: "The dog is changed by tender treatment and affectionate care . . . Rude human natures are correspondingly changed, and he who has great power of loving and exciting love may almost create anew whom he will."[56] Evangelical niceness has a telos that strives toward converting the uncongenial to the genial, the rude to the kind.

Henry Ward Beecher shared his sister's interest in niceness as a strategic and teleological "force" for Christian conversion, believing that persuasion depends on personal likability. In a lecture entitled "What is Preaching?" (1872), he explains that the early Christians succeeded in converting others because they recognized the power of niceness, or in other words, the need to "be so sweet, so sparkling, so buoyant, so cheerful, hopeful, courageous . . . so perfectly benevolent." You cannot "refashion men," argues Beecher, unless you have "social power in you."[57] As a preacher committed to the art of persuasion, Beecher understood, like his sister, the role niceness and likability play as forms of "social power" that have transformative effects.

The Likable Lincoln

The purpose of Stowe's theory of niceness is not just to embody God in a personable and lovable form but also to present the lineaments of a democratic nation. Stowe was part of an evangelical trend to make Christianity a Jesus faith, and the United States a Jesus nation. She speaks of the United States as a "Christian democracy," a concept she defines in her preface to The Lives and Deeds of our Self-Made Men (1872): "[T]he American government is the only permanent republic which ever based itself upon the principles laid down by Jesus Christ, of the absolute equal brotherhood of man, and the rights of man on the simple ground of manhood."[58] For Stowe, the individual who personified this fusion of Christian ideals and American democracy was Abraham Lincoln, whom she eulogized in biographical sketches in The Lives and Deeds and in her earlier collection, Men of Our Times (1868).

For the nineteenth century, Lincoln was the real-world incarnation of the nice Jesus. When Lincoln was shot on Good Friday in 1865, he quickly became sanctified in Easter Sunday sermons nationwide. "Jesus Christ died for the world, Abraham Lincoln died for his country," said one clergyman, which became a common refrain in the aftermath of the assassination.[59] Like her rendition of Jesus, Stowe's Lincoln was popular and likable, someone whose storytelling abilities and good nature made him a beloved neighbor as well as a welcome dinner guest: "Mr. Lincoln's kindness was unquestionably the rarest, the most wonderful. It may be doubted whether any human being ever lived whose whole nature was so perfectly sweet with the readiness to do kind actions; so perfectly free from even the capacity of revenge. He could not even leave a pig in distress."[60] Whether it was directed toward animals or rebels, Lincoln's "sweet kindness of feeling" was inexhaustible. His kindness toward the rebels was framed after his death as an act of Christian forgiveness. "He quickly came to symbolize," as John Stauffer writes, "an American Christ who forgave rebels their sins and allowed them to reenter the Union."[61]

Stowe is quick to frame Lincoln's kindness as a source of strength rather than weakness, an expression of what she refers to as "passive power": "Lincoln was a strong man, but his strength was of a peculiar kind; it was not aggressive so much as passive, and among passive things it was like the strength not so much of a stone buttress as of a wire cable. It was strength swaying to every influence, yielding on this side and on that to popular needs, yet tenaciously and inflexibly bound to carry its great end."[62] Like her notion of influence, Stowe understands Lincoln's passive power as strength through accommodation. Just as the liberal subject is always open to persuasion, remaining "pliable to the influences of the others," to quote Stowe in "Repression," so Lincoln personifies this notion of power by remaining flexible but not too flexible, since complete pliability would undermine his ethical principles.

As Marianne Noble notes in *The Masochistic Pleasures of Sentimental Literature*, Stowe does not want to eliminate or abandon power but seeks to reformulate it, rendering it an ally instead of an enemy.[63] Whether it is Jesus who governs personally or Lincoln who governs passively, both personify Stowe's theory of power as influence, an interpersonal mode of persuasion that becomes generalized as a model of democratic governance. The powerful mother, like the hegemonic state, is not one who has to threaten and strike the misbehaving child but one who quietly guides through affection. At one level then, Jesus and Lincoln—as the embodiment of benevolent authority—represent a nineteenth-century theory of hegemony, where authority operates invisibly through the internalization of shared meanings as consensus rather than through physical coercion.

Stowe's model of democratic governance relies on a notion of consensus based on interpersonal niceness, but this model is unique neither to Stowe nor to the nineteenth century. Whether it is Jürgen Habermas's deliberative democracy, which rests, in part, on a notion of "considerateness," or Martin Luther King, Jr.'s ideal of "civil dialogue," where disagreement is vital to democratic debate, democratic consensus requires a model of well-behaved citizens. For Stowe, writing in the aftermath of the Civil War, consensus-building is a way to reunify the nation through the standardization of a personality type that exemplifies democratic sociability. Niceness as a rule of conduct is a way to reimagine structures of community at a national as well as an interpersonal level, where disagreement and dissent can be communicated through "civil dialogue" rather than through war.

But what are the limits of niceness? When does persuasion fail? To put it into historical terms, when does "civil dialogue" collapse into Civil War? Even the phrase "civil war" is paradoxical, emphasizing a strained fusion of civility and violence, as if it were possible to have a polite and considerate war. What about a necessary war? Could slavery have been eradicated through "civil dialogue" and "civil listening"? In contrast to Henry Ward Beecher's brand of liberal Christianity that preached the nonexistence of Hell and avoided such unpleasant topics as the Crucifixion, Stowe grapples with catastrophe in its myriad forms, including the national catastrophe of the Civil War.[64]

In doing so, Stowe recognizes the necessity of war and argues that some good may come out of the destruction. In the immediate aftermath of the Civil War, in her preface to *Men of Our Times*, Stowe turns the fiery destruction of the Civil War into a cauldron of national cleansing: "The fierce fire into which our national character has been cast in the hour of trial, has burned out of it the lingering stain of compromise with anything inconsistent with its primary object, 'to ordain justice and perpetuate liberty.'"[65] Destruction is ultimately regenerative for Stowe; it redeems "our national character" of its sins, allowing it to be born again without the stain of slavery. American exceptionalism is a form of Christian redemption that ensures the reproducibility of innocence.

As a messianic figure of national redemption, Stowe's Lincoln shares a number of similarities with the nice Jesus: "Never since the times of Christian martyrs has history recorded a contrast more humiliating to humanity, between his kind words and kind intentions on the one hand, and infamous abusiveness and deliberate bloodthirsty ferocity in those who thus slew the best and kindest friend they had in the world."[66] Like Jesus, Lincoln's kindness could not protect him. How could someone so beloved, asks Stowe in *Footsteps*, "be put to so cruel a death in the very midst of a people whom he loved and for whom he labored?" This question, which for Stowe applies equally to Jesus and Lincoln, is answered in the next sentence: Their kindness, as a power over the hearts of men, "was the cause and reason of the conspiracy."[67] Jesus and Lincoln had to be killed because they were loved too much; they became powerful to the extent that their kindness inspired both affection and hatred.

This chapter began with Paul Coughlin's rejection of the nice Victorian Jesus, a model of divinity to which Stowe gave characterological form. But Stowe understands what Coughlin cannot acknowledge, namely that, whether it is niceness or kindness, there is something potentially dangerous, even revolutionary, in behavior that inspires good fellow feeling. Niceness, in other words, can be extremely powerful. As psychoanalyst Adam Phillips and historian Barbara Taylor write in *On Kindness* (2009), "Living according to our sympathies, we imagine, will weaken or overwhelm us; kindness is the saboteur of a successful life." It is, moreover, a "virtue for losers."[68] We find our own capacity for kindness terrifying, they argue, because it brings to light our susceptibility to the feelings of others, our vulnerability toward and dependence on others.

Rather than viewing niceness and kindness and the whole constellation of related terms of positive sociality with either suspicion or indifference, I want to offer a critique as well as a generous reading of Stowe's nice Jesus. On the one hand, Stowe's banality of niceness, epitomized in the figures of Jesus and Lincoln, describes how hegemonic ideology permeates the everyday to the extent that it becomes common sense, a nonanalytical category of habit. In the figure of Lincoln, it refers to a form of democratic governance based on carrot management rather than brute force, one that establishes cohesion and perhaps even coercion through consensus, that invisible display of authority that manipulates without appearing to do so. Stowe's theory of feminine power, where feminine also refers to feminized men like Lincoln and Jesus, exemplifies, at least in part, Richard Brodhead's concept of "disciplinary intimacy" or discipline through love, which represents a form of social control based on an "intensification of the emotional bond between the authority-figure and its charge." It creates well-behaved citizens for the industrial age through a sense of "affectional warmth," and what Brodhead calls the "personalization of authority," where power is more deeply imbricated in the psyche through the introjection of benignity. "Love-power" is a force of socialization, whereby authority instills norms and conventions in the one who is adored.[69] Brodhead usefully brings a hermeneutics of suspicion to traits associated with positive sociality in order to cast doubt on any form of power that claims to be benign.

However, in reading the nice Jesus exclusively through this paradigm of social control as a form of discipline that sustains consensus through the etiquette of well-behaved citizens, we preclude another possible reading of this figure, an equally important reading that acknowledges niceness as dangerous. To understand the religious significance of niceness, one has to turn to the language of crisis that begins *Footsteps*. Stowe tells us from the start that we must all suffer and we must all die. We must also witness the suffering and death of loved ones, as our social circle gradually becomes smaller, quieter, and lonelier. This somewhat bleak picture sounds distinctly Calvinist at one level because it forces us to acknowledge our mortality without any soothing reassurances. Religion is certainly not an opiate here but rather a sober reminder of the reality principle. Yet Stowe does not stop at this point. She goes on to ask whether we should respond to our common vulnerability either with shame and fear (as the result of Original Sin) or as the source of our humanity. In Stowe's opinion, it is precisely by acknowledging vulnerability that we can show compassion toward ourselves and toward others. The crisis of mortality, in other words, can also be a gift: it creates the conditions for kindness.

It is this doubled-edged quality to niceness—its ability to be both a form of democratic cohesion that can heal the nation in the aftermath of the Civil War and a perilous recognition of our common vulnerability—that makes Stowe such a nuanced theorist of religious modernism. By using the banal to rethink the sacred in terms of the trivial rather than the transcendental, Stowe differentiates herself dramatically from another religious modernist, William James, who defines banality as "the unprofitable delineation of the obvious."[70] Stowe refuses to dismiss the banal. For her, the banality of niceness is a way to reimagine both religious belief and national mourning through a model of democratic sociality that was urgently needed in the post-bellum period.

Elizabeth Stuart Phelps and the *Fin-de-Siècle* Jesus

Despite Stowe's importance, however, her influence on other writers was neither permanent nor complete; instead, the Jesus we find in the work of later nineteenth-century American writers reflects changing historical circumstances. For Elizabeth Stuart Phelps, whose spiritual biography *The Story of Jesus Christ: An Interpretation* (1897) appeared twenty years after Stowe's, Jesus was less an exemplar of a democratic ideal and more of an emblematic figure of *fin-de-siècle* angst. Phelps's Jesus embodied the conflicts and tensions of the period through various neurasthenic symptoms ranging from headaches to mood swings and from depression to elation. Where Stowe's Jesus represents a democratic mode of governance through consensus, Phelps's protagonist is a psychological study, employing all the fine detail of realist characterization, replete with interiority, or what Phelps calls "rounded development."[71] Phelps's Jesus is incredulous about his own powers of persuasion and skeptical toward his own authority. Where Stowe ultimately sanctifies feminine men as another form of the Mother-Savior suggesting an alternative model of hegemonic authority, Phelps explores the male psyche in order to show how traits associated with femininity—such as vulnerability, sensitivity, and doubt—are extremely difficult for men to bear. Androgynous qualities do not necessarily lead to a felicitous union but instead can create a warring psyche.

Phelps's Jesus marks the transition between a residual Victorianism, with its priority on sociality, and an emergent Modernism, with its internalized modes of reflection and angst. In good Victorian fashion, Phelps's Jesus is sociable and conversational, with a special affection for children: "[He was] very fond of children, and they of him; he was sometimes seen with them climbing over his lap and laughing." As with Stowe's characterization, Phelps's Jesus is an entertaining dinner guest with impeccable manners. At a dinner hosted by a Pharisee, for instance, "the conversation of Jesus was so remarkable, his mien so high, that mere social ease wilted before him." Despite his deft social skills, Phelps's Jesus was no extrovert nor, as she carefully adds, was he a hermit.[72] Phelps has to walk a fine line between portraying Jesus as a

Johann Michael Ferdinand Heinrich Hofmann, "Jesus the Christ" (from
Christ and the Rich Young Man). Reproduced from Elizabeth Stuart Phelps,
The Story of Jesus Christ: An Interpretation (Boston and New York:
Houghton, Mifflin and Company, 1897): Frontispiece.

sociable person who is not so social as to appear frivolous, and yet, at
the same time, show him as a serious, contemplative figure who prefers his own company without seeming to be a disturbed loner.

For Stowe and Phelps, the social and political are inextricably connected. For Stowe, Jesus's sociality implies that he genuinely loves
people, and his sociability functions metaphorically as a model for a
democratic state. For Phelps, Jesus's sociability does not redefine the
hegemonic but instead indicates a political and moral commitment to
socialism. He is a social and political outsider. In *The Struggle for
Immortality*, a collection of essays on Christianity published in 1889,
Phelps sums up the political stakes of sociality: "Christ was the

educated and sanctified socialist. He was the consistent democrat. He was the consecrated agitator. Social rank simply did not exist for him."[73] Jesus's sociality is a sign of his democratic sensibilities that have radical consequences in defying social class. Yet despite his love of people, Jesus, after his baptism, felt "overwhelmed with the events of the day" and "sought the solitude which it was his first and his second nature to love." Phelps's Jesus has an abiding need for solitude, a yearning to withdraw from the enervating world of social relations, a desire that Stowe's Jesus never expresses. But Phelps is careful to reassure her readers that Jesus ultimately cherishes the sacredness of human attachment and, in this way, conforms to the fundamental Victorian ethos of sociability. She insists that Jesus "was never anything of a recluse. While he had no interest in what could be called society, and no time for it, yet he never obviously shunned it. He believed thoroughly in the culture of human relations."[74] Phelps is an apologist for Jesus's introversion because it could be seen as a potential sign of behavioral deviance at a time when men, even divine men, had to be seen as socially normative.

But what is especially fascinating in Phelps's spiritual biography is how Jesus grapples with being perceived as a messiah. Is messianism a form of social madness? And isn't it equally mad to believe one is actually the Savior? Phelps is intrigued by how Jesus psychically works out this disjuncture between his own private angst and the public perception of him as a God. Where Stowe reflects on religious authority in terms of social persuasion and democratic consensus, Phelps turns inward to study the impact of fame on the psyche. To put it simply, Phelps's Jesus found being perceived as a deity to be deeply troubling. As a humble man who "think[s] so little of himself" he is "troubled" to see "Hebrew faces" idealize him as a Jewish hero.[75] Yet despite this tension between Jesus's private and public roles, Phelps assures her readers that he possesses "an intensely human, well-balanced mind."[76] A glimpse into Jesus's psyche should not call into question his sanity; self-doubt is a sign of health and not its opposite. This emphasis on Jesus's mind was consistent with liberal Christianity's focus on the person of Jesus. Henry Ward Beecher, for instance, defines Jesus's mission as the creation of a "psychological kingdom," but Phelps takes Beecher's curiosity about the interiority of Jesus a step further and develops it into a dimensional character from whose perspective the narrative is told.

Phelps frames her characterization of Jesus through the words of her father, Austin Phelps, who is quoted in the book's opening epigraph: "A man whose soul is absorbed in a great life's work is apt to disclose his own mental history only in glimpses. Christ was no exception to this." Phelps's spiritual biography offers "glimpses" into the "mental history" of her protagonist, glimpses that include Jesus's fraught relationship with his mother. Told from his vantage point, Jesus expresses concern at Mary's "loving surveillance" whose "love could thwart and perplex him at every step."[77] Where Stowe's Jesus has an idealized relationship with his mother, whom he lovingly describes as his "soul-friend," Phelps's Jesus finds maternal devotion to be smothering and intrusive, preventing him from discovering his own sense of self. There is a quality in Phelps's Jesus that is distinctly modern. She offers a character study of a sensitive Jewish man whose desire for autonomy creates a complex mixture of love and guilt toward his overprotective mother.

Despite their differences, Stowe's and Phelps's biographies of Jesus have a number of similarities. They wrote spiritual biographies late in their respective careers, with Phelps following in Stowe's footsteps. In both cases, a motherless daughter of a Calvinist minister, herself trained in scripture and biblical criticism, wrote a spiritual biography that transfigures the severe God of her father into a benevolent force of kindness. Their spiritual biographies of Jesus can therefore be read, in part, as acts of daughterly defiance against their father's God of fiery retribution and judgment, but they are also, to varying degrees, works of daughterly devotion. Phelps also saw herself as a devoted literary daughter to Stowe. In her autobiography, *Chapters from a Life* (1896), Phelps affectionately describes Stowe as "the most unselfish and loving of mothers." Her home in Andover was an expression of her kindness: "It was an open, hospitable house, human and hearty and happy."[78] Phelps also followed in Stowe's footsteps in terms of professional success. It is well-known that Stowe's *Uncle Tom's Cabin* was the best-selling literary work of the nineteenth century, but what is less well-known is that Phelps's first novel, *The Gates Ajar* (1868), was the century's second best-selling book by a female author.[79]

What is most striking is the different form that their feminism takes in their respective depictions of the nice Jesus. Where Stowe wants to feminize the nice Jesus in order to reclaim him as a Jewish mother, Phelps blatantly critiques the sexism of the Bible, while at the same time insisting on the masculinity of Jesus. In other words, Phelps is more explicitly critical of the institutional sexism of the Church and its most sacred document, while she is less willing than Stowe to feminize Jesus as a sign of the Mother-Savior. Jesus remains in the realm of the father but is a father figure who is emotionally and psychologically vulnerable.

Phelps begins her spiritual biography by making explicit what is implicit in Stowe's work, specifically, a critique of the sexism of the New Testament for occluding a woman's voice and perspective: "The story of the Gospels was written by men. Men have studied and expounded it for two thousand years. Men have been its commentators, its translators, its preachers. All the feminine element in it has come to us passed through the medium of masculine minds."[80] She praises Jesus for his feminism, which can be seen in his profound sympathy for women's plight, his compassion for their frustrated potential, and his recognition of their spiritual depth. He was "always treating women with respect, always recognizing their fettered individualism, their force of character if they had it, their undeveloped powers, their terrible capacity for suffering, their superiority in spiritual vigor." This emphasis on Jesus's respect and sympathy for women characterizes another feminist rereading of the Bible of the 1890s, Elizabeth Cady Stanton's controversial *The Woman's Bible* (1895). Phelps, Stowe, and Stanton all agree that Jesus should be praised for his patience with women, a trait that distinguishes him from his disciples, who were more dismissive of women's speech.[81]

Despite being outspoken about Christianity's sexism, Phelps seems rather defensive about protecting Jesus's masculinity. In contrast to Stowe, whose Jesus resembles a Jewish mother in drag, Phelps's Jesus, despite his mood swings and reclusive tendencies, is still manly. Beginning with his childhood, Jesus is described as a "manly boy," and then as an adult, he partakes in "the kindest and manliest deeds." Feminine attributes like niceness and tenderness can only be portrayed if they are coupled with modifiers of manliness, as epitomized in Phelps's phrase "mighty tenderness."[82] Even Jesus's mind is unequivocally masculine: "it [his well-balanced mind] was always attentive to practical affairs; he did not waste himself in speculation, or lose himself in aimless Oriental reverie." Phelps possesses a self-consciousness

and concern about the effeminacy of Jesus, which she wants to foreclose through descriptions of his body, whether it is his well-balanced
mind or his manly face: "His countenance was both winning and com-
manding." When Jesus weeps, Phelps is quick to add that he is a
"strong and sensitive man."[83] Stowe did not need to frame a weeping
Jesus as manly because tears were permitted within a mid-century
understanding of sentimental manhood. By the 1890s, however, sympathetic tears signified effeminate behavior. Hence, Phelps's defense of
the nice Jesus as manly was a way to expand the boundaries of acceptable masculinity at a time when such behavior was becoming increasingly circumscribed.

Jesus as a Hysterical Woman

In contrast to Stowe, who received complimentary reviews for
Footsteps of the Master, Phelps's spiritual biography was met with
hostility. One reviewer described it as a heretical act and accused the
author of suffering from "Ann Hutchinsonitis," meaning that Phelps
had sacrificed the sublime qualities of Christ and reduced him to a
"weak" figure who was "unbearably commonplace."[84] Progressive
theologian Shailer Mathews, dean of the School of Theology at the
University of Chicago, published the most scathing review of Phelps's
book. "The Christ we have before us," he wrote in his 1898 review of
the book in the *Biblical World*, "is an introspective, ambitious,
depressed, and at times almost hysterical woman! His strength, his
doubts and ambitions, his struggles with himself, his weakness, his
faintings, his sufferings are not those of a man . . . He may be a strong
woman of the intellectual, nervous spiritual type, but he is not a strong
man. He is feminine, not virile—a heroine rather than a hero."[85]
Phelps's crime, according to Mathews, is that she reduces a sacred
figure to a hysterical woman, a Victorian neurasthenic whose doubts
and internal struggles represent a paralysis of the will. This critique is
especially perplexing given the lengths to which Phelps underscores
Jesus's manliness, even remarking that he was a "manly boy." But ultimately, Phelps did not go far enough in masculinizing a sentimental
version of the Savior for the fin-de-siècle. Mathews's Jesus is a robust
and socially confident reformer whose force of personality inspires
others to action, not to self-introspection and private angst.

In "Ministerial Virility—And a Suggestion" (1901), Mathews makes a case for "Christian virility" not through athleticism but by "thinking manfully, by conversing manfully, by doing a man's work."[86] In contrast to the anti-intellectualism of Theodore Roosevelt's *The Strenuous Life* (1900), which criticizes the enervating effects of overcivilization and its body-denying intellectualism, Mathews's version of Muscular Christianity defends a "virile intellectual life," with muscularity as a sign of spiritual strength and vitality. Where Stowe uses the language of vitality to reenergize the life of Jesus through the language of motherhood, the term *vitality* became increasingly viewed as a distinctly masculine notion of power synonymous with force, agency, and assertiveness. Turn-of-the-century religious modernists like Mathews and his contemporary, Harvard chaplain Francis Peabody, appropriated the Victorian Jesus selectively: They kept the earlier generation's tendency to personalize Jesus as a friend and an amiable and social figure, while rejecting his sentimental and feminized traits. Peabody wanted "no gentle visionary" but rather "a Person whose dominating trait is force."[87] Mathews and Peabody rejected the feminist appropriation of Jesus, refusing to accept the reformulation of social power in Stowe's terms of "passive power" or "influence." They held onto the affective dimension of the Calvinist God, an uncompromising God of wrath and judgment, and linked him to modern modes of masculine embodiment, where incarnation meant muscularity. By the early twentieth century, Jesus had become the "manly redeemer" as a consequence of what Stephen Nichols describes as a "masculine revolution sweeping American Christianity's portrait of Christ."[88] This revolution is reflected in the titles of a number of books about Jesus published during this period, including R. W. Conant, *The Manly Christ* (1904), Carl Delos Case, *The Masculine in Religion* (1906), Jason Pierce, *The Masculine Power of Religion* (1912), and Bruce Barton, *A Young Man's Jesus* (1914).

Mathews's response to Phelps's spiritual biography represents part of a larger move within liberal Christianity in the late nineteenth and early twentieth centuries to make religion more appealing to men by distancing it from feminine traits such as niceness. One could be caring but not too caring. Christian *caritas* had become widely feminized by the late nineteenth century, and this affective shift, combined with the predominance of women in the church, threatened to subvert the established order of the institution. Christian kindness had to be reconfigured in terms of rugged masculinity. It was no longer about moral suasion, but about winning, heroism, and triumph. A century before Paul Coughlin, evangelical writer Josiah Strong remarked in 1901 that the Victorian Jesus does not "win young men to the church." They need the "heroic."[89] Similarly, Mathews's article on "virile Christianity" begins with the question, "How can we get men in our churches?" But as historian Gail Bederman points out, U.S. Protestant churches had been two-thirds women ever since the 1660s, so why should concerns over the feminization of religion become a crisis in the late nineteenth century? For Bederman, "the feminine church only became a problem after 1880, when the Victorian gender system had begun to lose coherence in the face of a cultural reorientation connected to the growth of a consumer-oriented, corporate order."[90]

This explains why Stowe can praise a feminized Jesus in the 1870s, one who prefers bouncing a baby on his knee to overturning tables in the temple, and attract no negative comments from her many reviewers. Her gendering of Jesus may appear boldly feminized to twenty-first century readers, but it seems not to have caused the slightest stir among her contemporaries. But why should it have? Just a generation earlier, Samuel Taylor Coleridge defined male genius as a man with a feminine face. Derived in part from the romanticism of an earlier era, sentimental manhood extolled the values of nurture, gentleness, and kindness. As Peter Gay remarked in his reading of Thomas Hughes's *The Manliness of Christ* (1879), a book published in Britain and widely read in the United States, Jesus's tears were seen as consistent with a Victorian notion of manliness rather than a threat to it.[91] This suggests that manliness was a far broader category in the 1870s than it would become by the 1890s, a decade in which the word *masculinity* would increasingly replace the older terms *manliness* and *manhood*.

But Stowe's sociable Jesus was not entirely anachronistic by the turn of the century. In many ways, it evolved into the Jesus of Social Gospel fiction, whose values would ideally shape the way middle-class Americans would lead their lives by leaving the Victorian parlor to assist the hungry and the suffering in the slums. Jesus transforms from a sociable character to a social reformer, committed to challenging a society dedicated to profit, greed, and ambition. The emphasis is less on introspection and more on action. Described by some as the third great awakening, the Social Gospel movement represents a public-spirited form of liberal Christianity dedicated to curbing the excesses of industrialization, inequality, and urban disparity.

One of the best-selling books of the 1890s was Charles Monroe Sheldon's *In His Steps: "What Would Jesus Do?"* (1896), whose title builds on Stowe's metaphor of footsteps as imitating the life of Christ. Sheldon's novel, according to historian Paul Boyer, ranks alongside Stowe's *Uncle Tom's Cabin* as among the books that have captured "some dominant current of popular feeling in their day."[92] Sheldon, who was a Congregational minister in Topeka, Kansas, begins his novel through his fictional counterpart Reverend Henry Maxwell, who implores his middle-class parishioners to ask themselves "What would Jesus do?" when confronted with a dilemma in their everyday lives for a full year. The task is to bring Jesus's teachings into practice, and the result is socially transformative but politically limited. Based in part on William Stead's popular *If Christ Came to Chicago* (1894), which urges interclass alliances through a politics of propinquity, so Sheldon's novel frames salvation through interclass rescue. One must feel the suffering of another to be truly Christian. For example, an upper-class girl named Virginia, known for being one of the most beautifully dressed girls in town, saves Loreen, a local drunk, by befriending her and taking her home to sober up. Loreen's salvation, however, is short-lived. During an angry mob scene, when a heavy bottle is thrown out of a saloon window, Loreen pushes Virginia out of the way and the bottle hits and kills Loreen instead. The working-class woman sacrifices her own life in order to save her wealthy friend. By staying safely within the sphere of the personal, where rich and poor can call each other friends, this novel unwittingly demonstrates how the religion of niceness can only go so far. It avoids a structural critique that would call into question how Virginia, for instance, can afford her beautiful dresses in the first place.

A more socialist strand of the Social Gospel movement combined the personal with the structural in praising the labor leader Eugene Debs as a figure who had replaced Lincoln as "the most Christlike character."[93] Although Debs had spoken critically about religion as well as the Church, his persona was framed using the language of Jesus. He also increasingly identified with Jesus as a living sacrifice, especially during his imprisonment for giving an antiwar speech during World War I, when he put a magazine image of Jesus on the wall of his cell. To religious figures who visited him in prison, Debs would say that the "[ruling class] nailed him to the cross and they threw me in here . . . If Christ could go to the cross for his principles, surely I can go to prison for mine." For Debs, Christianity and capitalism cannot coexist since economic conditions are predicated on competition and one must fight another for a job. Given these conditions, how can one love their neighbor? During this same period, Debs elaborated his views in "Jesus, the Supreme Leader" (1914), where he describes Jesus as "supremely human," and it was in his humanity that his divinity consisted. Repeating Stowe's association between Lincoln and Jesus and, as discussed below, Du Bois's analogy with John Brown, Debs wrote, "To me Jesus Christ is as real, as palpitant and persuasive as a historic character as John Brown, Abraham Lincoln, or Karl Marx." Jesus was the son of poor working people, born on a bed of straw "among asses and other animals," and his disciples were similarly of humble origin. He preached not to the scribes and Pharisees but to his own class of "ragged undesirables."

In contrast to Stowe's Jesus, who was well-liked among the rich and poor, Debs's Jesus is strictly committed to the proletariat. What is interesting is that in conveying Jesus's anger at injustice, Debs does not resort to the clichés of masculinity, nor does Jesus appear anxious about his virility. For Debs, Jesus was a revolutionary leader who combined the majesty of a god and the vision of a seer with the "loving heart of a woman." He was as "sweet and gentle as the noble mother who had given him birth."[94] Debs's socialist Jesus still possesses the Victorian gentleness that Stowe and others ascribed to him and his "love for the poor and the children of the poor" came from his maternal heart.

As Debs's characterization of Jesus demonstrates, the nice Jesus proved to be a resilient figure with multiple modernist afterlives in the early twentieth century. Debs's contemporary W. E. B. Du Bois similarly appropriated the gentle Jesus of the Victorian era to decry suffering and injustice, particularly racial violence that included lynching and mass incarceration. In the early twentieth century, the black Christ was a figure of critique rather than of triumph. Du Bois invokes the black Christ in various religious sketches and short stories, including "Jesus Christ in Georgia" (1911) and "The Gospel According to Mary Brown" (1915), as a way to represent the spiritual power of black kindness and condemn the virulence of white hatred. More than Stowe, Phelps, and even Debs, Du Bois's Black Jesus illustrates the dangerous consequences of niceness. Black amiability—like Indian hospitality—can be deadly.

W. E. B. Du Bois, the Black Jesus, and the Politics of Vulnerability

At the height of the modernist backlash against Victorian "namby-pambyism," to borrow a phrase from William James, Du Bois recuperates the Victorian legacy of the nice Jesus as a way to critique the hubris of white supremacy, while understanding and dramatizing the ethics of vulnerability. As Edward Blum observes, "depictions of Christ played a largely forgotten part in his battle against white supremacy, capitalism, violence, imperialism, and misogyny."[95] In *The Gift of Black Folk* (1924), Du Bois argues that vulnerability is part of a larger gift that black religion brings to American Christianity, specifically, an emotional vitality and passion that adds dimension and substance to the "cold formalism of upper class England and New England." The result is "kindliness and social uplift." For Du Bois, "the black man has brought to America a sense of meekness and humility which America never has recognized and perhaps never will." The black man, according to Du Bois, provides a crucial antidote to a white sense of their own entitlement. Where the traits of the American spirit, such as self-assertion and determination, can have dangerous consequences such as war and the imperial occupation of the "darker world," meekness and humility can provide an important "corrective," one based on a "deep sympathy with the wishes of the other man." Black Americans represent the "ethics of Jesus Christ," according to Du Bois, based on social compassion and the joy in serving others or what he calls a "poignant sympathy with men in their struggle to live and love which is, after all, the end of being."[96]

It is precisely this capacity to feel profound compassion, according to Du Bois, that constitutes black America's gift to the nation: the soulful expression of a democratic spirit that still has the capacity to love even in the midst of lynching, Jim Crow segregation, and poverty. In other words, African Americans are not the objects of Christian sympathy but its best practitioners. In *The Souls of Black Folk* (1903), Du Bois first introduces the phrase "gift of the spirit" as the last of three gifts that blacks have brought to the United States, the others being the "gift of story and song" and the "gift of sweat and brawn." In a land of dollars, the "gift of the spirit" provides an important antidote to capitalist greed by imagining qualities that exist beyond the profit motive, qualities that Cornel West, among others, have described as "nonmarket values."[97]

By accentuating vulnerability and hesitancy, Du Bois counters the self-assertion and determination of the American spirit with an alternative model of subjectivity, premised on doubt, questioning, and nonmastery. These are the very qualities that Shailer Mathews associates with an overly feminized Jesus who borders on hysteria. But for Du Bois, these same qualities are the basis of an anti-imperialist position that counters hubris with humility. Black male niceness as a form of vulnerability goes beyond individualism and inspires a sense of solidarity among those who suffer. Far more than either Phelps or Stowe, who stay within the conventions of biography, Du Bois's black Jesus is emblematic of a democratic spirituality that is collectivist, nurturing, and community-forming. This figure signifies, like Eugene Debs's version, sociality from below and solidarity among the powerless.

By making Jesus vulnerable and nonmasterful, Du Bois redeems these abject qualities and makes them worthy of dignity: "Jesus Christ was a laborer and black men are laborers; He was poor and we are poor; He was despised; He was persecuted and crucified, and we are mobbed and lynched."[98] Black Americans are the truest Christians who are able to identify with the suffering of Jesus most immediately and genuinely. Du Bois's Jesus is explicitly linked to a working-class identity, and particularly with the black poor, an identification that demonstrates a compassion for the misery of those who are economically marginalized and racially stigmatized. Du Bois's Jesus is part of what the legal scholar Michelle Alexander calls the "undercaste," a segment of the population permanently marginalized through law and custom.[99]

This is significantly different from the socialist tendencies of Phelps's Jesus, who may identify with the poor and disenfranchised but who is unequivocally not of them. Phelps is careful to assert his class pedigree as "the essence of good-breeding." He is a "courtly democrat." Stowe similarly qualifies Jesus's class genealogy by remarking that Joseph and Mary are "two members of the decayed and dethroned royal family of Judea," and this aristocratic bloodline, however decayed by the passage of time, still gave them a "nobility of feeling which distinguished them from common citizens."[100] The Victorian Jesus of Stowe and Phelps is the product of good breeding but humble circumstance, which illustrates the best of both worlds as it ensures that Jesus has impeccable manners while still being sensitive to plebian concerns. By contrast, Du Bois's black Jesus has no recourse to aristocratic bloodlines or any other form of genealogical redemption.[101]

Du Bois's ethics of vulnerability anticipate what Cornel West describes as "prophetic criticism," which "follows the biblical injunction to look at the world through the eyes of its victims." By looking at the victims of power, a vantage point that Du Bois calls a "democratic mode of being," prophetic criticism offers, according to West, a "critique of illegitimate authority and arbitrary uses of power; a bestowal of dignity, grandeur and tragedy on the ordinary lives of everyday people."[102] Whether in his essays "The Gift of the Spirit" and "Of the Culture of White Folk" or his literary transfigurations of the Gospels in "Jesus Christ in Georgia" (later titled "Jesus Christ in Texas") and "The Gospel According to Mary Brown," Du Bois's religious writing persistently asks which Americans would become representative if one were to frame a national type through the vulnerable Jesus. Du Bois's democratic type differs significantly from that of Walt Whitman, replacing the latter's exceptionalist language of "the best" with rhetorical humility.

Jesus's blackness plays a crucial role in encoding vulnerability not just in terms of an emotional state—an internalized mode of being as in Phelps's Jesus—but in terms of the subversiveness of Christian platitudes, such as "blessed are the meek." What happens when a black man utters the Sermon on the Mount? In "The Gospel According to Mary Brown" (1915), when Joshua repeats the familiar words "Blessed are the poor," the white mob becomes enraged and asks, "What does he mean that the 'weak will inherit the earth' when the weak are black? How dare he associate social equality with racial equality! 'Is God a Nigger?'" When Christian and democratic truisms are articulated by a black man, they suddenly become heretical. Harassed by an enraged white mob, Joshua's affect suddenly changes from humility to rage and he exclaims, "Woe unto you, Scribes and Pharisees Hypocrites!" And with these words, he is lynched. But the story does not end here but with the Resurrection, a metaphor of black resilience. When Joshua rises from the dead and visits his mother in her humble cabin and tells her of his heavenly triumph, his mother quietly dies at his feet. By moving the setting from Jerusalem to the rural South, Du Bois's retelling of the Crucifixion and the Ascension revitalizes the biblical narrative. Consequently, he defamiliarizes Christian clichés and reveals just how potentially radical they can be when the speaking subject is no longer assumed to be white.

Lynching Jesus

Du Bois was not alone in transfiguring the Crucifixion into a lynching. Over a decade later, Countee Cullen's poem "Black Christ" (1929) told the story of Jim, who punches a white man in self-defense and is hunted down by a white mob. Christ takes the place of Jim as the rope is tightened around his neck and is killed in his stead.[103] Where Cullen's poem focuses on divine immanence and racial redemption through the iconic figure of a lynched black man, Du Bois's short story "Jesus Christ in Georgia" (1911) emphasizes the living black Jesus rather than his transcendence. Du Bois turns to the physical experience of racism, and his Jesus is immersed in the social world of compassion and cruelty. This focus on social encounters aligns him with the Victorian tradition of Stowe and Phelps, but where social relations have a sacred valence for Stowe and (to a lesser extent) for Phelps, they acquire sadistic and violent qualities for Du Bois. Sociality can kill you.

"Jesus Christ in Georgia" begins *in medias res* inside a small-town jail, with a "stranger" overhearing a conversation among the local elites about how to turn black convicts into forced laborers to build the railroad. Du Bois already sees the legacy of slavery in the mass incarceration of black men and in the profitability of prison labor. The United States had already become a "prison nation."[104] In a gesture of Southern hospitality, the Colonel invites the stranger home to meet his wife and daughter at their mansion. The temporal setting is twilight, that transitional point between day and night that obfuscates visibility. The stranger appears to be cultured and gives the impression of being a teacher and a foreigner. The Colonel's wife invites him to stay for dinner and the stranger accepts due to their young daughter's insistence. But when the lights in the home are turned on and the stranger's mulatto skin is revealed, the invitation is tacitly rescinded. "He was tall and straight, and the coat looked like a Jewish gabardine. His hair hung in close curls far down the sides of his face, and his face was olive, even yellow." The stranger is suddenly familiar, both in terms of his coloring—"their practiced eyes knew" he had Negro blood—and in terms of his eyes. "Where had he [the Colonel] seen those eyes before?" The Colonel has a sudden flashback from the distant past of "the soft, tear-filled eyes of a brown girl."[105]

What is the connection between the tear-filled eyes of the brown girl and the eyes of the stranger? Perhaps the brown girl in the Colonel's flashback was once his rape victim and the stranger standing before him is his son. Initially perceived as a Jewish foreigner, the stranger embodies the uncanny—the incarnation of the plantation's sexual violence that still haunts the post-Reconstruction South. The flashback offers a glimpse of the repressed guilt of plantation violence, its traumatic impact on the psyche of the slave owner, who must disavow the tears of the black girl of his past by rejecting the visitor before him. Where Phelps describes Jesus's smile, Du Bois focuses on his eyes. In both instances, Jesus's face is the vehicle of his humanization, the point of contact between himself and others. But for Du Bois more than for Phelps, Jesus's face is a site of white projection and of the forbidden memories and guilt feelings that must remain repressed.

By framing the first half of his short story around the dinner invitation that is silently revoked, Du Bois adds an important new dimension to the sociability of the Victorian Jesus. As Stowe, Beecher, Phelps, and even Mathews make clear, Jesus was noted for his busy social life, a quality that was dramatized through his frequent invitations as a dinner guest among all ranks of society. He is both popular and a populist, a social democrat who is inclusive and accessible. Hospitality figures prominently in this Christian literature of sociability. In Du Bois's essay "Religion in the South" (1907), one of Jesus's first deeds upon arriving in Georgia is "to sit down and take supper with black men." But Du Bois doubts that Jesus would be welcomed with the same warmth if he dined among high-ranking whites in Georgia. This would be highly unlikely, since the "tremendous paradox of Christianity" is how white Christianity preaches all-inclusivity while at the same time closing its doors to blacks. The result is the "tendency to lie when the real situation comes up because the truth is too hard to face."[106] The Colonel's inability to look into the stranger's face because of "those eyes [that] kept burning into him" is itself symbolic of the white South's inability to acknowledge its traumatic history. The dinnertime scene, which represents a staple in Stowe's rendition of the ordinariness of Jesus, constitutes an impossible moment for Du Bois. It signifies a failed encounter as well as the limits of Southern hospitality.

Du Bois's short story has two parts. The first part, which I have just described, takes place inside the Colonel's home. The latter half occurs outdoors as the narrative follows the stranger after he leaves the Colonel's mansion and encounters a white farmer's wife. It is now night. The white woman cannot determine the stranger's race and assumes from his voice that he is white. The dinnertime scene that could not happen inside the Colonel's mansion occurs outdoors with the farmer's wife. She brings him cornbread and milk and joins him outdoors as he eats. She begins to confide in him "the things she had done, and had not done, and the things she had wished."[107] Here, Du Bois's Jesus is the embodiment of Stowe's good listener, the Jesus who patiently listens to the private desires and regrets of a woman. But when the stranger asks her if she loves her neighbors as herself, she explains that she tries but they are "niggers."

The Christian platitude "Love thy neighbor" uttered in the context of the Jim Crow South quickly triggers a crisis point in the narrative. As in "The Gospel According to Mary Brown," Du Bois shows how Christian clichés become heretical when the speaking subject is black. Du Bois conveys the bitter irony of Christian love when the farmer's wife lights the lamp in the doorway and realizes that the stranger is a mulatto: "She saw his dark face and curly hair. She shrieked in angry terror, and rushed down the path."[108] As with the earlier encounter in the Colonel's mansion, illumination does not transform sight into insight but instead exposes the blindness of prejudicial vision. The thin veneer of white Southern niceness can change suddenly and violently into blinding hatred.

Du Bois's use of the phrase "angry terror" to describe the white woman's response to the stranger's face demonstrates how terror—and its related term, vulnerability—is politically mediated and unevenly distributed. Who exactly is terrified of whom? And who is vulnerable? The "optics of race are tricky," writes Michael Eric Dyson in a *New York Times* op-ed piece, and he goes on to define racial terror in terms of two interlocking temporal registers: slow terror and fast terror. Slow terror represents everyday fears and micro-moments of injustice that "seep into every nook and cranny of black existence." They include such moments as Du Bois depicts above: a rescinded dinner invitation expressed in the politest of terms. Fast terror, by contrast, is "explosive and explicit; it is the spectacle of unwarranted black death." The latter is visible, and the former is often invisible. "Fast terror scares us; slow terror scars us."[109]

In the latter half of Du Bois's short story, we see how the "angry terror" of a white woman results in the fast terror of a lynching. At this crisis point, Du Bois's narrative accelerates and its various elements threaten to spin out of control. As the farmer's wife hysterically runs back to her home to tell her husband, she crashes into a black convict who has just escaped from the local jail and she falls down unconscious. At that moment, the farmer finds his wife collapsed on the ground in front of the runaway prisoner. A white mob immediately appears, and although the farmer's wife regains consciousness, she does nothing to stop the lynch mob from hanging the black renegade. While witnessing the gruesome act from her bedroom window, she suddenly sees the stranger with whom she had been confiding now nailed on a "crimson cross" and notices that his "calm dark eyes" were fastened on the "writhing, twisting body of the thief."[110] The crucified black Christ and the lynched prisoner are twinned figures, combining the racial violence of personal prejudice with the structural violence of racial incarceration. Where the story began with the black Christ eavesdropping on a conversation about how local whites in the Southern community planned to turn prisoners into forced laborers, it ends with the black Christ and the escaped prisoner dying side by side in a sadistic spectacle of black suffering. The fact that this story was republished in *The Crisis* every time a lynching was reported suggests that the story itself acquired a liturgical status through its repetition.[111]

Du Bois's Jesus not only enables a critique of racial violence in the United States, but also makes possible a reparative moment that facilitates white introspection. The story's final scene is described in terms of its emotional impact on the farmer's wife, much like Stowe's rendition of the Crucifixion that is told from Mary's perspective. Initially, the farmer's wife is overcome with emotion and unable to watch the violence outside. She cannot view race in real time, to quote Michael Eric Dyson, since "Americans prefer rose-tinted lenses and slow-motion replays in which we can control the narrative and minimize our complicity in the horrors of our history." By hiding her eyes from the spectacle in front of her—a spectacle that she, in part, created—she must disavow the horror of history, while refusing to acknowledge culpability. She then decides to look at the scene, and the final image of the farmer's wife is defined by physical and audible grief, with her outstretched arms mirroring the stranger's on the crimson cross: "She stretched her arms and shrieked."[112] These shrieks at the sight of the lynching/crucifixion are not the same as her earlier one, when she realized that the stranger who had become a friend was black. While the first shriek signals "angry terror," Du Bois suggests that the second shriek may signify her acknowledgment of guilt.

In "The Church and the Negro" (1913), Du Bois reflects on the importance of white guilt: "If the black men in America are what they are because of slavery and oppression, how cowardly for white Christians to deny their own guilt."[113] Guilty feelings are a necessary step toward national healing because they acknowledge white complicity in a history of racial violence. Guilt can be a productive emotion because it has the potential to demystify the lies of white Christianity and to encourage a period of reckoning. For Du Bois, Jesus's likability is a strategy for provoking this purgative guilt that breaks the habit of disavowal through acknowledgment.[114]

By coupling guilt with white womanhood, Du Bois applies to the era of lynching what Sarah Moore Grimké had asked a half-century earlier in the context of slavery: "Can any American woman look at these scenes of shocking licentiousness and cruelty, and fold her hands in apathy, and say, 'I have nothing to do with slavery'? *She cannot and be guiltless*" [original emphasis].[115] Du Bois sees this recognition of complicity as a form of grieving. White women need to acknowledge rather than disavow the violent consequences of race hatred, since lynching, as Ida B. Wells argued, was ostensibly done to defend white Southern womanhood. Race hatred was disguised through the chivalric rhetoric of honor. By witnessing that which is done in her name, the white Southern woman can no longer be innocent of how she is implicated in the racial violence that is committed in her honor. She can no longer be guiltless.

The final scene of Du Bois's story, however, remains ambiguous. The white woman clearly experiences grief at what she has witnessed, but it is unclear whether this grief will lead to revelation or to new forms of disavowal. The fact that Du Bois concludes this narrative in an open-ended manner, with the productivity of guilt being neither assumed nor foreclosed, suggests his own complex relation to the politics of vulnerability and the spectacle of black suffering. Can black suffering really be therapeutic for white people? How effective is the display of black vulnerability and racial injury in rectifying injustice? What the political scientist Alyson Cole says about vulnerability also applies to niceness: "[T]he language of vulnerability may not be able to perform the political work the most vulnerable require and deserve."[116] In other words, amiability may not be enough; and similarly, vulnerability does not provide an adequate political practice to challenge the production and reproduction of structural vulnerabilities.

Despite the ways in which Du Bois reimagines the figure of the gentle Jesus, his depiction is quite conventional in the sense that Jesus appears as a figure of suffering and a victim of racial violence. But imagine Jesus committing acts of violence in the name of love. Can Christian niceness take the form of ethical violence, especially when that violence is directed toward a federal government that enforces slavery? Where Stowe explores the relationship between the nice Jesus and the state through the figure of Lincoln, Du Bois turns to John Brown, the white abolitionist whose attack on the federal arsenal at Harper's Ferry in 1859 constitutes an important prelude to the Civil War. "Look at the history of human life," Du Bois proclaims, "who are the men before whom the world with one accord has bowed: Socrates, Seneca, Luther and Horace Mann, John Brown and Jesus Christ—poor men, paupers if you will, but *men*." Like Stowe and Phelps, Du Bois turns to biography as a way to explore the conflicts emerging from his ethics of vulnerability, adding biographical weight to Phelps's phrase "mighty tenderness" by asking how sympathetic men can justify violence.[117] By italicizing "men," Du Bois, like Phelps, expands the affective range of masculinity to include tenderness, sympathy, and kindness.

John Brown and Ethical Violence

When initially asked to contribute a volume to the *Century*'s biographical series, Du Bois wanted to write about Nat Turner, a person whom he studied while at college. But when the editors suggested instead that he write a biography on John Brown, Du Bois reluctantly agreed. He began writing in 1905 and *John Brown* was published in 1909, a fitting date, given that it marked the fiftieth anniversary of Harper's Ferry. It is ironic that a book Du Bois was originally averse to writing became his personal favorite, though it includes little in the way of original research and relies mainly on several secondary studies, such as R. J. Hinton's *John Brown and His Men* (1894). As Du Bois's biographer, Herbert Aptheker, notes, "In many ways, John Brown personified Du Bois's ideal of a religious person; he viewed Jesus as a rebellious Jew who was crucified for seeking to bring a just and humane society upon earth."[118] Following in the tradition of the Transcendentalists, who were among the first to compare John Brown to Christ, Du Bois saw John Brown as a Christ figure who committed race treason by sacrificing his life to bring about a just and humane society upon earth. He considered Brown's death a crucifixion. In the preface to *John Brown*, Du Bois writes, "John Brown worked not simply for Black Men—he worked with them; and he was a companion of their daily life, knew their faults and virtues, and felt, as few white Americans have felt, the bitter tragedy of their lot." According to Du Bois, John Brown came nearest of all Americans "to touching the real souls of black folk."[119]

Where Stowe and others sanctified Lincoln as a Christlike figure, Du Bois saw in Lincoln a contradictory and unreliable leader. He described him as "cruel, merciful; peace-loving, a fighter; despising Negroes and letting them fight and vote; protecting slavery and freeing slaves . . . —a big, inconsistent, brave man."[120] But as John Brown's biographer, David Reynolds, notes, Du Bois expressed unqualified admiration for Brown as one "who had lived with blacks and had died for them."[121] Du Bois was also careful to capture John Brown's role as a nurturing husband, father, and son. Similar to Stowe's use of domestic details to characterize a caregiving Jesus, Du Bois notes that when anyone in the family was sick, Brown would stay up and make sure they were cared for properly. His daughter affectionately referred to him as "a tender mother." She recounted with particular fondness how John Brown gently cared for his elderly father: "In cold weather he always tucked the bedclothes around grandfather when he went to bed, and would get up in the night to ask him if he slept warm—always seeming so kind and loving to him that his example was beautiful to see."[122] These intimate moments of the private John Brown as a nurturing caregiver to his family add dimension to Du Bois's portrait of the man as a figure of compassion and sacrifice.

John Brown embodied all of the Christian platitudes of niceness: love thy neighbor, the Golden Rule, the Sermon on the Mount. His decision to organize a twenty-two-man raid on the federal arsenal at Harper's Ferry, with the hope of inciting a widespread slave insurrection, was not an act of rage or revenge. Du Bois's underlying thesis in *John Brown* is that this act of violence was motivated by sympathy for the enslaved. What inspired John Brown was excessive compassion for the enslaved rather than rage at the slave owner. Du Bois uses John Brown's own words to explain the relation between kindness and violence: "I pity the poor in bondage that have none to help him. That is why I am here; not to gratify any personal animosity, revenge or vindictive spirit. It is my sympathy with the oppressed."[123] This makes John Brown the personification of Jesus, whose "natural sympathy" with the oppressed motivated his actions.

What Du Bois also takes from John Brown's example is that sympathy and niceness are not enough. Sympathy will not persuade Southern slave owners to manumit their slaves; niceness will not lead to social justice. Du Bois uses two quotations from John Brown to explain how ineffective persuasion is: first, "moral suasion is hopeless," and second, taken from Brown's last note before his execution, "I, John Brown, am quite certain that the crimes of this guilty land will never be purged away but with blood." Although considered legally guilty for the raid on the federal arsenal, Brown was innocent of a moral crime. His lack of guilt is a recurrent theme in Du Bois's biography, reflected in Brown's repeated admission in his letters that he sleeps soundly, with no remorse for taking up arms: "I feel quite cheerful in the assurance that God reigns and will overrule all for His glory and the best possible Good."[124]

John Brown is the incarnation of Christian niceness with a Calvinist inflection, with justice and righteousness ultimately reigning over liberal Christianity's understanding of sweetness as a tactic of moral suasion. Although Brown began as a pacifist, his antislavery passion overwhelmed his pacifism. He took the Golden Rule and demonstrated how this truism of Christian niceness could become radical and dangerous when applied to slavery. Stowe heralded the abolitionism of John Brown alongside William Lloyd Garrison and Wendell Phillips as "the spiritual children of the pilgrim fathers," whose work resulted in a "moral victory" that ended slavery.[125] Elizabeth Stuart Phelps witnessed the "soul" of John Brown in black schoolchildren singing "marching on."[126] Growing up in the New England theology, Stowe,

Phelps, and Du Bois all understood that it was New England Calvinism that inspired a sense of moral outrage and righteousness that generated the abolitionism of John Brown. But Du Bois also acknowledged the role of sentimental manhood in that Du Bois's John Brown, similar to Stowe's Jesus, was a nurturing mother.

Christian Niceness and the Gentilization of the Jew

Du Bois's black Christ was not ultimately a fighting warrior but a vulnerable outcast. In "Jesus Christ in Georgia," this figure was dressed in a "Jewish gabardine" with curls along the sides of his face. Du Bois's black Christ, in other words, was also a Jew. He was not a biblical Jew like Stowe's Jesus, with the dark Semitic features of the Middle East, but an immigrant Jew described as a "foreigner." He was contemporary rather than ancient. Du Bois was less interested than Stowe in Jesus's genealogy and his Semitic origins, and more intrigued by the relationship between being black and being Jewish in turn-of-the-century America. One was a religious outcast while the other was a racial one, but what Du Bois would learn in his three visits to Europe, the last of which was on the eve of Hitler's invasion of Poland, was the nonexceptionalism of the U.S. race problem. His European experiences allowed Du Bois to think beyond the "social provincialism" of the United States and instead to see how it "cut across lines of color and physique and belief and status and was a matter of cultural patterns, perverted teaching and human hate and prejudice."[127] Although Du Bois would make the relation between anti-Semitism and racism explicit in a speech about the Warsaw Ghetto in 1952, arguably he already understood the connections between Jewishness and blackness much earlier in the century.

Du Bois would make this connection explicit in 1934 during the last year of his editorship of *The Crisis* by publishing an essay by Jacob Weinstein, a labor activist, Chicago rabbi, and leader of the American Civil Liberties Union, entitled "The Negro and the Jew." Weinstein, who emigrated with his family from Poland as a young boy, argues that blacks and Jews share a minority mentality that seeks Gentile approval "by imitating Gentile manners." Assimilation, or gentilization, is born out of the need to please the Protestant status quo, or what Weinstein calls "the out-group's slavish obeisance to the approval of the in-group." Weinstein focuses not on passing but on minority impressibility or imitativeness in order to curry favor among the dominant group. "In Negro life, the man who looks and acts like white folks is assured of preference in almost any enterprise." But Weinstein saves his sharpest criticism for imitative Jews: "The Jew who attempts to gain his [the Gentile's] friendship by imitating Gentile manners and blindly adapting his standards, receives only the deepest contempt."[128] Imitating Gentile manners implies a cultural shame associated with being black or Jewish, a shame that is debilitating because of its internalized sense of self-abjection. Weinstein insists that blacks and Jews can overcome self-hatred by helping each other in the common struggle against becoming "toadies and lick-spittles." Drawing explicit connections between the rise of anti-Semitism in Germany and the lynchings in the South, this two-part series of articles on black and Jewish relations is ultimately a diatribe against assimilation, understood as the performance of white civility, with Gentile and genteel becoming synonymous terms.[129]

Read symptomatically, Weinstein's essay is more than a critique of assimilation, for it also betrays Jewish anxieties about modernization, which for the sociologist Talcott Parsons represents assimilation to a secularized form of Protestant Christianity. One form that this secularization takes is niceness: it gives shape and meaning to U.S. sociality, where Protestant civility becomes synonymous with good manners. As the sociologist John Murray Cuddihy argues in his monumental study *The Ordeal of Civility*, "the modernization process, the civilizational process, and the assimilation process were experienced as one— as the 'price of admission' to the bourgeois civil societies of the West at the end of the nineteenth century." Cuddihy goes on to define niceness as "the informally yet pervasively institutionalized civility expected—indeed, required—of members of that societal community called the civic culture." As the antithesis of obsession, fanaticism, and inwardness, or of any other affect that is considered to be too excessive and expressive, niceness is the behavioral corollary to modernization in the form of personal moderation and self-restraint. Niceness is the expression of what Cuddihy aptly calls the Protestant Etiquette, a pun on Max Weber's Protestant ethic, which signifies a "system of internal restraints" that monitor public presentation.[130] In this context, niceness becomes largely a performance of social conformity to a national status quo that appears to be neutral but is, in fact, deeply embedded in Christian mores and manners.

Diasporic Jewish intellectuals of the early twentieth century were among the first to critique niceness as a form of gentilization. Maurice Samuel, a British-Jewish intellectual, poignantly captures the fraught relationship between Jewishness and niceness in his 1932 book *Jews on Approval*. In one essay entitled "Jews, Be Nice," Samuel writes, "The Jews are probably the only people in the world to whom it has ever been proposed that their historic destiny is—to be nice." Such a goal is absurd, according to Samuel, since nice is a vacuous concept: "[T]he word *nice* indicates a pleasing absence of character. It is the best that a man can be without being anything." When niceness is applied to a people or a nation, it becomes even more insipid: "For a people consisting of nice individuals and of nothing more is not a people at all."

Although Stowe argues that niceness is precisely what holds a people together because superficial friendly encounters have a deeper unifying significance, Samuel finds the imperative to be nice to be insidious. Jews who refuse to assimilate to niceness and remain resolutely and proudly anti-nice are then blamed for fanning the flames of anti-Semitism: "If the Jews would only temper their voices, their table-manners and their ties, if they would be discreet and tidy in their enthusiasms, unobtrusive in their comings and goings, and above all reticent about their Jewishness, they would get along very well." Moreover, Jews are held responsible, through the careful cultivation of niceness, for the success or failure of their own integration within mainstream culture. The goal of this integration, as Samuel describes it, is not only happiness, but also to be "liked by everybody." Samuel finds in "the ideal of niceness" a "tragic problem" for Jewish people that can be summarized in the question "How can I get myself liked?"[131] Niceness and likability are connected for Samuel (as they were for his contemporary Dale Carnegie), since niceness is a strategy to improve one's chances of being liked; in turn, likability becomes an important index of social approval and integration.

Where Maurice Samuel sees niceness as distinctly not Jewish, as a vacuous term that actually poses a threat to "Jewish genius," an earlier generation of liberal American Jews took the opposite point of view. Niceness could not be more Jewish. In "Progressive Judaism and Liberal Christianity" (1899), the Reform rabbi Clifton Harby Levy argues that Jewish sociality was based on the Golden Rule: "As the Old Testament had it: 'Thou shalt love thy neighbor as thyself,' and as Hillel said, 'What is hateful unto thee do unto none.' So Jesus taught: 'Do unto others as you would that others should do unto you.'"[132] By situating the Golden Rule—a precept of Christian niceness—within a Jewish lineage from Hillel to the Hebrew Bible, Levy is effectively Judaizing both niceness and the Gentile. In doing so, Levy challenges the Christian monopoly on niceness by disclosing its Jewish origins. In a sense, Levy follows in the tradition of Stowe's philo-Semitism in showing how Christianity inherited Jewish patterns of sociality, of which niceness is an example. Christian niceness is unexceptional and even derivative, as it is based on Jewish teachings.

In *The Religion of Duty* (1905), Felix Adler, who renounced Judaism in 1876 when he founded the New York Society for Ethical Culture, argues that Christian sociality is a contradiction in terms, since Christianity is "clearly anti-worldly" in its attitude, by which he means that Christianity "seeks to exalt men by wooing them away from the world." In contrast to the Christian promise of transcendence and immortality, Judaism focuses on the actual world, with its emphasis on righteousness, justice, and law, together with its social dimension. Like Stowe and Stanton, Adler acknowledges Jesus's influence in terms of his ability to persuade others through his charming personality, and Adler wants to explore the basis of his charisma—"to grasp the subtle essence of that charm"—with its ability to convert "the most heterogeneous nations" through various historical epochs. The key to Jesus's charm, according to Adler, lies in his ability to exemplify the basic tenets of "Love thy neighbor." "'Thy neighbor thou shalt love as thyself,' was written by [Hebrew Prophets], and 'Have we not all one Father, has not one God created us all.'"[133] In showing how the Hebrew Bible contains an ethics of niceness, Adler not only aligns progressive Judaism with Liberal Christianity, but also counters the anti-Semitic stereotype of Jews as Christ-killers with an alternative image of Jewish neighborliness. Both Levy and Adler want to normalize Jewishness and counter its marginal status by showing how integral Jewishness is to the basic tenets of American niceness.

Despite differences in their respective arguments about Jesus and his niceness, what ultimately unites the progressive Jew with the liberal Christian is a shared interest in the charm of Jesus's personality as a powerful force of persuasion. This interest in the nice Jesus continues in the twenty-first century in the form of "the power of nice," a phrase coined by two advertising executives to describe carrot management skills, in which positive affirmation is seen as the key to productivity and profitability. This association between Jesus's charm and the advertising industry was established as early as the 1920s in Bruce Barton's bestseller *The Man Nobody Knows: A Discovery of the Real Jesus* (1925). Barton, an advertising executive and liberal Christian, turns Jesus into a marketing expert. "The parable of the Good Samaritan," Barton writes, "is the greatest advertisement of all time."[134] Jesus became the corporate American ad man, the master of the art of persuasion who could sell a parable like Barton could sell a book.

Although one trajectory of Christian niceness leads to an emergent advertising culture, it would be a mistake to reduce the Christology of niceness to Madison Avenue. It was and continues to be a far more multivalent sign. Whether Jesus is domesticated (Stowe), depressive (Phelps), an imprisoned socialist (Debs), or a lynched prisoner (Du Bois), all four types depict niceness as dangerous. In doing so, they challenge the status quo, including institutional Christianity, through what Adam Phillips and Barbara Taylor call "the subversive implications of *caritas*."[135] Niceness replaces the conventions of authority with alternative forms that are more humble and less masterful.

But what happens to niceness when the concept shifts from Jesus to women? Where Jesus's niceness threatens to undermine normative masculinity with the specter of effeminacy, it has a normalizing function for women. Christian niceness as a form of social etiquette reinforces the feminine through prescribed behavior. In moving from the Victorian Jesus to Victorian women, the next chapter tells the nineteenth-century story of feminine niceness, whose history is just as contested as its religious counterpart.

4

Feminine Niceness

> She has to please men if she is to succeed in her life as a woman.
>
> Simone de Beauvoir, *The Second Sex* (1949)

FOR A YOUNG WOMAN to be truly polite, she must take a lesson "in the school of Jesus Christ," wrote William Alcott in *The Young Woman's Guide to Excellence* in 1840. The "Saviour" represents, according to Alcott, "the purest specimen of good manners."[1] In his niceness, Jesus was both exceptional and exemplary, paradoxical traits that combine the sacred with the ordinary so that his divinity became accessible. Feminine niceness, by contrast, was mandated behavior, intended to typify women's conduct without the additional perk of being considered divine. Feminine niceness, moreover, kept women ordinary, typical, and conventional, but in order to be seen as normal, a woman had to behave like Jesus. In this sense, Christianity was as much about conduct as it was a system of belief; or to put it another way, belief was made visible through good manners.

Although the Cult of True Womanhood, with its four cardinal virtues—piety, purity, submission, and domesticity—was fading after the Civil War, its behavioral legacy epitomized in the implied social commandment of most women's conduct books—*thou shalt be agreeable*—was still very much alive. Even with the emergence of the New Woman in the late nineteenth century, which introduced more athletic and independent female types, there was nevertheless an affective dimension that defined ideal womanhood as "the gift to please."[2]

Niceness has been so deeply imbricated in the construction of the feminine and particularly, though not exclusively, with white womanhood that it is impossible to imagine being nice as distinct from being feminine. To be a woman in the nineteenth century was to be amiable, cheerful, and pleasant. The holy trinity of femininity depended on having a pliable temper, being gentle and always conciliating, characteristics that repeatedly surface in the etiquette manuals of the period. All three of these attributes emphasize the importance of accommodating to the wishes of others, a flexibility that works at an interpersonal level, but also more generally in terms of assimilating to a cultural script of gendered norms. Sarah Hale, who edited *Godey's Lady Book* for over forty years, wrote in *Manners; or, Happy Homes and Good Society All the Year Round* (1868) that the "first maxim of politeness is to be agreeable to everybody, even at the expense of one's own comfort." The following year, Reverend Daniel Wise, who authored *Guide to the Savior*, offered similar advice: "Breathe a kindly feeling for all . . . Live to scatter flowers of joy in every path you tread,—to be a golden beam of soft and mellow light in every home you visit. Aim to move as a loving seraph in every circle."[3] Published in the immediate aftermath of the Civil War, both books depict women as the domestic ambassadors of joy whose task was to heal the nation by spreading good cheer and cultivating fellow feeling. By being agreeable to everybody, women modeled a form of sociality that would overcome sectional animosities as well as personal grief.

Feminine niceness was not just a postwar panacea. Fifty years after the Civil War, a woman's moral duty still consisted of being the "sunshine in the home." In *Sunshine on Life's Highway*, part of the burgeoning genre of inspirational and self-help literature in the early twentieth century, James Henry Potts, a Methodist minister, reminds women that their mission is "to show joy, to radiate happiness, to cast light upon dark days," which a woman does "by rightly using her talent for pleasing." Pleasing is largely conveyed through a woman's smile, an attribute that has the ability to "embellish an inferior face and redeem an ugly one."[4] A woman's smile was considered the very foundation of Victorian society by implying stability, order, and contentment. "The whole fabric of civilization rested," according to the

New Woman writer Ella Hepworth Dixon, on the "acquiescent feminine smile."[5] A woman's smile was expected to produce an atmosphere
of cheerfulness that assured others that she consented to her own
subordination.

As with the African American smile, the "feminine smile" reassured
those in power that the subordinates feel only gratitude and happiness,
a point that second-wave feminist Marilyn Frye would make a century
later in noting that "[i]t is often a requirement upon oppressed people
that we smile and be cheerful. If we comply, we signify our docility and
our acquiescence in our situation." Compliance can also be a masquerade, functioning as a veil that conceals one's contempt for others as
in Constance Fenimore Woolson's epistolary confession to Henry James
in 1882: "I like so few people! Though I pass for a constantly smiling,
ever-pleased person! My smile is the basest hypocrisy."[6]

What differentiates feminine niceness from the other forms of niceness discussed thus far is that feminine niceness has to be taught and
continually practiced, hence the number of etiquette manuals dedicated to this purpose. Where Jesus's kindness was intrinsic to his
divine nature, and black amiability was understood as an essential
trait of being African, and Native American hospitality described a
bygone custom relegated to the Puritan past, feminine niceness represents a form of disciplined behavior that women had to aspire toward.
It did not refer to an essential character trait but to a cultural ideal that
had to be continually perfected through socialization.

In *Femininity* (1984), Susan Brownmiller describes the benefits of
assuming the feminine role: "The world smiles favorably on the feminine woman: it extends little courtesies and minor privilege. Yet the
nature of this competitive edge is ironic, at best, for one works at femininity by accepting restrictions, by limiting one's sights, by choosing
an indirect route, by scattering concentration and not giving one's all
as a man would to his own, certifiably masculine, interests." To be
feminine, Brownmiller elaborates, requires "a grand collection of com-
promises, large and small, that she simply must make in order to
render herself a successful woman."[7] The successful woman is one
who pleases others and whom others find pleasing; she both smiles
and is smiled upon. But what holds the feminine in place is the fear of
being perceived as unfeminine, or in nineteenth-century parlance, to
be seen as an "unsexed" or "mannish" woman.

According to Brownmiller, "femininity operates as a value system of niceness, a code of thoughtfulness and sensitivity." Niceness denotes the behavior that gives femininity its form. They share a basic commonality: both need to be continually performed and enacted. A woman cannot rest on past laurels but instead has to keep proving her feminine prowess as well as her niceness. Neither are ever guaranteed but always bestowed. As sociologist Greer Litton Fox argues, niceness is an *"achieved* rather than ascribed status," which is to say that women are under pressure to demonstrate their niceness anew in each social situation, since "one's identity as a 'lady' or a 'nice girl' is never finally confirmed."[8] As "a standard for and a goal of behavior," feminine niceness is simultaneously an ideal and an expectation, a paradox that points to its impossibility. And yet its ideological power stems from women's need for "continual compliance," a repetition of behavior that never actually reaches its goal.[9]

But unlike Jesus's amiability, considered to be a reliable aspect of his personality, feminine niceness was feared to be under threat. With the rise of the suffragette movement and women's call for equality, articles appeared in the mainstream press bemoaning the "loss of female amiability" and "feminine sweetness."[10] A cartoon from 1905 depicts an enraged Susan B. Anthony chasing after former President Grover Cleveland, trying to hit him over the head with an umbrella in response to Cleveland's controversial article in the *Ladies Home Journal* recommending that the middle-class women readers of the popular magazine stay away from the women's rights movement.[11] Cleveland went on to suggest that women ought to remain at home by the cradle and not meddle in public affairs. Public involvement would jeopardize femininity, an anxiety that found visual form in anti-suffrage postcards in the United States and the United Kingdom that mocked women activists for being undesirable and unappealing to men, a precursor to the ugly feminist stereotype. To be nice also meant to be nice looking, and anti-suffragette ideologues invoked ugliness, and particularly, the figure of the mannish lesbian as a way to discipline women politically and socially. The suffragette movement, moreover, tested not only the limits of the state but also the affective limits of feminine behavior, anticipating Marilyn Frye's observation that "anything but the sunniest countenance exposes us to being perceived as mean, bitter, angry or dangerous."[12]

Anxieties about the end of feminine niceness actually appeared long before the suffragette movement, thus illustrating the instability of this concept. At the start of the nineteenth century, feminine niceness was already considered conditional and fleeting, mirroring clichés about women as fickle and changeable. In 1806, an article entitled "On the Influence of Women" anticipated that gender equality would be the death knell of feminine charm: "[B]y becoming his rival, she would only lose that feminine sweetness, that amiable debility, and that retiring

Charles Lewis Bartholomew cartoon featuring Susan B. Anthony hitting former President Grover Cleveland over the head with an umbrella as Uncle Sam laughs in the background (1905). Reproduced from *The Minneapolis Journal* (Minneapolis: April 26, 1905). Cartoon Drawings Collection, Library of Congress Prints and Photographs Division, Washington, D.C., LC-DIG-ds-05624.

modesty, which form her empire."[13] The phrase "amiable debility" is especially noteworthy for the way it approvingly casts feminine niceness as a hindrance, emphasizing that amiability comes not from a position of strength but rather of weakness. By 1854, proslavery ideologue George Fitzhugh would similarly turn subordination into a strength: "So long as she is nervous, fickle, capricious, delicate, diffident and dependent, man will worship and adore her," since her "weakness is her strength, and her true art is to cultivate and improve that weakness."[14] Feminine niceness was a double-edged sword. What made a woman inferior also made her desirable. Adoration rewarded those who acquiesced.

There was, however, a price to be paid for being agreeable. The nineteenth century idealized feminine sweetness while at the same time understanding that such an ideal was also toxic. The feminine imperative to be nice actually made women sick, psychologically and physically. In an 1874 essay on "The Education of American Girls," Anna Brackett noted that a "thoroughly strong, able-bodied woman is almost an unknown ideal in American society."[15] In 1888, Susan B. Anthony wondered in a letter to a friend, "if it is woman's real, true nature always to abnegate self." Feminists began to question whether women's physical and behavioral weakness was natural or ideological. Women had internalized the debilitating script of femininity that had stunted their own growth. Harriet Beecher Stowe's grandniece Charlotte Perkins Gilman described femininity in terms of "the retarded development of [the] mother" as well as "the aborted development of women." The nineteenth-century investment in progress had found its limit in women, whose maturation to adulthood was characterized through tropes of malformation and arrested development. In 1884, Henry Adams explored femininity as a disability in his novel *Esther*, whose eponymous character "like most women, was timid, and wanted to be told when she could be bold with perfect safety."[16] Esther is based in part on Adams's wife, Clover Adams, who committed suicide in 1885 after a long bout of depression, a year after the publication of *Esther*. Training women like Esther to obey and become dependent upon outside authority illustrates how women become "dwarfed in capacity," according to early women's suffrage campaigner Matilda Gage, and are turned into "a retarding force in civilization."[17]

These examples taken from the nineteenth century point to the fact that U.S. Victorians already had a sense of femininity as mutilation, to use Simone de Beauvoir's mid-twentieth century metaphor.[18] As historian Douglas Baynton demonstrates, the concept of disability has been a powerful way in which women and minorities have been historically assigned inferior status. Just as Joan Scott maintains that gender is a "constitutive element of social relations," so Baynton has compellingly claimed that disability has been an important "marker of hierarchical relations."[19] That feminine niceness was commonly called an "amiable debility" illustrates how gender, disability, and race were intertwined discourses that maintained women's inferior status within the confines of what was considered natural and normal behavior. Femininity as disability was also a highly contested notion. Proslavery ideologues such as Fitzhugh argued for women's weakness and frailty to maintain normative notions of sexual difference, while feminists like Matilda Gage and Charlotte Perkins Gilman described women's development as a form of disability in order to make a larger case about the unnaturalness of women's socialization. If the fetters of inferiority were removed, they argued, girls could become healthy and well-adjusted women.

A fundamental claim of this chapter is that post–Civil War American women writers from Harriet Beecher Stowe, Louisa May Alcott, and Elizabeth Stuart Phelps to Jane Addams and Ida B. Wells explored a range of affects from grief and anger to disappointment and bitterness that were not typically seen within the narrow parameters of feminine propriety. Specifically, this chapter demonstrates how they grappled with the mandate for niceness as a fundamental attribute of normative femininity in ways that are not either clearly triumphant or destructive. They did not create ideal characters that heroically conquer and transcend the brutalizing effects of feminization. Instead, their narratives are often inconsistent, messy, and contradictory in ways that illustrate the difficulty of the feminine—and its social manifestation as niceness—without necessarily resolving its conflicts.

What unites these writers is that they share a highly pragmatic approach that is at once a critique as well as an affirmation. Their dissatisfaction with feminine niceness did not mean its rejection. To use a domestic cliché, they did not throw the baby out with the bathwater. Instead, they grappled with its limitations while teasing out its possibilities, however modest. In this sense, nineteenth-century U.S.

feminism represents a distinctly "unspectacular feminism," to quote
Nina Baym, as it emerged within a Victorian mindset that underscored
personal relationships where duty, self-control, and sacrifice were necessary ways to negotiate a harsh and often disappointing world.[20]

To illustrate the multiaccentual and dialectical dimensions of feminine niceness as both damaging and generative, this chapter argues
that some women writers after the Civil War developed a critique as
well as a reparative reading of their own socialization. Critique in this
context demonstrates how women recognized and addressed the toxicity of their own socialization, while Eve Kosofky Sedgwick's concept
of reparative reading allows for an exploration of how women retained
aspects of feminine niceness as a language of attachment, comfort, and
healing. On the one hand, feminine niceness functions as a behavioral
corollary to the corset that restricts the realm of possibility for women
by rewarding those who opt for "the smiles of society."[21] Long before
Simone de Beauvoir, nineteenth-century women already had an understanding of feminization as a form of mutilation. They acknowledged
the aggression embedded in feminine amiability. At the same time,
however, these writers understood that feminine niceness comprised
an ethical practice that provided a sense of social belonging and inter-
connectedness in a world that was rapidly becoming industrialized,
segmented, and atomized. This reparative understanding of feminine
niceness was not a naïve and guileless position but one that went
through critique and came out the other side. A reparative reading, as
Ellis Hanson notes, comes out of a depressive position of psychic
damage, and it "picks up the fragments to construct a sustainable
life."[22] For late nineteenth-century feminist writers, the ideological
and historical baggage of feminine niceness still contained the basis of
a social vision that emphasized the importance of solidarities, alliances, and interpersonal bonds.

More interested in critique than a reparative reading, the modernist
daughters of Victorian mothers profoundly understood femininity as a
pathology epitomized in the figure of the "angel in the house," which
Virginia Woolf defined as "intensely sympathetic," "immensely
charming" and "utterly unselfish." She elaborated, "If there was a
chicken, she took the leg; if there was a draft she sat in it—in short she
was so constituted that she never had a mind of her own, but preferred
to sympathize always with the minds and wishes of others."[23] Woolf's

contemporary Willa Cather similarly warned that such a feminine ideal was actually a form of self-effacement. Psychoanalyst Helene Deutsch gave scientific weight to this claim by noting that to be feminine was to be a masochist. The two are inextricably intertwined. There is a fundamental pathology to the feminine that defines women's behavior as passive, self-abnegating, and long-suffering, or to use Deutsch's own terms, "feminine masochism" and "feminine passivity."[24] From Woolf's "angel in the house" to Deutsch's analytic terms, the pathology of feminine niceness was powerfully named, diagnosed, and critiqued.

Understanding feminine niceness as a pathology has also informed an influential and long-standing account of feminist literary history that views nineteenth-century femininity as negative and debilitating. In *The Feminization of American Culture* (1977), Ann Douglas describes nineteenth-century American women as "oppressed and damaged" and claims that the influence they exerted on their society "was not altogether beneficial." "The cruelest aspect of the process of oppression," argues Douglas, "is the logic by which it forces its objects to be oppressive in turn, to do the dirty work of their society in several senses."[25] Women, in other words, were not only the victims of a sexist society that curtailed the possibility of realizing their full potential, but they also reproduced this toxicity by fitting their daughters and their daughters' daughters into the ideological corset of femininity. Two years later, Sandra Gilbert and Susan Gubar would publish *The Madwoman in the Attic* (1979), an influential study that carries on Ann Douglas's daughterly metaphor to express the anxiety surrounding female authorship as "profoundly debilitating." Their book, like Douglas's, is a caveat to the celebratory praise surrounding the newly constructed feminist literary canon. One should be wary about glorifying nineteenth-century women writers, they warn, for they come out of a literary tradition not of nurturing literary foremothers but of stern patriarchal fathers, and the literature of their "inferiorized" daughters contains the "germ of a dis-ease or at any rate, a disaffection, a disturbance, a distrust, that spreads like a stain throughout the style and structure of much literature by women."[26] One can only appreciate women's literary accomplishments by acknowledging the "infection in the sentence," a phrase that Gilbert and Gubar borrow from Emily Dickinson. The task of the feminist literary critic was to identify these germs and infections to understand the aesthetic forms that disaffection and distrust took.

Although this strain of feminist literary criticism created an important space in which to recover female authorship that cast new light on Victorian literature, there was, as Rita Felski observed in *Literature After Feminism,* a tendency toward projection, where feminist scholars saw in Victorian women writers their own struggles working in a patriarchal society. "Their description of Victorian women struggling against a repressive society to find their true selves often made these women sound remarkably like American feminists of the 1970s." This generation of critics created literary foremothers "very much after their own heart." They understood Victorian women writers as protofeminists, "unconsciously rebelling against their own confinement."[27] The feminist critic embarked on a form of reading dedicated to exposing the unconscious rebellion of the Victorian foremother and turning it into a conscious act of resistance for the feminist literary critic. Second-wave feminism's preoccupation with the nineteenth century was itself a revolt against the feminine, epitomized in Shulamith Firestone's evocative call for a *"smile boycott"* [original emphasis].[28] It illustrates the extent to which the Victorian "angel in the house" continued to haunt and influence feminist literary scholarship in the 1970s.

The structure of this chapter in many ways reflects the second-wave feminist gesture of looking backward in order to go forward. I begin with figures from the turn of century, such as Elizabeth Stuart Phelps, before looking further back into the nineteenth century toward their literary foremother Harriet Beecher Stowe, who was one of the central architects of feminine niceness and argued, like Louisa May Alcott, that it should be a behavioral standard for women and men, an equal opportunity socializer. This points to a fundamental connection between feminine niceness and American niceness, more generally, in that American niceness was always already feminized. Feminization should not be limited solely to women but should shape what Charlotte Perkins Gilman called "androcentric culture." Where feminization for Ann Douglas refers to the sentimentalism of nineteenth-century culture, with Calvinist intellectual toughness giving way to feminine anti-intellectual frivolity, feminization at its best for Stowe and others refers to a more positive form of socialization, one based on nonmarket values such as compassion and caring that tempered the cutthroat climate of laissez-faire capitalism. Feminine niceness, as a desirable attribute for both men and women, would become the social glue that would counter alienation with a sense of social connectedness.

These same writers, however, and particularly Elizabeth Stuart Phelps and Louisa May Alcott, also understood that the socialization of feisty girls into nice ladies represents a brutal process of what Pierre Bourdieu calls "symbolic violence," in which social structures of domination become embedded in the bodies of the dominated, "often unwittingly, sometimes unwillingly."[29] The dominated contribute to their own domination by tacitly accepting the limits imposed in terms of bodily emotions (shyness, anxiety, guilt) or passions and sentiment (love, admiration, respect). The writers in this chapter attempt to maneuver within these limits, while also challenging them at strategic moments, particularly in the case of Ida B. Wells. They also consent to them in ways that are both honest and instructive. To show the continuities and discontinuities between the fictional writers and their nonfictional counterparts, the chapter will then shift from mid-nineteenth century writers (Phelps, Stowe, and Alcott) to late nineteenth and early twentieth century reformers and social activists, such as Jane Addams and Ida B. Wells, to explore what happens to feminine niceness when it moves from fictional worlds to actual ones, when the context alters from individual characters and interpersonal relationships to more collective forms of sociality.

Memories of a Dutiful Daughter: Elizabeth Stuart Phelps

Whether Victorian women were mothers, daughters, or sisters, they were expected to subordinate their own desires and ambitions for the needs of their family. The dutiful daughter, like the good wife, was expected to live for others. This was largely an antebellum ideal, epitomized in Lydia Sigourney's short story "The Good Daughter" (1837), where little Ellen, after the death of her mother, sacrifices her own needs, including the need to grieve, in order to attend to those of her father. "[W]hen she saw her father looking so sad, she thought it was her duty to try to comfort him; and when he came in tired from his work, she would set a chair for him, and speak pleasantly to him as her mother used to do."[30] With the exception of Louisa May Alcott, who I will discuss later, there is no other American writer in the latter half of the nineteenth century whose identity centered so fundamentally on being a daughter than Elizabeth Stuart Phelps. Daughters figure in her fiction but more prominently in her autobiography, her biography of her father, as well as in her short fiction and essays, where she offers advice to young women who want to leave home to broaden their horizons but feel guilty about doing so. Daughters also figure metaphorically in her depiction of a divided female psyche, which she describes in terms of a "civil war of a dual nature" torn between duty and independence.

Phelps increasingly reflected on the daughterly role as she became older, especially after her father, theologian Austin Phelps, died in 1890. After his death, she went on to write *Austin Phelps: A Memoir* (1891) as well as her autobiography, *Chapters from a Life* (1896). Not unlike Phelps's first and best-selling novel, *Gates Ajar* (1868), which dealt with the afterlife and the process of grieving a loved one (in this case, the protagonist's brother, who was slain in the Civil War), her autobiographical writing in the 1890s was a form of grief-work, where she acknowledges the pain of losing her mother at the age of eight years old. Phelps's mother, who died three months after giving birth to her third child, had requested that her infant son be baptized at her funeral. The mother's funeral also signaled Phelps's own baptism, when she changed her name from Mary Gray to her mother's married name, Elizabeth Stuart Phelps. By taking her name, Phelps could keep her mother close, sustaining the intimacy of the mother-daughter bond that had been abruptly severed, while also occupying the discomfiting position of the wifely daughter, as in Sigourney's "Good Daughter," who is emotionally available to her grieving father as the one who listens.

In taking her mother's name, Phelps was also assuming her mother's vocation as a writer. Her mother's literary career spanned just three years (1851–1853), and her first book, *Sunny-Side*, sold 40,000 copies in its first two years. In *Chapters from a Life*, Phelps recounts how her mother would correct proof sheets one moment and then paint apostles for her children's first bible lesson the next. The struggle between being a popular writer and a tired mother, "crooning a sick child," ultimately ended her life.

> Her last book and her last baby came together, and killed her. She lived one of those rich and piteous lives such as only gifted women

know; torn by the civil war of the dual nature which can be given to women only. It was as natural for her daughter to write as to breathe; but it was impossible for her daughter to forget that a woman of intellectual power could be the most successful of mothers.[31]

Phelps's language is disturbingly frank: The book and the baby killed her. The effort to be all things to all people while at the same time pursuing her own creative ambitions drained the mother of energy and accelerated her death. Phelps describes her mother's decline and eventual death as if recounting a battle: "The struggle killed her, but she fought till she fell." This theme appears in the memoir of her father, "It is more than possible that if she had never written a book, the wife of his youth might have lived to share his age."[32]

What ultimately destroyed Phelps's mother was living up to an impossible ideal of female amiability and the multiple forms this imperative took in terms of hospitality, motherhood, and wifely duties. Interestingly, grief for her mother occupies a significant portion of the memoir about her father, going so far as to blame their marriage for her mother's early death at the age of thirty-seven. By devoting her life to pleasing Austin Phelps, Phelps (the mother) sacrificed her own: "[U]nder the movement of a nature like hers a woman may make a man divinely happy. But she may die in trying to do so."[33] Expressing resentment toward the father in a memoir devoted to him suggests that Phelps (the Good Daughter) grieves not only for her mother but also for her own childhood, which was spent trying to please a grieving and depressed father. She can only begin grieving properly for her mother once her father is dead. Phelps learned from an early age that feminine niceness could be deadly. By continuously giving to others, the mother had nothing left for herself, and the young daughter witnessed firsthand the tragedy of the "angel in the house."

Having seen the tragic implications of wifely niceness, how then does Phelps negotiate the demands of daughterly niceness? How much should a daughter sacrifice for the sake of her parents, or in Phelps's case, for her father? To handle the demands of the "Good Daughter," Phelps imagines the female psyche in terms of two different kinds of daughters: "the drawing-room girl" and "the girl in the garden." In Phelps's penultimate novel, *Confessions of a Wife* (1902), she defines these two types through an indoor/outdoor binary. Where the drawing-room girl "sits beside her father . . . doing the proper thing, saying what everybody says," the girl in the garden "disowned them, and didn't care a raindrop what they thought of her." By dividing the role of the daughter into two contrary types, Phelps was able to create a space for daughterly dissidence, where the Good Daughter could go to experience a temporary reprieve from the social gaze of propriety. These two competing types constitute the conflicting psyche of the protagonist, Marna Trent, who describes her own internal twoness, saying, "one girl stands off and judges the other girl." As a feminist counterpart to Du Bois's double consciousness, Phelps refuses to idealize either location since the garden is still a restricted space: "Why, if I were a man, I should be outside, in the clubs, the streets, the theaters,—God knows where,—doing bohemian things, watching people in the slums, going to queer places with policemen . . . But I am a girl; and I stay in the garden. And that's bad enough, for the other girls don't care about gardens."[34] The garden is still a female enclosure that permits a slight degree of autonomy but not nearly the amount of freedom permitted a man in the streets. Perhaps this is as far as a young woman who wants a degree of autonomy can go without incurring parental disapproval or societal wrath. That Phelps articulates the female psyche through the metaphor of daughters in a novel about a wife illustrates how the two roles, wife and daughter, were blurred in Phelps's own imaginative life.

The boundary defining daughterly duty and freedom preoccupied Phelps for much of her life. How can a daughter realize her full potential without alienating her father? As early as the 1870s, Phelps addressed this theme in two essays that appeared in *The Independent*, encouraging young women to break from the restrictions of feminine niceness. In "Unhappy Girls" (1871), Phelps describes women's conformity to type as a behavioral deformity: "Let us cease this foolish prattle about the sweet seclusion and the modest shelter of a deformed and wasted and wasting existence. Send your girls away from home. It will do them good. Urge them into the world." To keep girls at home is deforming because it stunts their growth and wastes their potential. "Individuality is the birthright of each human soul. This society crushes [it] out of women."[35] Six months later, Phelps published a related essay, "A Talk to the Girls" (1872), where she questions the daughter's role as the domestic burden-bearer for her family. She speaks to the Good Daughter directly: "Wash dishes till you die; and the world will leave you in peace." What should a woman do? "Not the thing which you can do most peacefully," she writes, "not the thing which you can do most easily . . . nor the thing which is expected of you, because it is expected of you."[36] Avoiding conflict by taking the road of least resistance is a recipe for disaster, Phelps warns. And she urges her young readers to assert their independence.

When a dutiful daughter has to confront her parents and tell them that her life will not be spent in domestic care, Phelps's advice becomes a bit implausible as she tries to reconcile confrontation with feminine niceness. This daughterly rebellion against parental authority can still, Phelps insists, be done sweetly: "Draw the line respectfully and affectionately between their convictions and yours."[37] Phelps's advice centers on how to fight the limitations of feminine niceness through feminine niceness, allowing the amiable daughter to say no to her parents with a firm but affectionate smile. This strategy, of course, assumes that the girl's parents will be amenable to such an arrangement, if the daughter approaches the topic delicately and kindly. But what if feminine niceness fails to persuade the parents? What should the Good Daughter do then? These are precisely the questions that Phelps cannot answer because she is too entangled in the very conventions of feminine niceness to address conflict and confrontation explicitly.

William James's Pragmatism and the Amiable Woman

Phelps's strategy to defuse conflict through the conventions of feminine amiability bears an uncanny resemblance to William James's description of pragmatism, a philosophy noted for its ability to accommodate conflict and negotiate limits. In "What Pragmatism Means" (1904), James defines pragmatism as an affable woman: "You see already how democratic she is. Her manners are as various and flexible, her resources as rich and endless, and her conclusions as friendly as those of mother nature." Pragmatism assumes the character of the Nice American Girl, who exudes a democratic personality: She has "no prejudices whatever, no obtrusive dogmas, no rigid canons of what shall count as proof. She is completely genial." Scholars have noted how James's metaphors are concrete and derived from everyday life, such as "truth's cash value."[38] James's choice of the amiable woman suggests the extent to which feminine niceness was a model for how niceness was conceptualized and talked about in the nineteenth century more generally. But James takes this feminine attribute, considered by some to be an "amiable debility" or a social ornament or "charm," and makes it an integral strategy of survivability in the modern world. Plasticity and adaptability allow pragmatism to function effectively in times of conflict and crisis as the "happy harmonizer." Sustaining continuity while adapting to change, pragmatism creates a bridge between the old and the new so as to minimize conflict: "New truth is always a go-between, a smoother-over of transitions."[39] James's choice of the amiable woman describes a philosophy as well as a worldview devoted to maneuvering in a dangerous and conflict-ridden world with a minimum of disagreement and obstruction. James, who opposed the rise in American militarism that resulted in the Spanish American War of 1898, saw in the conventions of femininity a constellation of traits that were essential in a modern world of flux and indeterminacy. To survive in this increasingly complex world, one has to reconceive authority as flexible and yielding, as something that is able to defuse conflict through diplomacy.

Pragmatism as a figure of female amiability recognizes the importance of limits. The genial woman is not "namby-pamby" and "wishy washy," James argues, nor does she simply say "yes, yes" in a gesture of unconditional agreeableness. In the second lecture of *Pragmatism*, James insists that pragmatism knows when to say no.[40] It represents a mixture of kindness and assertiveness, a notion of feminine niceness with boundaries. Rather than a figure of acquiescence and subordination, the amiable woman, for James, signifies a modern form of power as peaceable yet authoritative. She is emblematic not only of Jamesian pragmatism but also of democratic authority generally, an alternative to Theodore Roosevelt's hypermasculine Rough Riders.

Harriet Beecher Stowe on Repression

The nineteenth-century genealogy of Jamesian pragmatism typically begins with Ralph Waldo Emerson, but this elides an equally important lineage that has its origins in Harriet Beecher Stowe. As I argued in the previous chapter, Stowe was a major architect of the Christology of niceness in giving liberal Christianity a figurative form through the nice Jesus. She also feminized the authority of the state through a portrait of Lincoln, who embodied "passive power." For Stowe, and later for William James, amiability became a way to reconfigure authority in terms that were not defined by aggressivity and violence but by opposite traits such as flexibility and influence. Lincoln was a "strong man," but it was a strength "swaying to every influence, yielding on this side and on that to popular needs, yet tenaciously and inflexibly bound to carry its great end."[41] For both James and Stowe, and later for Jane Addams, whose father considered Lincoln an acquaintance, niceness—and specifically feminine niceness—was a way to reconfigure authority for the modern era.

But when shifting from Stowe's writing on Jesus and Lincoln to her postbellum sketches on domestic matters in *Little Foxes: Or, The Insignificant Little Habits Which Mar Domestic Happiness* (1866), one notices a change in her views on feminine niceness. She becomes more circumspect and less celebratory. Unlike Jesus's niceness, feminine niceness is more fraught and even debilitating. Full of Christian didacticism but without the figure of Jesus, Stowe's message in *Little Foxes* is clear: The phrase "little foxes" refers to the minor acts of thoughtlessness that accrue over time and have major consequences. "They seem to us too trifling to be remembered in church; they are like the red spiders on plants,—too small for the perception of the naked eye."[42] Where *Uncle Tom's Cabin* addresses systemic injustice and prophesies cataclysmic conflict, *Little Foxes*, published immediately after the Civil War, turns to the banal moments of disagreement in everyday life. It focuses on how we sustain relationships over time, navigating the joys and pitfalls of domestic attachments.

For Stowe, feminine niceness is potentially debilitating or therapeutic, depending on context. There is nothing inherent in amiability that makes it a debility, but it can certainly function in this way, especially among young wives. This is the subject of the third story in *Little Foxes*, entitled "Repression," which tells the story of a young married couple named John and Emmy. The story is told from the perspective of Emmy's older brother Chris, an old college friend of John's, whose name and manner bear an uncanny resemblance to Stowe's benevolent Christ. "Repression" narrates Emmy's decline from a state of marital bliss to deep depression, which begins when she and her husband move close to her in-laws in a New England town. Soon after their move, the tone of her letters to her brother becomes increasingly subdued, self-conscious, and measured. And yet despite this somber tone, Emmy only has positive things to say about her husband's mother and sisters. She refers to her mother-in-law as "such a good woman" and her sisters-in-law as "such nice women." In another letter, she describes the sisters as very kind "in their way" but then crosses out these words and writes over them "very kind indeed."[43] By carefully reading his sister's letters and noticing the points of self-censorship, Chris becomes increasingly concerned for his sister's well-being, and he decides to visit her. The empathetic brother becomes an analyst of sorts by detecting that the problem hinges on his sister's epistolary use of "nice" and "kind," terms that she. repeatedly invokes when describing her in-laws. Chris concludes to himself, "I am afraid these very nice people are slowly freezing and starving her."[44]

Stowe's narrator confides that there is a form of New England niceness that is excessively cold and severe, a niceness that can be compared to a white house "with all its window-blinds closed, with its neat white fences all tight and trim." Like the closed-up house, the inhabitants are exceedingly self-controlled, judgmental without saying a word, and living in an environment that has "not a wink or blink of life." Chris talks privately to his sister about the oppressive atmosphere of this "nice" home. Speaking to her brother face-to-face, Emmy is now able to confess all that she has had to repress in her letters: "What is the use of people's loving each other in this horridly cold, stingy, silent way?"[45] Chris describes them as "hopelessly crippled," emotionally stunted by their refusal to express affection. But what is of greater concern is the long-term impact of such an environment on his sister's loving nature: "[T]hey expect to weave, day after day, the fine cobweb lines of their cold system of repression around you, which will harden and harden, and tighten and tighten, till you are as stiff and shrouded as any of them." She cannot change her in-laws' habits through her warmth and amiability. Their wills are stronger, and they will ultimately transform her. The brother's advice is that his sister must forsake her feminine niceness and know when to say no, otherwise her own spirit will be crushed through excessive accommodation as the overly nice wife. "Do not always shrink and yield; do not conceal and assimilate and endeavor to persuade him and yourself that you are happy."[46] The traditional attributes of femininity that made her an appealing wife to begin with are here seen as poisonous and self-annihilating.

The brother's advice falls on deaf ears because Emmy's niceness has turned into a form of self-defeating masochism. Consequently, Chris speaks directly to her husband, John, to request that they move away from his family. Fortunately, the husband consents to move back to Emmy's hometown, resulting in her psychological transformation that allows her to regain her youthful vivacity and impulsive spirit. The final section of this short story is reserved for sermonizing, like so much of Stowe's fiction, and the moral of this story is that it is not enough to feel love; one also has to show it. Christianity requires an affective imperative—be demonstrative: "We can make it a Christian duty, not only to love, but to be loving,—not only to be true friends, but to *show* ourselves friendly."[47]

Revealingly, Stowe finds it easier to direct her final words toward undemonstrative Yankees—the inlaws should be nicer—rather than to the real failure: the overly nice wife who is too accommodating and is therefore nearly destroyed by the same behavioral mandate of femininity that made her an appealing prospect in the first place. Emmy's recovery is the result of her brother's actions rather than her own, since he literally speaks for her, which makes for a bittersweet end to Stowe's story. The actual moral of "Repression," which is ironically repressed by the story's happy ending, is that feminine amiability has a price that is potentially destructive to women and their families. In contrast to Jesus's niceness, which is unproblematic for Stowe, feminine niceness is far more complex. Like little foxes, feminine niceness may seem too trivial to be seen as a problem, but like the barely detectable red spider on a plant, it may eventually prove harmful.

Stowe's *We and Our Neighbors*: Feminine Niceness as "Mission Work"

Where Stowe explores the toxic aspects of feminine niceness in "Repression," she represents its therapeutic potential in her novel *We and Our Neighbors* (1873). The novel portrays a far more socially oriented understanding of feminine niceness as part of a Christian ethics of neighborliness. The protagonist, Eva Henderson (formerly Eva van Arsdel), a newlywed who comes from a respectable New York family, has just moved with her husband, Harry, into one of the unfashionable streets in New York City, while Harry starts out as an editor. Just as marriage converts Eva van Arsdel from a fashionable flirt to a Christian do-gooder in *My Wife and I* (the prequel to *We and Our Neighbors*), so she now converts strangers into friends as a way to transform the alienation of urbanization into the familiarity of neighborliness. For her, feminine niceness is "mission work," a politics of engagement that gradually brings disparate people together through sociality. If Little Eva hadn't died in *Uncle Tom's Cabin*, she would have grown up to be Eva Henderson in *We and Our Neighbors*. She is the Good Samaritan who converts through kindness. "Everybody is running to me, every hour," she admits, "I am consulter, sympathizer and adviser." Eva is the female incarnation of the nice Jesus, though without the humility. She is the sociable Jesus rather than the transcendent one, whose quotidian contact with others is the source of religious inspiration. "Conversion, when real, is a solution of all difficulties in our days as it was in those of the first apostles," writes Stowe, because it can lead to "permanent change of character."[48]

Stowe's *We and Our Neighbors* epitomizes the core nineteenth-century belief that sociality was women's business. To quote from an article on women's influence that appeared in 1851, it is women's responsibility *"to regulate the forms and control the habits of social life"* [original emphasis].[49] As Harry says to his wife, "That's what you women are for—at least such women as you. It's your mission to interpret differing natures—to bind, and blend, and unite." According to Stowe, women are naturally more sociable than men and therefore more capable of countering the fragmentation of the industrial age through communitarianism: "Women are naturally social and gregarious, and have very little experience of the kind of shyness that is the outer bark of many manly natures, in which they fortify all the more sensitive part of their being against the rude shocks of the world."[50] Feminine niceness signifies a therapeutic view of sociality that compensates for the alienation and loneliness of modern urban life by cultivating a communitarian ethos based on neighborliness.

Emmy in "Repression" and Eva Henderson in *We and Our Neighbors* illustrate antithetical notions of feminine niceness. One is damaging, while the other is therapeutic; one is self-destructive, while the other is self-affirming; one is a sign of pathological masochism, while the other is an example of what William James calls "healthy-mindedness." Where Emmy has taken the dictates of feminine niceness and turned them inward so that her own will has been destroyed, Eva shifts the ethos of femininity outward and turns it into a Christian social ethics, converting strangers into neighbors, where people are no longer afraid of each other but connected through friendship.

For Stowe, Eva is more than a good Christian woman; she also personifies a distinctly American form of feminine niceness that fuses the feminine with democratic sociability. Eva acquires her specifically American cast in a series of exchanges with an Englishman named Mr. Selby, who observes, "[T]he best class of American girls [has] that noble frank manner, that fearless giving forth of their inner nature, which comes from the atmosphere of a free democratic society."[51] Stowe translates Eva's feminine niceness into the hospitality of the American home, which is open and accessible (in contrast to the severe Yankee home in "Repression"). Eva conveys this democratic sensibility through her choice of home furnishings: "I always hate to drop very dark shades over my windows in the evening . . . I like to have the firelight of a pleasant room stream out into the dark, and look cheerful and hospitable outside; for that reason I don't like inside shutters."

Eva's femininity expresses a nascent consumerist ethos, where shopping and sociality become the twin functions of the middle-class housewife. She then goes on to oppose what she perceives as the antisocial English tradition of high stone walls with broken bottles on top to prevent anyone from climbing over them. Why should the sight of his trees or the odor of his flowers be denied to his poor neighbors? Mr. Selby defends the high stone walls as an expression of British privacy, but he is ultimately a foil in Stowe's plot whose purpose is to highlight Eva Henderson as the good democrat, who sees such walls as "the enemy of brotherly kindness and charity."[52] This transatlantic comparison of domiciles is a thinly veiled endorsement of American niceness, defined against its favorite bogeyman, the British class system.

In his review of *We and Our Neighbors*, Henry James considered the novel superficial and tedious, with the characters talking endlessly about home décor, plumbing, and new carpeting.[53] But the novel's emphasis on home décor draws an important analogy between American domesticity and feminine niceness (i.e., hospitality), with the nice home being equated with the nice woman in that they both aim to please and impress others. Nice homes and nice women also have something else in common: They are intended to be looked at. This conflation of the woman's body and her home was part of a more general trend in the latter half of the nineteenth century to link women's appearance and home decoration as the outward signs of inner character. The house is the personification of Stowe's ideal of the American woman: cultivated and tidy, which is to say, maintaining bourgeois standards of propriety while behaving in a warm and accessible (i.e., democratic) way. The American woman's demeanor and her domestic space are fully inscribed within class codes of good taste and proper conduct, while she denies through her friendliness that such codes are exclusive. After all, the curtains remain open at night, permitting passersby to catch a glimpse of her domestic idyll.

Stowe's version of feminine niceness as a form of Christian ethics inserts into industrialism those values that are in danger of disappearing: communitarian bonds of belonging, a belief in nurturing, and a commitment to others. But Eva Henderson's *caritas* is more compensatory than critical, in the sense that the novel offers a personal understanding of structural inequities that can be pacified through individual acts of caring. Interpersonal amiability can placate class tensions. Stowe's version of feminine niceness, therefore, functions in the service of a model of capitalism where profit can be reconciled with social bonds and exploitation can be mollified through niceness. Interpersonal relations—the female domain of sociality—can make capitalism more humane. Feminine niceness palliates the destructive effects of exploitation by making everyone feel neighborly; in this way, it sustains the status quo by countering alienation with geniality. You may not have much money, but at least you are invited to the Hendersons' parlor.

On the Limits of Niceness: Stowe's Rosebud Feminism

Whether it was liberal Christianity and the formation of the amiable Jesus or female sociality and the ethics of neighborliness, Harriet Beecher Stowe was a major theorist of American niceness. Through her narratives, she gave it form, content, and purpose. One could even say that it was her "mission work." But as William James's foundational metaphor suggests, there is a point when the amiable woman must say no. The limits of Stowe's own amiability are disclosed in an exchange she and her half-sister Isabel Hooker had with Elizabeth Cady Stanton over *The Revolution*, a feminist newspaper that Stanton and Susan B. Anthony founded in 1868. To garner greater support and respect for the publication, which addressed women's issues ranging from the vote to divorce and workers' rights, Stanton and Anthony sought Stowe's and Hooker's endorsement on the masthead nearly two years after its initial publication. Stowe expressed discomfort at the radical nature of the newspaper's title.

According to Stowe's biographer, Joan Hedrick, "They inquired of Stanton and Anthony whether the name might be changed to something a trifle less shocking to public taste."[54] Stanton was outraged at such a suggestion and what it implied in terms of the content, style, and political vision of the newspaper, and she wrote Anthony on December 28, 1869, insisting that they keep the name of their publication:

> As to changing the name of the *Revolution*, I should consider it a great mistake. If all these people who for twenty years have been afraid to call their souls their own begin to prune us and the *Revolution*, we shall become the same galvanized mummies they are. There could not be a better name than *Revolution* . . . A journal called *Rosebud* might answer for those who come with kid gloves and perfumes to lay immortal wreaths on the monuments which in sweat and tears others have hewn and built.[55]

Although not naming Stowe outright, Stanton certainly had her in mind when she defended the title of their newspaper to Anthony. But this distinction between "Revolution" and "Rosebud," the latter being Stanton's mocking alternative for a less offensive title, reveals a significant division in nineteenth-century feminism between those who wanted to challenge the boundaries of feminine propriety to varying degrees and those who wanted to work within the conventions of the feminine. Stowe's brand of feminism, which we might call "Rosebud feminism," signifies a "nice" form of social protest that is concerned with its own respectability and is deeply committed to Christian conventions of femininity. This type of feminism stays within the boundaries of good taste, much like Stowe's Eva Henderson, whether in aesthetic, religious, or behavioral terms.

Stowe's "Rosebud feminism," which was far tamer than her abolitionism, appears in her praise for another suffrage publication during this same time called *The Woman's Journal,* a long-running (1870–1917) periodical based in Boston, whose editors and contributors included such notable figures as Mary Livermore, Julia Ward Howe, Lucy Stone, Henry Blackwell, Thomas Wentworth Higginson, and William Lloyd Garrison. In contrast to *The Revolution,* which published articles (largely written by Stanton) on the rise of a woman's Ku Klux Klan in Georgia, the corruption of Wall Street, and the intensifying conflict between capital and labor, *The Woman's Journal* was the epitome of respectable feminism, often printing passages of biblical verse on the front page, as well as translations of poetry by Goethe, Herder, and other renowned European male poets. It included articles on the vote as well as pedantic essays endorsing conventional models of femininity, such as "A Nice Girl" (1871), a short diatribe that bemoans the disappearance of this female type: "There is nothing half so sweet in life, half so beautiful or delightful or so lovable, as a nice girl. Not a pretty or a dashing girl; but a nice girl."[56]

Louisa May Alcott: Editing as a Form of Feminization

When it came to women's writing, Stowe was deeply conservative, a tendency that becomes acutely apparent in her work as an editor. Although she criticized feminine niceness in the context of a vulnerable young wife in *Little Foxes,* she clearly policed the boundaries of female characterization when reading the work of younger women writers. She wanted American women writers to create nice American girls who were feisty and independent but also asexual. When Stowe read Louisa May Alcott's first novel, *Moods* (1864), a novel that was highly influenced by Brontëan themes of adulterous longing, female desire, and a woman's surrender to a powerful, charismatic man, Stowe was deeply critical. According to Janet Zehr, Stowe "attacked the morality of *Moods* in vague terms in a conversation with Thomas Niles," an editor who would later commission *Little Women.* When Alcott went to revise *Moods* in 1880, she implemented Stowe's suggestions, as Michelle Ann Abate has argued, by making "the new version more universally appealing by excising objectionable elements."[57] Alcott, in other words, sought to make *Moods* nicer by replacing the tragic ending with a happier one, where the heroine doesn't die but instead repents her adulterous longings, returns to her husband, and lives happily ever after, learning that "love and duty go hand in hand."[58]

The revised novel conforms to a Victorian template of feminine virtue and self-restraint that emphasizes repentance and warns against impulsivity. By rewriting the ending to fit with middle-class ideas of propriety, Alcott's revision of *Moods* can be seen as a form of assimilation, transforming a potentially explosive narrative about female desire into a formulaic story of a well-behaved, apologetic woman who marries out of duty. This transformation from a Brontëan-style novel to girls' fiction reflects at the level of narrative the process of feminization as a story of female assimilation to a conventional script of little womanhood.

A morality tale emerges from this editing anecdote, in which literary form mirrors Alcott's biography. Described by Bronson Alcott as his "dutiful daughter," Louisa May Alcott sought to please her literary mother, Stowe, as well as the class of readers who shared Stowe's literary sensibilities, by repenting her youthful rebellion and rewriting one of her most daring and introspective works so that it conformed to the dictates of feminine propriety. Alcott had to do at the level of literary form the same thing that was expected of her at the level of gender, namely, conform to type in order to please others. Like women generally, the novel as a commercial form was expected "primarily to please."[59] Where Stowe prescribed feminine niceness as a mandate for literary characterization, Alcott had a far more fraught relationship with feminine niceness, both in terms of characterization as well as in her own inclination to please. Stowe, moreover, could prescribe niceness without herself being crippled by the need to please, whereas Alcott never escaped this paradox. For Alcott, feminine niceness represented a powerfully normative force of socialization, which she initially questioned but ultimately accepted with resignation and a degree of bitterness.

This acquiescence to cultural norms can be seen in Alcott's revised edition of *Little Women* in 1880. The slang, regionalisms, and colloquialisms were replaced, according to Elaine Showalter, "by a blander, refined and 'ladylike' prose. Jo now calls her father 'Papa' rather than 'Pa.'" Editors omitted the New England vernacular expressions for a national audience, replacing "prim as a desk," for instance, with "prim

as I can." What is especially noteworthy is the transformation of
Marmee from (and here Showalter is quoting Alcott's original 1868
edition of *Little Women*) "a stout, motherly lady, with a 'can-I-
help-you' look about her which was truly delightful" to a tall, genteel
and fashionable figure in the 1882 version.[60] The refinement of prose
matched the refinement of feminine beauty. Similar to Emmy's cross-
outs in her letters to her brother in Stowe's "Repression," there is a
parallel between textual editing and social restraint evident in the
silence surrounding the second edition of *Little Women* in Alcott's
own letters and journals. Just as the revised language of the novel converts slang to a more ladylike style of prose, so *Little Women* narrates
the process of refinement that turns tomboys into little women. Jo
March freely uses slang, much to the disapproval of her sisters Amy
and Meg, who describe it as "so boyish" and "unlady-like." [61]

This gendered tension between ladylike diction and boyish slang,
including the frequent use of the slang term *nice*, enacts at the level
of speech precisely the tensions and conflicts that characterize Jo's difficult conversion from a feisty American Girl to Mrs. Bhaer, a well-
behaved married lady. Jo March demonstrates that feminization can be
done, at least to a limited extent, on her own terms, suggesting a degree
of flexibility and accommodation, where one could breathe a bit easier
in the ideological corset of little womanhood since it no longer appears
to fit so tightly. On the one hand, Jo March is an ideal in that she goes
through the socialization process with her feisty spirit still intact, but
on the other hand, her feistiness and independence seem to dissipate in
her married persona as Mrs. Bhaer, the protagonist in the sequels to
Little Women. The married Jo March is a far blander character, fully
domesticated and desexualized while promulgating a regime of feminine niceness for a new generation of girls.

The Feminization of Jo March

Little Women is about the feminization of Jo March, a process that is
synonymous with the word *nice*, as when Jo warns her friend Laurie,
"I am not quiet and nice." Although it is fine for Jo to describe Laurie
as a "nice boy," she rejects the use of that word to define herself.[62]
Why? The term *nice* is synonymous with the feminine, with the mandate to be agreeable to others. Nice girls are those who assume the

conventions of femininity and are rewarded by being considered "love-worthy," a term that appears in the novel as a euphemism for being desirable to men and therefore free from the fate of the spinster.

Feminist critics have been divided on *Little Women*, disagreeing on whether Jo March's transition from adolescence to young womanhood is tragic or inspirational. Judith Fetterley, one of Alcott's most astute critics, regards the novel as Alcott's personal civil war, torn between conflicting impulses about femininity and creativity. Ultimately, for Fetterley, Jo March ends the novel in "self-denial, renunciation, and mutilation." Alcott's biographer Martha Saxton considers Alcott's most famous novel to be "a regression for Louisa as an artist and as a woman," a position that is even more dramatically stated by Nina Auerbach, who claims that *Little Women* depicts a "pilgrimage to submission." Many feminist critics have concluded that *Little Women* marks a turning point in Alcott's own career, when she sold out, so to speak, to commercial success by writing standard girls' fiction. "They see the domestic drama of *Little Women*," according to Elaine Showalter, "as a capitulation to middle-class ideals of female self-sacrifice." But Showalter differs from this critical appraisal by attributing the novel's long-standing appeal to the fact that it is "both convincing and inspiring."[63]

Critical disagreement over *Little Women* and its protagonist Jo March raises important questions about how we interpret Victorian womanhood as a problem of feminine niceness. There is, moreover, a genealogy of feminism that can be traced through women's reflections on the feminine mandate to be nice, which would include Simone de Beauvoir, who saw in Jo March a "glimpse of my future self": "I identified myself passionately with Jo, the intellectual. Brusque and bony, Jo clambered up into trees when she wanted to read; she was much more tomboyish and daring than I was, but I shared her horror of sewing and housekeeping and her love of books." Not only did *Little Women* inspire the young de Beauvoir to be a writer, but Jo March, the intellectual, gave de Beauvoir the language with which to understand her strained and ambivalent relation to feminine niceness, in contrast to her sister and cousins, who seemed to master the cultural script of femininity with more ease and grace. Jo March taught de Beauvoir that one could understand a woman's life as an "endless disputation" with feminine niceness and as an ongoing argument with the conventions of femininity.[64]

Little Women also seems to have inspired many of Alcott's late Victorian readers. A fifteen-year-old Jane Addams confided to a friend that she read *Little Women* several times and "it never seems to grow old." Charlotte Perkins Gilman, who grew up poor once her father abandoned the family, appreciated that in Alcott's work "the heroes and heroines were almost always poor, and good, while the rich people were generally bad."[65] And Ida B. Wells listed Alcott among her favorite authors, alongside Charles Dickens and Charlotte Brontë. Only Edith Wharton disagreed. She was forbidden from reading Alcott's work due, in part, to the excessive use of slang, or as Wharton describes it: "[T]he children spoke bad English *without the author's knowing it.*" When Wharton finally did read *Little Women,* she was "exasperated by the laxities of the great Louisa."[66]

But Wharton was the exception. Most readers have appreciated how *Little Women* portrays the process of socializing girls into little women as fraught and difficult, but few readers, with the exception of de Beauvoir, have acknowledged explicitly Alcott's critique of feminization as a process largely implemented by sisters toward each other. More commonly, *Little Women* has been praised for celebrating sisterhood, as reflected in Jo's poem "In the Garret," where sisterhood is "Made by love's immortal power."[67] But *Little Women* also captures the aggression, hatred, and anger embedded in sisterly relationships. Alcott's best-loved novel, in other words, conveys the painful aspects of feminization, a process that is largely instigated and monitored not by the parents but by the youngest sister Amy, with her blond, bouncy curls and impeccable dress sense, who has mastered the performance of femininity with comparative ease. It is through her conflictual relationship with Amy that Jo expresses her anger and defiance at becoming a lady. Jo's acculturation into little womanhood doesn't happen without a fight, and her personal struggle with societal norms, which at times is expressed with remarkable humor, is experienced and dramatized through the intimacy of a sibling bond.

In *Siblings,* feminist psychoanalyst Juliet Mitchell notes how formative sibling relationships are and how they have been largely ignored in psychoanalytic literature. This is true in literary analysis as well, where the intergenerational dynamics between parent and child have been seen as more significant than lateral relations. But lateral relations, argues Mitchell, are precisely how socialization takes place within the home—one becomes a social being by becoming aware of where one stands in relation to others. The sibling relationship teaches a child how to see oneself through another's eyes, and in this sense, socialization bears an uncanny resemblance to feminization. But more than this, sibling relationships also teach one how to negotiate the power of antithetical feelings and how one can feel both aggression and affection for a sister or a brother. As Mitchell writes, "An actual sibling is considered important in allowing the access to hatred in a way that can be resolved so that sociality results. Siblings provide a way of learning to love and hate the same person."[68]

Although Alcott largely identified herself as a daughter and biographers have frequently emphasized the parent-child bond in studies of her life, Alcott's most famous novel focuses on the relationship of four sisters: Meg, Jo, Beth, and Amy.[69] *Little Women* is as much, if not more, about the lateral relationship of siblinghood than the vertical one of parent and child. In fact, the novel's opening pages describe a fight between Jo and Amy, with the latter criticizing Jo's use of slang and her boyish demeanor, saying, "I detest rude, unlady-like girls." Jo retorts by saying to her ultra-feminine sister, "I hate affected, niminy piminy chits."[70] The other two sisters act as mediators, with Meg, the eldest, assuming the role of mother and Beth, "the peace-maker," reassuring Jo that being a tomboy is just fine. This opening chapter depicts a sibling conflict, its mediation, and ultimately by the end of the first chapter, its resolution, where all four sisters sing along with Marmee, a trajectory that dramatizes the process of Jo's feminization over the course of the novel as a whole.

In the struggle to become a little woman, Jo must repress her anger, a quality for which she is notorious in her family. In the chapter "Jo Meets Apollyon," for example, when Amy burns Jo's beloved manuscript of fairy tales because of Jo's irritability, the narrator is careful to introduce the chapter by acknowledging the aggressivity of their bond: "She and Amy had many lively skirmishes in the course of their lives, for both had quick tempers, and were apt to be violent when fairly roused. Amy teased Jo, and Jo irritated Amy, and semi-occasional explosions occurred, of which both were much ashamed afterward." Jo refuses to forgive her sister for destroying her manuscript, and on the following day, she goes ice-skating with Laurie, while Amy decides to follow along with her skates. Jo, who knows her younger sister is trying to catch up with them, refuses to alert her to the thin ice and Amy falls in—but when Jo sees that her sister has fallen through the ice and is struggling to stay afloat, she is overcome with fear and shock, unable to call for help or even initially to move. Laurie manages to take charge of the rescue operation and they both pull Amy out of the water. This scene captures the violence at the heart of sibling love— and the tremendous grief Jo feels afterward for nearly causing the death of her youngest sister. She feels guilty for her anger, and the final scene of the chapter involves no words but simply an exchange of gazes, when Amy, recovering in her bed, begins to smile and holds out her arms to her older sister, and they "hugged one another close, in spite of the blankets, and everything was forgiven and forgotten in one hearty kiss."[71]

Although this chapter features Jo's self-recrimination for her negative emotions and includes Marmee's famous advice to repress one's anger, there is in this final image—the sisters' silent embrace—a recognition of the simultaneity of negative and positive emotions. The resolution of this chapter promises a form of forgiveness that is not actually based on forgetting but instead on accepting the fundamental ambivalence that structures the sibling bond. Sibling love can only occur, to paraphrase psychoanalyst D. A. Winnicott, if sisters and brothers first have sufficient hatred for each other.[72]

The Symbolic Violence of Sisterhood

Alcott's *Little Women* points to a fundamental paradox of feminine niceness: Although it demands the repression of unladylike anger, it is nevertheless a violent process of socialization that depends in large part on micromoments of female aggression, most notably expressed in the March family through sisterly criticism and judgment. The violence of *Little Women* is not confined to examples of Jo's temper but is also present in the banal remarks of her sisters, or what Harriet Beecher Stowe would describe as "little foxes," that daily undermine domestic happiness. Amy, and to a lesser extent Meg, routinely criticize Jo's conduct, her speech, and her clothing. "Hold back your shoulders, and carry your hands easily, no matter if your gloves do pinch." In contrast to Jo, whose aggression is direct, loud, and explosive, Amy's hostility is expressed through the seemingly innocuous category of sisterly advice. At one point, Amy explains to her older sister the social perks of feminine niceness: "I want people to like you, and they would if you'd only try to be a little more agreeable. Do your hair the pretty way, and put the pink rose in your bonnet."[73] Niceness is intertwined with prettiness, a behavioral standard that also requires the internalization of the Victorian beauty myth, which will, in turn, lead to likability. Amy's own mastery of this standard leads to various social benefits, including popularity: "Everybody liked her, for among her good gifts was tact. She had an instinctive sense of what was pleasing and proper, always said the right thing to the right person." Jo confides in Amy, "I wish it was as easy for me to do little things to please people, as it is for you."[74]

Amy is the opposite of Beth, who refuses to judge her sisters and instead praises Jo's talents unconditionally and accepts her idiosyncratic behavior with a generous heart. Amy, by contrast, is always critical of her elder sister, giving her advice that rarely strays from this central line: "Women should learn to be agreeable, particularly poor ones; for they have no other way of repaying the kindnesses they receive." Amy betrays her own conventionality when she adds a bit later, "I don't like reformers, and I hope you will never try be one."[75] Amy's judgmental and even cruel remarks to her older sister illustrate "that not pleasing others is social suicide," as sociologist Mary Pipher notes. Girls, rather than mothers, become the primary bullies of femininity: "Like any recent converts to an ideology girls are at risk of becoming the biggest enforcers and proselytizers for the culture."[76] Part of the peer pressure of girlhood is learning to admonish those who do not conform to the feminine standard.

But what keeps Amy's criticisms and the values they represent from being taken too seriously in *Little Women* is the fact that the personification of feminine niceness is, to quote de Beauvoir, "blond, vain, and stupid."[77] Because advice about how to be a "successful" woman comes primarily from her youngest sister, Jo is able to laugh at the conventions of femininity. Consequently, the novel depicts feminization as both pernicious and ridiculous. This is most apparent in the chapter "Calls," when Amy and Jo pay visits to the respectable families in town. Anxious about the impression her sister will make, Amy advises Jo, "Just be calm, cool and quiet,—that's safe and ladylike; and you can easily do it for fifteen minutes." Jo reassures her sister that she has played the role of a "prim young lady on stage," so she needn't worry, but when they enter the Chester home, one of the ladies at the reception audibly remarks that Jo is a "haughty, uninteresting creature." While Amy is mortified and blames her sister for failing to please the ladies, "Jo laughed noiselessly all through the hall." Jo reassures her sister that when they visit the respectable Lamb family, she will act the part of a "charming girl," and the Lambs will exclaim, "What a lively, nice creature that Jo March is!"[78] And in fact, Jo does manage to charm the Lamb family but by telling amusing stories at Amy's expense. The chapter ends, in part, with the realization that one sister will never entirely change the other, and despite her nagging advice, Amy will never get her older sister to conform to the conventions of femininity.

The chapter's lesson, and arguably the lesson of *Little Women* as a whole, is that siblings must recognize the fundamental autonomy of the other, and they must learn to accept each other on their own terms. Jo's laughter at the Chesters, together with her ability to talk back to Amy while they both learn to accept each other's differences, all illustrate the ways in which *Little Women* is an allegory of feminization: The symbolic violence of socialization as personified by Amy is never entirely effective, and subsequently, femininity often fails. Jo, despite Amy's efforts, remains unrepentantly herself. Yet Jo has acquired sufficient skills in the feminine masquerade to allow her to function in a normative way in New England society.

In contrast to Stowe's Eva Henderson, whose niceness is as natural as having an Irish maid, Alcott's Jo March denaturalizes feminine niceness and draws attention to it as a process of socialization by which girls are converted into little women. This conversion is a fraught experience, but it can also be negotiated on Jo's own terms, and this is where Alcott provides her young women readers with a happy ending. *Little Women* concludes on a positive note not in the conventional sense of Jo's marriage to Mr. Bhaer, a scene that is quickly described in a terse sentence, but in the sense of her own personal triumph of young womanhood; she did it her way.

Revealingly, what characterizes Alcott's work and that of all the women in this chapter is that they do not throw out the feminine completely. It can be critiqued, exposed, and expanded to include a wider range of attributes for women's behavior, but it is not dismissed as a value. From Eva Henderson to Jo March, all see a redemptive quality in

the feminine that has to do with sociality and the importance of feeling
a sense of connectedness beyond one's immediate family. In other
words, there is a contradictory attitude toward the social, which is at
once oppressive in the form of feminization, and yet its product—"social intercourse"—is considered absolutely vital. Charlotte Perkins
Gilman, sounding very much like her great-aunt Stowe, best summarizes this value when she praises women for cultivating social intercourse, because it represents "the essential condition of civilization. It
is not merely a pleasure or an indulgence; it is the human necessity."[79]
In this sense, what unites the women writers in this chapter is this
dialectical sense of critique and reparative reading, where feminine
niceness signifies a form of symbolic violence on the one hand and the
basis of human sociability on the other.

The Symbolic Violence of Mrs. Bhaer

But where *Little Women* demonstrates a complex response toward
feminization that is at once violent and playful, pernicious yet absurd,
its sequel, *Little Men* (1871), is merely prescriptive. Published two
years after *Little Women*, *Little Men* turns explicitly to the theme of
disciplining through affection at Plumfield, a boarding school for predominantly at-risk boys (and a few female students) that is funded
through Laurie and Amy's philanthropic munificence. In the novel's
opening pages, the lively and spirited children at the school repeatedly
describe Plumfield as a "nice" school: "It seems a very nice place
indeed," "It's the nicest place in the world," "it *is* a very nice place to
be in." Jo and her husband, Professor Bhaer, run the school with the
affection of a loving family, where "manners and morals were insinu-
ated, without the pupils exactly knowing how it was done."[80] Jo, who
is characterized at the outset as "jolly," sums up their pedagogical
ethos: "[W]e don't believe in making children miserable by too many
rules, and too much study." This approach to learning is best encapsulated in Professor Bhaer's aphorism: "Kindness is always better than
force. Try it and see."[81] If the students are happy, they will obey, and
thus niceness, kindness, and an array of related terms become rules
without ever being perceived as such.

Where feminine niceness in *Little Women* is praised, detested,
argued with, challenged, and even laughed at, niceness within the pedagogical domain of Plumfield is a religion. Niceness becomes a truism

in *Little Men* rather than part of an ongoing debate between two strong-willed sisters; its value is now considered both self-evident and sacrosanct. Alcott gives the reader a hint of what is to come at the end of *Little Women*, when Plumfield is first introduced as a utopian community, based in large part, or so it is implied, on Bronson Alcott's pedagogy. The task of Professor and Mrs. Bhaer is to convert "wild" and rebellious children into kind, self-regulating individuals: "[T]he most rampant ragamuffin was conquered in the end."[82] All students must be inculcated in the school of niceness: "Kindness in looks and words and ways is true politeness."[83] Feminization is an equal opportunity socializer, where both boys and girls are considered suitable grist for the niceness mill.

In contrast to *Little Women*, where the conversion of Jo March into little womanhood is not entirely complete or convincing, Mrs. Bhaer seems to lack Jo's fiery temperament and her "crotchety" behavior, even though the narrator at the start reassures the reader that there is a great deal of continuity between the two: "She was not at all handsome, but she had a merry sort of face that never seemed to have forgotten certain childish ways and looks, any more than her voice and manner had."[84] But when Jo March becomes "Mother Bhaer," as she is frequently called in *Little Men*, she loses her sense of humor. Jolliness has now replaced her acerbic wit. She is now a proselytizer of niceness rather than its playful critic. She is a believer rather than a skeptic.

The most troubling aspect of Jo's transformation to Mrs. Bhaer is seen in the taming of Little Annie Harding, who becomes known at the school as "Naughty Nan." The Bhaers recruit her to Plumfield after her mother died and she had been "running wild at home." She immediately reminds Mrs. Bhaer of herself as a feisty young girl who is "full of spirits, and only needs to be taught what to do with them to be as nice a little girl as Daisy."[85] The conversion of Naughty Nan from a wild child into a nice girl (she grows up to be a doctor) is portrayed through the metaphor of the garden, a highly feminized and aestheticized trope: "[F]or this little garden was full of sweet flowers, half hidden by the weeds; and when kind hands gently began to cultivate it, all sorts of green shoots sprung up, promising to blossom beautifully in the warmth of love and care, the best climate for young hearts and souls all the world over."[86] The garden metaphor implies that the process of feminization is organic and natural, a combination of growth and pruning that produces feminine niceness through a consensual process of "love and care." In contrast to Elizabeth Stuart Phelps's garden that is merely a temporary respite from the pressures of female propriety, Nan's garden illustrates a comfortable mode of being from which relief is neither desired nor sought.

Although Alcott describes Nan's transformation into "nice Nan" as a natural process of cultivation, it is in fact far more pernicious than its counterpart in *Little Women*. Where Alcott in *Little Women* depicts feminization in lateral terms from the perspective of the tomboy who mockingly ridicules the process of her own socialization, feminization is represented in *Little Men* vertically from the perspective of Mother Bhaer, who oversees Naughty Nan's conversion in a far more involved and controlling way than Marmee ever did in *Little Women*.

But what would Nan's transformation from naughty to nice look like if told from Nan's perspective? How would Nan narrate her own feminization? This is precisely the perspective that is suppressed in *Little Men*. Unlike the first novel, the little women do not speak of their socialization, and it is this silence, combined with the absence of anger, which makes niceness in *Little Men* unsettling. In this novel, Plumfield becomes a laboratory of manufactured niceness, producing a behavioral sameness that is destructive and disturbing. Alcott's utopia verges on becoming a dystopian nightmare. Jamesian pragmatism, with its versatility and flexibility, has turned into orthodoxy, and niceness has become obligatory.

In the final paragraph of *Jo's Boys* (1886), published two years before Alcott's death, the narrator imagines an apocalyptic end to Plumfield: "It is a strong temptation to the weary historian to close the present tale with an earthquake which should engulf Plumfield and its environs so deeply in the bowels of the earth that no youthful Schliemann could ever find a vestige of it." But she admits that such a "melodramatic conclusion might shock my gentle readers."[87] This destructive ending to the trilogy suggests that the aggressivity that could be expressed in the March home but not at Plumfield can no longer be suppressed. The fantasized destruction of the school indicates the extent to which Alcott had learned to hate her fictional world and the readers who demanded more of the same. But she pulls back from the ramifications of this violent end to return in tone and theme to the orthodox niceness of Plumfield, concluding in a perfunctory manner that "all the marriages turned out well." Nan, however, remained "a busy, cheerful, independent spinster and dedicated her life to her suffering sisters and their children, in which true woman's work she found abiding happiness."[88] In describing Nan's life, Alcott is describing her own, but in a sarcastic tone that rehearses the clichés about women's happiness through service to others.

There is a quiet seething throughout this terse conclusion that captures Alcott's contempt for the fictional world she has created and threatens to break through the polite veneer of respectability in the last paragraph of her final novel. This concluding paragraph harks back to Jo's temper in *Little Women*, a reminder that women's rage can be disciplined but not entirely eradicated. Jo's defiant voice returns in the final words of Alcott's trilogy, suggesting that feminine niceness is not guaranteed behavior; it is not as comforting and constant as one would like to think it is. There is also a potentially explosive quality to feminine niceness that can only be repressed for so long. Jo's aggression lies just below the surface of Mrs. Bhaer's cheerful demeanor.

Toward a Pragmatic Theory of Feminist Niceness: Jane Addams

As I have argued, nineteenth-century American women writers had a complex and dynamic interpretation of the concept of feminine niceness. They reflected on whether it was a behavioral form of mutilation or a necessary and effective force of social cohesion. They thought about its debilitating consequences as well as its productive uses. The women in this chapter understood that it could go both ways. Their approach was critical as well as reparative. Even Harriet Beecher Stowe, who believed most fervently in its potential as a social therapeutic, admitted that feminine niceness could also be toxic when internalized by a young wife desperate to please her husband and his relations.

This ambivalence about feminine niceness took one of two forms in the early twentieth century: It was either critiqued as the "angel in the house" that modernist writers like Virginia Woolf poignantly rebuked, or it inspired social movements that sought to institutionalize feminine niceness in terms of policies for maternal and child welfare as well as formulations of social ethics, where feminine niceness became a way for both men and women to live peacefully together. To put it differently, by the turn of the century, feminine niceness shifted from the interpersonal world of intimate relationships to the social world of policy, reform, and institutions. What happens to feminine niceness when it leaves the fictional world of characters and moves to the actual world of impersonal relations, populations, and social policy? These questions define, in part, the life work of a woman who once wrote of her enduring affection for Alcott's *Little Women*, Jane Addams.

A philosopher, activist, pragmatist, and sociologist, Addams institutionalized a form of pragmatism with feminine niceness at its core. Her life and writings intersect with several of the figures in this chapter, most notably Ida B. Wells, who referred to her friend as "the greatest woman in the United States." William James positively reviewed her work and frequently praised her in his correspondence to her. In one letter from 1909, after reading her study of urban youth subcultures in *The Spirit of Youth*, James succinctly articulates his praise: "You inhabit reality."[89]

In "The Subjective Necessity for Social Settlements" (1892), Addams describes her outlook in terms that resonate with Jamesian pragmatism: "The one thing to be dreaded in the Settlement is that it lose its flexibility, its power of quick adaptation, its readiness to change its methods as its environment may demand. It must be open to conviction and must have a deep and abiding sense of tolerance. It must be hospitable and ready for experiment." This same strategy also applies to democracy, a point she makes in *Newer Ideals of Peace* (1906), in discussing the risks of inflexibility: "[I]t is so easy to commit irreparable blunders because we fail to correct our theories by our changing experience."[90] Hull House is emblematic of democracy in the sense that both are anchored in a pragmatic philosophy of adjustment and accommodation, a philosophy that is considered key for moral development.

Founded in 1889, Hull House was based on the belief that social and labor strife could be ameliorated if the wealthy understood how the other half lives. Addams rejected charity because the way in which giving was structured impersonally meant that the wealthy were never in contact with the poor. Addams was ultimately a reformer and she understood Hull House as a meeting ground for affluent Americans to recognize their dependency upon the poorer classes for their own wealth and comfort. The ethics of care requires more than a monetary donation; it also needs active involvement and social obligation. Class antagonism must be replaced by reciprocity, a transformation that relies on the wealthy acknowledging their moral responsibility to help the less fortunate. In many respects, Addams takes Alcott's worldview, epitomized in Marmee's motto for a happy marriage in *Little Women*— "mutual helpfulness"—and applies it to civic institutions and ultimately to the nation. Addams takes the conventions of Victorian interpersonal relations and institutionalizes them so that Hull House functions as a "go-between," to borrow William James's phrase, linking domesticity with civic responsibility.

Like Plumfield, Hull House represents an evangelical institution committed to the conversion of hearts and minds. Hull House did so at two levels: It turned immigrants into productive citizens while also converting wealthy patrons from philanthropists to reformers. Its social ethics were premised on the power of persuasion: Once the wealthy came into contact with the immigrant poor in the respectable setting of Hull House, then they would be persuaded to alter their views of the other half and cultivate what Addams calls "sympathetic knowledge."[91] This faith reveals an important quality about individuals as Addams understood it: A person wants to be agreeable toward others because man desires "to be at unity with his fellow-creatures." Addams takes agreeableness, that mainstay of Victorian etiquette manuals, and makes it part of a democratic theory of social ethics. Furthermore, she earnestly takes the feminine virtue of self-abnegation, which Alcott perfunctorily ironizes in the concluding paragraph of *Jo's Boys*, and turns it into a core value of women's social citizenship. In 1907, when defending municipal suffrage for women, Addams wrote, "As men earned their citizenship through their readiness and ability to defend their city, so perhaps woman, if she takes a citizen's place in the modern industrial city, will have to earn it by devotion and self-abnegation in the service of its complex needs."[92] The same qualities that have conventionally defined the feminine—agreeableness, sociality and self-abnegation—can also define the new liberalism and the emergent welfare state, in which public institutions curtail corporate greed and protect the vulnerable.

Jane Addams shares a certain intellectual kinship with Harriet Beecher Stowe. Both see feminine niceness as a way to theorize power (rather than weakness), and specifically as a template for modeling state authority, based in part on a feminized notion of democratic authority that values listening, reciprocity, and conciliation. Like Stowe, Addams believes that the individual embodies the foundation for social and political change. Although a more secular thinker than Stowe, she nonetheless understood U.S. democracy as a Christian practice based on helping the vanquished. She also shares with her Victorian foremother an evangelical faith in conversion and she would have wholeheartedly agreed with Stowe's words: "Conversion, when real, is a solution of all difficulties in our days as it was in those of the first apostles."[93] Addams's conversion occurred as an awakening to class disparity while slumming in East London on a midnight tour in an omnibus in 1883. Although she would later reject the voyeurism of slumming, she found it personally transformative, as it led to her decision to create a settlement house in Chicago.[94]

Like Stowe, Addams believed in the power of conversion to change the hearts and minds of people. Affective experience can be a powerful force of moral suasion. But as an abolitionist during the Civil War, Stowe recognized the limits of persuasion: The slave owner could not be persuaded in most cases to manumit his slaves voluntarily despite the heroic example of her characters George Shelby and Edward Clayton. Far more than Stowe, Addams trusted that personal revelation could occur by constructively engaging with the urban subaltern. According to Maurice Hamington, "Addams had a deep faith in humanity—people were fundamentally good and society could improve. This is the progressive spirit. Democracy was an organizing principle for Addams and it was funded by social exchanges."[95] Addams's notion of civic religion depended on the capacity of people to change for the better.

Addams's faith in the powers of moral suasion, however, found its limit with the Pullman Strike of 1894, one of the most important examples of labor upheaval in U.S. history and a turning point in the development of Addams's social ethics. I want to turn to this strike and the subsequent exchange that resulted between Addams and her friend John Dewey because it points to Addams's reluctance to address conflict and specifically the limits of conciliation. Centered in Chicago, the Pullman strike crippled the national economy and brought Addams into a new role as public mediator.[96] From Addams's perspective, a key player in this social disaster was the founder and president of the Pullman Palace Car Company, George Pullman, one of the wealthiest men in the United States, whose company was estimated to be worth

$62 million. Pullman came from poverty, and his rise to wealth confirmed a rags-to-riches narrative of American mobility, a storyline that Horatio Alger's novels featuring Ragged Dick made famous during this time. But unlike the typical Alger hero, Pullman was shrewd, controlling, and unpopular.

The main cause of the strike was the severe wage cut enacted after the Panic of 1893, when the demand for the construction of new luxury train cars plummeted. Prior to the Panic, the corporation enjoyed unprecedented prosperity, earning profits of over six million dollars and employing 5,500 workers. After the Panic of 1893, however, the car manufacturing division sustained losses, but the more lucrative operating division still continued to yield large revenues, which is to say, affluent travelers still preferred luxury railway travel despite the decline in the demand for new construction. George Pullman refused to utilize profits from the lucrative surplus acquired before 1893. He also refused to use the profits from one part of the business to cushion the losses of the other, so he made all of his workers bear the brunt of the decline with a 25 percent wage cut, while also reducing hours. This retrenchment policy reduced workers' wages to a pittance, while the salaries of Pullman officials remained the same.[97]

After the workers presented their grievances and the leaders were immediately fired, the American Railway Union, founded by Eugene Debs a year earlier and consisting of four thousand workers, called for a general strike of all railroads with Pullman cars. The railways from Mississippi to California shut down. After six days, President Grover Cleveland ordered in the military over the objections of the Illinois governor and violence erupted, resulting in the death of twelve people in the Chicago area from clashes between protestors and the police and federal troops. Determined to break the union, George Pullman, who had left town for New York City, refused to negotiate with the American Railway Union or agree to arbitration. The strike ended three months later on the company's terms: A drastic wage cut and no membership in the union.

Jane Addams was appointed to the Civic Federation of Chicago and its Board of Conciliation of the Industrial Committee, and although she persuaded representatives from the railway union to come to the negotiating table, she could not persuade George Pullman to attend. The conciliation committee failed at voluntary arbitration, and Debs was arrested for violating the no-strike injunction and eventually served a six-month sentence. The American Railway Union could have been, if it had succeeded, the most powerful union in the nation, but instead it quickly faded. This failed attempt at arbitration initiated an intriguing conversation between Addams and John Dewey, who had just been appointed the first chair of the Department of Philosophy at the University of Chicago. In a letter to his wife, Alice, Dewey described how he defended the inevitability of conflict and even argued that it could be a productive force for greater truth and consciousness. But Addams adamantly disagreed, claiming, "[A]ntagonism was not only useless and harmful, but entirely unnecessary." She argued that conflict was based not on "objective differences," to use Dewey's words, but by "a person's mixing in his own personal reactions."[98] In other words, all conflict can be reduced to personal antagonism rather than competing interests and structural tensions, such as those between capital and labor.

Although Addams repeatedly defined herself against dogmas of any kind and called for flexibility in temperament, she tenaciously held on to her "ideal of social intercourse," where conflict could be resolved through dialogue, compassion, and reciprocity. This ideal that the social sphere could meliorate economic and political conflicts demonstrates her abiding faith in a Victorian model of feminine niceness adapted to the public sphere. Two years before the Pullman Strike, the young Addams idealistically outlined the value of dialogue to ameliorate class conflict:

> Is it possible for men, however far apart in outward circumstances, for the capitalist and the working-man, to use the common phrase, to meet as individuals beneath a friendly roof, open their minds each to each, and not have their 'class theories' insensibly modified by the kindly attrition of a personal acquaintance? In the light of our experience I should say not.[99]

Addams prefers to think in terms of individuals as opposed to classes or theories. The personal can convert the impersonal; likability can trump profits. All that is needed is to meet beneath a "friendly roof" for this personal conversion to take place, epitomized in her credo "[W]e look all men in the face."[100]

Limited by a view of social ethics based on individual persuasion, with a tendency toward reducing political and social dynamics to interpersonal matters, Addams bemoans the selfishness of George Pullman, describing him obliquely in "Modern Lear" as a stubborn and foolish patriarch who refuses to understand his daughter Cordelia. Capital and labor are cast in terms of a father-daughter relationship, with a family tragedy allegorically describing an industrial tragedy. As her biographer Louise Knight notes, "Addams disapproves of capitalism but not because of its effects on the workers. What troubles her are the moral failings of the individual capitalist."[101] Addams's "Modern Lear" is poignant and nuanced, depicting a daughter's reckoning with a cruel father, an analogy that allowed Addams to reflect firsthand on the brutality of power. Her "friendly roof" approach to interpersonal conversion failed in this context: Nothing could bring George Pullman to the bargaining table.

The failure of conciliation in the Pullman Strike led Addams to rethink her aversion to argument, antagonism, and what Leo Tolstoy called "moral force" (versus physical force).[102] As a well-mannered patrician, Addams had internalized her culture's dislike of outspoken and angry women who challenged political limits through behavioral dissidence. Her investment in feminine niceness made her hesitant to disagree, and yet social ethics required a limit point: the ability to say no to unjust practices. Like William James's amiable woman who knows when to say no, Addams had to learn how to draw firm limits when the situation demanded it. The test came with her opposition to World War I. Her pacifism was not what she called the "goody-goody" variety, but a tough-minded position that attracted a tremendous amount of criticism that affected Addams profoundly. As a public intellectual, Addams experienced for the first time the feeling of being hated that went far beyond the interpersonal level of gossip and came from a force that was powerful, impersonal, and faceless, namely, public opinion. Addams recounts what it was like to be a pacifist at a time of war: "social opprobrium and wide-spread misunderstanding which brought me very near to self pity, perhaps the lowest pit into which human nature can sink." She realized that "we are all much more dependent upon our social environment and daily newspaper than perhaps any of us realize."[103] She was warned by friends that she was committing "intellectual suicide" by opposing the war and that her credibility would never recover. And in many respects, this was true.

Yet what fueled the social opprobrium was, ironically, her defense of niceness: that human beings would rather befriend each other than kill each other. Addams's opposition to the war was based on the argument that human nature was not primarily or even fundamentally based on violence but on something more potentially radical—on kindness. Her public vilification resulted in her belief that human beings are kind, loving, and altruistic. In "Personal Reactions in Time of War," she boldly challenged the Social Darwinism of the age by denaturalizing aggression: "War is in fact not a natural process and not a struggle for existence in the evolutionary sense."[104] As part of the International Congress of Women at The Hague in 1915, she had the opportunity to speak to injured German soldiers who were soon to return to the battlefield and who admitted that they intentionally aimed their bayonets so that they would not shoot an enemy soldier. In her famous address at Carnegie Hall in 1915, she noted that in order to get soldiers to kill, to transform a man into a killing machine, they had to take stimulants in the form of alcohol and other drugs.

At the core of Addams's antiwar writings is a redefinition of what it means to be human. She believed human beings are fundamentally social, committed to solidarity and sympathy, or what Addams called the "humane instinct," an innate quality that has allowed human beings to survive over time.[105] Paradoxically, Addams had to learn how to fight in order to make a case against war. She had to sacrifice at a personal level her investment in feminine niceness in order to make a courageous case for human kindness. During the period between the Pullman Strike and the end of World War I, Addams developed into William James's pragmatic figure—the amiable woman who knows when to say no. This ability to combine cooperation with disagreement, accommodation with limits, served as the basis of her democratic ethics, as well as influencing her own personal evolution as a feminist activist.

Ida B. Wells, Social Justice, and the Limits of Niceness

Described by a Danish traveler in Chicago as the "Jane Addams among Negroes," Ida B. Wells was a Progressive reformer who worked with Jane Addams on a number of issues, including the racial integration of Chicago public schools.[106] Wells also founded a black settlement house, worked for women's suffrage, and helped create the first national black women's organization, the National Association of Colored Women (NACW). But before settling down in Chicago in 1895, when she married lawyer Ferdinand Barnett, Ida B. Wells campaigned against racial violence in the South, edited the militant *Free Speech,* and contributed regularly to the local white press in Memphis and black weeklies nationally. Becoming increasingly more radical as racial violence escalated, she wrote in the *Detroit Plaindealer* in 1889, on the eve of her antilynching campaign, that the black community must respond to the "outrages which daily occur" and she called for her readers to "[a]gitate and act . . . until *something* is done."[107] Wells's brand of activism differed from Addams's in an important way: Wells knew the importance of expressing moral outrage at racial injustice. "Unfeminine" anger rather than feminine amiability motivated her actions. Far less idealistic than Addams, Wells recognized the limits of persuasion. She understood the parameters of niceness in the struggle for civil rights.

Known as a "difficult woman," Ida B. Wells reveals the contradictions surrounding feminine niceness for women of color in the late nineteenth century. As Hazel Carby has argued, black women were placed outside the construction of womanhood, a term that included only white women.[108] Wells knew that the category of womanhood was politically contested and racially and economically stratified, and she laid claim to this category as a way to counter the black female stereotype of the hypersexual female who was promiscuous and amoral. Middle-class black womanhood was indeed a fragile construct in the late nineteenth century. In one of her earliest journalistic pieces, "The Model Woman: A Pen Picture of the Typical Southern Girl," Wells expands the language of the feminine type as well as the regional language of southernness to include black women and she praises the "typical girl" for her "womanly modesty, dignity of deportment, and refinement of manners; and the whole enveloped in a casket of a sweetness of disposition, and amiability of temper that makes it a pleasure to be near her." And unlike Jo March, she is "beautiful because of the absence of slang."[109] Privately and publicly, Wells sought to expand the rhetoric of feminine types to include black women, where typicality would be part of the long revolution to recognize the full humanity of black women. Wells claimed the language of femininity for black women and, in doing so, she highlighted the intersection of feminine etiquette with racial etiquette.

Wells, however, had a difficult time with conventional femininity. On the one hand, she identified with the rebelliousness and originality of her favorite fictional character, Jo March, sharing a "besetting sin" in possessing a strong temper. At sixteen years old, she described her temperament in terms of a "tempestuous, rebellious, hard headed will-fulness" connected to her "disposition to question . . . authority." In one instance, when social slander circulated in Memphis about her, she wrote in her diary, "I was so angry that I foamed at the mouth, bit my lips & then realizing my impotence—ended in a fit of crying."[110]

Although her anger resonates with Jo March's impetuous tempera-ment, Wells did not identify as a tomboy. She was in many ways more akin to Amy than Jo in terms of her predilection for fashion. Her diary regularly records her expenditures, most often for dresses, and she writes on multiple occasions about her disappointment at not being able to afford various accessories such as a parasol, hat, and gloves. "My expenses are transcending my income," she wrote, "I must stop."[111] As a teacher in her twenties, she often spent her meager pay-checks at a downtown Memphis department store instead of paying her rent. She was petite, attractive, and stylish, invested in a version of the Victorian beauty myth. She also observed how other black women dressed, occasionally remarking in her diary the names of women who were especially pretty.

Where Harriet Beecher Stowe, Louisa May Alcott, and Jane Addams understood feminine niceness primarily in terms of moral goodness, Wells saw feminine niceness in physical terms as being nice looking. There was a power to being pretty, and she realized early on that her authority as a public figure would depend, in part, on how others per-ceived her body. In the 1880s, publisher T. Thomas Fortune would remark that she combined intelligence with attractiveness, and she knew that her powers of persuasion as a writer and later as an orator would depend on this combination.[112]

For Wells, it was important to be treated as a lady, which is to say, with respect and good manners. Stowe, Alcott, and Addams could expect such treatment from men, given their race and class position, but Wells could not. In 1886, Ida B. Wells attended a racially mixed Knights of Labor meeting in Memphis, and she recounted in the

Memphis Watchman that it was the first time she was ever welcomed "with the courtesy usually extended to white ladies." She continued, "It was the first assembly of the sort in this town where color was not the criterion to recognition as ladies and gentlemen."[113] This example illustrates not only Wells's identification with labor organizations and the working-class, but it also discloses the importance she placed on conduct and middle-class propriety for black men and women. Although she never felt at ease among the black elite in Memphis, she nonetheless was committed to their ideals of racial uplift, which placed a premium on respectability, self-control, and good manners.

Yet Wells also understood the limits of niceness. She knew that activism against racial injustice required at times that one behave in a distinctly unladylike manner. She continually had to negotiate between niceness and outrage while combating Jim Crow in the post-Reconstruction South. One particular incident includes her 1885 lawsuit against the Chesapeake, Ohio & South Western Railroad Company. According to court transcripts, the conductor, William Murray, entered the first-class ladies' car to collect tickets. When Wells handed him hers, he told her to leave the coach, insisting that it was for whites only. The only black women permitted in the first-class car were nannies and maids traveling with their white employers. Wells's biographer Paula Giddings describes the scene: "Wells told him that she was not moving. Murray, saying that he did not want any trouble, told Ida that he wanted to treat her like a lady, but that she would have to go to the colored car. 'I replied,' Ida recounted, 'that if he wished to treat me like a lady, he would leave me alone.' When the train paused on the Wolf River trestle, just before its first stop at Frazier's Station, Murray again beseeched Wells to leave the car. Once more, she refused. At that point, the conductor attempted to physically pull her out of the seat, tearing the sleeve off her dress in the process." Wells hooked her feet under the seat in front of her and began scratching the conductor with her nails and then bit his hands deeply enough that they started to bleed. "He tried to drag me out of the seat, but the moment he caught hold of my arm I fastened my teeth in the back of his hand."[114] The conductor asked the white passengers to help and some did, while others stood on the seats to get a good view and applauded the conductor.

Wells, who preferred to leave the train rather than sit in the smoking car, was left at the platform of the first station, still holding onto her

Ida B. Wells (circa 1887). Reproduced from I. Garland Penn.
The Afro-American Press and its Editors (Springfield, Mass.: Willey & Co.,
Publishers, 1891): 409. Visual Materials from the NAACP Records, Library
of Congress Prints and Photographs Division, Washington, D.C.,
LC-DIG-ppmsca-23823.

first-class ticket. She notes in her autobiography, "[A]lthough the
sleeves of my linen duster had been torn out and I had been pretty
roughly handled, I had not been hurt physically." In remarking on the
state of her body as well as her dress, Wells underscores the fact that
racism is experienced physically and that it is "a visceral experience,"
to quote writer Ta-Nehisi Coates, that "cracks bones, breaks teeth."[115]

Although Wells would eventually lose her lawsuit against the railroad company, what is striking about this scene is how Wells frames her
refusal to leave the car through the language of femininity, saying to the
conductor that she wanted to be treated like a lady. But resisting the

conductor required that she forsake the feminine by aggressively scratching and biting Murray to the point that he could no longer use his hands and others had to lift her out of the coach. In this context, Wells gives women's anger—that bugbear of Victorian femininity—a seminal role to play in the struggle against racial injustice. Furthermore, this scene reveals the politically conservative side of niceness in the sense that it helps sustain the status quo by keeping other values, such as fairness, at bay. Niceness is overrated as a virtue, writes Malcolm Gladwell: "Fairness sometimes requires that surfaces be disturbed, that patterns of cordiality be broken, and that people, rudely and abruptly, be removed from their place. Niceness is the enemy of fairness."[116] Wells invokes the language of feminine niceness while also disclosing its limits by showing how Jim Crow could only be challenged through the "unlady-like" behavior of kicking and biting.

In the nineteenth century, women's anger signaled the limit point of femininity. "An enraged woman," according to *The Young Lady's Own Book* (1833), "is one of the most disgusting sights in nature." Much of Jo March's angst derives from the fear she has of her own anger, that her temper will drive her to "do something dreadful, and spoil [her] life, and make everybody hate [her]."[117] Although Jo detests the mandate for girls to be nice, she is terrified by her own capacity for anger because of its explosive potential to do harm to others in addition to the social costs of being hated. But Wells, far more than Alcott and her fictional counterpart, understands that sometimes you have to be hated. Women's anger is precisely what is needed to challenge sexist and racist laws and customs. Elizabeth Cady Stanton recollects a revealing anecdote about the necessity of women's anger in bringing about social change: "A friend of mine, a professor and a wise man, says our movement will never come to anything until the women are mad enough to swear." Labor activist Mary "Mother" Jones exposed the class politics behind the etiquette of being a lady most saliently when she declared, "No matter what your fight, don't be ladylike! God Almighty made women and the Rockefeller gang of thieves made the ladies."[118] Rage and femininity were thought to be at opposite ends of the spectrum of sanctioned behavior, a belief that made an angry lady an oxymoron, an absurd impossibility.

Speaking out, whether in a railway car or on a platform before thousands of people, required forsaking niceness at another level. In the nineteenth century, print was seen as more socially acceptable for women than oratory because it did not violate social conventions. As Sandra Gustafson has argued, "For a woman who wished to break out of her constricted domestic role without directly challenging social expectations, print provided a relatively safe venue." Oratory, by contrast, exposed women's bodies directly to derision and criticism. It was deemed an "unfeminine activity."[119] Speaking in public threatened one's femininity, evident from the angry responses toward suffragettes and abolitionists, such as Angelina Grimké, who was threatened by an angry mob outside of the auditorium where she was lecturing. From her first speech in 1853, Susan B. Anthony was regularly "ridiculed for her looks, her clothes, her marital state, her speeches, her voice, and her ideas." Black women speakers such as Sojourner Truth and Frances Harper were both seen as masculinized figures for speaking before "promiscuous" audiences comprised of men and women.[120] As Philip Foner writes in his introduction to *The Voice of Black America* (1972), "although oratory is only one form that black Americans have used throughout history to assert their worth and to validate their claim to human rights, it is a singularly important one. Perhaps even more than writers, black orators helped to demolish the myth of the natural inferiority of black people."[121] Black women felt these strictures more deeply as their femininity and morality were explicitly impugned for speaking out.

With that said, Wells demonstrates that both writing and public speaking were dangerous for black women. Her inflammatory editorial published in *Free Speech* in 1892 led to the destruction of the *Free Speech* office, the near-lynching of its editor Mr. Fleming, and death threats to Wells, who at the time was attending a conference in Philadelphia and staying with Frances Harper. In this editorial, she questioned the white southern explanation for lynching as a way to protect white womanhood from black rapists; she suggested that there also existed consensual unions between white women and black men. The most damaging sentence was the final one: "If Southern white men are not careful, they will over-reach themselves and public sentiment will have a reaction; a conclusion will then be reached which will be very damaging to the moral reputation of their women."[122] With these printed words, she became an overnight exile from the South, not returning for thirty years.

Middle-class black women orators had to confront the conventions of femininity when it came to public speaking, since these ideals made it nearly impossible to speak out against racism and sexism without compromising their femininity. In one of her first formal lectures, given at New York's Lyric Hall in 1892, Wells spoke about the lynching of three Memphis businessmen, including her friend Tom Moss, and when her anger combined unwittingly with grief, she began to cry while reading aloud her prepared lecture. Although Wells was mortified by her emotional outburst, she was reassured afterward that such emotion only made her words more powerful and also more feminine. She successfully combined genuine emotion with rhetorical authority to convey the horrors of lynching. But Wells aspired to a style of oratory that was self-controlled, logical, and unemotional, a style that underscored composure and respectability.

Although Wells understood the power of emotion as a means of persuasion, she wanted that emotion to come not from her performance but from the details of her lectures. She wanted the facts surrounding the events to be the conveyers of affect, not her voice or manner. "I am only a mouthpiece through which to tell the story of lynching," she later told Frederick Douglass, "I do not have to embellish, it makes its own way." By speaking about the sexual violence of lynching, she knew she would have to replace the language of sentiment with that of empirical fact and substitute "false delicacy" with statistics. She was, as Paula Giddings points out, one of the few women reformers who used the word *rape* without qualification or apology.[123]

Yet in contrast to her direct rhetorical style, which rarely used the passive voice, Wells was carefully dressed as a Victorian lady, replete with accessories, including a handkerchief and jewelry. She brilliantly navigated the dynamics of sexuality and race to negotiate between propriety and outrage, feminine convention and unfeminine activism, decorum and directness. She carried a gun in her purse, a purchase she made after the Memphis lynching of the three businessmen, and she advised black families to have a Winchester in their home. Wells, who Frederick Douglass affectionately referred to as a "brave little woman," is the incarnation of Naughty Nan if she were allowed to leave her Plumfield garden and enter the public sphere.[124] Naughtiness is not just about misbehaving; it can also supply the courage to fight injustice.

Wells, who traveled to Britain twice in the 1890s to raise awareness and support for her antilynching crusade, invokes not American niceness (as Stowe did when comparing the two countries) but its opposite—British niceness versus American nastiness. Wells contrasts British kindness and hospitality with American cruelty and rudeness, thus inverting the more familiar structure of transatlantic comparison. Her preference for Britain was political but also deeply personal. In an interview with the New York *Sun*, she jubilantly admitted that she experienced no "race prejudice anywhere in Great Britain . . . [I]t was like being born again in a new condition."[125] She told Liverpool audiences that in Britain, "a colored person can ride in any sort of conveyance in any part of the country without being insulted, stop at any hotel, or be accommodated at any restaurant one wishes without being refused with contempt; wander into any picture gallery, lecture room, concert hall, theater, or church and receive the most courteous treatment from officials and fellow sightseers." She had a freedom of mobility that she did not have in the United States, a point that she repeated in her column "Ida B. Wells Abroad" in the Chicago *Inter-Ocean* for American readers.

Where refined manners and a fashionable dress could not protect her from being physically thrown out of the first-class ladies car in the United States, Wells's self-presentation inspired a favorable reaction from the British elite. Sir Edward Russell, a prominent citizen of Liverpool and editor of the *Liverpool Daily Post*, which provided enthusiastic coverage of Wells's visit, noted that she was "adorned by every grace of womanhood." In her letters as well as in her column, she mentioned the warm welcome she received throughout her visit and praised British hospitality. She was made to feel like a lady, a feeling that fueled her Anglophilia as well as her condemnation of U.S. racism.

Meanwhile, the U.S. press published slanderous articles attacking Wells's reputation as a way to discredit her words during her UK tour in the spring of 1894. The white-owned *Memphis Commercial* kicked off the wave of insulting attacks by publishing a libelous article on Wells with the subheading "The Record of This Notorious Courtesan," while a story in the *New York Times* described her as "a slanderous and nasty-minded mulatress."[126] The U.S. press, both Northern and Southern, sought to punish Wells for exposing the nation's dirty laundry abroad. They had hoped that by discrediting the messenger, the message would be discarded. The opposite, in fact, happened. The British press reacted strongly against such attempts to discredit her antilynching lectures, with the *Liverpool Daily Post* calling the American articles "coarse" and "libelous."[127] The negative U.S. coverage actually backfired when it created greater media attention surrounding Wells's visit in Britain, resulting in thirty-five speaking invitations in London and a total of 102 lectures throughout Britain, according to Wells's count.

Wells was pleased by the support she received from the British press as well as the capacity of her British audiences to share her outrage at racial injustice in the United States, or what she called "United States atrocities." She also frequently experienced warm hospitality from notable British citizens, including her hosts in Liverpool, Charles F. Aked, a young pastor and Christian Socialist, and his wife. They sensed, to quote Wells, "that I did not like, or rather had no confidence in, white people, and they set themselves to work to uproot my natural distrust and suspicion."[128] British niceness sought to convert Wells's animosity into affection, successfully transforming her deep suspicion of white people into interracial friendships.

British hospitality also extended to Wells's depiction in the British press. She was repeatedly described as speaking with "refinement, dignity and self-restraint." Her oratorical style was powerful, poignant, and measured, stirring a deep emotional response in her British audiences, which ranged from small drawing-room gatherings to large lecture halls of four thousand people. What is striking is how British praise for her rhetorical manner was coupled with compliments regarding her appearance. The London *Chronicle* mentioned her mixed blood as well as her attractiveness: "She is under 30 years of age, very vivacious in manner, and decidedly good looking."[129] One paper referred to her as "a young lady of little more than 20 years of age," while another portrayed her as "a good-looking mulatto, dressed with uncommonly good taste." Such frequent remarks about her youth amused Wells, who was thirty-two years old at the time. She collected the clippings of British newspapers describing her speeches, from *The Birmingham Daily Post* to the *Manchester Guardian*. But she also included clippings of articles that referenced her ladylike demeanor and attractive appearance, including one from *The Ladies Pictorial* (May 1893): "She has attractive manners and a pleasant voice."[130] The fact that she carefully assembled and annotated each article suggests how important such comments were to Wells.

The British press acknowledged what the U.S. press could not, namely that Wells could be nice looking and a lady. Wells embraced this in large part because, as her earliest forays into journalism attest, she wanted to lay claim to feminine types—Southern lady, True Womanhood—as inclusive of black women. That she did this while lecturing on the controversial topics of lynching, sexuality, and rape is further testimony to the open-mindedness of her British audience as well as her own ability to use her body as a rhetorical tactic. Wells was fully aware of how black women's bodies were watched, commented on, and frequently insulted. By contrast, Stowe, Alcott, and Addams did not need to address their own bodies in their work as deliberately as Wells did. Nor were they preoccupied with being perceived as pretty, but rather quite the opposite. Wells knew that her success as a public figure depended on how she used her body. Like the fictional Amy March, Wells understood that a woman needed to look pleasing in order to please and persuade others. Continually reduced to her body as the site where racism and sexism intersect, Wells wanted to take that site and turn it into a sign of respectability. The British newspaper clippings demonstrate that she did precisely that.

Feminine niceness as a Victorian ideal represents conflict-averse behavior, and yet the women writers, orators, and activists in this chapter take this ideal and plunge it into the real world of familial, market, and race relations to make it conflict-immersed. The "angel in the house" is not so much killed but pragmatized: Her wings are clipped and she is forced to maneuver in a world filled with animosity, cruelty, and war. Feminine niceness undergoes a critique by women and men concerning its toxic effects on women's sense of what is possible in their own lives. This critique creates reparative possibilities that extend from filial relations to ethical practices that culminate in antilynching and antiwar crusades. Feminine niceness, moreover, signifies a debility as well as a strength, as it serves as a way to reimagine power from democratic authority to global movements of nonviolence.

But feminine niceness can only explore its potential as an ethical model of interconnection and belonging when it, paradoxically, lets go of the mandate to please.

Although the advice to let go of the need to please may seem therapeutic in relation to women and the Victorian legacy of the "angel in the house," it can become rather dangerous in the context of empire building. The next chapter turns to the relation between niceness and imperialism during the U.S. occupation of the Philippines in the aftermath of the Spanish American War of 1898. In response to overseas colonies, American intellectuals and U.S. periodical culture were preoccupied with reconciling democracy with colonization. Is it possible to be friendly invaders and conquer a nation democratically? Can there be a consensual empire? The next chapter explores what happens to American niceness when it arrives on the shores of Luzon.

5

The Likable Empire from Plymouth Rock to the Philippines

> We are not just any hegemon. We run a uniquely benign
> imperium . . . it is a fact manifest in the way others
> welcome our power.
>
> Charles Krauthammer, "The Bush Doctrine" (2001)

For at least the first half of the nineteenth century, the lanky and awkward Brother Jonathan was the iconic figure of the independent nation. As the rejected son of the cantankerous John Bull, Brother Jonathan symbolized the perennial underdog who preferred to work quietly and independently on his farm rather than fight like his father. But with the annexation of Hawaii and then the invasions of Cuba, Puerto Rico, Guam, and the Philippines in the Spanish American War of 1898, the United States was now competing with John Bull as an imperial power in its own right. The nation sought to reconcile its new imperial role with its exceptionalist self-image as a beacon of democracy for the world to emulate. But how could a nation that was founded on overthrowing the tyrannical fetters of British imperialism justify its new identity as an imperial nation?

This was the question that David Starr Jordan, President of Stanford University, grappled with in his commencement address to the class of 1898 entitled "Lest We Forget": "We have come to our manhood among the nations of the earth. What shall we do about it?" Jordan, who opposed the U.S. annexation of the Philippines, feared that the United States would follow Britain's "habit of domination."[1] This fear is alluded to in the title of Jordan's address, "Lest We Forget," which invokes the refrain from Rudyard Kipling's popular poem "Recessional" (1897), where Kipling warns Britons about the dangers of imperial hubris at a time when the empire was waning. Americans on the eve of their own overseas expansion, Jordan's title implies, would do well to heed Kipling's advice.

Jordan's fears were partly allayed by his belief that American men were simply too nice to be effective imperialists. Unlike British soldiers, who could kill the king of Zanzibar simply because the king was anti-British, democratic ideals prevented American men from "doing such things as this." According to Jordan, the British stubbornly insist on "civic order" while Americans never lose sight of the individual, a fact that "unfits America for certain tasks for which England is prepared."[2] Jordan's anti-imperialism, then, stems in part from his belief that American men are not temperamentally suited to the ruthless task of empire building, a belief that illustrates just how deeply entrenched the ideology of American niceness had become by the end of the century. Even in the face of years of military aggression on the part of the United States, Americans such as Jordan still believed that their countrymen were so nice that they lacked the capacity to be cruel.

This insistence on American niceness during the age of empire characterized not just anti-imperialists like David Starr Jordan but also those who supported America's imperial ambitions. In his "Proclamation to the Philippine People" in late December 1898, President William McKinley justified the U.S. invasion of the Philippines on the grounds of friendship: "[W]e come, not as invaders or conquerors, but as friends . . . to win the confidence, respect, and affection of the inhabitants of the Philippines by assuring them in every possible way that full measure of individual rights and liberties which is the heritage of free peoples, and by proving to them that the mission of the United States is one of benevolent assimilation, substituting the mild sway of justice and right for arbitrary rule."[3] Americans were not brutal imperialists like the Spaniards but liberators who would instill in the Philippines the basis of democratic citizenship and governance. Americans represented a nicer and gentler form of imperialism, one based on democratic principles and the pedagogical mission of tutelage.

McKinley's model of "benevolent assimilation" introduces a new imperial model of authority, one that replaces brute force with persuasion, or what he terms "mild sway." American imperialism, according to this model, depends not on fear but on affection, not on colonial hierarchy but on winning the confidence of the Filipinos. To describe this new form of empire, American intellectuals came up with various phrases, such as "democratic empire" or "imperial republic," neologisms that sought to convince skeptics that Americans could rebrand imperialism as a benevolent activity. Within this context, democracy was understood primarily in terms of popular consent, not in the political sense of a Filipino referendum on the U.S. occupation, but in the interpersonal sense of popularity. American imperialism, in other words, was implemented through and ideologically depended on a display of American likability.

The concept of a likable empire is the culmination of a process that this book has been tracing throughout the nineteenth century, expressly how the exercise of authority was conveyed through the language of niceness. Whether it was the transformation of God's authority from the Calvinist God who smites to a personable and friendly Jesus, or Harriet Beecher Stowe's personification of state authority in the form of Lincoln as a maternal figure who patiently listens, the nineteenth century worked hard to establish a homology between Americanness and niceness. My focus in this final chapter is to explore what happens to the concept of American niceness when it is exported abroad. I turn specifically to the Philippines as the colonial site where the multiaccentuality of American niceness took conflicting forms that both justified and challenged empire. Niceness, in other words, was not intrinsically imperial or anti-imperial; it was not unswervingly loyal to any side. The rhetoric of niceness was instrumental in formulating a model of liberal imperialism that appeared more egalitarian than the form of imperialism practiced by European powers and that understood the task of empire building in terms of friendship. A democratic empire also depoliticized imperial policy, making it an interpersonal matter of likability rather than something motivated by political, economic, and military interests abroad. This demonstrates that the new imperial age was less a break from the past than its reformulation, with earlier forms of American niceness, ranging from hospitality to Southern niceness, being recast in global terms.

But American niceness was not solely an imperial strategy. The latter half of this chapter explores its alternative uses as either a direct expression of moral outrage and anti-imperial critique or a deeply ambivalent response to U.S. policy as conveyed in the personal observations of the first generation of American teachers, who arrived on the shores of Manila in 1901 to be dispersed throughout the islands for three-year terms. Their experiences working in small, remote communities illustrate a complex relationship to colonialism. Modeled on American Indian education, the implementation of public education in the Philippines was seen as part of a benevolent imperial policy dedicated to educating not only the elite but also the masses.[4] Commonly assigned to regions far from Manila, American teachers were often isolated from other Americans and encouraged to reach out to Filipinos. This socially interdependent relationship between the teacher and the villagers created, in some cases, personal bonds of friendship and attachment for both Filipinos and Americans that complicated colonial hierarchies as well as the teachers' imperial mission as "agents of assimilation."[5] The teachers' diaries, letters, and some of their publications detail experiences and insights that at times worked against the *telos* of imperialism to tell another story, namely that "mild sway" could work both ways. Filipino hospitality could, in fact, be a native form of "benevolent assimilation," which raises the question of who exactly was changing whom?

From Southern Niceness to Imperial Niceness

In Chapter 2, I discussed the fantasy of consensual slavery, where the United States was seen as having the "best and mildest form" of slavery, to quote Oliver Wendell Holmes.[6] This proslavery fantasy required two main actors: the benevolent slave owner and the happy slave who consented to his or her own enslavement through their smiles and gratitude. In this chapter, I argue that this fantasy expanded in the 1890s in the form of imperial niceness, which depended on a similar combination of actors, the kind American imperialist and the grateful colonized. As corporate interests enlarged their sphere of influence, both the plantation economy and the ideological apparatus that justified the plantation were transported to new American colonies to produce a consensual empire, to which the colonized supposedly wanted to belong. My focus will be on the Philippines because this is where the United States articulated its mission of "benevolent assimilation" most explicitly, while also committing large-scale atrocities, most notably the Balangiga Massacre (1901) and the Moro Crater Massacre (1906). The incorporation of this colonial archipelago throws the contradictions of American niceness into sharp relief against the background of the brutal policies it enabled.

During Senate hearings investigating war crimes in 1902, Governor William Howard Taft explained that the U.S. war with the Philippines was exceptional for its civility: "[T]here never was a war conducted, whether against inferior races or not, in which there was more compassion and more restraint and more generosity." Taft made this claim after admitting that the U.S. military had employed the "water cure," involving U.S. soldiers forcibly pouring water into the mouths of Filipinos to extract information. But even after conceding the use of torture, Taft added that there were a few amusing instances when Filipinos would come in and say that "they would not say anything until they were tortured; that they must have an excuse for saying what they proposed to say."[7] In using waterboarding, the American soldiers were merely fulfilling the wishes of the Filipinos. It was torture by consent. The Filipinos were literally asking for it.

Both President McKinley's promise of friendship and Governor Taft's claim of a compassionate war articulate the ideology of imperial niceness, a reiteration of American niceness for the global age.[8] This global reiteration was defined in and through a range of conflicting articulations that included the frontier and Plymouth Rock, as I will discuss below. But it was also largely influenced by the antebellum model of Southern niceness that had been used to justify white-minority rule over a nonwhite population. What novelist and human rights attorney Albion Tourgée said about American literature in the late nineteenth century also holds true for its foreign policy during this same period: The nation had become confederized. As Tourgée wrote in his 1888 essay "The South as a Field for Fiction," "Our literature has become not only Southern in type, but distinctly Confederate in sympathy."[9] Some of the best-selling fiction of the 1880s and 1890s

consisted of the Lost Cause novels of Thomas Nelson Page, who celebrated the antebellum plantation by creating a romanticized world
peopled by chivalric men, Southern belles, and contented slaves.

This antebellum idyll, where class and race hierarchy not only
maintained social order but also added picturesque charm, became
especially useful as a way of justifying a world order based on industrial
castes. Nostalgia for the Southern plantation could be used to legitimate its modern incarnation on the international stage. Well before
1898, the world was becoming confederized through Southern knowledge of race management and plantation culture, evident in the large
number of former slave owners and slave traders who found work in
managing coerced labor in Fiji and Queensland, Australia.[10] "The world
today," wrote W. E. B. Du Bois in 1920, "consists, not of races, but of
the imperial commercial group of master capitalists, international and
predominantly white; the national middle classes of the several nations,
white, yellow, and brown . . . the international laboring classes of all
colors; the backward, oppressed groups of nature-folk, predominantly
yellow, brown, and black."[11] Du Bois enables us to see the parallel
between the hierarchical structure of the Southern plantation economy
and its global counterpart, a parallel that allows the "master capitalists" to learn from the genteel slaveholder how to rule in a brown world.

Just as the fantasy of consensual slavery needed the happy slave to
confirm the kindness of the master and, by extension, the benevolence
of the system, so the consensual empire needed the affirmation of the
colonized to sanction the mildness of U.S. military occupation. The
democratic empire needs to be liked by those it exploits. Filipino
approval validated the democratic nature of Americans and by extension, their superiority over their interimperial competitors. In this
way, imperialism became sutured with the long-standing ideology of
American exceptionalism, in which national specialness is predicated
on generosity and likability. In *Facts about the Filipinos* (1901), a collection of poorly cited quotations compiled by a small group of U.S.
academics with moderate anti-imperialist leanings, an anonymous
source is quoted as saying, "The people [Filipinos] do not hate the
Americans . . . The Americans are better than the Spaniards. The
Spaniards never paid for what they took; they never cured the wounded;
and when they captured prisoners, they treated them badly, starved
them, and put them in dungeons. The Americans never do this."

Quotations such as these confirm the fantasy of a consensual and likable empire but in fact American likability was a decidedly unstable notion. In the same collection, another unspecified source claims just the opposite: that the Filipinos hate the Americans. "The majority of the people realize that they are over-powered and helpless, and so maintain a passive sullenness . . . The people don't like the Americans . . . It is doubtful whether they hated the Spaniards as much as they hate the Americans."[12] Either way, the U.S. occupation of the Philippines is framed not in structural or factual terms but primarily through the interpersonal language of liking and hating.

Facts about the Filipinos uses "facts" to depict both Filipino consent and dissent. American niceness is either a stunning success or a miserable failure. One notion, however, becomes clear, that the highly fraught discourse of American likability in the Philippines reflects not American insularity but interimperial dynamics, in which Americans are measured against other colonial powers, either erstwhile or contemporary, such as the Spanish and the English. As *The Times* declared in 1899, "America is on her trial in the eyes of the world as an Imperial Power."[13]

Perceptions of empire are intermeshed with stereotypes of national character. The British actively construct an empire, whereas for Americans it happens accidentally; the British are gung-ho imperialists, while Americans are reluctant ones. The British temperament is more suited to empire-building, given their royal traditions and aristocratic history, whereas Americans are good democrats with a more egalitarian sensibility. This belief persisted throughout much of the twentieth century. As late as 1965, an article in *The New York Times* posed the question "Is America an empire? It is a question which no American cares to ask himself and, if you ask it of him, he returns a hasty negative. 'Imperialism is not in our blood. You are still thinking in terms of the British Empire.'"[14] This illustrates a form of "violent innocence," where Americans disavow their own imperial culpability by displacing it onto the British. This discomfort in admitting imperial motives, as historian Louis Perez claims, informs much of the historiography of the Spanish American War of 1898. Twentieth-century historians still bought into the McKinley line that U.S. intentions were altruistic and that the United States practiced a democratic form of imperialism. Southern educator Louis B. Wright remarked during the height of the Cold War, "American imperialism was the most enlightened of any in the world." During this same period, noted historian H. Wayne Morgan rejected the word *imperialism* and instead claimed that the U.S. objective "involved altruism toward native peoples considered unready for self-rule."[15]

This long-standing assumption that the United States represents a benign power can be traced back to British self-conceptions of their own benevolence in relation to the brutality of Spanish imperialism in the New World. From the beginning of the British imperial venture with Sir Walter Raleigh, the English saw themselves as liberating the New World from tyrannical Spaniards. The British signified a kinder and gentler form of colonialism inaugurated by "planters" rather than *conquistadores*. This became known as the Black Legend, which developed a strong anti-Catholic current as Protestant England battled with Spain in the Americas. With the Spanish American War, this grand narrative acquired a modern inflection, with the United States liberating the Filipinos from the brutal rule of the Spanish crown, an updated version that depended on contrasting familiar stereotypes: the democratic and freedom-loving Americans versus the corrupt, elitist, and slothful Spaniards. To signal the further decline of the Spanish empire after the war at Manila Bay, Commodore George Dewey referred to Spain as a "fast growing old woman."[16]

National types are clichés that depend on reiteration, and like clichés, they function as mental shortcuts for organizing the world. But types are not merely shortcuts, as Walter Lippmann warned, they also project onto the world certain cultural values that are emotionally charged.[17] Social types, more generally, map out what is acceptable and unacceptable behavior in a given society. They are prescriptive as much as they are descriptive of what it means to be a normative American. National types are narratives in concentrated form, in that they always already contain an explanatory impulse, a desire to repeat that which we already know. Their function is to affirm the familiar and to convert the strange into the recognizable. Their predictability is a source of comfort as well as an explanation. Gertrude Stein observed the pervasiveness and therapeutic function of repetition in *The Making of Americans:* "Repeating is the whole of living, and it makes of living a thing always more familiar." People are defined by their habits of thought, as they live according to behavioral scripts, each one patterned and repetitive. For William James, with whom Stein studied as an undergraduate at Radcliffe, habits are the "fly-wheel of society, its most precious conservative agent," which maintain the status quo however unjust it may be.[18] In this sense, repetition actually facilitates forgetting, turning disavowal into a habit of thought. Within the context of empire, such patterns of thought and behavior enable one not to see what is right in front of them, just like Herman Melville's Captain Delano, who is blinded by the habit of typological seeing.

Plymouth Rock Revisited: Filipinos as Indians on the Asian Frontier

As a constellation of clichés and truisms that depend on repetition, nationalism requires that habits of thought are mapped onto physical space. Within an imperial context when nationalist thought is exported abroad, it becomes especially important that symbolic forms become materially marked on the new land. One way this was done was to imagine Plymouth Rock as a portable object, one that appeared in *fin-de-siècle* sermons, periodicals, and books about Hawaii as well as the Philippines with equal ease. The Philippines became a reiterative site where U.S. race relations were restaged, not solely along a black-white axis but also in red-white terms. The Philippines, moreover, combined the Southern plantation with the western frontier. Governor Taft's testimony before the U.S. Senate committee referred to the Filipinos in terms of "tribes" and assured the skeptical senators that "[i]t is possible for us to govern them as we govern the Indian tribes." Theodore Roosevelt similarly compared the Filipinos to the Apaches and the Sioux. Roosevelt confidently added that the "doctrine I preached in my 'Winning of the West' was equally applicable in the Philippines."[19]

This pairing of the American West and the Philippines was more than a convenient analogy. Between 1899 and 1902, 87 percent of the generals serving in the Philippine-American War and all four of the military governors (Wesley Merritt, Elwell S. Otis, Arthur MacArthur, and Adna Chaffee) had been involved in overseeing Indian policy, including, in the case of Colonel Jacob Smith, the Wounded Knee Massacre in 1890. Not surprisingly, the Philippine-American War, also known as the Philippine Insurrection, was called another "Indian War." General Henry Lawten said that he and General Samuel Young "were seasoned Indian fighters who knew how to deal with savages and who would 'pursue the rebel Filipinos just as they had relentlessly pursued the Modocs and Apaches in the triumph of civilization.'"[20]

The Spaniards had referred to the Filipinos with the derogatory term *indios,* which Americans continued to use. The fusion of *indio* with Indian is best seen in an interview with an American soldier in the Philippines that appeared in the *Kansas City Times.* He explained that the Americans had adapted the old frontier adage into a new form: "[T]he only good Filipino is a dead one. Take no prisoners; lead is cheaper than rice."[21] Now that the American frontier had been officially declared closed in 1890, the Philippines afforded Americans the opportunity to continue what Herman Melville had called "the metaphysics of Indian-hating" in a modified form.

The Philippines designated a site of repetition not only in terms of Indian-hating, with westward expansion at the expense of Native Americans being reenacted in the jungles of the Philippines, but also in terms of rewriting the primal scene of national origins. By going to the tropics, Americans could reimagine the first encounter at Plymouth Rock. In an issue of *The American Monthly Review of Reviews* from 1899, Winthrop Marvin, a Boston-based journalist who would go on to become secretary of the Merchant Marine Commission, draws an explicit parallel between the Yankee missionaries who landed on the Hawaiian coast in 1820 and the "band of 'imperialists' [who] landed on Plymouth Rock." There would be "no backward steps," only the goal of winning the land for "Christianity and civilization."[22] In the fall of 1899, when the U.S. war in the Philippines had turned particularly gruesome, President McKinley invoked the Pilgrims in defending the presence of U.S. troops as part of a divine plan: "From Plymouth Rock to the Philippines the grand triumphant march of human liberty has never paused . . . May we not feel assured that if we do our duty, the Providence which favored the undertakings of the fathers and every step of our progress since, will continue His watchful care and guidance over us."[23]

Whether it was the conquest of a continent or a cluster of islands, the narrative of U.S. empire did not signify a radical break but was instead understood as part of a continuum, as a repetition of the Ur-encounter at Plymouth Rock. By framing the imperial venture in the Philippines as a continuation of manifest destiny in North America,

Americans could make its first significant intervention in Asia seem familiar. Whether Plymouth Rock was now in Hawaii or the Philippines, Americans were simply rediscovering themselves. Recycling the rhetoric of settler colonialism—replete with references to pioneers, the frontier, and unfriendly Indians—justified a familiar and seemingly benign form of colonialism as opposed to a distinctly European-style of aggressive imperial domination through alien rule. Settler colonialism fused with imperialism. The tired clichés associated with Indian encounter combined with the all-too-familiar military tactics of Indian removal resurfaced in the Philippines. As the legal scholar Aziz Rana argues, the settler structure of U.S. society did not end with Indian removal as the "original sin" of the nation but became the nation's "basic governing framework for American life for over three centuries." U.S. expansion to the Philippines—with its rhetorical and military reliance on an earlier epoch of manifest destiny— reveals what the United States has historically disavowed, namely, that it has always been a "settler empire."[24]

For sociologist Franklin Giddings, a direct link existed between Plymouth Rock and Luzon, the largest island in the Philippines. Manifest destiny on the North American continent and imperialism on tropical islands continue the same practice of "the Christian art of exploitation" that has characterized U.S. relations with Native Americans from the beginning. In *Democracy and Empire* (1900), Franklin Giddings makes a case that democracy and empire are not mutually exclusive phenomena; on the contrary, they have been historically intertwined, starting with the frontier. There is a deeply cynical tone to Giddings's manifesto on globalization because he understands the process as entirely fueled by commercial interests searching for new markets to exploit.

We long ago became weary of sowing and reaping, and also of legitimate trading; we are beginning now to weary even of our protected manufactures. We must find new opportunities for making fortunes by jobs and government contracts. The reservations allotted to our unhappy red men have nearly all been appropriated by rough riders, and we naturally turn to the sunny lands and gentle savages of Hawaii and Luzon for further practice of the Christian art of exploitation . . . they offer something better than an honest living, earned in the sweat of one's brow.[25]

According to Giddings, the natives of Hawaii and the Philippines serve the same function as the native population in the United States: Appropriating native lands, or what Theodore Roosevelt called "wasted spaces," facilitates investment, speculation, and government contracts in order to avoid physical labor. By the end of the century, Brother Jonathan had exchanged his farming tools for stocks and bonds because physical labor had become "irksome," to quote Thorstein Veblen in *The Theory of the Leisure Class* (1899). To make money without work is precisely what attracted the United States to both Hawaii and Luzon. Capitalist interests shifted from the wild west to the tropics, as the frontier represented not only a dynamic concept but also a portable one that could be exported across oceans from continents to islands.

Despite the fact that Giddings perceptively analyzes what is motivating the new era of globalization, he also apologizes for it. Just as Henry Clay bemoaned the disappearance of the Native American as an inevitable yet necessary stage of national development, so Giddings understands the "economic conquest of the natural resources of the globe" as inevitable. The only issue is what form this exploitation should take. Will the United States turn the Philippines into plantations "to be exploited remorselessly in the old-fashioned way for the benefit of their owners, without regard to the well-being of their native populations"? Or will the United States embark on a model of tutelage, which Giddings sees as preferable on moral grounds, where northern nations will govern "firmly, in the interest both of the world at large and of their own native inhabitants"? Giddings imagines a model of consensual empire based on "consent without consent," or what he also refers to as "probable consent," which is delayed consent that "may be given years later." Giddings employs the analogy of a child who is critical of her parents' firmness until she becomes an adult and then is grateful for her strict upbringing. According to this model, imperial conquest has a happy ending. The "democratic empire" will eventually evolve into a nice empire, where "spiritual brotherhood" will prevail and "the kingdom of heaven [will] be established on the earth."[26]

Natty Bumppo Goes to the Philippines

The problem with this model of imperialism animated by American niceness, a model that assumes the apparent consent of the conquered, is that it is very difficult to tell what the other is thinking. This was precisely the lesson I drew in Chapter 2 from the way Edgar Allan Poe's friendly Tsalalians and Herman Melville's smiling Babo use niceness as a colonial form of deception in luring the white travelers in *The Narrative of Arthur Gordon Pym* and the gullible Captain Delano in *Benito Cereno* into a false sense of security. Facial expressions of consent such as the smile may deceive more than they enlighten because expressions cannot be taken at face value. One U.S. veteran explained the Janus-faced quality of Filipinos in terms of "that particular faculty of all Orientals to say one thing and meaning [sic] another."[27] Like the noble/ignoble binary that shaped white perceptions of Indians as either friendly or hostile, so Americans in the Philippines divided the natives into the friendly *amigos* and the hostile *insurrectos*.

But such binaries were unstable in the context of guerilla war. Similar to Pym's distrust of Tsalalian friendliness, one U.S. soldier wrote of Filipino duplicity, saying that they "professed to be 'mucho amigo' (good friends) to our faces, while secretly aiding the insurrection with all the means at their hands."[28] Other military men, such as Brigadier General J. Franklin Bell, who took charge of destroying villages in Batangas Province in southern Luzon, complained that the Batangans were more numerous than the Sioux and did not wear war paint to assist Bell in deciphering "the actively bad from the only passively so." Colonel Frederick Funston mocked the idea of imperial benevolence and McKinley's concept of "mild sway" as he did the notion of Filipino friendship: "The Filipino doesn't love us a bit. He doesn't know what gratitude is. He has no sense of appreciation, and I believe he'd like us better if we dealt more severely with him."[29]

With the possible exception of Funston, who confidently asserted that the Filipinos hated the Americans, these military responses stem from a common anxiety based on their inability to read Filipino faces with the same ease with which they claimed to have been able to read Indians. From the U.S. perspective, the same person could be either a friend or foe. The Americans condescendingly referred to this duplicity as "amigo warfare," but historian Reynaldo Ileto argues that feigning friendship was a Filipino survival strategy that needs to be understood as a mode of resistance within the context of the U.S. invasion: "Amigo warfare was an attempt to come to terms with the new colonizer—to deflect its massive power by being friends and negotiating with its representatives in the town centers, while maintaining commitment to the revolutionary project."[30] Although the United States claimed to be coming to the Philippines as friends rather than invaders, the U.S. military response to "amigo warfare" was brutal. For them, friendship meant either complete Filipino submission to U.S. authority or being labeled an enemy and destroyed, together with the destruction of livestock, crops, and entire villages.

Although some Americans, particularly military leaders, described the Filipinos as duplicitous, believing that their niceness was a subterfuge for revolutionary activities, other Americans insisted on the genuineness of Filipino niceness. In an article that appeared in *National Geographic* entitled "The Philippines and Their People," which was reprinted as a U.S. Senate document at the request of Senator Henry Cabot Lodge, Henry Gannett noted how safe most of the islands were by 1904 (75 percent of the islands). Based largely on his own experience as a government geographer, surveyor, and census-taker in the Philippines, he commented, "a white man is as safe in traveling or living as in Arizona or Colorado or Montana. He may go about with perfect freedom." To convey how safe he felt traveling alone, Gannett invokes an Indian analogy, not of the savage but rather of the nice Indian on a reservation: "[T]here is no more danger than in traveling on the reserve of a tribe of friendly Indians." He credits Filipino hospitality for the safety of the islands. When hotels are few, the white traveler must depend on the generosity of local villagers, where "the people are ready and anxious to show him hospitality."[31]

Walter W. Marquardt, who arrived as a teacher in 1901 and spent the next eighteen years in the Philippines as a principal, superintendent of schools, and eventually Director of Education in the Philippines, confidently noted, "the courtesy and hospitality of the Filipino people is almost proverbial." He recalled several occasions where he depended on a Filipino family housing him for an evening as a school inspector who traveled extensively and he remembered one poor family who had to go to the house next door to borrow knives and forks in honor of their American guest. He would at first offer payment to the families for the food and lodging, but a Filipino friend advised him "most strongly" to cease making such offers, as it always insulted the host's feelings.[32] Just as American niceness was a highly contested and multiaccentual concept, so was Filipino niceness. It was both feigned and sincere, a source of suspicion and of safety, a guerilla strategy of resistance, and a genuine gesture of hospitality.

But just as Americans attempted to interpret Filipino niceness—is it duplicitous or genuine?—so Filipinos sought to understand the Janus-faced quality of American niceness. They too tried to distinguish friend from foe. They also tried to make sense of the Jekyll-and-Hyde dynamic of U.S. policy in the Philippines, where the American was a twinned figure—a nice American who came in friendship and the Ugly American who came to kill. Furthermore, American duplicity took the form of conflicting tactics between the civilian leadership who invoked the rhetoric of friendship to build consensus and the military hawks who incited fear through the barrel of a gun. At stake in this division was the form U.S. authority should take in the Philippines: "mild sway" or military aggression.

These competing modalities of authority within the colonial government exposed fissures and contradictions at the heart of the U.S. imperial venture, contradictions that are apparent in the oxymoron of a "democratic empire." In the Philippines, for every brutal military man such as General Frederick Funston, there was an amiable American charming the Filipinos through the interpersonal sphere of sociality. Military aggression and a charm offensive went hand in hand, with the soldier's bayonet acting as the necessary counterpoint to the nice American's winning smile.

William Howard Taft: The Icon of the Nice American

The person who embodied the American charm offensive most successfully was the first civilian governor, William Howard Taft, who served in the Philippines from 1901 to 1904. A graduate of Yale, Taft was appointed Solicitor General of the United States, and by the age of thirty-five, he became a judge for the Sixth Federal Circuit. Six years later, President McKinley would ask Taft to head the second Philippine Commission and to oversee the implementation of a colonial infrastructure. He was at first reluctant to accept McKinley's offer. He strongly opposed the U.S. occupation of the Philippines because it represented, according to Taft, "a burden by us contrary to our traditions [,] and at a time when we had quite enough to do at home." McKinley, who admitted his own ambivalence about the endeavor, stressed the importance of civic duty, and he responded to Taft's reluctance with the retort, "I can trust the man who didn't want them better than I can the man who did." This conversation, which appeared in the magazines of the period, frames U.S. leaders as reluctant imperialists, the political counterparts to Natty Bumppo's persona as the reluctant Indian killer who would rather avoid conflict than seek it. But Taft, who would go on to write "Civic Duty," ultimately accepted McKinley's offer on the grounds of duty to one's country.[33]

Taft gave the likable empire a figural form as the gentle giant, whose three-hundred-pound frame was both strong and active. His face was frequently described as kindly and avuncular, hardly the face of terror. His very persona exuded the ethos of American imperialism: an authoritative figure that combined warmth with strength, someone who possessed a personable style that attracted people to him effortlessly. Taft's early biographer, Edward Cotton, noted that Taft's greatest achievement in the Philippines was turning native hostility into friendliness through the power of his magnetic personality. "When [Taft] left, not only had the rebels surrendered, but those whose hatred of the United States had been most intense had become enthusiastic supporters of the American policy." Taft, in other words, personified American niceness, with its power to convert animosity into affection. At the end of his three and a half years as governor of the Philippines, Taft had built a consensual empire to which the Filipinos wanted to belong.

Taft, the icon of the nice American, became the poster boy of a distinctly American brand of imperialism, one based on friendship rather than fear, on likability rather than aggression. He gave an interpersonal dimension to the U.S. occupation of the Philippines that drew a polite veil over the less picturesque elements of military brutality and economic plunder. Sociality played as much of a role in the Philippines—and in the presentation of U.S. imperialism to Anglophone readers—as the bayonet and the dollar.

In the years after the Spanish American War, American readers were losing interest in the Philippines after the dramatic capture of the leader of the Filipino nationalists, Emilio Aguinaldo, and his subsequent swearing of allegiance to the United States in 1901. For the vast majority of Americans, indifference replaced the initial wave of outrage or jingoism, depending on whether one supported the war or not.

American satirist Finley Peter Dunne's "Mr. Dooley" captured this indifference when he wondered if the Philippines were "islands or canned goods." William Taft's wife, Helen Herron Taft, acknowledged in her memoir that the Philippines did not "seem to have impressed themselves very forcibly upon the general American mind."[34]

When articles about the Philippines did appear in U.S. periodicals in the early twentieth century, it was largely from a human-interest angle, frequently featuring Governor Taft and Helen Taft with descriptions of their banquets, their social life, and especially Taft's magnanimous personality. The fact that U.S. imperial policies were primarily depicted through an interpersonal lens—focusing on the personalities of individual Americans in the Philippines, from the affable Tafts to well-intentioned American teachers—emphasizes the role that American niceness played during this period. Imperialism was framed primarily as a social encounter rather than an economic and military strategy with distinct interests and aims. While this interpersonal lens omitted significant details about U.S. policy, it also highlighted potentially unsettling details that both challenged Jim Crow sociality in the United States and affirmed the importance of interracial friendships between Filipinos and American teachers.

The rendering of Taft's popularity in the Philippines for consumption in U.S. periodicals illustrates how the United States understood empire as a media event. Taft and his wife mastered the new visual media, and they frequently had journalists and photographers accompany them to public events. American niceness could be visually packaged and disseminated internationally through gestures of amiable sociality. It was a mediagenic encounter ripe for the global age of incorporation. When Taft and his wife returned to the Philippines in 1905, they were accompanied by American photographer Harry Fowler Woods, who immortalized the Taft handshake when Taft greeted a Moro chieftain. This greeting had particular symbolic significance because the Moros were considered to be the most resistant to the U.S. occupation (and would become the targets of a brutal massacre the following year). Taft's charm offensive, this photograph suggests, could even work among the most defiant.[35] Taft's biographer, Edward Cotton, reinforced the impact of these images by remarking that the Filipinos "had never encountered anything like the Taft smile and the Taft handshake."[36]

Photograph of William Howard Taft and Moro Chieftain. Photograph by
Harry Fowler Woods, 1905. © Trustees of H. F. Woods Camp Trusts.
Reproduced by Permission of the Trustees.

In *Overland Monthly*, Robert Westcott tells how the Filipinos revered Taft and frequently called him "Santo." "In their eyes, he is indeed a saint. They have canonized him by popular consent, and there is no doubt but that Taft's name will go down through the Filipino generations to come alongside those of their numerous religious saints." Westcott also adds that the Filipino natives showered Taft's family with gifts, some of which were quite valuable, while the majority consisted of chickens and fresh eggs. How did Taft cultivate the affection of the Filipinos? At first, according to Westcott, the Filipinos were taken aback by Taft's enormous size, and they expected him to rule as the Spaniards did, with an "iron hand." But Taft won them over when he began "to assert his democracy and smile their fears away."[37] Democracy and smiles go hand in hand, the latter being an expression of the former. Taft embodied McKinley's ideal of "mild sway," with his likable personality being a powerful force of persuasion.

Westcott's portrait of Taft in the Philippines adapts older forms of benign authority for the mass media age, namely the figure of the beloved patriarch of Southern paternalism. Taft, we are told, was adored by his "little brown brothers," a term that Taft used affectionately to refer to the Filipinos. Westcott's portrayal of Taft bears an uncanny resemblance to the kind slave master of proslavery novels and later Lost Cause fiction: "He handled them [the Filipinos] like they were so many children, in an affectionate earnestness of manner that simply compelled them to look up to him. This is the way he won the natives and caused himself to be universally loved by the people."[38] This recycling of a familiar type but now in the setting of the Philippines underscores the continuity involved in refashioning older forms of American niceness for the new era of imperial conquest. Not only was Plymouth Rock portable but so was Dixie.

Taft's magnanimity exemplified a concept that I call "manifest cheerfulness," a national affect that John O'Sullivan defined in 1839 as the "cheerful creed of high hope and universal love."[39] Taft conveyed this spirit of optimism and hope through his facial expressions, such as his ubiquitous smile and his contagious laughter. In the Philippine newspaper *El Progreso*, an article entitled "Señor Taft" claims "Mr. Taft has the same respectful smile for all, the same courtesy." The fact that Helen Taft included a clipping of this article in her memoir suggests that she understood the importance of her husband's jollity for

U.S. globalization. American journalist Walter Wellman similarly reported that Taft molded the Philippines into a nation largely through his amiable manner: "He smiled upon those people, and won their liking; he laughed with them, and won their good humor." Cotton claimed that Taft's uproarious laughter was "known and loved around the world. . . . It was heard in America, Europe, and Asia. It oiled the machinery; and carried as much influence as anything he said." Taft's contagious laugh became the soundtrack of Americanization that coheres the world through interpersonal skills.

It is not enough, however, for Cotton to emphasize Taft's likability; he also has to compare it to other imperial powers, thus illustrating how American niceness was a tactic in interimperial rhetoric: "'Why,' exclaimed the Filipinos, 'the Spanish never laughed like that!'"[40] Revamped for the twentieth century, the Black Legend was no longer primarily about Spanish brutality, but about who had the best sense of humor, the Americans or the Spaniards. Notice how Cotton claims to quote the Filipinos directly as a way to give voice to the colonized in a democratic gesture that contributes to the fantasy of the consensual empire.

Media portrayals of Taft's smile and his overall sense of good cheer illustrate the process by which U.S. hegemony was constructed in the Philippines for an Anglo-American audience. Just as journalists described the building of roads and bridges, so they also depicted how the hearts and minds of the Filipinos were won. The sheer repetition of articles about Taft's popularity among the Filipinos raises the question of what cultural work was being done through the narrative frame of sociability. Scenes that dramatize Filipino affection for Taft function metonymically to illustrate Filipino legitimation of the U.S. presence in the Philippines for an American reading public thousands of miles away. But why was Filipino consent so important? Was it to assuage American guilt? Was it to vindicate the invasion in order to show that Franklin Giddings's ideal of a democratic empire was in fact a reality?

Filipino legitimation of U.S. occupation was a way to cultivate U.S. consent for imperial policies. If the Filipinos liked Taft, who personified America's imperial presence in the country, then that presence is legitimated for Americans as well as Filipinos. Legitimation is a democratic form of authority in which leaders depend on the consent of the governed, and, in the case of a democratic empire, the colonized have to agree to their own colonization. They did so by cheering Taft. By personalizing the political, U.S. periodical articles collapsed the distinction between liking Taft and liking the U.S. occupation of the Philippines. In this way, U.S. media coverage of the Philippines focused largely on human-interest stories, sidestepping policy and military issues. Taft's popularity, in other words, compensated for justice rather than expressed it. The interpersonal lens of likability obscured political questions of power. Democratic legitimacy was reduced to a popularity spectacle. Taft, together with the American media industry, anticipated Dale Carnegie's formula for individual (and national) success by knowing how to make friends and influence people. One article in particular seemed to encapsulate Carnegie's advice: "Mr. Taft is a peace-maker, and his jolly, unassuming, yet dignified personality wins him thousands of friends among Asiatics, as well as Occidentals."[41]

Modeling Multiracial Hospitality in the Era of Jim Crow

When William and Helen Taft arrived in the Philippines in June 1900, they were immediately struck by an atmosphere of racial antagonism and segregation. "Whites only" signs appeared on the front windows of restaurants, barbershops, and bars in Manila, and the two thousand black volunteers serving in the Philippines were routinely harassed with racist taunts, epithets, and songs. As historian Jonathan Lurie points out, over 60,000 U.S. soldiers had brought their racism with them, frequently calling the Filipinos "niggers" and shooting at them randomly. "I feel sorry for these people and all that have come under the control of the United States," an African American sergeant wrote. "The first thing in the morning is the 'Nigger' and the last thing at night is the 'Nigger.'"[42] A Filipino physician noted that white soldiers would push Filipinos off the streets, spit at them, call them "niggers," and generally "abuse them in all manner of ways." White soldiers would also rob Filipinos on the street, steal from the fruit vendors, and loot Filipino homes. One black soldier wrote home in 1899: "The whites have begun to establish their diabolical race hatred in all its home rancor in Manila, even endeavoring to propagate the phobia among the Spaniards and Filipinos."[43] Historians Stuart Creighton Miller and especially Paul Kramer understand the Philippine-American

War as primarily a race war, and Kramer has argued that U.S. colonial violence depended on racial ideologies that took new forms within the context of the Philippines.

It is within this highly charged atmosphere that the Tafts moved into their new home in the Malacañang Palace, and Taft immediately made it clear that racial discrimination was unacceptable. "The color line," noted one of Taft's early biographers, "was never drawn at the numerous official or unofficial dinners or receptions required by his office." "We insisted on complete racial equality," recalled Helen Taft, "We made it a rule from the beginning that neither politics nor race should influence our hospitality in any way."[44] Although Taft's private letters refer to the Filipinos as "unfit for self-government" and "the greatest liars it has ever been my fortune to meet," his public persona was highly inclusive. The openness of Taft's receptions, for instance, "signaled a sharp break with ongoing military encounters as well as with domestic U.S. forms." Kramer calls these multicultural affairs "fiesta politics," which played an important role in establishing an "inclusionary racial formation," a symbolic expression of cross-racial empire building that countered both military conduct and Jim Crow segregation in the United States.[45]

Human-interest stories about the Tafts' hospitality seemed to have had an afterlife far exceeding the time the Tafts actually spent in the Philippines and such stories resurfaced in 1908, while Taft campaigned for the U.S. presidency and won the election. In his portrait of Taft in *The Outlook* in 1908, Lyman Abbott portrayed him as a man "free from the race and class prejudices of every description of any man I have ever known . . . His friendship for the Filipino is not a patronizing friendship. It is that of a big, wise, helpful brother."[46] Abbott described Taft dancing with Filipino ladies, who appeared diminutive alongside his large frame. Soon after arriving in the Philippines, Taft studied the country's most popular dances, such as the Spanish *quadrille* or the *rigodon.* "In forty days he attended a score of state balls, literally dancing and smiling his way into the hearts of the people."[47] Helen Taft admitted that they made a "poor display in our first attempts at the *rigodon,* but by dint of watching others night after night both my husband and I became most proficient at it." Reflecting on the importance of such social events more generally, Helen Taft recalled how "Americans and Filipinos mingled together in perfect amity" and how the Filipinos seemed pleased with such "friendly co-operation," because it demonstrated to them that "America was in the Philippines as a friend rather than as an arbitrary ruler."[48]

In 1906, *The Independent* published an article recounting the Taft years, when the Malacañang Palace was a multicultural contact zone, in contrast to what it became in the two years after the Tafts' departure. Entitled "American Snobbishness in the Philippines," the article, written by sociologist Elsie Clews Parsons, featured a daughter of one of the prominent native officials who looks nostalgically at a photograph taken of her with Mrs. Taft, both in traditional Filipino dress. "Between this native aristocracy and the Americans in Manila there is at present little or no social intercourse, altho [sic] the natives have a deep sense of hospitality and are devoted to social festivity."[49] Americans rarely left their own social bubble, and there were American ladies who had never visited a Filipino home. The democratic multiculturalism of the Taft years was quickly replaced by American "race snobbishness" that resulted in a heightened sense of social segregation between the Filipino elite and their American counterparts.

Taft understood the significance of sociality in the construction of hegemony. The consent of the governed within an imperial republic required pleasure as well as compulsion. As Ann Laura Stoler has argued, "colonialism produced both its colonizers and its colonized in the banal and humble intimacies of the everyday."[50] U.S. hospitality was one way in which cross-racial social relations were produced and reproduced. Such relations reflected the emergence of a multicultural empire, with local elites mingling with "master capitalists," to quote W. E. B. Du Bois.[51] In contrast to the streets of Manila, where U.S. soldiers would frequently harass and taunt the Filipinos, the Malacañang Palace represented an alternative space of American niceness, an inclusive interracial colonial space in which power between the global and the local was made visible through the mundane pleasures of dancing the *rigodon*.

Although the Tafts' multiculturalism in the Philippines undoubtedly served the interests of the colonial endeavor, it is important not to underestimate the impact that these human-interest stories had on American readers, who were consuming these stories within a segregated nation. In Asia, the Tafts modeled an alternative form of sociality, one that was far more racially inclusive than their subsequent years in the White House (1909–1913). In other words, the Tafts were able to reimagine an inclusive racial formation in Asia for U.S. consumption in ways that were socially prohibited in the United States in the context of Jim Crow and Chinese Exclusion. The fact that there were several testimonials attesting to Taft's lack of bigotry, regardless of whether or not they were accurate, suggests that, for the first time, being seen as a racist by the mainstream press was considered a liability for a politician.

"The Filipinos Hate Us"

The triumphant and self-congratulatory periodical accounts of Taft's popularity in the Philippines contrast with other articles that emphasize Filipino contempt for Americans. *The Arena*, a progressive magazine from Boston, published a symposium in 1902 entitled "Why I am opposed to Imperialism." One of the four participants was Ernest Crosby of Rhinebeck, New York, who wrote:

> We have already made the Filipinos hate us as much in four years as the Spaniards did in four hundred, and our troops had hardly entered Manila and Santiago before they began to call the natives 'niggers' and 'monkeys.' What hate, jealousy, wounded pride, and sullen misery on the one hand, and cruelty, disdain, and oppression on the other, that word 'Imperialism' has denoted ever since the dawn of history![52]

Another contributor to the symposium, Bolton Hall, similarly noted, "Imperialism's other name is *Brutality*." Taft's charm offensive, which includes all the necessary gestures of niceness, such as handshakes, smiles, and laughter, ultimately conceals the cruelty of the U.S. occupation of the Philippines. Upon his return from a fact-finding mission in the Philippines, Senator Fred DuBois of Idaho concluded, "The Filipinos hate us."[53]

British periodicals were particularly critical of U.S. treatment of the Filipinos. Although initially, as Geoffrey Seed has argued, the British press was highly supportive of the U.S. presence in the Philippines, seeing it as part of the white man's burden, they began to change their views in the first decade of the twentieth century. Britons living in the Philippines were shocked at U.S. corruption, cruelty, and violence and charged that the Spaniards were more humane rulers than the Americans. The *Spectator* unapologetically acknowledged this: "[T]he Americans will never succeed in the Philippines unless they banish cruelty, and make clemency, and not reprisals, the distinguishing mark of the ruling race . . . The Americans are not by nature cruel . . . but 'the brightness of Columbian air' has given them . . . a certain fierceness which makes them liable to act in hot blood, and in hot blood there is little equity."[54] Hugh Clifford, a colonial civil servant in Southeast Asia who had eagerly welcomed the U.S. annexation of the Philippines, soon became highly critical of it. By 1906, Clifford wrote in *Macmillan's Magazine* that he believed the Filipinos were "far worse off than . . . under the dominion of Spain." A writer in the *Fortnightly Review* similarly noted that the Americans were "more hated than the Spaniards ever were." John Foreman, who wrote extensively on the Philippines and had lived as a merchant in the country for many years, was especially appalled by the American treatment of Filipinos that he personally witnessed. He commented on the drunken behavior of American soldiers, their rudeness toward the Filipinos, and the frequency of rape, robbery, and murder committed by them with impunity.[55] Although he noticed an improvement among U.S. troops after Taft's arrival, he nonetheless declared the U.S. imperial venture a failure and urged the Americans to withdraw from the islands.

What is significant about the debate over the U.S. occupation of the Philippines is the distinctly social cast that it took. The main focus of the debate was whether the Filipinos liked or hated Americans. The interpersonal dynamics of likability were inseparable from the political debate about annexation. Whether it was a domestic critique of U.S. imperialism as published in the *Arena* or interimperial condemnation in the British press, the success or failure of the U.S. imperial venture was framed within the terms of popularity. Why should the question of American popularity be so prominent in the context of the Philippines? One reason is that the United States framed the entire colonial venture around the concept of a democratic empire, a concept that was based implicitly on the ideal of the consent of the governed. For a colony without political representation, both consent and its failure were understood in terms of likability, while hatred became a euphemism for colonial dissent.

In addition to informing discussions about the relations between the invading Americans and Filipinos, the American likability factor also influenced debates about the racial divisions between white and black American soldiers. Black soldiers' letters, many of which were published in the African American press, underscored the fact that Filipinos distinguished between the friendly treatment they received from black soldiers versus hostility from white soldiers. In 1900, the *Savannah Tribune* published a letter from F. H. Crumbley, who wrote, "The natives are very friendly to the Negro soldiers" and he encouraged the black middle class—professionals and missionaries—to emigrate to the Philippines. Infantryman James Booker wrote in his letter, published in the *Richmond Planet* in 1900, "Wherever we have been stationed on the islands we have made friends with the natives and they always express regret when we are ordered from amongst them."[56] General Robert P. Hughes made a similar observation in his statement before the U.S. Senate committee on the Philippines in 1902: "[T]he colored troops taken to Samar mixed readily with the natives [and] many of the latter shed tears when the colored soldiers were removed." Filipinos would refer to black soldiers affectionately as "negritos Americanos," while black soldiers would call the Filipinos "cousins."[57]

Letters from black soldiers also provide insight into the brutal everyday encounters between white soldiers and Filipinos, thus illustrating how the U.S. color line was exported to the islands. John W. Galloway, a sergeant major in the 24th U.S. Infantry, saw a direct connection between the treatment of the Filipino and the black southerner: "He is kicked and cuffed at will and he dare not remonstrate." The *New York Age* published an anonymous letter from a black soldier who similarly noted how white Americans applied "home treatment for colored peoples: cursed them as damned niggers, steal [from] and ravish them, rob them on the street of their small change, take from the fruit vendors whatever suited their fancy, and kick the poor unfortunate if he complained, desecrate their church property, and after fighting began, looted everything in sight, burning, robbing the graves."[58]

Although it is important to remember that black soldiers were not merely innocent bystanders but were implicated in the brutality of colonial war alongside white soldiers, their personal observations complicate their relationship to Americanism and imperialism.[59] Black niceness worked as an implicit critique of white racism that lumped together both blacks and Filipinos under the epithet "nigger." Furthermore, black likability created a way to talk about their own friendships and identification with Filipinos, evident in a letter by a black soldier writing home: "Tell my friends that I am just the same as a Filipino."[60]

This link between blacks and Filipinos is not only a significant interpersonal bond but also an important symbolic analogy that anti-imperialists used in their critique of annexation. The cruelty of imperialism includes the everyday encounters described in the letters of black soldiers, together with punctuated moments of crisis. And it is in these latter moments of egregious violence—such as the Moro Crater Massacre of 1906—that we see another strain of American niceness surface, namely, the use of niceness as a critique of imperialism. Although Theodore Roosevelt had officially declared the end of the Philippine-American War on July 4, 1902, the Moro Crater Massacre points to the fact that opposition to the U.S. presence on the islands continued long after the official end of the conflict.

With the northern part of the Philippines largely pacified, the U.S. military turned its attention to the south, with General Wood declaring, "The Moros would either submit or suffer harsh consequences." Jolo Island in particular was a site of ongoing resistance to the U.S. occupation in this largely Muslim region. It came to Wood's attention that 800 to 1000 Moros, including many women and children, had taken refuge in an inactive volcano called Bud Dajo, and he dispatched 600 troops to bombard them, which they did over the course of two days. By March 7, 1906, the United States reported fifteen killed and thirty-two wounded, but with the release of photographs of mass graves, it became clear that there were nearly one thousand people dead. The *New York Times* headline read: "WOMEN AND CHILDREN KILLED IN MORO BATTLE PRESIDENT WIRES CONGRATULATIONS TO TROOPS."[61]

Among the first to respond to the news of this massacre of Muslim men, women, and children was Mark Twain, who wrote in a tone of utter disgust and shame: "The enemy numbered six hundred—including women and children—and we abolished them utterly, leaving not even a baby alive to cry for its dead mother. *This is incomparably the greatest victory that was ever achieved by the Christian soldiers of the United States.*"[62] Twain was especially horrified at the murder of women and children, and he goes on to create a picture in prose of the terrified children clinging to their mothers for protection: "We see a picture. We see the small forms. We see the terrified faces. We see the tears. We see the small hands clinging in supplication to the mother; but we do not see those children that we are speaking about. We see in their places the little creatures whom we know and love." He sarcastically adds, *"Death List is now 900. I was never so enthusiastically proud of the flag till now!"* [original emphasis].[63] By creating through words a visual image of the children's "terrified faces," Twain seeks to humanize the statistics, to put a human face on the enormous scale of the massacre of nine hundred people. Twain's sympathetic portrait of the child is intended to catalyze moral outrage at the cruelty of U.S. policy in the Philippines through an analogy of the American child. His camera lens is focused on the youngest victims of the crime, not on the patriotic killers. By concentrating on the innocence of the Moro child, he exposes the pretense of national innocence. His concluding image is the U.S. flag, forever stained in the blood of innocent civilians in this tragic act of egregious cruelty.

Similarly, Moorfield Storey, president of the Anti-Imperialist League in Boston and one of the founders of the NAACP, wrote in "The Moro Massacre" that "our flag [has] so many indelible stains of which the blood shed in the massacre of Jolo is the latest!"[64] Like Twain, he highlights the victims to express his outrage at this instance of ethnic cleansing, with no women and children spared and no prisoners taken. "They have been exterminated," he concludes. He then exposes the cruelty that lies just below surface of the official rhetoric of "benevolent assimilation" in the form of a question: "Is it possible that this is all the greatest and freest nation in the world, as we like to believe ourselves, can do for a people over whom we insist on extending our benevolent sway?" Although Twain had published a scathing critique of lynching in "The United States of Lyncherdom" (1901), Storey makes an explicit connection between the Moro Massacre in the Philippines and the lynching of black men in the United States: "The spirit that slaughters brown men in Jolo is the spirit which lynches black men in the South . . . When a man is lynched the community which tolerates the offence suffers more than the victim."[65] Where Twain focuses on the youngest victims of U.S. violence, Storey turns to the damaging impact such violence has on the United States as a whole.

In a letter to Storey, W. E. B. Du Bois describes the experience of looking at a photograph of the mass graves that appeared in U.S. newspapers in the aftermath of the carnage: "It was the most illuminating thing I have ever seen. I want especially to have it framed and put upon the walls of my recitation room to impress upon the students what wars and especially Wars of Conquest really mean."[66] At the center of the photograph is a corpse of a Moro woman, with a bare breast, and her dead baby on her lap. No doubt Du Bois had the Philippines in mind when he wrote in *Darkwater* (1920):

> It is curious to see America, the United States, looking on herself, first, as a sort of natural peacemaker, then as a moral protagonist in this terrible time. No nation is less fitted for this role. For two or more centuries, America has marched proudly in the van of human hatred,—making bonfires of human flesh and laughing at them hideously, and making the insulting of millions more than a matter of dislike,—rather a great religion, a world war-cry: Up white, down black; to your tents, O white fold, and world war with black and parti-colored mongrel beasts![67]

Du Bois combines the spectacle of lynching—bonfires of human flesh—with the large-scale carnage of imperial wars. His description of the grotesque laughter of the American lynchers building bonfires recalls the image of American soldiers burning the dead in Balangiga, Philippines, after an earlier massacre in 1901. Two elderly women emerged from hiding, pleading unsuccessfully with U.S. soldiers to give the dead a "Christian burial" rather than stack their bodies and soak them with kerosene before igniting the funeral pyre.[68] The hideous laughter in Du Bois's apostrophe is the soundtrack of American hatred, the grotesque shadow-side of Taft's affable laughter of American niceness.

One month after the Moro Crater Massacre, an interview appeared in *The Arena* (the same Boston periodical that included the symposium on anti-imperialism) about U.S. involvement in the Philippines, featuring the suffragist, temperance activist, and travel writer Helen Gougar. A celebrity in her day, she served twenty-three years as the president of the Woman's Suffrage Association of Indiana, having worked with Susan B. Anthony and Elizabeth Cady Stanton, among others. Noted for her acerbic wit and elegant oratory, Gougar made an

Trench at Bud Dajo, Philippines, March 1906. This photograph appeared
several months after the Battle of Bud Dajo in Johnstown, Pennsylvania's
Weekly Democrat on January 25, 1907. The Anti-imperialist League
immediately reprinted 3,000 copies and distributed them to the press.
This is more than likely the image that Moorfield Storey sent to W. E. B.
Du Bois. The U.S. National Archives and Records Administration,
Local Identifier No. 111-SC-83648.

easy transition to travel writing. In *Forty Thousand Miles of World
Wandering* (1905), she remarks that a civilization can be gauged by
how well they treat women.[69] In the Philippines, her feminism found
its global articulation through her anti-imperialism. Not addressing
the massacre explicitly, she chastises American soldiers for looting the
homes of Filipinos and stealing their furnishings and art. She describes
the Filipinos in Manila, where she was based, as cultivated and educated, with men treating their wives respectfully. In this article as well
as in her travel book, she recounts her sixteen days in the Philippines,
including an experience attending the national theater to see a play in
Tagalog by Severino Reyes entitled *Walang Sugat* (*Not Wounded*). Set
in 1896, the play depicts the cruelties of Spanish rule and how an outraged and long-suffering people finally found retribution. When the

Spanish friars were killed off in one act, Gougar notes, "the audience went wild with cheering."[70] One does not have to read too closely into the play's plot and the audience's response to understand it as an allegory of the U.S. occupation. By the first decade of the twentieth-century, Spanish friars were a safe way to vocalize colonial rage and bitterness after eight years of U.S. occupation.

Gougar's views about the economic plunder of the Philippines brought her sharp rebuke in the U.S.-dominated press in Manila. She criticized former Governor Taft for supporting a contract-labor system that would reduce Filipinos to modern slaves, working on sugar and tobacco plantations for far below a living wage: "Its enactment would be a crime not second to that of African slavery." Gougar also attacked the plan to bring in Chinese labor to work on plantations under contract-labor because it would lower wages more generally: "If the Chinese are to come to the Philippines and Hawaii, let them come as free men, work as free men, go as free men. Let there be no slave-labor under the whip of capital in any corner of the earth over which the stars and stripes wave."[71] Contract labor was the imperial equivalent of slavery, argued Gougar, and the United States was merely repeating the same tactics of colonization used by France and the United Kingdom. Gougar condemned the establishment of the plantation economy in the Philippines, a policy that Franklin Giddings had cynically predicted nearly a decade earlier. Taft's amiability certainly "oiled the machinery," to borrow Edward Cotton's metaphor, in the sense that it facilitated the investment of capital for the underdevelopment of the Philippines as a corporate plantation dependent on contract-labor and the importation of U.S. goods.

Gougar's words, when combined with those of Du Bois, Storey, and Twain, demonstrate the multiaccentuality of American niceness, which exposes what the Tafts' geniality attempted to deflect. In doing so, it models a different notion of the nice American, one predicated on anti-imperialism, where justice predominates over affability. American niceness, in other words, can critique as well as facilitate imperialism. The analogy between Filipinos and Black Americans features extensively in American rebukes of U.S. imperialism, whether in terms of lynching (Storey and Du Bois) or enslavement (Gougar). This alternative tradition of American niceness also shares a genealogy with U.S. critiques of Indian policy, ranging from Washington Irving's outrage at the Creek massacres in Florida to Helen Hunt Jackson's extensive documentation of U.S. human rights abuses against Native Americans in *A Century of Dishonor*. In both instances, niceness took the form of moral outrage and national shaming, a collective form of self-rebuke at the cruelty of manifest destiny.

The Return of the Nice Indian

The use of the Indian analogy to contextualize and explain American conduct in the Philippines can be found not only in terms of how the rhetoric of amiability facilitates both the establishment of a settler nation and resistance to it, but also in the form of indigenous hospitality. In other words, Plymouth Rock and the nice Indian reemerge in the Philippines. When Governor Taft appeared before the Senate Committee on the Philippines to report on war crimes in 1902, he began his statement by commenting on the genuineness of Filipino hospitality: "The Filipino is an exceedingly hospitable person. The Spaniard says, 'My house is yours.' Sometimes there is a question whether he means it; but when a Filipino who has a house says it is yours he turns out his family and puts you in, and he expects you to appreciate it by accepting his offer."[72] In fact, Secretary of War Elihu Root placed an entire section of documents relating to the Philippines under the heading "Filipino Hospitality." Similarly, Helen Taft mentions her "long acquaintance with Filipino hospitality" in her memoir *Recollections of Full Years*.[73]

The American elite were not the only ones to comment on Filipino niceness. The letters of black soldiers repeatedly stress Filipino friendliness. W. Cordin with Company B, 25th Infantry wrote, "They [Filipinos] are friendly and hospitable . . . There are here some of the best mulatto people I have ever seen in my life. They are handsome. It is common for the women to wear their hair hanging down." Chaplain Theophilus G. Steward wrote in 1901, "The [Filipinos] are hospitable to a fault, and they have too the full color sympathy, and appear to entertain a decided fondness for colored Americans, many of whom having come to Manila with the colored regiments, have married handsome Filipino belles." Governor Taft observed that black soldiers "got along fairly well with the natives" and "too well with the native women," which led to "a good deal of demoralization in the towns where they have been stationed." In response, Taft ordered the with-drawal of black soldiers from the Philippines in 1902.[74]

But hospitality also entails risk, as noted in Chapter 1, in that min-gling with the stranger can also be dangerous and even deadly. The ambiguity surrounding the concept of hospitality was borne out in the Balangiga Massacre on the island of Samar in 1901, less than three months after the Tafts arrived in the Philippines. When U.S. troops from Company C of the 9th Infantry arrived in the coastal town of Balangiga, the mayor warmly welcomed the soldiers, while secretly coordinating with the *insurrectos*. The army's task was to stop the flow of supplies to the Filipino resistance in Samar. On September 26, 1901, while the U.S. soldiers were eating dinner, Filipinos ambushed the men and killed seventy-four, confirming for many Americans their fears about Filipino duplicity.[75] This led to a series of reprisals in the days and weeks following that became genocidal campaigns, which included destroying villages and killing thousands of civilians. After the Balangiga Massacre, orders were given to reduce the region to a "howling wilderness" by killing anyone able to bear arms, including women and children aged ten years and older.[76] The press considered it one of the great failures of U.S. military history alongside the Alamo and Custer's defeat.

Some military leaders blamed Taft's friendliness toward the natives for encouraging such dissent. General Chaffee, who had extensive experience fighting Native Americans, denounced Taft's "soft molly-coddling of treacherous natives" and was determined to end resistance in Samar with "shot, shells and bayonets."[77] For U.S. military leaders, American niceness was naive and misplaced because they believed colonial authority needed to terrorize the colonized into obedience. The Balangiga Massacre exposed civilian leaders like Taft to military scorn and confirmed precisely the point made by military strategists about the dangers of "amigo warfare." The massacre revealed how ineffective American niceness was in the colonial setting and how it actually risked the safety of U.S. soldiers.

This gap between civilian "soft mollycoddling" and military aggression would only widen with the increase of U.S. civilians in the Philippines, most notably the arrival of over five hundred school-teachers in August 1901. Traveling on the U.S. Army transport *Thomas*, the teachers, who were branded "Thomasites," landed just a few months after the Tafts. A precursor to the Peace Corps, the American teachers represented the colonial carrot to the military's stick; they were the benevolent face of conquest, a personification of American niceness whose mission was to set up primary schools throughout the archipelago to teach English literacy as well as basic math skills. In contrast to the Spaniards, who remained in the more densely populated port cities and never embarked on a policy of mass public education, the Americans were sent to the remotest regions of the islands to implement the ideal of colonial tutelage. Some of the teachers had prior experience teaching in Indian and black training schools, while others arrived immediately out of college. They comprised the ideological wing of U.S. imperialism, dedicated to legitimizing the colonial endeavor to the Filipinos directly through culture, language, and sociality. They would mediate U.S. imperialism not through a bayonet but through pedagogy, with the interpersonal playing a vital role in the everyday relations sustaining imperial rule.

Educator Walter Marquardt described the Thomasites as having the "pioneer spirit" and he saw their work as educators following that of the soldier.[78] While some Thomasite accounts share this mission as the cultural accomplice to the soldier, others demonstrate a more nuanced and complicated relationship to the imperial endeavor. They were neither unambiguously pro-imperialist nor vehemently anti-imperialist. Instead, some Thomasites represented a third category combining elements of both positions, resulting in a hybrid attitude that epitomized "colonial ambivalence," where the very presence of the Filipino undermined the authority of the colonial position and exposed the contradictions and ambivalence that lay at the heart of the imperial project.[79]

The teachers lived in the Philippines for a minimum of three years, though some stayed longer, while others married into local Filipino families and spent the rest of their lives in the archipelago. Soon after their arrival in Manila, the teachers were assigned to remote villages, often the only Westerners in the immediate region, and for many, this was the first time they experienced life as a minority. Many became culturally and socially integrated into Filipino society as they adapted to the manners and mores of what was commonly called "Filipino Hospitality." Some of the American teachers learned the local dialect of Tagalog or Visayan. To be effective persuaders, teachers had to immerse themselves in their immediate surroundings, and this immersion was itself a form of integration and incorporation, in which many were transformed through their encounter with the host culture. Just as American niceness, according to the biographical sketches of Taft, converted anti-Americanism into affection, so Filipino hospitality altered American teachers' relationship to their colonial mission. They received a cultural education that stayed with them long after they returned, with a few not returning at all.

The Thomasites' immersion into Filipino society illustrates what Vicente Rafael calls "the promise of the foreign." Filipino nationalism, forged within a colonial context, has been "inseparable from the hosting of a foreign presence to which one invariably finds oneself held hostage." Filipinos, argues Rafael, have taken their country's foreign influences and converted foreignness from "a sign of shame into a signal of impending sovereignty."[80] By incorporating the foreign, Filipino culture absorbs and domesticates otherness. How did Filipino incorporation work when the foreigner was a young American teacher, equipped with little more than a few notebooks and chalk, oftentimes without a school room, assigned the task of teaching English to a population who greeted her with suspicion? What happened to the American abroad in her encounter with Filipino hospitality in the remote provinces of the archipelago?

Just as Taft's Filipino popularity became fodder for human-interest stories in U.S. periodicals, so the role of American teachers in the Philippines also appeared in the pages of U.S. magazines during the first decade of the twentieth century. In 1906, James Le Roy, a writer on the Philippines and a high-ranking diplomatic aide to Taft in Manila, published an article in *The Outlook* entitled "The American Teacher in the Philippines." He admits that some of the original Thomasites proved "uncongenial or unfitted for the work," and they were subsequently removed from the classroom. But Le Roy focuses on the success stories. He describes the ideal type of American teacher as one who has an assortment of personality traits that bears an uncanny resemblance to Taft's nice American: "a broad-minded, tactful, generous, and approachable *neighbor*" [original emphasis]. Anticipating the critique of the Ugly American, Le Roy, who was fluent in Spanish, adds that the ideal teacher should teach English in the classroom but should also learn the native dialect so that "he may the better put himself *en rapport* with his pupils and parents, and may understand their mental processes the better also."[81] Like the good diplomat, teachers practice a form of ambassadorship in order to ingratiate themselves into the hearts and minds of their students.

In "American Teachers and the Filipinos," also published in *The Outlook*, Helen Beattie, one of the original Thomasites, stresses the importance of a teacher's appearance in making her a successful educator in the Philippines. "The successful American teacher for the Philippines must be socially attractive, possessing diplomacy, executive ability, tact, persistence, patience, hopefulness, and, last of all, teaching ability." Social skills are especially important in the Philippines, argues Beattie, because the Filipinos are "an eminently social people." American teachers must be a "diplomat," by which she means warm and welcoming, if they expect to be invited to Filipino dinners, balls, and theaters. For Beattie, American niceness is understood as a form of diplomacy, a necessary social tactic in converting Filipino suspicion into warmth: "It has been no uncommon thing to see cold, indifferent towns changed most marvelously in a few months' time in this way."[82] She has witnessed firsthand the power of the interpersonal to turn animosity into friendship. For Beattie, likability matters.

Beattie was one of 165 women who arrived in 1901, and although women constituted a distinct minority among the 365 men, they were seen as especially effective educators. Described by scholars as "maternal soldiers of empire," the female Thomasites embody what Amy Kaplan calls "manifest domesticity," where the traditional sphere of domesticity expanded—like the trajectory of Manifest Destiny—onto foreign ground. Domesticity, argues Kaplan, became an important force of imperial incorporation, converting the foreign into the familiar terms of family and nation. Given women's association with domesticity, they became ideal vehicles for the promulgation of what Funie Hsu and others have called "maternal colonialism." But Helen Beattie's account is not particularly maternal; instead, she resembles Ida B. Wells in her emphasis on prettiness as a tactic of persuasion.[83] She also observes Filipino sociality not in the familial sense of white mothering or fathering but rather in more lateral terms, such as receiving invitations to attend dances and the theater. There is little of the hearth in Beattie's account and far more about the youthful pleasures of Filipino sociality. Her article serves as an advice piece for other American teachers on how to be liked by the Filipinos: "He [the American teacher] must have tact for a prouder, more sensitive people than these never lived. He must not assume that he is of a superior race, and that things not American are hopelessly bad."[84] Beattie, as the personification of the nice American, advises her male compatriots on how to avoid being perceived as the Ugly American, since she admits that some of her fellow teachers had turned to drink and gambling.

What is interesting is that many of the articles by or about American teachers in the Philippines focus more on the warmth of Filipino sociality than on American niceness. In these articles, Filipino friendliness is not a source of suspicion, as it was among the military, but a sincere mode of hospitality. Some American teachers took Filipino niceness at face value, appreciating the way in which they were greeted and integrated into local life. One such article appeared in the *Congregationalist and Christian World* in 1902, and it consists of extracts from a personal letter of a Boston University student who teaches in Negros. He writes, "The people are kind to me and considerate in many ways of my well-being. Many Americans might take lessons from these people in hospitality."[85] His homesickness is abetted, in part, due to the invitations he received to participate in local community life. Another teacher comments in *The Outlook*, "Seldom does he enter a town without finding a spirit of increased friendliness and confidence pervading. He always finds the wonderful Filipino hospitality awaiting him, and is everywhere treated with the greatest of courtesy and respect."[86] What differentiates these periodical articles from those featuring Taft is that they are less about charming and impressing the Filipinos with a likable personality and more about Filipino sociality and inclusivity. There is a tone of humility in these articles, which counters the imperial hubris of both Taft and the American military leadership by suggesting that Americans can learn much about niceness from Filipinos rather than vice versa.

One of the most poignant accounts written by a Thomasite is by Albert Leslie Pitcher, who wrote "The Need of Good Men in the Philippines," which appeared in the progressive magazine *The Independent* in 1907. One of thirty-five teachers from Massachusetts and a graduate of Harvard (1896), Pitcher begins by reflecting on his two years of teaching in Pampanga, a province of Luzon. He describes the pleasure of reminiscing about his time in the Philippines by looking at photographs of his friends from those days. But the response of his American friends troubles him: "[W]hen I have declared strong feelings of friendship for people in the town where for two years I lived familiarly with them, my declaration has been taken as a good joke."[87] Their mockery is a sign of their racism, as is their skepticism that Pitcher could have developed deep friendships with a colonial people. Friendship implies a degree of equality, and his earnest assertion of interracial friendship unsettles such presumptions among his white American peers.

Pitcher admits that he arrived in the Philippines with a colonial mentality: "to help show the natives something about American schools and to teach them English." But he was soon "surprised to find in a peasant community so high an intellectuality." He then goes on to describe how he was transformed through his intimate encounters with Filipino domestic and social life:

> I was admitted to their family life, an intimacy that proved to me their respect for old age; their love for their children; their reverence for the family, accountable for monogamy, legitimate children and a wholesome observance of marriage. I visited their ceremonies, religious and secular . . . I went with them into the country, hunted, ate, slept just as they did. I found in their relations, one with the other, their conduct was marked by a dignified courtesy and a constant good nature.[88]

Not only was Pitcher invited into the homes of Filipinos, but he also welcomed Filipinos into his own home, a gesture of reciprocity that was consistent with the manners and mores of Filipino hospitality. "My house was always open to them, my ear ever ready to listen to a grievance—too often caused by American injustice—and my advice at their service. Possibly coming and living alone in their town brought out to me all the charm of Filipino hospitality, and led to our understanding." As he became fluent in the local dialect, he played the role of mediator, listening to the injustices inflicted by Americans upon the townspeople. He also became their confidante, and the final lines of his article are perhaps the most moving: "[M]y life with them was shorn of its loneliness and became one of pleasure."[89] While living alone in Pampanga, Pitcher never felt lonely because he was fully integrated into their social world, where he found acceptance, companionship, and happiness.

As the anthropologist Mary Racelis and literary scholar Judy Celine Ick have argued in their collection entitled *Bearers of Benevolence: The Thomasites and Public Education in the Philippines,* the American teachers often lived alone. "Seeing American teachers alone, the Filipino values of hospitality and compassion would quickly come to the fore, 'Poor thing! S/He doesn't have anyone with her' ('*Kawawa naman! Wala man lang siyang kasama.*')." Given how dispersed the American teachers were throughout the islands, Julian Encarnacion similarly notes, "If the American teacher wanted to talk to somebody he had to talk to a Filipino. If he needed a friend, that friend had to be a Filipino."[90] In this situation, where the American teacher was dependent on Filipino sociality, apparently stable colonial power relations could quickly become reversed. According to Racelis, "In the classroom the Americans were the teachers and the Filipinos the students. In the community, the Filipinos became the teachers and the Americans took the role of students learning how to live and enjoy life in that foreign environment."[91] The teacher-student bond was one of interdependency rather than a rigid colonial hierarchy.

This emphasis on a personal frame to evaluate the bonds between teachers and students has been critiqued for replacing colonial hierarchy with a notion of reciprocity. This results in academic sentimentalism that brackets off the structural dynamics of colonialism for "the niceties of student-teacher relationship" [sic].[92] Although I understand this concern, it is problematic to elide the personal entirely. There is a contingent element to the personal that unsettles paradigms and complicates theories, particularly within the context of colonialism. I want to recover a dialectical sensibility between the structural and the personal in understanding some Thomasites as paradoxical figures who combine an imperial mission with personal vulnerability, because the latter represents an important and undervalued attribute of niceness as curiosity and risk-taking. This understanding of niceness is particularly helpful in exploring the dynamic between American curiosity and Filipino sociality: How do some American teachers become Filipinoized in trying to navigate their new social world? Although the Thomasites have been called "agents of assimilation," their accounts demonstrate how the contingencies of the colonial situation, which include the teachers' own need for social attachments, require that they adjust and assimilate to the very communities that they were sent to Americanize. This illustrates the historian Nicholas Thomas's caveat that colonial policy, including pedagogical practices, is often projected rather than realized.[93]

The significance of Filipino sociality is born out in Albert Pitcher's depiction of village life in his article "Hunting in Luzon: A Search for Game, Not for Men" (1902), which appeared in the *Boston Evening Transcript*, the same newspaper that published William James's anti-imperialist writing among others.[94] Pitcher spends little time on the hunt and far more time detailing food preparation and dining rituals in the remote village. He carefully notes the making of *naci* (cooked rice) in the evening, and then women preparing *bibinka* (pancakes) in the morning with a fluency that suggests his own familiarity with the culture he describes. After dinner, there was storytelling about former hunts that were told in Pampangan and then in Spanish. He depicts a rich and busy social scene of a village outing to the mountains that includes men, women, and children, together with two Americans, a teacher (who we assume to be Pitcher) and a nonthreatening police inspector, who is invited because of his guns, which ironically prove ineffective since the *carabao* (water buffalo) are killed using traditional methods—a spear and netting. Pitcher epitomizes the cultural ambassador, explaining culinary practices with the same informal knowledge with which he translates Pampangan expressions to his American readers. He also represents an alternative model of American masculinity, one that breaks with a militaristic stereotype and unabashedly recounts the pleasures of domestic bachelorhood.

Not all Thomasites had such a profound experience in the Philippines as Albert Pitcher. In a confidential letter to W. E. B. Du Bois on August 28, 1902, H. M. Butler, an African American educator in the Philippines, wrote requesting the names of potential teachers of color who could serve in the Philippines. Writing from the province of Pangasinan, Butler remarks that there are only four black teachers in the entire archipelago and the Department of Education is possibly interested in recruiting more because the white teachers are "discouraged" and "returning home." Du Bois wrote back a brief note enthusiastically saying that he would do what he could.[95] Although there is little information on whether more teachers of color were actually recruited in the ensuing years, Butler remained in the Philippines for the rest of his life despite the fact that his American wife returned to the United States soon after their arrival. Butler eventually retired from the Department of Education at the University of Manila in 1933 and died in the Philippines in 1944. Butler's letter to Du Bois, written soon after his arrival in the Philippines, discloses two things: first, his observation that a number of white teachers were discouraged by the job and wanted to return to the United States; second, his belief that black teachers would be better able to adapt to the Philippines, as his own life would illustrate.

Despite Butler's observation that white recruits were dismayed by the challenging conditions, there were a number of Thomasites who decided to stay in the Philippines or who returned after spending a few years back in the United States. Ralph Wendell Taylor, a University of Michigan graduate, was an original Thomasite who remained in the Philippines far beyond his three-year commitment and eventually brought his elderly mother to live with him. In his extensive correspondence with his mother, he admits that he questions the impact that they were having among the Filipinos: "I doubt very much if native peoples are benefitted very much by the coming of another civilization to overwhelm them. As you suggest the Americans here (and I would say at home also) need missionaries as much as the natives do—which is one reason why I am not particularly in favor of foreign missions."[96]

Bess Taylor Thompson, who also arrived on the SS *Thomas* in 1901, taught until 1904, when she returned to California to work in the Oakland schools. She then decided to return to the Philippines because "I had never ceased being homesick for the Islands." Here, Thompson echoes Pitcher in that both feel homesick for a place that was not literally their home yet functioned as one at an emotional level. Dr. Gilbert Perez arrived in the Philippines as a young teacher planning eventually to travel the world but decided to spend his life in the archipelago because he "liked the country and the people."[97] What these brief anecdotes illustrate is the extent to which some of the early American teachers decided to spend all or a significant part of their professional lives in the Philippines. Pitcher's article, together with the several references to Filipino sociality in published and unpublished letters and diaries, point to the profound and transformative changes that Americans across the color line experienced in the Philippines.

Filipino scholars have explored and discussed the importance of Filipino hospitality as part of a national recovery program of social values in the post-Marcos era. To understand key Filipino concepts and cultural characteristics, scholars such as psychologist Virgilio Enriquez claim that one must begin with the Tagalog language and the variety of terms that describe social relations. He argues that the term *kapwa* is ultimately the most important as well as the most comprehensive, as it means "the unity of the one of us and the other," the recognition of a shared identity. Enriquez explains that in English the self is defined in opposition to the other, and therefore, the self is understood as a separate identity. But in Tagalog, both are integrally fused together in the formation of a social identity that does not distinguish between "ego" and "other." The concept of *pakikipagkapwa* includes the root word *kapwa* but also goes beyond it, as it refers to human interaction at the highest level.[98] It refers to an idea, a value, and an ethics that acknowledge the dignity of the other, regardless of their station in life. It defines a democratic worldview that is other-oriented.

For Filipino scholars such as Enriquez, the translation of Filipino hospitality to *pakikipagkapwa* represents a mode of sociality that is also indicative of the culture as a whole. Or as Raymond Williams would put it, *kapwa* describes a whole way of life. This Tagalog term includes niceness, amiability, and social harmony, all of which are inscribed within a larger ethical framework that also emphasizes justice. According to Enriquez, *pakikipagkapwa* includes resistance among the powerless. "He [the Filipino] knows the meaning of co-operation and concerted action. He knows that *pakikibaka* (joining the struggle) is a valid aspect of *pakikipagkapwa* in the face of injustice and adversity."[99] This term encompasses Filipino dissidence to the U.S. occupation, such as the Balangans surreptitiously sending supplies to the *insurrectos* or the Moros in Mount Dajo taking refuge inside an inactive volcano on the eve of their massacre. But if *pakikipagkapwa* refers to human relations at the highest level, what would it mean to embrace the human element of this Tagalog term to include U.S. dissidence to such imperial policies? In other words, the moral outrage of Mark Twain, Moorfield Storey, W. E. B. Du Bois, and Helen Gougar could serve as transpacific examples of *pakikipagkapwa*.

Thomasites like Albert Pitcher were sent to the provinces of the Philippines to Americanize the Filipino, to replace indigeneity with "civilization." But in this encounter, Pitcher was himself transformed through the deep friendships and rich social experiences that he had over the course of his two years in Pampanga. Enriquez's essay on *kapwa* concludes with a proverb originally from the region of Pampanga, perhaps a proverb that Pitcher knew and would likely understand as a speaker of the local language: *Malagua ing maguing tao, masaquit ing magpacatau.* It means, "It is easy to be born *tao* [human], but it is not as easy to act like one."[100] Pitcher's story is ultimately paradoxical. Through an imperial mission, Pitcher became Filipinoized, which in turn had a transformative effect on him. He became more fully human by becoming decolonized. He expressed genuine longing and sadness for the Filipino friends whom he left behind, much to the astonishment of his friends in the United States, who were bemused by his earnest attachment to a colonized other. The depth of this attachment illustrates a sensibility that is akin to *kapwa.*

Throughout this book, American niceness has been related to the exercise of power and authority. But the writings of American teachers in the Philippines, such as Pitcher, reveal how cultural missionaries of Americanization were in turn profoundly transformed through their experiences with Filipino hospitality. To repeat the words of the American teacher from Boston University: "Many Americans might take lessons from these people in hospitality."[101] If American niceness incorporated indigenous modes of hospitality as part of a national history of manners, as discussed in Chapter 1, then this final chapter on empire illustrates just the opposite, namely, how a minority culture incorporated an imperial one.

If apologists for American imperialism saw the invasion of the Philippines as the continuation of a "civilizing" mission that began at Plymouth Rock, both nascent and committed anti-imperialists could also invoke the primal scene of American niceness by reintroducing the trope of the kind Indian in the form of the hospitable Filipino. Moreover, the experiences of many of the Thomasites in the Philippines raise the tantalizing possibility that this time the white settler could embrace indigenous hospitality rather than destroy it. To put it another way, the Narragansett term *wunnégin* that Roger Williams first introduced to Anglophone readers in 1643 could now be realized through the Tagalog term *pakikipagkapwa*. Both terms link niceness with cooperation, sociability, and moral goodness, and, in doing so, they offer a trans-indigenous model of sociality that could serve as a counterbalance to a history of colonialism.[102]

Returning to the Primal Scene of Indigenous Niceness

If such a possibility seems overly optimistic, perhaps even idealistic, consider the evocative question that Mahmood Mamdani poses in his essay "Settler Colonialism: Then and Now" (2015): "What does it mean for America, the world's first settler colony, to be decolonized?" He then goes on to answer the question with an analogy from German history: "For those who think that such a question is anachronistic in the aftermath of the Indian genocide—given that a small number survive today—it is well worth asking: what did it mean to de-Nazify Germany in the aftermath of the genocide of Jews?"[103] What would it mean then to decolonize the United States? And what role would niceness play in this process of decolonization? On the one hand, niceness has enabled a pattern of forgetting, a way to disavow both the nineteenth-century wounds of genocide and slavery and their ongoing legacy today. This national habit of disavowal has depoliticized the violence of a white settler nation and its imperial manifestations by focusing instead on interpersonal moments of likability, epitomized in the media spectacle over Governor Taft's popularity in Asia. On the other hand, however, over the course of its highly contested history, niceness has also been the vehicle of critique, a way to challenge, unsettle, and contest manifest destiny by insisting on the necessity of what Toni Morrison famously called "rememory," an antidote to selective amnesia that revisits the past and confronts its darkest moments. By highlighting the critical aspects of the multiaccentual terrain of American niceness, this book challenges the dominant pattern of historical disavowal and forgetting by evoking "long memory," which as Dylan A. T. Miner has remarked, is "at the core of Indigenous modes of knowing."[104] Long memory, as an indigenous epistemology, both acknowledges and engages with the legacy of suffering, in the vein of William Apess and Zitkala-Sa, together with their allies Washington Irving and Helen Hunt Jackson.

How effective could such a countervailing strategy of niceness ultimately be? Native American hospitality did little to curb genocide and Filipino hospitality did little to turn the tide of American imperialism. But questioning the effectiveness of indigenous niceness, either in the form of Native American *wunnégin* or Filipino *kapwa*, is not to wallow in pessimism; instead, it is to confront that pessimism head on by grappling with the contradictions embedded in the concept of niceness and acknowledging its strengths as well as its limits.

In linking *kapwa* with *wunnégin*, this book concludes with a trans-indigenous model of niceness that brings Plymouth Rock together with the Philippines in an anti-imperialist embrace of indigenous hospitality, where niceness merges with ethics. To be nice, in this model, is to be fully human. This understanding of niceness comprises an ethics of the nonmarket, a term that Cornel West aptly uses to acknowledge those values, such as mercy, justice, caring, nurturing, solidarity, and fidelity, that are denigrated in a society dedicated solely to profit but which are nonetheless vital for a healthy democracy. As part of a constellation of terms denoting positive sociality, niceness is precisely what binds individuals together; it is an expression of our desire to connect with others, to feel a sense of belonging, or what Jane Addams called "the solidarity of the human race."[105] Consequently, niceness represents both the foundation and precondition for new forms of economic and political justice, reminding us that if the interpersonal can disavow the structural, it can also help us reimagine the world.

Notes

INTRODUCTION

1. Canadian government's travel and tourism information for the United
   States: http://travel.gc.ca/destinations/united-states; "Bahamas Issues
   Travel Advisory to Citizens Travelling to US, Young Males Asked to
   Exercise Extreme Caution," *The [Jamaican] Gleaner,* July 8, 2016; Angela
   Waters, "Overseas Travel Warnings about the USA Mount," *USA Today,*
   August 11, 2016; Joan Beck, "The Ugly American is Being Displaced by the
   Deadly American," *Chicago Tribune,* May 27, 1993.
2. "Current History in Caricature," *Review of Reviews* 25 (January 1902): 16.
3. José Martí, "The Truth About the United States" (1894), in *José Martí:
   Selected Writings,* ed. Esther Allen (New York: Penguin, 2002), 329.
4. Twain's first foray into the theme of conjoined twins as contrarian types
   was "The Personal Habits of the Siamese Twins" (1869), which first
   appeared in *Packard's Monthly* in 1869 and was later republished in *Mark
   Twain's Sketches, New and Old* (Hartford, CT: The American Publishing
   Company, 1875), 208–212. Thanks to Shosuke Kinugawa for this source.
   Twain would return to the theme of conjoined twins as contrarian types in
   Pudd'nhead Wilson and *Those Extraordinary Twins,* but without explicit
   reference to their views on slavery.
5. Richard Peake's play *Americans Abroad* was actually a collaboration with
   British comedian Charles Mathews. It was performed under the title
   Jonathan in England; or Jonathan Doubikins. According to Francis Hodge,
   this may have been the first antislavery play. Francis Hodge, *Yankee
   Theatre: The Image of America on the Stage, 1825–1850* (Austin: University
   of Texas Press, 1964), 73–74. See also Maura L. Jortner, "Throwing Insults
   Across the Ocean: Charles Mathews and the Staging of 'the American' in
   1824," in *Portrayals of Americans on the World Stage: Critical Essays,* ed.
   Kevin Wetmore, Jr. (Jefferson, NC: McFarland & Co., 2009), 41.
6. Fanny Trollope, *Domestic Manners of the Americans* (New York: Penguin,
   1997), 40; D. H. Lawrence, *Studies in Classic American Literature* (New
   York: Cambridge University Press, 2003), 65. The phrase "Ugly American"
   first appeared in the best-selling novel *The Ugly American* (1958), written

by William Lederer, a Navy captain, and Eugene Burdick, a political scientist, at the height of the Cold War.

7. Henry James, letter to his mother, Mrs. Henry James, Sr., October 13, 1869. Quoted in "Background and Sources" in the Norton Critical Edition of *The American*, by Henry James, ed. James W. Tuttleton (New York: Norton, 1978), 321–322.

8. On national fantasy and affect, see Lauren Berlant, *The Anatomy of National Fantasy: Hawthorne, Utopia, and Everyday Life* (Chicago: University of Chicago Press, 1991).

9. Alexis de Tocqueville, *Democracy in America* (New York: Penguin, 2003), 653, 656.

10. Karen Horney, *The Neurotic Personality of Our Time* (1937) (New York: W. W. Norton, 1964), 116 (footnote 1).

11. Geoff Dyer, "My American Friends," *New York Times*, January 3, 2010, p. BR23.

12. Rudyard Kipling, *American Notes* (New York: Arno Press, 1974), 126.

13. Fanny Wright, *Views of Society and Manners in America* (Cambridge, MA: Harvard University Press, 1963). Quoted in Christina Kotchemidova, "From Good Cheer to 'Drive-by Smiling': A Social History of Cheerfulness," *Journal of Social History* 39.1 (2005): 11.

14. Charles Dickens, letter to John Forster from Washington, DC, March 15, 1842. In the same letter, Dickens qualifies his praise of the United States with a revealing confession: "But I don't like the country. I would not live here, on any consideration. It goes against the grain with me. I think it impossible, utterly impossible, for any Englishman to live here, and be happy." Quoted in *The Life, Letters, and Speeches of Charles Dickens*, vol. 1 (Boston: Houghton, Mifflin and Company, 1894), 159.

15. Robert Louis Stevenson, *Across the Plains with other memories and essays* (1892) (New York: Charles Scribner's and Sons, 1905), 40-41. I am grateful to Ann Colley for this source.

16. "President Bush Addresses the Nation," *Washington Post*, September 20, 2001. http://www.washingtonpost.com/wpsrv/nation/specials/attacked/transcripts/bushaddress_092001.html

17. Christopher Bollas, *Being a Character: Psychoanalysis and Self Experience* (New York: Hill & Wang, 1992), 165–192. For a discussion of Bollas's concept of "violent innocence" in the context of post-9/11 thought, see Jacqueline Rose, "Psychoanalysis, Politics and the Future of Feminism: A Conversation" (with Juliet Mitchell and Jean Radford), *Women: A Cultural Review* 21:1 (7 April 2010): 90.

18. By contrast, I could not find one article in the British press during the heyday of the IRA bombings in England during the 1970s and 1980s that asked the question: "Why do the Irish hate us?" When I asked British friends why this was so, their answer was consistently the same: "The English know very well why the Irish hate us." The consistency of the British response is just as revealing as the ubiquity of the American question. While the immediate U.S. response to 9/11 through the question "Why do they hate us?" is based on disavowal, the absence of this question in the British context is not a sign of denial, but conversely, an acknowledgment of historical consequences.

19. This question—why do they hate us?—is not limited to the immediate aftermath of 9/11. It has now been transposed into a declarative statement—Islam hates us—to justify ongoing military operations in the Middle East and to push for banning Muslim refugees. In a March 2016 interview with Anderson Cooper, Donald Trump said: "I think Islam hates us. There's a tremendous hatred there. We have to get to the bottom of it." But in his inaugural speech, Trump mystified the reasons for such hatred by saying: "This is something nobody can even understand." In 2013, John F. Kelley, now Trump's head of the Department of Homeland Security, expressed similar sentiments in a speech: "I don't know why they hate us and I frankly don't care, but they do hate us and are driven irrationally to our destruction." This emphasis on 'them' hating 'us' is a way to avoid acknowledging what the CIA calls "blowback," namely the acknowledgment that U.S. foreign policy has consequences. Jon Schwarz, "Why Do So Many Americans Fear Muslims? Decades of Denial About America's Role in the World," *The Intercept* (February 18, 2017), accessed February 18, 2017.

20. Graham Greene, *The Quiet American* (New York: Penguin, 1992), 40.

21. George Shulman, "Acknowledgment and Disavowal as an Idiom for Theorizing Politics," *Theory & Event* 14.1 (2011), accessed July, 28, 2016, https://muse.jhu.edu/. Shulman references Michael Rogin's notion of "motivated forgetting" from Rogin's "'Make My Day!': Spectacle as Amnesia in Imperial Politics," *Representations* 29 (Winter 1990): 103; Ernest Renan, "What Is a Nation?" (1882), accessed October 1, 2015, http://ucparis.fr/files/9313/6549/9943/What_is_a_Nation.pdf.

22. This quote from Marilyn Monroe is taken from Jacqueline Rose, "A Rumbling of Things Unkown," *London Review of Books* 34 no. 8 (2012): 29–34. In this same article, Rose reminds the reader that Arthur Miller in *The Misfits* gave Monroe's character Roslyn a variation of the same expression: "Hello, how are you, what a nice day."

23. Thomas De Quincey, "English Dictionaries," in *The Notebook of an English Opium-Eater* (Boston: Ticknor and Fields, 1855), 277; Julius Charles Hare, "On English Orthography," *Philological Museum* 1 (1832): 650.

24. Brander Matthews, "New Words and Old," *Harper's New Monthly Magazine* 97 (June 1, 1898): 307–312.

25. Noah Webster, William Webster, and William Wheeler, *An American dictionary of the English language* (Springfield, MA: G. & C. Merriam, 1868), 286. For a British example, see John Ogilvie, *The Imperial dictionary of the English language* (London: Blackie & Son, 1884), 257. In British dictionaries, the colloquial definition of *nice* as pleasing does not typically appear until the final definition of the term. The older definitions predominate.

26. Walt Whitman, "Slang in America," *North American Review* 141 (Nov. 1, 1885): 431, 435.

27. V. N. Voloshinov, *Marxism and the Philosophy of Language*, trans. Ladislav Matejka and I. R. Titunik (Cambridge, MA: Harvard University Press, 1986), 23.

28. V. N. Voloshinov, *Marxism and the Philosophy of Language*, 23

29. V. N. Voloshinov, *Marxism and the Philosophy of Language*, 23–24. [original emphasis]

30. Barbara Alice Mann, *George Washington's War on Native America* (Westport, CT: Praeger, 2005); David E. Stannard, *American Holocaust: Columbus and the Conquest of the New World* (New York: Oxford University Press, 1992), 124.

31. David Blight, "The Civil War Isn't Over," *The Atlantic*, April 8, 2015, accessed July 23, 2015, https://www.theatlantic.com/politics/archive /2015/04/the-civil-war-isnt-over/389847/

32. Quoted in Blight, ibid.

33. Philip Taft and Philip Ross, "American Labor Violence: Its Causes, Character, and Outcome" (1969), in *The History of Violence in America: A Report to the National Commission on the Causes and Prevention of Violence*, ed. Hugh Davis Graham and Ted Robert Gurr, http://www.ditext. com/taft/vio-con.html. Karl Liebknecht also acknowledged the exceptional brutality suffered by American labor in his 1907 monograph *Militarism*, a publication that earned him eighteen months in a German prison. See Alex Gourevitch's review essay, "Happy Consciousness in the Gilded Age," *Historical Materialism* 21.2 (2013): 179–190.

34. W. E. B. Du Bois, *The Souls of Black Folk* (New York: Oxford University Press, 2007), 104.

35. Jacqueline Rose, *On Not Being Able to Sleep* (Princeton, NJ: Princeton University Press, 2003), 202.

36. Amanda Anderson, "Character and Ideology: The Case of Cold War Liberalism," *New Literary History* 42 (2011): 209–210.

37. Jeffrey Stout, *Democracy and Tradition* (Princeton, NJ: Princeton University Press, 2004), 3.

38. Kate Field, *Hap-Hazard* (Boston: James R. Osgood and Co., 1873), 252.

39. Walt Whitman, *Democratic Vistas, and Other Papers* (London: Walter Scott, 1888), 21.

40. Julian Go and Anne L. Foster, "Introduction: Global Perspectives on the U. S. Colonial State in the Philippines," in *The American Colonial State in the Philippines: Global Perspectives*, ed. Julian Go and Anne L. Foster (Durham, NC: Duke University Press, 2003), 23; for Noam Chomsky on American exceptionalism, see his lecture "On Power and Ideology" at the New School of Social Research, September 19, 2015. For a discussion of comparative exceptionalisms, see Carrie Tirado Bramen, "Flirting in Yankeeland: Rethinking American Exceptionalism through Argentine Travel Writing," *The Latino Nineteenth Century*, ed. Rodrigo Lazo and Jesse Alemán (New York: New York University Press, 2016), 230–254.

41. Theodor Adorno, *The Authoritarian Personality* (New York: Norton, 1993), 346.

42. Max Weber, *The Protestant Ethic and the "Spirit" of Capitalism* (New York: Penguin, 2002), 34, 14, 218; original emphasis.

43. David E. Stannard, "American Historians and the Idea of National Character: Some Problems and Prospects," *American Quarterly* 23:2 (May 1971): 202.

44. Fanny Trollope, *Domestic Manners of the Americans*, 18.

45. Robert R. McCrae, "Personality Profiles of Cultures: Patterns of Ethos," *European Journal of Personality* 23 (2009): 205–277.

46. Elizabeth Stuart Phelps, *The Struggle for Immortality* (Boston: Houghton Mifflin, 1889), 192.

47. Otto Bauer, *The Question of Nationalities and Social Democracy*, trans. Joseph O'Donnell (Minneapolis: University of Minnesota Press, 2000), 22.

48. Joep Leerssen, "The Rhetoric of National Character: A Programmatic Survey," *Poetics Today* 21:2 (Summer 2000): 280.

49. *Encyclopédie* of Diderot and d'Alembert is cited in Joep Leerssen, *National Thought in Europe: A Cultural History* (Amsterdam: Amsterdam University Press, 2006), 69. On the relational quality of national character within a transatlantic context, see Susan Manning, *The Poetics of Character: Transatlantic Encounters, 1700–1900* (Cambridge, UK: Cambridge University Press, 2013).

50. Jonathan as the archetypal Yankee actually appeared in the late eighteenth century in Royall Tyler's 1787 play *The Contrast*. The relationship between Jonathan and John Bull seems to vary. According to some, it is a father-son relationship as it is in Spaulding's work; for others, John Bull is a cousin or Jonathan's uncle. Brother Jonathan mostly appeared in political satire as well as on the stage; his theatrical heyday was the 1820s. Winifred Morgan, *An American Icon: Brother Jonathan and American Identity* (Newark: University of Delaware Press, 1988).

51. John Kirke Paulding, *The Diverting History of John Bull and Brother Jonathan* (New York: Inskeep & Bradford, 1812), 3–4.

52. Ibid., 19.

53. This is quoted from a later version of Paulding's transatlantic allegory, entitled *The Bulls and the Jonathans*, ed. William Paulding (New York: Charles Scribner and Co., 1867), 47.

54. John Kirke Paulding, *The Diverting History of John Bull and Brother Jonathan*, 15, 9.

55. Barry Rubin and Judith Colp Rubin, *Hating America: A History* (New York: Oxford University Press, 2004), viii.

56. See Philippe Roger, *The American Enemy: The History of French Anti-Americanism*, trans. Sharon Bowman (Chicago: University of Chicago Press, 2005), 1.

57. Barry Rubin and Judith Colp Rubin, *Hating America*, 29.

58. Thomas Jefferson, *The Writings of Thomas Jefferson*, vol. 1, ed. H. A. Washington (Washington, DC: Taylor & Maury, 1853), 561.

59. Thomas Jefferson, *Writings*, ed. Merrill D. Peterson (New York: Library of America, 1984), 854.

60. Christopher Hitchens recounts this anecdote of Jefferson being rebuffed by King George in *Thomas Jefferson: Author of America* (New York: Harper Collins, 2005), 54–56.

61. Thomas Jefferson, *Autobiography of Thomas Jefferson*, ed. Paul Leicester Ford (New York: G. P. Putnam's Sons, 1914), 97.

62. Ibid., 157.

63. Thomas Day is quoted in Simon Schama, "The Unloved American," *New Yorker* 79.3 (March 10, 2003): 3.

64. Fanny Trollope, *Domestic Manners of the Americans*, 57–58.

65. Ibid., 168.

66. Ibid., 314.

67. Glenn Kessler, "Campaign Methods Put to Test in Tour to Boost U.S. Image: Bush Policies Remain Obstacle for Hughes," *Washington Post*, September 30, 2005; Lucy Jones and Fawaz Turki, "Two Views: Karen Hughes' 'Listening Tour' and Its Aftermath: Selling America to the Muslim World," *Washington Report on Middle East Affairs* (December 2005): 24–26.

68. Thomas Paine, *Common Sense* (Girard, KS: Appeal Publishing Co., 1920), 15; Thomas Jefferson, *The Declaration of Independence* is cited in Appendix C: "The Declaration of Independence: The Jefferson Draft with Congress's Editorial Changes," in Pauline Maier, *American Scripture: Making the Declaration of Independence* (New York: Random House, 1998), 235–241.

69. Jacques Rancière, *Disagreement: Politics and Philosophy*, trans. Julie Rose (Minneapolis: University of Minnesota Press, 1998), 107–108.

70. Pauline Maier, *American Scripture: Making the Declaration of Independence* (New York: Random House, 1998), 8, 21.

71. For a discussion of the colonial relation as a familial metaphor between father and son, see Jay Fliegelman, *Prodigals & Pilgrims: The American Revolution against Patriarchal Authority, 1750–1800* (New York: Cambridge University Press, 1982). For a discussion of the rhetoric of affect in Jefferson, Paine, and others, see Jay Fliegelman, *Declaring Independence* (Stanford: Stanford University Press, 1993), 127–129.

72. Carl Becker, *The Declaration of Independence: A Study in the History of Political Ideas* (New York: Harcourt, Brace & Co., 1922), 19–23.

73. Thomas Jefferson, *Writings*, 18.

74. Quoted in Pauline Maier, *American Scripture*, 122.

75. Julie Ellison, *Cato's Tears* (Chicago: University of Chicago Press, 1999), 17.

76. Henry Dwight Sedgwick, *The New American Type: And Other Essays* (Boston: Houghton, Mifflin & Co., 1908), 21.

77. John O'Sullivan, "The Great Nation of Futurity," *The United States Magazine and Democratic Review* 6:23 (November 1839): 426–430.

78. In a similar vein, Philip Fisher remarks that Americans do not constitute a *Volk*. They lack "those features that any romantic theory of the nation-state required." Philip Fisher, "Democratic Social Space: Whitman, Melville, and the Promise of American Transparency," *Representations* 24 (Autumn 1988): 60–101.

79. Kathleen Smith Kutolski, "Freemasonry and Community in the Early Republic," *American Quarterly* 34 (1982): 24.

80. Tocqueville, *Democracy in America*, 593–594.

81. Ibid., 662.

82. Catharine Maria Sedgwick, *The Poor Rich Man, and The Rich Poor Man* (New York: Harper & Brothers, 1836), 111. For an essay situating Sedgwick's novel within the class-conscious sentimentalism of the 1830s, see Joe Shapiro, "The Providence of Class: Catharine Maria Sedgwick, Political Economy and Sentimental Fiction in the 1820s," *American Literary History* 27:2 (Summer 2015): 199–225. Melville parodies Sedgwick's sentimental view of poverty in his 1854 diptych "Poor Man's Pudding and Rich Man's Crumbs." See Paul Lewis, "'Lectures or a Little Charity': Poor Visits in

Antebellum Literature and Culture," *The New England Quarterly* 73:2 (June 2000): 266–268.

83. Hannah Arendt, "The Social Question," *On Revolution* (New York: Viking, 1965), 15.

84. Catharine Maria Sedgwick, *The Poor Rich Man*, 32–33.

85. Ibid., 39.

86. For a contemporary discussion of the emotional labor of niceness, see Madeleine Bunting, *Willing Slaves: How the Overwork Culture Is Ruling Our Lives* (New York: Harper Collins, 2004). See also Bunting, "Sweet Smiles, hard labour," *The Guardian* (UK), June 12, 2004.

87. Sedgwick, *The Poor Rich Man*, 27. Although Sedgwick describes the process of converting animosity into friendliness as the "benevolent principle," I would argue that niceness and benevolence are not synonymous. Benevolence is something that the privileged offer the have-nots; the poor cannot be benevolent toward the rich. Niceness, however, is a more reciprocal exchange, or at least it is perceived that way. Although Sedgwick uses the word benevolent here, she is describing more generally a reciprocal notion of niceness—where Susan the seamstress is nice to her boss and vice versa. The exchange of niceties establishes a democratic social sphere, and this exchange—even if it is just a habituated social ritual—still plays a vital role in allaying Sedgwick's own anxieties and guilt about an increasingly class-ridden society. On the significance of benevolence in the antebellum period, see Susan Ryan, *The Grammar of Good Intentions: Race and the Antebellum Culture of Benevolence* (Ithaca, NY: Cornell University Press, 2004).

88. Catharine Maria Sedgwick, *Letters from Abroad to Kindred at Home*, vol. 1 (New York: Harper, 1841), 117.

89. Ibid., 117.

90. Catharine Maria Sedgwick, *Means and Ends: Or Self-training* (London: Charles Tilt, 1839), 140.

91. Pierre Bourdieu, "Codification" (1986), *In Other Words: Essays Towards a Reflexive Sociology*, trans. Matthew Adamson (Stanford: Stanford University Press, 1994), 78.

92. Tocqueville, *Democracy in America*, 654.

93. Harriet Beecher Stowe, "Home Religion" (1864), in *Household Papers and Stories* (Boston: Houghton, Mifflin and Co., 1896), 213–214.

94. Ralph Waldo Emerson, "Experience" (1844), in *Essays* (Boston: Ticknor and Fields, 1856), 62–63.

95. W. E. B. Du Bois, "The Problem of Amusement" (1897), in *Du Bois on Religion*, ed. Phil Zuckerman (Walnut Creek, CA: AltaMira Press, 2000), 25.

96. Anna Julia Cooper, *A Voice From the South* (New York: Oxford University Press, 1988), 93–94; original emphasis. For her remarks about train conductors folding their arms and refusing to help black women off the train, see p. 90.

97. Frances Harper, "True and False Politeness" (1898), in *A Brighter Coming Day: A Frances Ellen Watkins Harper Reader*, ed. Frances Smith Foster (New York: Feminist Press, 1990), 397–398.

98. Ida B. Wells, *Crusade for Justice: The Autobiography of Ida B. Wells*, ed. Alfred M. Duster (Chicago: University of Chicago Press, 1970), 113. This episode is recounted in Paula J. Giddings, *Ida: A Sword Among the Lions* (New York: Harper Collins, 2008), 268.

99. Maya Angelou, "Preacher, Don't Send Me," *Maya Angelou: The Complete Poetry* (New York: Random House, 2015), 249–250.

100. The phrase "the nonmarket" comes from Cornel West, and it defines values that bind us together in democratic community, irreducible to profit and market value. Parenting, he argues, illustrates a nonmarket activity because "so much sacrifice and service goes into it without any assurance that the providers will get anything back." Cornel West, "The Moral Obligations of Living in a Democratic Society," in *The Good Citizen*, eds. David Batstone and Eduardo Mendieta (New York: Routledge, 1999), 11.

101. Ralph Waldo Emerson, "Friendship," in *Essays* (Boston: J. Munroe & Co., 1841), 159–160.

CHAPTER ONE

1. For a seventeenth-century account of Puritan experiences with Native Americans, see Edward Winslow, *Mourt's Relation* (1620–1621). In the 1850s, the poet and historian Henry Howard Brownell popularized the Puritan-Native encounter in *The Discoverers, Pioneers and Settlers of North and South America* (1853). John Smith is more closely associated with the colonization of Virginia than New England, where he spent less than three months, yet the latter became of equal importance to him. He is credited with giving the region the name "New England" and he produced the most accurate map made of the New England coastline at that time. See Neal Salisbury, *Manitou and Providence: Indians, Europeans and the Making of New England, 1500–1643* (New York: Oxford University Press, 1982), 97–98.

2. The historian Jean O'Brien describes the New England preoccupation with origins, and originary places, as "firsting," a process whereby the English and their descendants are responsible for erecting the proper institutions of social order. *Firsting and Lasting: Writing Indians Out of Existence in New England* (Minneapolis: University of Minnesota Press, 2010). For an interesting discussion of how the significance of national origins in Native American history contrasts with the current skepticism toward origins in American studies as part of a critique of American exceptionalism, see Sarah Rivett, "The Spectral Indian Presence in Early American Literature," *American Literary History* 25.3 (Fall 2013): 625–637.

3. George Henry, *An Account of the Chippewa Indians, Who Have Been Travelling among the Whites, in the United States, England, Ireland, Scotland, France and Belgium* (1848), in *American Indian Nonfiction: An Anthology of Writings, 1760s–1930s*, ed. Bernd C. Peyer (Norman, OK: University of Oklahoma Press, 2007), 203–204. This pamphlet first appeared in Leeds, England, in 1847 and was published in Boston a year later.

4. For a discussion about public shaming as a tool to rebuke government policies and corporate actions today, see Jennifer Jacquet, *Is Shame Necessary? New Uses for an Old Tool* (New York: Pantheon Books, 2015).

5. Zitkala-Sa, "Side by Side" (1896), in *American Indian Stories, Legends, and Other Writings*, ed. Cathy Davidson and Ada Norris (New York: Penguin, 2003), 223.

6. Donald E. Green, *The Politics of Indian Removal: Creek Government and Society in Crisis* (Lincoln: University of Nebraska Press, 1977); Russell Thornton, "Cherokee Population Losses During the Trail of Tears: A New Perspective and a New Estimate," *Ethnohistory* 31 (1984): 289–300, cited in Ward Churchill, *Indians Are Us? Culture and Genocide in Native North America* (Monroe, ME: Common Courage Press, 1994), 36. Zitkala-Sa, "California Indian Trails and Prayer Trees" (1922), in *American Indian Stories*, 251.

7. On September 8, 2000, Assistant Secretary of the Bureau of Indian Affairs, Kevin Gover, admitted that westward expansion was an outright war: "[I]t must be acknowledged that the deliberate spread of disease, the decimation of the mighty bison herds, the use of the poisoned alcohol to destroy mind and body, and the cowardly killing of women and children made for tragedy on a scale so ghastly that it cannot be dismissed as merely the inevitable consequence of the clash of competing ways of life." http://www.bia.gov/idc/groups /public/documents/text/idco11935.pdf. Some have criticized the Bureau of Indian Affairs for using the phrase "ethnic cleansing" as a polite euphemism for genocide, a word that historians have claimed in such works as David Stannard's *American Holocaust* and in multiple works by Ward Churchill.

8. Ward Churchill, *A Little Matter of Genocide: Holocaust and Denial in the Americas 1492 to the Present* (San Francisco: City Lights Books, 1998), 97.

9. Philanthropist, E. D. "INDIANS." *Philanthropist, a Weekly Journal Containing Essays, on Moral and Religious Subjects* 6.6 (Jun 09, 1821): 92. https://search -proquest-com.gate.lib.buffalo.edu/docview/137664406?accountid=14169.

10. Zitkala-Sa, "Side by Side," in *American Indian Stories, Legends, and Other Writings*, ed. Cathy Davidson and Ada Norris (New York: Penguin, 2003), 225.

11. Fernand Braudel, "History and the Social Sciences: The *Longue Durée*," in *On History*, trans. Sarah Matthews (Chicago: University of Chicago Press, 1980), 25–54. Zitkala-Sa's emphasis on destruction as process anticipates scholarly definitions of settler colonialism, where invasion is a "structure not an event." Duncan Bell, *Remaking the World: Essays on Liberalism and Empire* (Princeton: Princeton University Press, 2016), Chapter 2; Patrick Wolfe, "Settler Colonialism and the Elimination of the Native," *Journal of Genocide Research* 8:4 (2006): 338.

12. Walter Benjamin, *Walter Benjamin: Selected Writings*, vol. 1 (1913–1926), ed. Marcus Bullock (Cambridge, MA: Harvard University Press, 1996), 184.

13. Henry Clay, "Speech on the Seminole War" (1819), cited in Susan Scheckel, *The Insistence of the Indian: Race and Nationalism in Nineteenth-Century American Culture* (Princeton: Princeton University Press, 1998), 4. Although Henry Clay's views toward the Indian would change in the 1830s when he read reports about relocation and how one in four Cherokees died during the Trail of Tears, he was an ardent supporter of manifest destiny.

14. Logan's speech is cited in Henry Howe, *Historical Collections of Virginia* (Charleston, SC: Babcock & Co., 1845), 108.

15. Edward D. Seeber, "Critical Views of Logan's Speech," *The Journal of American Folklore* 60: 236 (April–June 1947): 130–146; Carolyn Eastman, "The Indian Censures the White Man: 'Indian Eloquence' and American

Reading Audiences in the Early Republic," *The William and Mary Quarterly* 65:3 (July 2008): 535–564.

16. Quoted in Alexis de Tocqueville, *Democracy in America*, 395.

17. Alexis de Tocqueville, "Two Weeks in the Wilderness," in *Democracy in America and Two Essays on America*, ed. Isaac Kramnick (New York: Penguin, 2003), 878.

18. Black Elk, *The Sixth Grandfather: Black Elk's Teachings Given to John G. Neihardt*, ed. Raymond J. DeMallie (Lincoln: University of Nebraska Press, 1984), 289–290.

19. Rauna Kuokkanen, "Toward a New Relation of Hospitality in the Academy," *American Indian Quarterly* 27:1–2 (Winter/Spring 2003): 267.

20. There are multiple versions of Simon Pokagon's *Red Man's Rebuke* (1893). This passage citing Columbus appears in the version reprinted in the appendix of Cheryl Walker, *Indian Nation: Native American Literature and Nineteenth-Century Nationalisms* (Durham: Duke University Press, 1997), 215.

21. Simon Pokagon, "Red Man's Rebuke," in Cheryl Walker, *Indian Nation*, 233.

22. Jacques Derrida, *Of Hospitality*, trans. Rachel Bowlby (Stanford: Stanford University Press, 2000), 45.

23. Ibid.

24. Ibid., 25. In contrast to Émile Benveniste, who understands hospitality as a pact of reciprocity between the host and guest, Derrida sees hospitality and gift giving as practices not based on the expectation of return. This is similar to my understanding of Indian hospitality (especially Charles Eastman's version of it) as giving without the expectation of return. See Tracy McNulty, *The Hostess: Hospitality, Femininity, and the Expropriation of Identity* (Minneapolis: University of Minnesota Press, 2007), vii–xvii.

25. Ibid., 72–73, 81; original emphasis.

26. Thomas Hutchinson and Bartlett's *Dictionary of Americanisms* are cited in the *Oxford English Dictionary* under "Indian gift" and "Indian giver."

27. Mary E. Stuckey and John M. Murphy, "By Any Other Name: Rhetorical Colonialism in North America," *American Indian Culture and Research Journal* 25:4 (2001): 75. See also David Murray, *Indian Giving: Economies of Power in Indian-White Exchanges* (Amherst: University of Massachusetts Press, 2000).

28. Robert Montgomery Bird, *Nick of the Woods; or, The Jibbenainosay: A Tale of Kentucky*, vol. 2 (Philadelphia: Carey, Lea & Blanchard, 1837), 71.

29. Richard Slotkin, *Regeneration through Violence: The Mythology of the American Frontier, 1600–1860* (Middletown, CT: Wesleyan University Press, 1973), 21.

30. Alden T. Vaughan, "Frontier Banditti and the Indians: The Paxton Boys' Legacy, 1763–1775," *Pennsylvania History* 51 (1984): 2.

31. Lorenzo Veracini, *Settler Colonialism: A Theoretical Overview* (New York: Palgrave, 2010), 14.

32. Quoted in David Stannard, *American Holocaust: The Conquest of the New World* (New York: Oxford University Press, 1992), 244.

33. Herman Melville, *The Confidence-Man* (1857), ed. Stephen Matterson (New York: Penguin 2005), 192, 198.

34. Minnie Myrtle [Anna Cummings Johnson], *The Iroquois; Or, The Bright Side of Indian Character* (New York: D. Appleton & Company, 1855), 24. Myrtle met Red Jacket's granddaughter at church and learned about her experiences of racism in the East Coast, where she was forced to eat in a separate space at her boarding house.

35. Ibid., 252.

36. For more on the contested congressional debate on Indian removal, see David Mayers, "Removals," in *Dissenting Voices in America's Rise to Power* (New York: Cambridge University Press, 2007): 80–108.

37. Minnie Myrtle, *The Iroquois*, 23.

38. Ibid., 29.

39. Lewis Henry Morgan, *The League of the Iroquois* (1851) (New York: Corinth Books, 1962), 141–143. On the influence of Lewis Henry Morgan's work on Marx and Engels, see William Shaw, "Marx and Morgan," *History and Theory* 23: 2 (May 1984): 215–228.

40. Lewis Henry Morgan, *House and House-Life of the American Aborigines* (Washington: Government Printing Office, 1881), 45.

41. Ibid., 61, 76.

42. Michael Rogin, *Fathers and Children: Andrew Jackson and the Subjugation of the American Indian* (1991) (New Brunswick: Transaction Publishers, 2009), 13.

43. Rosa Luxemburg, *The Accumulation of Capital* (New York: Monthly Review Press, 1968), 370–371.

44. David Harvey, *The New Imperialism* (New York: Oxford University Press, 2003).

45. Thomas Durfee, "Oration: A Historical Discourse," in *Two Hundred and Fiftieth Anniversary of the Settlement of Providence* (June 23–24, 1886) (Providence: Providence Printing Co., 1886), 125. Honorable Thomas Durfee was Chief Justice of the Supreme Court of Rhode Island.

46. Roger Williams, *A Key into the Language of America* (Bedford, MA: Applewood Books, 1997), 9, 17, 47.

47. Scott L. Pratt, *Native Pragmatism* (Bloomington: Indiana University Press, 2002), 103. "*Wunnetu nitta*" is cited in Roger Williams, *A Key into the Language of America*, 51.

48. Roger Williams, *A Key into the Language of America*, 7, 16.

49. Ibid., 10.

50. James Fenimore Cooper, *The Deerslayer* (1841) (New York: Penguin, 1987), 60.

51. Scott Pratt, *Native Pragmatism*, 92. Pratt's source for this Micmac story is "The Chenoo, or the Story of a Cannibal with an Icy Heart," in Charles G. Leland, *The Algonquin Legends of New England* (Boston: Houghton Mifflin & Co., 1884), 233–245.

52. Scott Pratt, *Native Pragmatism*, 91.

53. H. H. "The Conestoga Massacre," *The Independent*, June 3, 1880. This piece was written by Helen Hunt Jackson, who was a frequent contributor to *The Independent*. The essay was an excerpt from her forthcoming book, *The Century of Dishonor* (1881), which appeared the following year. For more on Jackson's relation to *The Independent* and to periodical writing,

more generally, see Kate Phillips, *Helen Hunt Jackson: A Literary Life* (Berkeley: University of California Press, 2003), 93–117.

54. Susan Kalter, "Introduction," in *Benjamin Franklin, Pennsylvania, and the First Nations, The Treaties of 1736–62*, ed. Susan Kalter (Urbana: University of Illinois Press, 2006), 37.

55. Benjamin Franklin, *A Narrative of the Late Massacres in Lancaster County, of a Number of Indians* (1764), 13. https://archive.org/stream/narrativeoflatemoofran#page/14/mode/2up

56. Ibid., 9

57. Ibid., original emphasis.

58. Ibid., 26.

59. Benjamin Franklin was fascinated with the ceremonial rituals and oratory of Native American diplomacy. Between 1736 and 1762, Franklin (together with his partner David Hall after 1753) published fourteen Indian treaties, which consisted of approximately 25 percent of the Indian treaties published during the colonial era. See Timothy J. Shannon, "Benjamin Franklin and Native Americans," in *A Companion to Benjamin Franklin*, ed. David Waldstreicher (Malden, MA: Blackwell, 2011), 164–182.

60. Benjamin Franklin, *A Narrative of the Late Massacres*, 29.

61. Ibid., 28. On the classical distinction between guilt and shame, see E. L. Constable, "Shame," *MLN* 112.4 (1997): 655–656. Constable cites Bernard Williams, *Shame and Necessity* (Berkeley: University of California Press, 1993), 90. Jacqueline Rose's distinction is useful here: "People feel guilty when they violate other people, shame when they fail themselves or the group." Jacqueline Rose, "Introduction: Shame," in *On Not Being Able to Sleep: Psychoanalysis and the Modern World* (Princeton, NJ: Princeton University Press, 2003), 4.

62. Karl Jaspers, *The Question of German Guilt*, trans. E. B. Ashton (1948) (New York: Fordham University Press, 2000), 115–116.

63. Gudrun Grabher, Roland Hagenbüchle, Cristanne Miller, eds., *The Emily Dickinson Handbook* (Amherst: University of Massachusetts Press, 1998), 328.

64. Susan Kalter, "Introduction," 1–44.

65. Wai Chee Dimock, "Hemispheric Islam: Continents and Centuries for American Literature," *American Literary History* 21.1 (Spring 2009): 37. Wai Chee Dimock characterizes Washington Irving as deeply empathetic toward Native Americans: "Irving seemed to understand exactly what it meant for Indians to have lost out, to be victims of circumstances beyond their control. They are the scum of the earth in the nineteenth century, ground down by poverty, dead to the world by a social death" (40). Dimock goes on to link Irving's sympathy toward Native Americans with his similar feelings toward the vanquished Moors in the Iberian Peninsula.

66. Quoted in Dimock, "Hemispheric Islam," 37–38.

67. Washington Irving, "Traits of Indian Character," *Analectic Magazine* 3 (February 1, 1814): 145–157.

68. Jill Lepore, *The Name of War: King Philip's War and the Origins of American Identity* (New York: Vintage Books, 1998), x.

69. Ibid., xiii.

70. Washington Irving, "Traits of Indian Character," *Analectic Magazine*, 154.

71. Ibid.

72. Ronald Takaki, *Iron Cages: Race and Culture in Nineteenth-Century America* (Seattle: University of Washington Press, 1979), 96.

73. Washington Irving, "Traits of Indian Character," *Analectic Magazine*, 156.

74. Elias Boudinot, *A Star in the West: or, A humble attempt to discover the long lost ten tribes of Israel, preparatory to their return to their beloved city, Jerusalem* (Trenton, NJ: D. Fenton, 1816), iv. https://archive.org /stream/starinwestorhumbooboud#page/n5/mode/2up

75. Elias Boudinot, *A Star in the West*, 186, 179.

76. For more on Lydia Maria Child and the connection between her antiremoval activism and abolitionism, see Carolyn Karcher, *The First Woman in the Republic: A Cultural Biography of Lydia Maria Child*. For a study of women's activism in the antebellum period and the relation between antiremoval petitions and abolition, see Alisse Portnoy, *Their Right to Speak: Women's Activism in the Indian and Slave Debates* (Cambridge, MA: Harvard University Press, 2005). On the role of sympathy in Child's American Indian writings, see Laura Mielke, *Moving Encounters: Sympathy and the Indian Question in Antebellum Literature* (Amherst, MA: University of Massachusetts Press, 2008).

77. Lydia Maria Child, *The First Settlers of New England* (Boston: Munroe and Francis, 1829), 65, 169.

78. Ibid., 171.

79. E. M. Winslow, *The Pattern of Imperialism: A Study in the Theory of Power* (1948), cited in Victor Gordon Kiernan, *America: The New Imperialism: From White Settlement to World Hegemony* (1978) (London: Verso, 2005), xv.

80. Irving's "Philip of Pokanoket" has been seen as lamenting the inevitability of Indian demise. Michelle Sizemore accuses Irving of a "more subtle form of colonialist violence." Michelle Sizemore, "'Changing by Enchantment': Temporal Convergence, Early National Comparisons, and Washington Irving's Sketchbook," *Studies in American Fiction* 40. 2 (Fall 2013): 157–183.

81. Christopher Castiglia, *Interior States: Institutional Consciousness and the Inner Life of Democracy in the Antebellum United States* (Durham: Duke University Press, 2008).

82. Washington Irving, "Traits of Indian Character," *Analectic Magazine*, 156.

83. Quoted in Scott Pratt, *Native Pragmatism*, 67.

84. James B. Twitchell, *For Shame: The Loss of Common Decency in America* (New York: St. Martin's, 1997), 27.

85. Charles Darwin, *The Expression of the Emotions* (New York: D. Appleton & Co., 1873), 318. Babel.hathitrust.org

86. Martin Delany, *Principia of Ethnology: The Origin of Races and Color* (Philadelphia: Harper & Brother, 1879. Rpt. Baltimore: Black Classic Press, 1991), 23, 29.

87. Frederick Douglass, "Inhumanity of Slavery" (1850) in Appendix to *My Bondage and My Freedom*, in *Frederick Douglass: Autobiographies*, ed. Henry Louis Gates, Jr. (New York: The Library of America, 1996), 428.

88. Lydia Maria Child, *An Appeal for the Indians* (New York: Wm. P. Tomlinson, 1868), in *A Lydia Maria Child Reader*, ed. Carolyn L. Karcher (Durham: Duke University Press, 1997), 88.

89. Quoted in Sean P. Harvey, "'Must Not Their Languages Be Savage and Barbarous Like Them?' Philology, Indian Removal, and Race Science," *Journal of the Early Republic* 30:4 (Winter 2010): 514.

90. Lewis Cass, "Review of *Travels in the Central Portion of the Mississippi Valley [&c.,]*, By Henry R. Schoolcraft; "Review of *A Vindication of the Rev. Mr. Heckewelder's History of the Indian Nations*, By William Rawle," *North American Review* 26 (1828): 366, 372–373.

91. Sean P. Harvey, *Native Tongues: Colonialism and Race from Encounter to the Reservation* (Cambridge, MA: Harvard University Press, 2015), 150–151.

92. Reverend John Heckewelder, *History, Manners, and Customs of The Indian Nations* (Philadelphia, 1876. Rpt. Bowie, MD: Heritage Books, 1990), 79.

93. Ibid., 76; original emphasis.

94. Lewis Cass, "Review of *Travels in the Central Portion of the Mississippi Valley*," 374.

95. Quoted in John Twitchell, *For Shame: The Loss of Common Decency in America*, 34–35.

96. Lewis Cass, *North American Review* 46 (1828): 375–376.

97. W. H. Gardiner quoted in John McWilliams, *New England's Crises and Cultural Memory: Literature, Politics, History, Religion, 1620–1860* (New York: Cambridge University Press, 2004), 17; Lewis Cass, *North American Review* 46 (1828): 376.

98. "Review." *North American Review* 46 (January 1838): 11, quoted in Steven Conn, *History's Shadow: Native Americans and Historical Consciousness in the Nineteenth Century* (Chicago: University of Chicago Press, 2004), 156.

99. Thomas Carlyle refers to James Fenimore Cooper as the most "original" and "most thoroughly American" in his review essay "The Works of James Fenimore Cooper," in *The North American Review* 74 (1852): 147. Melville's comments are from "Cooper's New Novel" (review), *New York Literary World*, April 28, 1849. Francis Parkman's description of Cooper is from "Memorial of James Fenimore Cooper," held in New York in 1851 (New York: Putnam, 1859).

100. Leslie Fiedler, *Love and Death in the American Novel* (Champaign, IL: Dalkey Archive, 2008), 192.

101. Ibid., 192.

102. James Fenimore Cooper, *The Deerslayer*, 66.

103. Ibid., 123.

104. Leslie Fiedler, *Love and Death in the American Novel*, 195.

105. For Cooper's financial risks and faulty investments, see Steven Watts, "'Through a Glass Eye, Darkly': James Fenimore Cooper as Social Critic," *Journal of the Early Republic* 13. 1 (Spring 1993): 55–74.

106. Leslie Fiedler, *Love and Death in the American Novel*, 26.

107. Richard Slotkin, *Regeneration through Violence*, 515.

108. Jill Lepore, *The Name of War*, 197. Edwin Forrest is quoted in Lepore, 194.

109. John Augustus Stone, *Metamora; or, The Last of the Wampanoags*, in *Staging the Nation: Plays from the American Theater, 1787–1909*, ed. Don B. Wilmeth (Boston: Bedford Books, 1998), 63. The fact that Metamora is attacked by a wolf is significant in that Indians were long likened to wolves from Cotton Mather to Andrew Jackson. See Stannard, *American Holocaust*, 241.

110. Ibid., 74.

111. Ibid., 77.

112. Ibid., 98.

113. Laurence Hutton, "The American Play," *Lippincott's Monthly Magazine*, March 1886, 37.

114. George William Curtis, "Editor's Easy Chair," *Harper's New Monthly Magazine* 28 (December 1863): 132.

115. Review of Metamora in *The Ariel. A Semimonthly Literary and Miscellaneous Gazette*, Jan 9, 1829, 3, 19.

116. *London Times* review quoted in William R. Alger, *Life of Edwin Forrest, the American Tragedian*, vol. 2 (Philadelphia: Lippincott, 1877), 476–477.

117. Gabriel Harrison, *Edwin Forrest: The Actor and the Man. Critical and Reminiscent* (Brooklyn, NY: 1889. Rpt. Ithaca: Cornell University Press, 2009), 43–44.

118. Gabriel Harrison, *Edwin Forrest*, 37, 33.

119. James Murdock, *The Stage; or, Recollections of Actors and Acting from an Experience of Fifty Years* (Philadelphia: Stoddard, 1880), 298.

120. Gordon M. Sayre, *The Indian Chief as Tragic Hero* (Chapel Hill: University of North Carolina, 2005), 122. For a discussion of *Metamora* in relation to antebellum Indian policy, see Scott C. Martin, "Interpreting 'Metamora': Nationalism, Theater, and Jacksonian Indian Policy," *Journal of the Early Republic* 19.1 (Spring 1999): 73–101.

121. Cited in Jill Lepore, *The Name of War*, 212.

122. Sacvan Bercovitch, *The American Jeremiad* (Madison: University of Wisconsin Press, 1978), xi.

123. Gabriel Harrison, *Edwin Forrest*, 41.

124. John McWilliams, *New England's Crises and Cultural Memory*, 120.

125. William Apess, *Eulogy on King Philip* in *On Our Own Ground: The Complete Writings of William Apess, A Pequot*, ed. Barry O'Connell (Amherst: University of Massachusetts Press, 1992), xx.

126. William Apess, *Eulogy on King Philip*, 307, 280; Philip F. Gura, *The Life of William Apess, Pequot* (Chapel Hill: University of North Carolina Press, 2015), 108.

127. William Apess, *Eulogy on King Philip*, 279, 281.

128. Ibid., 305.

129. Ibid., 302.

130. Ibid., 286.

131. Ibid., 301.

132. Deborah Gussman, "'O Savage, Where Art Thou?': Rhetorics of Reform in William Apess's "Eulogy on King Philip,'" *The New England Quarterly* 77.3 (September 2004): 468. Deborah Gussman refers to this form of rebuke as the "Native American jeremiad." See my discussion of the "heathen's

jeremiad" in *The Uses of Variety: Modern Americanism and the Quest for National Distinctiveness* (Cambridge, MA: Harvard University Press, 2000), 269–276.

133. William Apess, *Eulogy on King Philip*, 306.

134. Ibid., 310.

135. Ibid.

136. Jacqueline Rose, "Introduction: Shame," in *On Not Being able to Sleep* (London: Chatto & Windus, 2003), 7. Rose quotes the poet Christina Rossetti.

137. My reading of Apess's conclusion in *Eulogy* was influenced by Adam Phillips's reading of Albert Camus's *The Myth of Sisyphus* in *Missing Out: In Praise of the Unlived Life* (New York: Farrar, Straus and Giroux, 2012), xi-xx.

138. Zitkala-Sa, "Americanize the First Americans" (1921), *American Indian Stories, Legends, and Other Writings*, 244.

139. Zitkala-Sa, "Bureaucracy versus Democracy" (1922), *American Indian Stories*, 246.

140. Zitkala-Sa, Selections from *American Indian Magazine* in *American Indian Stories*, 210.

141. Zitkala-Sa, "The California Indians of Today" (1922), in *American Indian Stories*, 260.

142. James W. Baker, *Thanksgiving: The Biography of an American Holiday* (Lebanon, NH: University of New Hampshire Press, 2009).

143. J. L. G. Ferris, "Autobiography," *The Literary Digest* 98:1 (July 1928): 25–26; Warren W. Brown, "J. L. G. Ferris: America's First Painter Historian," *The Print Connoisseur* 4 (April 1924): 84–109.

144. Michael Rogin has shown how the rhetoric of Manifest Destiny uses metaphors of devouring to describe expansion. Michael Rogin, *Fathers and Children: Andrew Jackson and the Subjugation of the American Indian*, 9.

145. On the figure of the hostess, see Tracy McNulty, *The Hostess: Hospitality, Femininity, and the Expropriation of Identity* (Minneapolis: University of Minnesota Press, 2006).

146. Stephen Turner, "Settlement as Forgetting" in *Quicksands: Foundational Histories in Australia and Aotearoa New Zealand*, ed. Klaus Neumann, et al. (Sydney: University of New South Wales Press, 1999), 20–38.

147. According to Edward Winslow in *Mourt's Relation*, there were 53 surviving Pilgrims and 90 native men who attended the three-day event in 1621. Lillian Eichler similarly mentions that Indians outnumbered the Puritans by nearly two to one. Lillian Eichler, *The Customs of Mankind: With Notes on Modern Etiquette and the Newest Trend in Entertainment* (New York: Doubleday, 1924), 442. I am grateful to Prentiss Clark for bringing this source to my attention.

148. Edward Winslow, *A Relation or Journall of the Beginning and Proceedings of the English Plantation Settled at Plimoth in New England [Mourt's Relation]*, 1622, p. 61, quoted in James W. Baker, *Thanksgiving: The Biography of an American Holiday* (Durham, NH: University of New Hampshire Press, 2009), 12. According to Baker, *Mourt's Relation* had become so rare by the eighteenth century that there were no extant copies

in New England. It was not until 1820, when an original pamphlet was discovered in Philadelphia, that the famous description of the first Thanksgiving of 1621 was recovered. It was not republished in full until 1841, in Reverend Alexander Young's *Chronicles of the Pilgrim Fathers*. See Baker, 11–13.

149. Warren W. Brown, "J. L. G. Ferris; America's Painter-Historian," *The Print Connoisseur* (April 1924): 90–91.

150. Yael Ben-zvi, "Where Did Red Go?: Lewis Henry Morgan's Evolutionary Inheritance and U.S. Racial Imagination," *CR: The New Centennial Review* 7.2 (Fall 2007): 203.

151. Steven Conn, *History's Shadow*, 1–2.

152. Lewis Meriam, *The Problem of Indian Administration* (Baltimore: Johns Hopkins University Press, 1928), 3. In 1928, the Meriam report was released, commissioned by the Institute for Government Research, which concluded that "an overwhelming majority of the Indians are poor, even extremely poor, and they are not adjusted to the economic and social system of the dominant white civilization." http://www.narf.org/nill/documents /merriam/d_meriam_chapter1_summary_of_findings.pdf.

153. Lillian Eichler, *The Customs of Mankind*, 334.

154. Laura Claridge, *Emily Post: Daughter of the Gilded Age, Mistress of American Manners* (New York: Random House, 2008), 262–263.

155. Lillian Eichler, *The Customs of Mankind*, 334.

156. Ibid., 334–335. Surprisingly, Eichler does not acknowledge the importance of Indian hospitality in her later chapter on Thanksgiving. The year 1621–1622 is told entirely from the Puritan perspective.

157. In 2011, the U.S. Mint produced a one-dollar coin designed to honor the 1621 treaty between the Wampanoags and the Puritan Separatists as part of the "Native American Golden Dollar Program."

158. Roxanne Dunbar-Ortiz, *An Indigenous Peoples' History of the United States* (Boston: Beacon Press, 2014), 5.

159. Charles Eastman, *The Soul of the Indian* (Mineola, NY: Dover, 2003), 26–27.

160. Cornel West, *Keeping Faith: Philosophy and Race in America* (New York: Routledge, 2009), 126.

CHAPTER TWO

1. George Eliot, "Review of *Dred: A Tale of the Great Dismal Swamp*" in *The Westminster Review* (October 1856), rpt. in *Critical Essays on Harriet Beecher Stowe*, ed. Elizabeth Ammons (Boston: G. K. Hall, 1980), 43; the Chris Rock epigraph is from his stand-up performance at the University at Buffalo, November 16, 2003, cited in Brian Herberger and Mike Flatt, "Alumni Arena Rocks with Laughter," *UB Spectrum*, November 17, 2003, http://www.ubspectrum.com/article/2003/11/alumni-arena-rocks -with-laughter.

2. Charles Dickens, letter to Harriet Beecher Stowe, July 17, 1852, quoted in Laurie L. Harris, *Nineteenth Century Literary Criticism*, vol. 3 (Detroit: Gale Research Company, 1983), 537.

3. George Fredrickson's *The Black Image in the White Mind* is quoted in Harriet Beecher Stowe, *Uncle Tom's Cabin: Authoritative Text*,

Backgrounds and Contexts, ed. Elizabeth Ammons (New York: Norton Critical Edition, 2010), 437.

4. Harriet Beecher Stowe, *Dred: A Tale of the Great Dismal Swamp*, ed. Robert Levine (New York: Penguin, 2000), 146.

5. Robert S. Levine has argued that Stowe's *Dred* is a courageous revision of *Uncle Tom's Cabin*, showing how she was able to rethink and modify her earlier views on slavery and race during the turbulent decade of the 1850s. Robert S. Levine, introduction to *Dred: A Tale of the Great Dismal Swamp*, ed. Robert S. Levine, ix-xxx. Also see Robert S. Levine, *Martin Delany, Frederick Douglass, and the Politics of Representative Identity* (Chapel Hill: University of North Carolina Press, 1997).

6. Harriet Beecher Stowe, *Dred: A Tale of the Great Dismal Swamp*, 211.

7. Ibid., 499.

8. Martin R. Delany, *The Origin of Races and Color* (Baltimore: Black Classic Press, 1991), 90.

9. Anthony Benezet, *A Short Account of that Part of Africa, Inhabited by the Negroes* (1762) (Bedford, MA: Applewood Books, 2008), 13, 79. For more on Benjamin Franklin and Anthony Benezet, see Gordon Wood, *The Americanization of Benjamin Franklin* (New York: Penguin, 2005), 227.

10. Ezra Tawil, *The Making of Racial Sentiment: Slavery and the Birth of the Frontier Romance* (New York: Cambridge University Press, 2008), 156.

11. Frederick Douglass, "Inhumanity of Slavery" (1850), in *Frederick Douglass: Autobiographies* (New York: The Library of America, 1996), 425–426. [original emphasis].

12. John W. Blassingame, ed. *Slave Testimony: Two Centuries of Letters, Speeches, Interviews, and Autobiographies* (Baton Rouge: Louisiana State University, 1977), 323.

13. Nathaniel Hawthorne and Oliver Wendell Holmes are quoted in Greg Grandin, *Empire of Necessity* (New York: Picador, 2015), 271. As an old man, Oliver Wendell Holmes reflected on his reluctance to join the abolitionist cause, and he recalled his father's memories of living in Georgia where he "came in contact with slavery in its best and mildest form." *Life and Letters of Oliver Wendell Holmes*, ed. John T. Morse, vol. 1 (Cambridge, MA: Riverside Press, 1896), 304. For a comparison between Holmes's attitude toward slavery and Captain Delano, see Grandin, 271.

14. John W. Blassingame, *The Slave Community: Plantation Life in the Antebellum South*, revised edition (New York: Oxford University Press, 1979), 230. According to Blassingame, Sambo was a combination of Uncle Tom, Jim Crow, and Uncle Remus.

15. Ellen Cushman, "Face, Skins, and the Identity Politics of Rereading Race," *Rhetoric Review* 24.2 (2005): 389.

16. Josiah Nott and George Gliddon, *Types of Mankind* (Philadelphia: Lippincott, Grambo & Co., 1854), 52. Josiah Nott is quoting from "The Slavonians and Eastern Europe," *North British Review* 11 (August 1849): 528.

17. Facialization, for Gilles Deleuze and Félix Guattari, refers to the overcoding of the face over other parts of the body, "so that the body, head included, has been decoded and has to be *overcoded* by something we shall

call the Face." See Deleuze and Guattari, "Year Zero: Faciality," in *A Thousand Plateaus: Capitalism and Schizophrenia*, trans. and ed. Brian Massumi (Minneapolis: University of Minnesota Press, 1987), 170. For a useful discussion of Deleuze and Guattari's notion of facialization in relation to nineteenth-century slave portraiture, see Agnes Lugo-Ortiz and Angela Rosenthal, ed., introduction to *Slave Portraiture in the Atlantic World*, (Cambridge, UK: Cambridge UP, 2013), 7. For a discussion of our contemporary era of post-faciality, where other body parts can become overcoded, see Bernadette Wegenstein, "Getting Under the Skin, or, How Faces Have Become Obsolete," *Configurations* 10:2 (Spring 2002): 221–259.

18. Michelle Ann Stephens, *Skin Acts: Race, Psychoanalysis and the Black Male Performer* (Durham: Duke University Press, 2014), 222.

19. Eric Lott, *Love and Theft: Blackface Minstrelsy and the American Working Class* (New York: Oxford University Press, 1993), 36–37. I would emphasize perhaps more than Lott that Frederick Douglass's enthusiasm for blackface minstrelsy is highly qualified. It pertains to black performers appearing before a white audience as he saw in Rochester with Gavitt's Original Ethiopian Serenaders in 1849. A year earlier, Douglass disapprovingly described white performers in blackface as "the filthy scum of white society, who have stolen from us a complexion denied to them by nature, in which to make money, and pander to the corrupt taste of their white fellow citizens" (quoted in Lott, 15).

20. Frederick Douglass, *My Bondage and My Freedom*, in *Frederick Douglass: Autobiographies*, ed. Henry Louis Gates, Jr. (New York: Library of America, 1996), 152.

21. Ethnology, for Douglass as it was for the Englishman Prichard, underscored the commonality of the human race, a point Douglass made in a speech on ethnology in 1854: "Human rights stand upon a common basis [and] they are supported, maintained and defended for *all* the human family; because all mankind have the same wants, arising out of a common nature." Frederick Douglass, "The Claims of the Negro Ethnologically Considered," (Rochester, NY: Lee, Mann & Co., 1854), 34.

22. Frederick Douglass, *My Bondage and My Freedom*, 155. On the muteness of the typological image, see Brian Wallis, "Black Bodies, White Science: Louis Agassiz's Slave Daguerreotypes," *American Art* 9:2 (Summer 1995): 38–61.

23. Frederick Douglass, *My Bondage and My Freedom*, 151, 155. For a discussion of Douglass's recognition of his mother in Prichard's book in comparison to the portrayal of his mother in his earlier work *Narrative of the Life of Frederick Douglass*, see Michael A. Chaney, "Picturing the Mother, Claiming Egypt: *My Bondage and My Freedom* as Auto(bio)ethnography," *African American Review* 35.3 (Autumn 2001): 391–408.

24. Robert S. Levine, *The Lives of Frederick Douglass* (Cambridge: Harvard UP, 2016), 119–120. See also John Stauffer, "Creating an Image in Black: The Power of Abolition Pictures," in *Beyond Blackface: African Americans and the Creation of American Popular Culture, 1890–1930*, ed. W. Fitzhugh Brundage (Chapel Hill: University of North Carolina Press, 2011), 66–94; John Stauffer, Zoe Trodd, and Celeste-Marie Bernier, *Picturing Frederick*

Douglass: An Illustrated Biography of the Nineteenth Century's Most Photographed American (New York: Liveright-Norton, 2015); Maurice O. Wallace and Shawn Michelle Smith, ed. *Pictures and Progress: Early Photography and the Making of African American Identity* (Durham: Duke University Press, 2012).

25. Frederick Douglass, *Life and Times of Frederick Douglass*, in *Frederick Douglass: Autobiographies*, 896–897.

26. Harriet Beecher Stowe, *Dred: A Tale of the Great Dismal Swamp*, 447.

27. Robert S. Levine has compellingly argued that while writing *The Heroic Slave*, Frederick Douglass was moving away from a Garrisonian faith in moral suasion toward a more militant notion of black resistance. Robert S. Levine, *The Lives of Frederick Douglass* (Cambridge, MA: Harvard University Press, 2016), 119–178.

28. Frederick Douglass, *The Heroic Slave* (1853), ed. Robert Levine, John Stauffer, and John R. McKivigan (New Haven, CT: Yale University Press, 2015), 7.

29. Frederick Douglass, *My Bondage and My Freedom*, 450.

30. Harriet Beecher Stowe, *Dred: A Tale of the Great Dismal Swamp*, 206.

31. As Eric Lott noted, the figure of Uncle Tom originated in the minstrel shows of the 1830s and 1840s with the sentimental slaves of Old Uncle Ned and Old Black Joe in Stephen Foster's "Plantation Melodies." Eric Lott, *Love & Theft: Blackface Minstrelsy and the American Working Class* (New York: Oxford University Press, 1993), 33.

32. Harriet Beecher Stowe, *Uncle Tom's Cabin*, Norton Critical Edition, ed. Elizabeth Ammons (New York: Norton, 1994), 18, 154.

33. Harriet Beecher Stowe, *Dred: A Tale of the Great Dismal Swamp*, 49.

34. Harriet Beecher Stowe, *Uncle Tom's Cabin*, 362–363.

35. William Ellery Channing, *Slavery* (Boston: James Munroe and Company, 1835), 103.

36. George Boulukos, *The Grateful Slave: The Emergence of Race in Eighteenth-Century British and American Culture* (New York: Cambridge University Press, 2008), 235. I am grateful to my colleague Ruth Mack for recommending this source.

37. Harriet Beecher Stowe, *Uncle Tom's Cabin*, 7–9.

38. Harriet Beecher Stowe, *A Key to Uncle Tom's Cabin* (1853) (Mineola, NY: Dover, 2015), 115. This Dover edition is an unabridged replication of the original (Boston: John P. Jewett & Co., 1853).

39. Harriet Beecher Stowe, *Uncle Tom's Cabin*, 8.

40. Harriet Beecher Stowe is cited in Charles Dudley Warner, "The Story of Uncle Tom's Cabin," *The Atlantic Monthly* 78 (September 1896): 311–321. Rpt. in Elizabeth Ammons, ed. *Critical Essays on Harriet Beecher Stowe* (Boston: G. K. Hall & Co., 1980), 65.

41. Harriet Beecher Stowe, "Introduction to the New Edition," in *Uncle Tom's Cabin* (Boston: Houghton Mifflin & Co., 1890), xviii.

42. Charles Dudley Warner, "The Story of *Uncle Tom's Cabin*," in Elizabeth Ammons, ed., *Critical Essays on Harriet Beecher Stowe* (Boston: G. K. Hall, 1980), 69, 65.

43. Harriet Beecher Stowe, *The Life of Harriet Beecher Stowe, Compiled From Letters and Journals*, ed. Charles Edward Stowe (Boston: Houghton, Mifflin & Co., 1891), 171. Scholars seem torn on the question of Southern hatred of Stowe. Thomas Gossett claims that in journals, at least, animosity toward Stowe lessened significantly within two years after the publication of *Uncle Tom's Cabin*, though Gossett admits that the debate may have continued in Southern newspapers. Joseph Roppolo emphasizes the longevity of Southern white hatred of Stowe, especially in New Orleans. See Joseph Roppolo, "Harriet Beecher Stowe and New Orleans: A Study in Hate," *The New England Quarterly* 30.3 (Sept. 1957): 346–362; Thomas Gossett, *Uncle Tom's Cabin and American Culture* (Dallas, TX: Southern Methodist University Press, 1985).

44. Harriet Beecher Stowe, *Uncle Tom's Cabin*, 380.

45. Kevin Pelletier, *Apocalyptic Sentimentalism: Love and Fear in U.S. Antebellum Literature* (Athens: University of Georgia Press, 2015).

46. Cited in Owen Muelder, *Theodore Dwight Weld and the American Anti-Slavery Society* (Jefferson, NC: McFarland 2011), 64.

47. Harriet Beecher Stowe, *Uncle Tom's Cabin*, 381.

48. Harriet Beecher Stowe, *A Key to Uncle Tom's Cabin*, 20. The concept of "ethical witnessing" comes from contemporary feminist scholarship on the use of terror in Latin American. See Rosa-Linda Fregoso, "Witnessing and the Poetics of Corporality," *Kalfou* 1:1 (2010): 21–31; Anne Cubilié, *Women Witnessing Terror* (New York: Fordham University Press, 2005); Kelly Oliver, "Witnessing and Testimony," *Parallax* 10.1 (2004): 79–88.

49. Charles Dickens, *American Notes*, 249.

50. Frederick Douglass, *My Bondage and My Freedom*, 401–403.

51. Frederick Douglass, "Inhumanity of Slavery," in *My Bondage and My Freedom*, 425–426.

52. Frederick Douglass, *My Bondage and My Freedom*, 409.

53. Ibid., 425–426.

54. Samuel Ringgold Ward, "Men and Women of Mark," in *The Heroic Slave*, ed. Robert Levine et al. (New Haven, CT: Yale University Press, 2015), 147–148.

55. See James B. Salazar, *Bodies of Reform: The Rhetoric of Character in Gilded Age America* (New York: New York University Press, 2010), 5.

56. Harriet Beecher Stowe, *A Key to Uncle Tom's Cabin*, 177.

57. Ibid., 86.

58. Ibid., 177, 181.

59. These quotations from runaway slave advertisements were found in the American Antiquarian Society Database on Historical Newspapers, in *Charleston Mercury* (SC), 50 (March 25, 1858): 3 and *Macon Weekly Telegraph* (GA), 33:17 (January 11, 1859).

60. John W. Blassingame, *Slave Community*, 314.

61. Frederick Douglass, "The Nature of Slavery," in *My Bondage and My Freedom*, 422.

62. Ibid.

63. Frederick Douglass, *Life and Times*, 602.

64. The phrases "Magnolia Curtain" and the "Sable Curtain" come from historian David Robertson's *Denmark Vesey: The Buried Story of America's Largest Slave Rebellion and the Man Who Led It* (New York: Knopf, 1999), 78. According to Robertson, the Southern charade lost legitimacy as early as 1822 with Denmark Vesey's failed slave rebellion in Charleston, South Carolina.

65. For a discussion of anti-Uncle Tom novels, see Thomas Gossett, *Uncle Tom's Cabin and American Culture* (Dallas, TX: Southern Methodist University Press, 1985).

66. Robert Criswell, *"Uncle Tom's Cabin" Contrasted with Buckingham Hall, The Planter's Home, OR, A Fair View of Both Sides of the Slavery Question* (New York: D. Fanshaw, 1852), 37 38, 43; original emphasis.

67. Robert Criswell, *Buckingham Hall*, 381; original emphasis.

68. Ibid., 142.

69. Quoted in Joy Jordan-Lake, *Whitewashing Uncle Tom's Cabin: Nineteenth-Century Women Novelists Respond to Stowe* (Nashville, TN: Vanderbilt University Press, 2005), 85. Originally cited in Ronald Takaki, *A Different Mirror* (Boston: Little, Brown, 1993), 111.

70. Robert Criswell, *Buckingham Hall*, 149–150.

71. Stephen A. Hirsch, "Uncle Tom's Companions: The Literary and Popular Reaction to *Uncle Tom's Cabin*," (Ph.D diss., State University of New York at Albany, 1975), 21. Referenced in Thomas Gossett, *Uncle Tom's Cabin and American Culture* in Elizabeth Ammons, ed. *Uncle Tom's Cabin: Authoritative Text, Backgrounds and Contexts, Criticism*, 447.

72. W. L. G. Smith, *Life at the South, Or "Uncle Tom's Cabin" As It Is* (Buffalo, NY: George H. Derby and Co., 1852), 516.

73. Unlike Stowe's *Uncle Tom's Cabin*, W. L. G. Smith's proslavery novel *Life at the South, or "Uncle Tom's Cabin" As It Is* actually stays within the eighteenth-century conventions of the grateful slave, where the happiness of the slave's face is a sign of his kind master. See George Boulukos, *The Grateful Slave: The Emergence of Race in Eighteenth-Century British and American Culture* (New York: Cambridge University Press, 2008).

74. Caroline Hentz, *The Planter's Northern Bride* (Philadelphia: T. D. Peterson, 1854), vii.

75. George Boulukos, *The Grateful Slave*, 235.

76. Caroline Hentz, *The Planter's Northern Bride*, v–vi.

77. For a discussion of the nineteenth-century Southerner as the representative American, see *The Southerner as American*, ed. Charles Grier Sellers, Jr., especially Sellers's essay, "The Travail of Slavery" (New York: E. P. Dutton, 1966), 40–71.

78. See discussion of John O'Sullivan and what I am calling "manifest cheerfulness" in the introduction. John O'Sullivan, "The Great Nation of Futurity," *The United States Magazine and Democratic Review* 6:23 (November 1839): 426–430.

79. Elizabeth Keckley and Henry Watson are quoted in John W. Blassingame, *The Slave Community*, 257.

80. Mrs. Austa Malinda French, *Slavery in South Carolina and the Ex-Slaves Or, The Port Royal Mission* (New York: Winchell M. French, 1862), 208.

81. John Brown, *Slave Life in Georgia: A Narrative of the Life, Sufferings, and Escape of John Brown, a Fugitive Slave* (1855), ed. F. N. Boney (Savannah, GA: Beehive Press, 1991), 98–100.

82. Quoted in Maurie D. McInnis, *Slaves Waiting for Sale: Abolitionist Art and the American Slave Trade* (Chicago: University of Chicago Press, 2011), 126–127.

83. Harriet Beecher Stowe, *A Key to Uncle Tom's Cabin*, 157.

84. Harriet Beecher Stowe, *Uncle Tom's Cabin*, 283–284.

85. Joel Dinerstein, "'Uncle Tom Is Dead!': Wright, Himes, and Ellison Lay a Mask to Rest," *African American Review* 43.1 (Spring 2009): 83; Orlando Patterson, *Slavery and Social Death: A Comparative Study* (Cambridge, MA: Harvard University Press, 1980), cited in Dinerstein, 86.

86. Frederick Douglass, *My Bondage and My Freedom*, 172, 309–310.

87. John W. Blassingame, *The Slave Community*, 304, 314, 305. Lundsford Lane is quoted in Blassingame, *The Slave Community*, 314.

88. John W. Blassingame, *The Slave Community*, 313.

89. Mary Boykin Chesnut, *A Diary from Dixie*, ed. Ben Ames Williams (Cambridge, MA: Harvard University Press, 1980), 293.

90. Ibid., 433, 524, 536.

91. James M. McPherson, *The Negro's Civil War: How American Blacks Felt and Acted During the War for the Union* (1965) (New York: Penguin, 2003).

92. Elizabeth R. Varon, *Southern Lady, Yankee Spy. The True Story of Elizabeth Van Lew, a Union Agent in the Heart of the Confederacy* (New York: Oxford University Press, 2003).

93. Leslie Fiedler, *Love and Death in the American Novel* (1960) (Champaign, IL: The Dalkey Archive, 2008), 399.

94. David Walker, *David Walker's Appeal* (1830) (Baltimore, MD: Black Classic Press, 1993). For a discussion of David Walker's *Appeal* that examines his reconciliatory vision of interracial friendship and harmony, see Kevin Pelletier, *Apocalyptic Sentimentalism*, 40–41.

95. Edgar Allan Poe, *The Narrative of Arthur Gordon Pym*, 166.

96. Ibid., 180.

97. George Eliot, "Review of *Dred*," 43.

98. Herman Melville, *Benito Cereno*, 39.

99. Ibid., 44–45.

100. Ibid., 70.

101. Peter Coviello, "The American in Charity: 'Benito Cereno' and Gothic Anti-Sentimentality," *Studies in American Fiction* 30 (2002): 159.

102. Herman Melville, *Benito Cereno*, 71.

103. Ibid., 41, 35.

104. Leslie Fiedler, *Love and Death in the American Novel*, 400.

105. My reading of Melville's novella is closely aligned with C. L. R. James's conclusion: "Melville . . . in the opinions of the capable, well-meaning, Negro-loving Captain Delano, itemized every single belief cherished by an advanced civilization . . . about a backward people and then one by one showed that they were not merely false, but were the direct cause of his own blindness

and stupidity." *Mariners, Renegades, and Castaways: The Story of Herman Melville and the World We Live In* (1953) (London: Allison & Busby, 1985), 133. I would add that Melville is not only critical of Delano's stupidity but he is also an astute critic of the ideology that enables and sustains Delano's bafflement, that is, an abiding faith in his own magnanimity.

106. Herman Melville, *Benito Cereno*, 55.

107. Ibid., 82, 66.

108. María DeGuzmán, *Spain's Long Shadow: The Black Legend, Off-Whiteness, and Anglo-American Empire* (Minneapolis: University of Minnesota Press, 2005), 4–5.

109. Herman Melville, *Benito Cereno*, 101. Dan McCall, editor of the Norton Critical Edition of *Benito Cereno*, references Daniel Webster's praise of the nation after the Compromise of 1850: "A long and violent convulsion for the elements has just passed away, and the heavens, the skies, smile upon us," (101).

110. Herman Melville, *Benito Cereno*, 101.

111. Albion Tourgée, "The South as a Field for Fiction," in *Undaunted Radical: The Writings and Speeches of Albion W. Tourgée*, ed. Mark Elliott and Mark David Smith (Baton Rouge: Louisiana State University Press, 2010), 204.

112. Kevin Phinney, *Souled American: How Black Music Transformed White Culture* (New York: Billboard Books, 2005), 60–61.

113. "Old Aunt Jemima," composed by James Grace, originally sung by Billy Kersands (Boston: John F. Perry and Co., 1875), Brown University Library.

114. Marilyn Kern-Foxworth, *Aunt Jemima, Uncle Ben, and Rastus: Blacks in Advertising, Yesterday, Today, and Tomorrow* (Westport, CT: Praeger, 1994), 6. For a discussion of Nancy Green at the 1893 Columbian World's Fair, see M. M. Manring, *Slave in a Box: The Strange Career of Aunt Jemima* (Charlottesville: University Press of Virginia, 1998), 60–78. Nancy Green was fatally hit by a car in Chicago in 1923.

115. Marilyn Kern-Foxworth, *Aunt Jemima, Uncle Ben, and Rastus*, 71.

116. Kimberly Wallace-Sanders, *Mammy: A Century of Race, Gender and Southern Memory* (Ann Arbor: University of Michigan, 2008), 59.

CHAPTER THREE

1. Paul Coughlin, *No More Christian Nice Guy: When Being Nice Instead of Good Hurts Men, Women and Children* (Ada, MI: Bethany House, 2005), 26.

2. Terry Eagleton, introduction to *The Gospels: Jesus Christ* (London: Verso, 2007), xxiv–xxv.

3. Giorgio Agamben, *The Time That Remains: A Commentary on the Letter to the Romans* (Stanford: Stanford University Press, 2005), 2; Jacob Taubes, *The Political Theology of Paul* (Stanford: Stanford University Press, 2003). In the original French edition, Taubes still refers to Jesus as a "nice guy" in English.

4. Henri Lefebvre, "The Everyday and Everydayness," *Yale French Studies* 73 (1987): 9; Maurice Blanchot, "Everyday Speech," *Yale French Studies* 73 (1987): 13.

5. David Morgan, "The Masculinity of Jesus in Popular Religious Art," in *Men's Bodies, Men's Gods: Male Identities in a (Post-) Christian Culture*, ed. Bjorn Krondorfer (New York, New York University Press, 1996), 251.

6. Harriet Beecher Stowe, *Footsteps of the Master* (New York: J. B. Ford, 1877), 186.

7. Susan Curtis, "The Son of Man and God the Father: The Social Gospel and Victorian Masculinity," in *Meanings of Manhood: Constructions of Masculinity in Victorian America*, ed. Mark C. Carnes and Clyde Griffen (Chicago: University of Chicago Press, 1990), 26.

8. Nathan O. Hatch, *The Democratization of American Christianity* (New Haven: Yale University Press, 1989), 7.

9. Harriet Beecher Stowe, preface (first edition) to *Uncle Tom's Cabin*, Norton Critical Edition, ed. Elizabeth Ammons (New York: W. W. Norton & Company, 1994), xiii.

10. "The Preacher and the Forces of Democracy," *The Methodist Review* (Jan. 1918): 94.

11. "The Modern Novel," *The Methodist Quarterly Review* (Apr 1860): 12.

12. Bryan Garsten, *Saving Persuasion: In Defense of Rhetoric and Judgment* (Cambridge: Harvard University Press, 2003), 2.

13. Francis Greenwood Peabody, *Jesus Christ and the Christian Character* (1905) (New York, The Macmillan Company, 1910), 42.

14. William Ellery Channing, *Discourse on the Evidences of Revealed Religion* (Liverpool, UK: F. B. Wright, 1830), 22. See Richard Wightman Fox, *Jesus in America: Personal Savior, Cultural Hero, National Obsession* (New York: HarperCollins, 2004), 188.

15. Horace Bushnell, *The Character of Jesus: Forbidding His Possible Classification With Men* (1861) (New York: Charles Scribner's, 1898), 20. This work was originally a chapter of Bushnell's earlier book, *Nature and the Supernatural* (1858).

16. See also Charles Beecher's *The Incarnation*, with an introduction by Harriet Beecher Stowe (New York: Harper, 1849). This book offers a far more vivid portrait of Mary than it does of Jesus, demonstrating a Marianism similar to that found in the work of his sister Harriet.

17. Henry Ward Beecher, *The Life of Jesus, the Christ* (New York: J. B. Ford, 1871), 5, 11, 112.

18. Albert Schweitzer, *The Quest for the Historical Jesus*, trans. W. Montgomery (London: A. & C. Black, 1910), 193–194.

19. Selden Lincoln Whitcomb, *The Study of a Novel* (Boston: D. C. Heath & Co., 1905), 111.

20. Thomas Carlyle, "Essay on Biography" (1832), *Little Masterpieces*, ed. Bliss Perry (New York: Doubleday & McClure, 1902), 3.

21. Scott Casper, *Constructing American Lives: Biography & Culture in Nineteenth-Century America* (Chapel Hill: University of North Carolina Press, 1999), 2

22. Harriet Beecher Stowe, "Introductory Note," in *Religious Studies: Sketches and Poems. The Writings of Harriet Beecher Stowe*, vol. 16 (New York: AMS Press, 1967), ix

23. "Harriet Beecher Stowe," *Current Literature* 20:3 (Sep 1896): 221.

24. Michael McKeon, *Secret History of the Domestic* (Baltimore: Johns Hopkins University Press, 2006), 338. See also Catherine Sanok, *Her Life Historical: Exemplarity and Female Saints' Lives in Late Medieval England* (Philadelphia: University of Pennsylvania Press, 2007).

25. On the Renaissance topos of footsteps and imitation theory, see Timothy Hampton, *Writing from History: The Rhetoric of Exemplarity in Renaissance Literature* (Ithaca: Cornell University Press, 1990), 66.

26. Terry Eagleton, *The English Novel: An Introduction* (Oxford, UK: Blackwell, 2005), 3.

27. Harriet Beecher Stowe, *Footsteps of the Master*, 68, 288.

28. J. Hillis Miller, *The Form of Victorian Fiction* (Notre Dame, IN: University of Notre Dame Press, 1968), 94.

29. Harriet Beecher Stowe, *Footsteps of the Master*, 185.

30. Joanne Dobson, "Reclaiming Sentimental Literature," *American Literature* 69 (1997): 263–288.

31. Ian Watt, *The Rise of the Novel* (Berkeley: University of California Press, 2001), 177.

32. F. O. Matthiessen, *Henry James: The Major Phase* (1944) (New York: Oxford University Press, 1963), 140. For Henry James Sr.'s philosophical work on spirituality and society, see his *Society: The Redeemed Form of Man* (Boston: Houghton, Osgood and Company, 1879).

33. Harriet Beecher Stowe, *Footsteps of the Master*, 176; original emphasis.

34. Theodore Parker, *A Discourse Occasioned on the Death of Daniel Webster* (Boston: Benjamin B. Mussey & Co., 1853), 16.

35. Susan Bordo is here quoting Don Hanlon Johnson, "The Body: Which One? Whose?" *Whole Earth Review* (Summer 1989): 408. Susan Bordo, *Unbearable Weight: Feminism, Western Culture and the Body* (10th Anniversary Edition) (Berkeley: University of California Press, 2004), 17.

36. Richard Wightman Fox, *Jesus in America*, 258–259.

37. Harriet Beecher Stowe, *Footsteps of the Master*, 136.

38. Ibid., 70.

39. Walter Kaufmann, "Editor's Preface to *The Antichrist*," in *The Portable Nietzsche*, ed. Walter Kaufmann (New York: Penguin, 1976), 566.

40. Harriet Beecher Stowe, *Footsteps of the Master*, 120.

41. Harriet Beecher Stowe, *Woman in Sacred History* (New York: J. B. Ford, 1873), 20; original emphasis.

42. Harriet Beecher Stowe, *Woman in Sacred History*, 20.

43. Henry Ward Beecher, *The Life of Jesus, The Christ*, 35.

44. Octavius Brooks Frothingham wrote in 1852, "The real Christ is the spiritual, or the Spirit. Without the Spirit, the historical Christ is naught. Without the historical Christ, the Spirit is himself." Quoted in Richard Wightman Fox, *Jesus in America*, 276.

45. Thomas Loebel, *The Letter and the Spirit of Nineteenth-Century American Literature: Justice, Politics, and Theology* (Montreal: McGill-Queen's University Press, 2005), 138.

46. Harriet Beecher Stowe, *Footsteps of the Master*, 137.

47. Leslie Fiedler, *What Was Literature? Class Culture and Mass Society* (New York: Simon and Schuster, 1982), 172.

48. See John Gatta, *American Madonna: Images of the Divine Woman in Literary Culture* (New York: Oxford University Press, 1997).

49. Catherine Clément and Julia Kristeva, *The Feminine and the Sacred* (1998), trans. Jane Marie Todd (New York: Columbia University Press, 2001), 62.

50. Harriet Beecher Stowe, *Footsteps of the Master*, 182.

51. Ralph Waldo Emerson, "The Authority of Jesus" (1830), in *Young Emerson Speaks: Unpublished Discourses on Many Subjects*, ed. Arthur Cushman McGiffert, Jr. (Boston: Houghton Mifflin Co, 1938), 97.

52. Ralph Waldo Emerson, *The Journals and Miscellaneous Notebooks of Ralph Waldo Emerson* (August 25, 1843), vol. 9 (Cambridge, MA: Harvard University Press, 1971), 7.

53. Harriet Beecher Stowe, *Little Foxes: or, the Insignificant Little Habits Which Mar Domestic Happiness* (London: Bell and Daldy, 1866), 140.

54. Harriet Beecher Stowe, *Footsteps of the Master*, 182.

55. Catharine Beecher, *An Essay on Slavery and Abolitionism* (Philadelphia: Henry Perkins, 1837), 46.

56. Harriet Beecher Stowe, *Footsteps of the Master*, 133.

57. Henry Ward Beecher, "What is Preaching?" in *Yale Lectures on Preaching* (New York: J. B. Ford, 1872), 192.

58. Harriet Beecher Stowe, *Men of Our Times; Or, Leading Patriots of the Day* (Hartford, CT, Hartford Publishing Co., 1868), vi.

59. John Stauffer, *Giants: The Parallel Lives of Frederick Douglass and Abraham Lincoln* (New York: Hachette, 2008), 298–301. See Fox, *Jesus in America*, 246.

60. Harriet Beecher Stowe, *Men of Our Times*, 63.

61. John Stauffer, *Giants*, 301.

62. Harriet Beecher Stowe, *Men of Our Times*, 110.

63. Marianne Noble, *The Masochistic Pleasures of Sentimental Literature.* (Princeton: Princeton University Press, 2000), 9–10. Noble cites Elizabeth Grosz's discussion of the relationship between feminism and power: "[P]ower has been seen as the enemy of feminism, something to be abhorred, challenged, dismantled, or at best something to be shared more equally, a thing which can be divided in different ways. Power is not the enemy of feminism but its ally . . . Power is not something that feminism should disdain or rise above for it is its condition of existence and its medium of effectivity." From "Feminism, Women's Studies and the Politics of Theory," a paper delivered at American University, November 6, 1997.

64. This is not to say that Henry Ward Beecher was complaisant during the Civil War. He was a committed abolitionist who used the pulpit to argue for emancipation in the United States and abroad. Rather, my point addresses Beecher's and Stowe's respective versions of liberal Christianity that Thomas Jenkins describes: "Henry Ward Beecher was the premiere nineteenth-century writer in this form of sentimental incarnationalism. Harriet Beecher Stowe, however, represents sentimentalism at its most dramatic. Whereas her brother sought a way around difficult passages in the Gospels, she delved into them. Where her brother's work demonstrates a facile ingenuity, her work shows some dramatic profundity. By contrasting their

writing, we can take a measure of the shallows and depths of the character of God in sentimental incarnationalism." Thomas E. Jenkins, *The Character of God: Recovering the Lost Literary Power of American Protestantism* (New York: Oxford University Press, 1997), 64.

65. Harriet Beecher Stowe, *Men of Our Times*, vi–vii.

66. Ibid., 97.

67. Harriet Beecher Stowe, *Footsteps of the Master*, 248.

68. Adam Phillips and Barbara Taylor, *On Kindness* (New York: Farrar, Straus and Giroux, 2009), 4–5, 9.

69. Richard Brodhead, *Cultures of Letters: Scenes of Reading and Writing in Nineteenth-Century America* (Chicago: University of Chicago Press, 1993), 18–19.

70. Quoted from Bliss Perry, *The American Mind* (Boston: Houghton Mifflin Co., 1912), 15.

71. Elizabeth Stuart Phelps, *The Story of Jesus Christ, An Interpretation* (Boston: Houghton Mifflin & Co., 1897), 111; Elizabeth Stuart Phelps, *The Struggle for Immortality* (Boston: Houghton Mifflin & Co., 1889), 63.

72. Elizabeth Stuart Phelps, *The Story of Jesus Christ*, 224, 189, 99.

73. Elizabeth Stuart Phelps, *The Struggle for Immortality*, 186–187.

74. Elizabeth Stuart Phelps, *The Story of Jesus Christ*, 77, 188.

75. Ibid., 96.

76. Ibid., 118.

77. Ibid., iii, 101–102.

78. Elizabeth Stuart Phelps, *Chapters from a Life* (Boston: Houghton Mifflin & Co., 1897), 134–135.

79. Christine Stansell, "Elizabeth Stuart Phelps: A Study in Female Rebellion," *The Massachusetts Review* 13:1–2 (Winter-Spring 1972): 239.

80. Elizabeth Stuart Phelps, *The Story of Jesus Christ*, 11.

81. Elizabeth Stuart Phelps, *The Story of Jesus Christ*, 200. Elizabeth Cady Stanton writes, "His patience with women was a sore trial to the disciples, who were always disposed to nip their appeals in the bud." Elizabeth Cady Stanton, *The Woman's Bible* (Amherst, NY: Prometheus Books, 1999), 121.

82. Elizabeth Stuart Phelps, *The Story of Jesus Christ*, 47, 199, 237.

83. Ibid., 118, 236, 282.

84. "The Story of Jesus Christ," *The Chap-Book: Semi-Monthly* (Feb 1, 1898): 249.

85. Shailer Mathews, "Review of *The Story of Jesus Christ* by Elizabeth Stuart Phelps," *The Biblical World* 11:1 (Jan 1898): 60.

86. Shailer Mathews, "Ministerial Virility—And a Suggestion," *The Biblical World* 17 (1901): 3.

87. Quoted in Clifford Putney, *Muscular Christianity: Manhood and Sports in Protestant America, 1880–1920* (Cambridge, MA: Harvard University Press, 2001), 93.

88. Stephen Nichols, *Jesus Made in America: A Cultural History from the Puritans to the Passion of the Christ* (Downers Grove, IL: InterVarsity Press, 2008), 107.

89. Susan Curtis, "The Son of Man and God the Father: The Social Gospel and Victorian Masculinity," in *Meanings of Manhood: Constructions of*

Masculinity in Victorian America, ed. Mark C. Carnes and Clyde Griffen (Chicago: University of Chicago Press, 1990), 68.

90. Gail Bederman, "'The Women Have Had Charge of the Church Work Long Enough': The Men and Religion Forward Movement of 1911–1912 and the Masculinization of Middle-Class Protestantism," *American Quarterly* 41:3 (September 1989): 436.

91. Peter Gay, "The Manliness of Christ," in *Religion and Irreligion in Victorian Society,* ed. R. W. Davis and R. J. Helmstadter (London: Routledge, 1992), 113. See also *Sentimental Manhood: Masculinity and the Politics of Affect in American Culture,* ed. Mary Chapman and Glenn Hendler (Berkeley: University of California Press, 1999); E. Anthony Rotundo, *American Manhood: Transformations in Masculinity from the Revolution to the Modern Era* (New York: Basic Books, 1993).

92. Paul S. Boyer, "In His Steps: A Reappraisal," *American Quarterly* 23:1 (Spring 1971): 60; Charles Monroe Sheldon, *In His Steps: "What Would Jesus Do?"* (1896) (Chicago: Advance Publishing Co., 1898); Erin A. Smith, "'What Would Jesus Do?' The Social Gospel and the Literary Marketplace," *Book History* 10 (2007): 193–221; Gregory S. Jackson, "'What Would Jesus Do?': Practical Christianity, Social Gospel Realism and the Homiletic Novel," *PMLA* 121: 3 (May 2006): 641–661.

93. Jacob H. Dorn, "'In Spiritual Communion': Eugene V. Debs and the Socialist Christians," *The Journal of the Gilded Age and Progressive Era* 2:3 (July 2003): 305.

94. Jacob H. Dorn, "'In Spiritual Communion,'" 313; Eugene V. Debs, "Jesus, the Supreme Leader," *The Coming Nation* [Chicago], 1:5 (March 1914): 2. https://www.marxists.org/history/usa/parties/spusa/1914/0300-debs-jesus-supreme.pdf

95. Edward J. Blum, "'There Won't Be Any Rich People in Heaven': The Black Christ, White Hypocrisy, and the Gospel According to W. E. B. Du Bois," *The Journal of African American History* 90:4 (Autumn 2005): 372.

96. W. E. B. Du Bois, *The Gift of Black Folk* (Garden City Park, NY: Square One Publishers, 2009), 160–161.

97. Cornel West defines "nonmarket values" as "love for others, loyalty to an ethical ideal and social freedom," in *Keeping Faith: Philosophy and Race in America* (New York: Routledge, 2008), 126.

98. W. E. B. Du Bois, "The Church and the Negro" (1913), in *Du Bois on Religion,* ed. Phil Zuckerman (Walnut Creek, CA: AltaMira Press, 2000), 99.

99. I am borrowing from Michelle Alexander's evocative notion of the American undercaste in *The New Jim Crow: Mass Incarceration in the Age of Colorblindness* (New York: The New Press, 2011), 13.

100. Elizabeth Stuart Phelps, *The Story of Jesus Christ,* 189; Harriet Beecher Stowe, *Footsteps of the Master,* 52.

101. In one of his later works, *The World and Africa* (1946), W. E. B. Du Bois describes Jesus as a distinct ethnic type, as a "Syrian Jew" with a "hooked nose and curly hair." He was a mixture of "Mongoloid and Negroid elements." See Edward J. Blum, "'There Won't Be Any Rich People in Heaven': The Black Christ, White Hypocrisy, and the Gospel According to W. E. B. Du Bois," *The Journal of African American History* 90:4 (Autumn 2005):

369. For a discussion of whiteness and nineteenth-century Jesus portraiture, see Jefferson J. A. Gatrall, "The Color of His Hair: Nineteenth-Century Literary Portraits of the Historical Jesus," *Novel: A Forum on Fiction* 42.1 (2009): 109–130.

102. Cornel West, *Keeping Faith: Philosophy and Race in America* (New York: Routledge, 2008), xi, 119.

103. Countee Cullen, *The Black Christ & Other Poems* (New York: Harper & Brothers, 1929).

104. For a discussion of the phrase "prison nation," see Erinn Gilson, "The Perils and Privileges of Vulnerability: Intersectionality, Relationality, and the Injustices of the U.S. Prison Nation," *philoSOPHIA* 6:1 (Winter 2016): 44–45.

105. W. E. B. Du Bois's "Jesus Christ in Georgia" was published in *The Crisis* in December 1911 and a slightly revised version appears as "Jesus Christ in Texas" in *Darkwater* (1920). Du Bois, "Jesus Christ in Georgia," *Du Bois on Religion*, 93. It is not clear whether Du Bois is intentionally trying to blur "Jewish gabardine" with "Jewish gaberdine," the latter phrase used in Shakespeare's *The Merchant of Venice* to refer to Shylock's garments.

106. W. E. B. Du Bois, "Religion in the South," in *Du Bois on Religion*, 85.

107. W. E. B. Du Bois, "Jesus Christ in Georgia," in *Du Bois on Religion*, 97.

108. Ibid.

109. Erinn Gilson argues that vulnerability is "politically mediated: it is politically framed and differently distributed." By emphasizing the politics of vulnerability, she differentiates her use of the term from the understanding of vulnerability as inherent to the human condition. Erinn Gilson, "The Perils and Privileges of Vulnerability," 45. Michael Eric Dyson, "Racial Terror: Fast and Slow," *New York Times*, April 17, 2015, p. A31.

110. W. E. B. Du Bois, "Jesus Christ in Georgia," in *Du Bois on Religion*, 98.

111. Edward J. Blum, "Lynching as Crucifixion: Violence and the Sacred Imagination of W. E. B. Du Bois," in *The Souls of W. E. B. Du Bois: New Essays and Reflections*, ed. Edward J. Blum and Jason R. Young (Macon, GA: Mercer University Press, 2009), 204.

112. Michael Eric Dyson, "Racial Terror: Fast and Slow"; W. E. B. Du Bois, "Jesus Christ in Georgia," in *Du Bois on Religion*, 98.

113. W. E. B. Du Bois, "The Church and the Negro," in *Du Bois on Religion*, 100.

114. W. E. B. Du Bois's understanding of the productive uses of guilt anticipates Robert Jay Lifton and Leslie Farber's concept of "animating guilt," which is a productive form of guilt that heals and revitalizes, and it "always connects with an image beyond the guilt and beyond the atrocity and moves toward change and transformation." To be fully human, they argue, requires "the capacity to be in touch with our guilt." Robert Jay Lifton and Leslie Farber, "Questions of Guilt," *Partisan Review* 39 (1972): 517, 519, 518.

115. Sarah Moore Grimké, *Letters on the Equality of the Sexes and the Condition of Women* (1838), quoted in *Root of Bitterness: Documents of the Social History of American Women*, ed. Nancy Cott (Boston: Northeastern University Press, 1996), 126.

116. Alyson Cole, "All of Us Are Vulnerable, but Some Are More Vulnerable than Others: The Political Ambiguity of Vulnerability Studies, an Ambivalent Critique," *Critical Horizons* 17:2 (May 2016): 274.

117. W. E. B. Du Bois, "The Joy of Living," in *Writings by W. E. B. Du Bois in Periodicals Edited by Others*, vol. 1, ed. Herbert Aptheker (Millwood, NY: Kraus-Thomson Organization, 1982), 218, quoted in Edward Blum, "'There Won't Be Any Rich People in Heaven,'" 375; Elizabeth Stuart Phelps, *The Story of Jesus Christ*, 237; original emphasis.

118. Manning Marable, *W. E. B. Du Bois: Black Radical Democrat* (Boston: Twayne Publishers, 1986), 65–66; Herbert Aptheker, "W. E. B. Du Bois and Religion: A Brief Reassessment," *Journal of Religious Thought* 39 (1982): 10.

119. W. E. B. Du Bois, *John Brown* (Philadelphia: George W. Jacobs & Co., 1909), 7–8. For a discussion of how John Brown's contemporaries understood his acts of violence as expressions of love, see Kevin Pelletier, *Apocalyptic Sentimentalism: Love and Fear in U.S. Antebellum Literature* (Athens: University of Georgia Press, 2015), 153-192. Du Bois' praise of John Brown can be seen as part of a genealogy of a U.S.-styled liberation theology, dating back to Thoreau and Whittier, and culminating with James Baldwin's admiration of Brown as an "American prophet," who sought to "liberate a *country*, not simply the black people of that country." Baldwin quoted in Pelletier, 178.

120. W. E. B. Du Bois, "Opinion of W. E. B. Du Bois," *The Crisis* 24:3 (July 1922): 103.

121. David Reynolds, *John Brown, Abolitionist: The Man Who Killed Slavery, Sparked the Civil War, and Seeded Civil Rights* (New York: Random House, 2005), 495.

122. W. E. B. Du Bois, *John Brown*, 36.

123. Ibid., 348.

124. Ibid., 365, 368.

125. Harriet Beecher Stowe, *The Lives and Deeds of Our Self-Made Men*, vol. 2 (Hartford, CT: Worthington, Dustin & Co., 1872), 326.

126. Elizabeth Duquette points out that Elizabeth Stuart Phelps could be referring to "John Brown's Body" or "The Battle Hymn of the Republic," two Union marching songs that were sung to the same tune with some of the same lyrics. Elizabeth Stuart Phelps, *Selected Tales, Essays, and Poems*, ed. Elizabeth Duquette (Lincoln: University of Nebraska Press, 2014), 164, 249, n 3.

127. W. E. B. Du Bois, "The Negro and the Warsaw Ghetto," in *Du Bois on Religion*, 197. Du Bois delivered this speech in New York City in 1952 to honor the Jewish resistance fighters of the Warsaw Ghetto.

128. Jacob Weinstein, "The Jew and the Negro: A Comparative Study in Race and Prejudice," Part II, *Crisis* 41 (July 1934): 197–198.

129. Jacob Weinstein, "The Jew and the Negro: A Comparative Study in Race and Prejudice," Part II, *Crisis* 41:7 (July 1934): 198. According to Eric Goldstein, American Jews in the 1930s were in an increasingly difficult position, in the sense that they were "encouraging a heightened sense of Jewish identification with blacks but also pushing them to secure their uncertain position as whites." Eric Goldstein, *The Price of Whiteness: Jews, Race, and American Identity* (Princeton: Princeton University Press, 2007), 158.

130. John Murray Cuddihy, *The Ordeal of Civility*, 13–14.
131. Maurice Samuel, "Jews Be Nice," in *Jews on Approval* (New York: Liveright, 1932), 9–11, 14.
132. Maurice Samuel, *Jews on Approval*, 20. Clifton Harby Levy, "Progressive Judaism and Liberal Christianity," *The New World; a Quarterly Review of Religion, Ethics and Theology* (Sept 1899): 502.
133. Felix Adler, *The Religion of Duty* (New York: McClure, Phillips & Co., 1905), 113, 160.
134. Bruce Barton, *The Man Nobody Knows* (New York: Bobbs-Merrill, 1925), quoted in Richard Wightman Fox, *Jesus in America*, 318; Linda Kaplan Thaler and Robin Koval, *The Power of Nice: How to Conquer the Business World through Kindness* (New York: Random House, 2006).
135. Adam Phillips and Barbara Taylor, *On Kindness*, 21.

CHAPTER FOUR

1. William Alcott, *The Young Woman's Guide to Excellence* (Boston: George W. Light, 1840), 258.
2. At the end of her seminal essay "The Cult of True Womanhood" (1966), Barbara Welter acknowledges that in the latter half of the nineteenth century, the True Woman evolved into the New Woman "[a]nd yet the stereotype, the 'mystique' if you will, of what woman was and ought to be persisted, bringing guilt and confusion in the midst of opportunity." Barbara Welter, "The Cult of True Womanhood, 1820–1860," *American Quarterly* 18:2 (Summer 1966): 174. For the "gift to please," see Charles Wagner, *The Simple Life*, trans. Mary Louise Hendee (New York: McClure, Phillips & Co, 1903), 146.
3. Sarah Hale, *Manners; or, Happy Homes and Good Society All the Year Round* (Boston: Tilton, 1868), 89; Rev. Daniel Wise, *The Young Lady's Counsellor* (New York: Carlton & Lanahan, 1868), 121.
4. James Henry Potts cites the French sixteenth-century poet Clément Marot: "[W]hat the sunbeam is to the landscape: it embellishes an inferior face and redeems an ugly one." James Henry Potts, ed. *Sunshine on Life's Highway* (Philadelphia: Uplift Publishing, 1911), 151.
5. Ella Hepworth Dixon, *The Story of a Modern Woman* (1894), ed. Steve Farmer (Toronto: Broadview, 2004), 122, 142.
6. Marilyn Frye, *The Politics of Reality: Essays in Feminist Theory* (Trumansburg, NY: Crossing Press, 1983), 2, quoted in Sara Ahmed, *The Promise of Happiness* (Durham, NC: Duke University Press, 2010), 66; Constance Fenimore Woolson, letter to Henry James (August 30, 1882), in Leon Edel, ed., *Henry James Letters*, vol. 3 (Cambridge, MA: Harvard University Press, 1980), 545. Woolson committed suicide in Italy in 1894.
7. Susan Brownmiller, *Femininity* (New York: Simon & Schuster, 1984), 15–16.
8. Greer Litton Fox, "'Nice Girl': Social Control of Women through a Value Construct," *Signs* 2:4 (Summer 1977): 805, 809, 812.
9. Jacqueline Rose has written on "the failure or difficulty of femininity for women" in "Femininity and its Discontents," in *Sexuality in the Field of Vision* (London: Verso, 1986), 102.

10. "On the Influence of Women," *The Literary Magazine, and American Register,* June 1806, 403.

11. Cleveland warned, "This particular movement is so aggressive, and so extreme in its insistence that those whom it has fully enlisted may well be considered as incorrigible." Quoted in Lynn Sherr, *Failure Is Impossible: Susan B. Anthony in Her Own Words* (New York: Times Books, 1995), 142–143.

12. Quoted in Ahmed, *The Pursuit of Happiness,* 66. Kenneth Florey argues that U.S. suffragettes were depicted in anti-suffrage postcards in a far more flattering light than their British counterparts. While the British suffragettes were often portrayed as grotesque and aggressive, American suffragettes were more often seen as young and pretty, though misguided in their views. Kenneth Florey, *American Woman Suffrage Postcards—A Study and Catalog* (Jefferson, NC: McFarland & Co., 2015), 213–214.

13. "On the Influence of Women," *The Literary Magazine, and American Register,* June 1806, 403.

14. George Fitzhugh, *Sociology for the South; or, The Failure of Free Society* (1854; rpt. New York, 1865), 213–217, cited in Elizabeth Moss, *Domestic Novelists in the Old South: Defenders of Southern Culture* (Baton Rouge: Louisiana State University Press, 1992), 33–34.

15. Anna C. Brackett, "The Education of American Girls," in *The Education of American Girls,* ed. Anna C. Brackett (New York: G. P. Putnam's Sons, 1874), 124.

16. Henry Adams, *Esther* (1884) (New York: Scholars' Facsimiles, 1938), 65–66.

17. Matilda Gage is quoted in Douglas C. Baynton, "Disability and the Justification of Inequality in American History," in *The New Disability History: American Perspectives,* ed. Paul K. Longmore and Lauri Umansky (New York: New York University Press, 2001), 45.

18. In *A Very Easy Death,* a tribute to her mother, Simone de Beauvoir imagines her mother as a girl squeezing her body, heart, and mind into the armature of normative femininity: "She had been taught to pull the laces hard and tight herself. A full-blooded, spirited woman lived on inside her, but a stranger to herself, deformed and mutilated." Simone de Beauvoir, *A Very Easy Death,* trans. Patrick O'Brian (New York: G. P. Putnam's, 1966), 43.

19. Joan Scott is quoted in Douglas C. Baynton, "Disability and the Justification of Inequality in American History," 34.

20. Nina Baym, *Woman's Fiction: A Guide to Novels by and about Women in America, 1820–1870* (Ithaca: Cornell University Press, 1978), 17–19.

21. Eve Kosofky Sedgwick associates the reparative process with "nourishment and comfort" and refers to Melanie Klein's understanding of reparative as a term akin to love (128). Eve Kosofky Sedgwick, "Paranoid Reading and Reparative Reading, or, You're So Paranoid, You Probably Think This Essay Is About You," in *Touching Feeling: Affect, Pedagogy, Performativity* (Durham, NC: Duke University Press, 2003), 123–152. The phrase "smiles of society" comes from an 1870 advertisement for Elizabeth Stuart Phelps's novel *Hedged In:* "Can a woman who has fallen from virtue be restored not only to the favor of God, but to the smiles of society?" *The Woman's Journal* (March 26, 1870): 93.

22. Ellis Hanson, "The Future's Eve: Reparative Reading after Sedgwick," *South Atlantic Quarterly* 110:1 (Winter 2011): 102.

23. Virginia Woolf, "Professions for Women," in *Women and Writing,* ed. Michèle Barrett (New York: Harcourt Brace Jovanovich, 1979), 59.

24. Helen Deutsch, *The Psychology of Women,* vol. 1 (New York: Grune & Stratton, 1944).

25. Ann Douglas, *The Feminization of American Culture* (1977) (New York: Farrar, Straus & Giroux, 1998), 11.

26. Sandra Gilbert and Susan Gubar, *The Madwoman in the Attic: The Woman Writer and the Nineteenth-Century Literary Imagination* (New Haven: Yale University Press, 1979): 51.

27. Rita Felski, *Literature After Feminism* (Chicago: University of Chicago Press, 2003), 66–67.

28. Shulamith Firestone, *The Dialectic of Sex: The Case for Feminist Revolution* (New York: Farrar, Straus & Giroux, 1970), 81.

29. Pierre Bourdieu, *Masculine Domination,* trans. Richard Nice (Stanford: Stanford University Press, 2001): 38.

30. Lydia Sigourney, "The Good Daughter," in *The Girls Reading Book, in Prose and Poetry,* 14th ed. (New York: Turner, Hughes and Hayden, 1847), 48.

31. Elizabeth Stuart Phelps, *Chapters from a Life,* 12.

32. Elizabeth Stuart Phelps, *Austin Phelps: A Memoir* (New York: Scribner's, 1891), 87.

33. Ibid., 87, 53.

34. Elizabeth Stuart Phelps, *Confessions of a Wife* (New York: Century, 1902), 9, 67, 10. Phelps published *Confessions of a Wife* under the pseudonym "Mary Adams."

35. Elizabeth Stuart Phelps, "Unhappy Girls," *The Independent,* July 27, 1871, 23.

36. Elizabeth Stuart Phelps, "A Talk to the Girls," *The Independent,* January 4, 1872, 24.

37. Ibid.

38. William James, "What Pragmatism Means," in *Writings 1902–1910* (New York: Library of America, 1987), 40, 522. On James's banking metaphors, see "Pragmatism's Conception of Truth," in *Writings 1902–1910,* 573.

39. William James, "What Pragmatism Means," 513.

40. William James, "Pragmatism and Humanism," in *Writings 1902–1910,* 604. William James writes, "Pragmatism says no, and I fully agree with her," in "What Pragmatism Means," 521.

41. Harriet Beecher Stowe, *Men of Our Times; Or, Leading Patriots of the Day* (Hartford: Hartford Publishing Co., 1868), 110.

42. Harriet Beecher Stowe, *Little Foxes: or, The Insignificant Little Habits Which Mar Domestic Happiness* (London: Bell and Daldy, 1866), 90.

43. Ibid., 66.

44. Ibid., 67.

45. Ibid., 67, 78.

46. Ibid., 79, 81.

47. Stowe, *Little Foxes,* 89.

48. Harriet Beecher Stowe, *We and Our Neighbors*, 464, 432–433.
49. H. H. Agnew, "Woman's Office and Influence," *Harper's New Monthly Magazine* 3:17 (October 1851): 656.
50. Harriet Beecher Stowe, *We and Our Neighbors*, 148, 173.
51. Ibid., 287.
52. Ibid., 290–291.
53. Henry James, "Review of Harriet Beecher Stowe, *We and Our Neighbors*," in Henry James, *Literary Criticism: Essay on Literature, American Writers & English Writers*, vol. 1, ed. Leon Edel (New York: Library of America, 1984), 618–620. For more on the house/body conflation of the nineteenth century, see Beverly Gordon, "Woman's Domestic Body: The Conceptual Conflation of Women and Interiors in the Industrial Age," *Winterthur Portfolio* 31.4 (Winter 1996): 281–301.
54. Joan D. Hedrick, *Harriet Beecher Stowe: A Life* (New York: Oxford University Press, 1994), 361.
55. Elisabeth Griffith, *In Her Own Right: The Life of Elizabeth Cady Stanton* (New York: Oxford University Press, 1984), 145.
56. "A Nice Girl," *The Woman's Journal*, May 13, 1871. During this early period *The Woman's Journal* did not reference Susan B. Anthony and only occasionally republished pieces by Elizabeth Cady Stanton, and yet it was heartily endorsed by Stowe, whose work was frequently mentioned in its pages and who also wrote short articles for it. *The Woman's Journal* was the unofficial organ of the American Woman Suffrage Association (AWSA), and by 1910, the official organ of the National American Woman Suffrage Association (NAWSA).
57. Janet S. Zehr, "The Response of Nineteenth-Century Audiences to Louisa May Alcott's Fiction," *American Transcendental Quarterly* 1.4 (1987): 331; Michelle Ann Abate, "Topsy and Topsy-Turvy Jo: Harriet Beecher Stowe's *Uncle Tom's Cabin* and/in Louisa May Alcott's *Little Women*," *Children's Literature* 34 (2006): 60.
58. The "love and duty" sentence is taken from Louisa May Alcott's preface to the 1882 revision of *Moods*. Critics such as Elizabeth Lennox Keyser claim that the revised version of *Moods* was actually truer to Alcott's original manuscript than the 1864 version. Alcott supports this claim in her 1882 preface by maintaining that the editors of *Moods* in 1864 "so altered" the plot "to suit the taste and convenience of the publishers, that the original purpose of the story was lost sight of, and marriage appeared to be the theme instead of an attempt to show the mistake of a moody nature, guided by impulse, not principle." Louisa May Alcott, *Moods*, in *The Portable Louisa May Alcott*, ed. Elizabeth Lennox Keyser (New York: Penguin, 2000), 157. Christine Doyle argues that Alcott's revision of *Moods* demonstrates an increasing distance from Brontëan themes and a shift toward American ideals that were particularly Emersonian, specifically, the replacement of passion and melodrama with pragmatism, to make "love and duty go hand in hand." Christine Doyle, *Louisa May Alcott and Charlotte Brontë: Transatlantic Translations* (Knoxville: University of Tennessee Press, 2000), 225. In the vein of Showalter, Alcott's biographer Harriet Reisen considers the revision of *Moods* a "betrayal of the [original] work,"

transforming an adult novel about marriage and its limitations into a formulaic story for teenagers. Harriet Reisen, *Louisa May Alcott: The Woman Behind Little Women* (New York: Henry Holt, 2009), 279–280.

59. "The Modern Novel," *The Methodist Quarterly Review* (Apr 1860): 12.

60. Elaine Showalter, introduction to *Little Women*, ed. Elaine Showalter (New York: Penguin, 1989), xxi.

61. Louisa May Alcott, *Little Women*, ed. Elaine Showalter (New York: Penguin, 1989), 3.

62. Ibid., 48, 56.

63. Elaine Showalter, introduction to *Little Women*, xxiii. Martha Saxton and Judith Fetterley are quoted in Showalter, introduction to *Little Women*, xxii; Nina Auerbach, "Reviews," *Nineteenth-Century Fiction* 33.4 (March 1979): 476. See Judith Fetterley, "*Little Women*: Alcott's 'Civil War,'" *Feminist Studies* 5 (1979): 369–383.

64. Simone de Beauvoir, *Memoirs of a Dutiful Daughter* (1958), trans. James Kirkup (New York: Harper Collins, 2005), 89–90. In her autobiography, de Beauvoir writes movingly of her younger sister who was, like Jo March's younger sister Amy, fair-haired with blue eyes (42). The phrase, "endless disputation," comes from de Beauvoir's description of the antithetical mores she inherited from her parents in *Memoirs of a Dutiful Daughter*, 41.

65. Quoted in Barbara Sicherman, "Reading *Little Women*: The Many Lives of a Text," in *U.S. History as Women's History: New Feminist Essays*, ed. Linda K. Kerber, Alice Kessler-Harris, and Kathryn Kish Sklar (Chapel Hill: University of North Carolina Press, 1995), 245, 256.

66. Quoted in Barbara Sicherman, "Reading *Little Women*," 261.

67. Susan Naomi Bernstein, "Writing and Little Women: Alcott's Rhetoric of Subversion," *American Transcendental Quarterly* 7:1 (March 1993): 478.

68. Juliet Mitchell, *Siblings* (Cambridge, UK: Polity Press, 2003), 205, 225.

69. Biographies of Louisa May Alcott that highlight the parent-child bond include Eva LaPlante's *Marmee & Louisa: The Untold Story of Louisa May Alcott and Her Mother* (New York: Simon & Schuster, 2012) and John Matteson's *Eden's Outcasts: The Story of Louisa May Alcott and Her Father* (New York: W. W. Norton, 2008).

70. Louisa May Alcott, *Little Women*, 3.

71. Ibid., 74, 82.

72. D. A. Winnicott is quoted from Juliet Mitchell, *Siblings*, 37–38.

73. Louisa May Alcott, *Little Women*, 288–289.

74. Ibid., 257, 295.

75. Ibid., 295–296.

76. Mary Pipher is quoted in Daniel Delis Hill, *Advertising to the American Woman, 1900–1999* (Columbus: Ohio State University Press, 2002), 203.

77. Simone de Beauvoir, *Memoirs of a Dutiful Daughter*, 104.

78. Louisa May Alcott, *Little Women*, 289–290.

79. Charlotte Perkins Gilman, *Women and Economics*, 2nd ed. (Boston: Small, Maynard & Co., 1899), 295, quoted in Carl Degler, "Charlotte Perkins Gilman on the Theory and Practice of Feminism," *American Quarterly* 8:1 (Spring 1956): 25.

80. Louisa May Alcott, *Little Men* (1871) (New York: Signet, 1986), 10, 13.

81. Ibid., 20, 311.

82. Louisa May Alcott, *Little Women*, 485.

83. Louisa May Alcott, *Little Men*, 109, 107. As Elizabeth Young argues, "These little men are feminized into adulthood, not so much by their literal exposure to the authoritative Mother Bhaer as by their psychic imitation of female self-control." Elizabeth Young, "A Wound of One's Own: Louisa May Alcott's Civil War Fiction," *American Quarterly* 48.3 (1996): 485–486.

84. Louisa May Alcott, *Little Men*, 11.

85. Ibid., 102.

86. Ibid., 111.

87. Louisa May Alcott, *Jo's Boys* (1886) (New York: Penguin, 1994), 349.

88. Ibid., 349–350.

89. Maurice Hamington, "Public Pragmatism: Jane Addams and Ida B. Wells on Lynching," *The Journal of Speculative Philosophy* 19.2 (2005): 172. William James is cited in Maurice Hamington, *Embodied Care: Jane Addams, Maurice Merleau-Ponty, and Feminist Ethics* (Urbana: University of Illinois Press, 2004), 97.

90. Jane Addams, "The Subjective Necessity for Social Settlements" (1892), in *The Jane Addams Reader*, ed. Jean Bethke Elshtain (New York: Basic Books, 2002), 26; Jane Addams, *Newer Ideals of Peace* (New York: Macmillan, 1907), 186. On the relationship between Jane Addams's social philosophy and William James's pragmatism, see Charlene Haddock Seigfried, *Pragmatism and Feminism: Reweaving the Social Fabric* (Chicago: University of Chicago Press, 1996).

91. Maurice Hamington, "Toward a Theory of Feminist Hospitality," *Feminist Formations* 22:1 (Spring 2010): 29.

92. Jane Addams, *Newer Ideals of Peace*, 206, quoted in Wendy Sarvasy, "Social Citizenship from a Feminist Perspective," *Hypatia* 12: 4 (Autumn 1997): 58.

93. Harriet Beecher Stowe, *We and Our Neighbors*, 432–433.

94. Seth Koven, *Slumming: Sexual and Social Politics in Victorian London* (Princeton, NJ: Princeton University Press, 2004), 8.

95. Maurice Hamington, "Two Leaders, Two Utopias: Jane Addams and Dorothy Day," *NWSA Journal* 19:2 (Summer 2007): 180.

96. Maurice Hamington, *The Social Philosophy of Jane Addams* (Urbana: University of Illinois Press, 2009), 133.

97. Almont Lindsey, "Paternalism and the Pullman Strike," *The American Historical Review* 44.2 (January 1939): 272–289.

98. Louise W. Knight, *Citizen: Jane Addams and the Struggle for Democracy* (Chicago: University of Chicago Press, 2005), 323.

99. Jane Addams, "The Objective Value of a Social Settlement" (1892), in *The Jane Addams Reader*, 44.

100. Jane Addams, "A Modern Lear," in *The Jane Addams Reader*, 176.

101. Louise W. Knight, *Citizen*, 328; Jane Addams, "A Modern Lear" (1912), in *The Jane Addams Reader*, 163–176.

102. For a discussion of Jane Addams's meeting with Tolstoy in Russia in 1896 and how she found his argumentative manner disagreeable, see Louise

Knight, *Citizen*, 372–374. See also Jane Addams, *Twenty Years in Hull House with Autobiographical Notes* (New York: Macmillan, 1910), 268. Toward the end of her life, however, Addams does positively employ the phrases "moral force" and "moral energy" (both terms associated with Tolstoy) in her essay "Tolstoy and Gandhi" (1931), in *The Jane Addams Reader*, 436–441.

103. Jane Addams, "Personal Reactions in Time of War" (1922) in *The Jane Addams Reader*, 320.

104. Ibid., 323.

105. Jane Addams used the language of instincts to refer to all sorts of human behavior from Thorstein Veblen's "instinct of workmanship," to the "brutal instinct" and the "humane instinct." The latter she includes in *Newer Ideals of Peace*, 144.

106. Linda O. McMurry, *To Keep the Waters Troubled: The Life of Ida B. Wells* (New York: Oxford University Press, 1998), 296.

107. *Detroit Plaindealer*, 18 October 1889, quoted in Paula Giddings, *Ida: A Sword Among Lions*, (New York: Harper Collins, 2008), 160.

108. Hazel V. Carby, "'On the Threshold of Woman's Era': Lynching, Empire, and Sexuality in Black Feminist Theory," in *Dangerous Liaisons: Gender, Nation, and Postcolonial Perspectives*, ed. Anne McClintock, Aamir Mufti, and Ella Shohat (Minneapolis: University of Minnesota Press, 1997), 336.

109. Ida B. Wells, "The Model Woman: A Pen Picture of the Typical Southern Girl," *New York Freeman*, Feb. 18, 1888. Reprinted in *The Memphis Diary of Ida B. Wells*, ed. Miriam Decosta-Willis (Boston: Beacon Press, 1995): 188.

110. Ida B. Wells, *The Memphis Diary of Ida B. Wells*, 73, 88.

111. Ida B. Wells, *The Memphis Diary of Ida B. Wells*, 59. For more on Ida B. Wells's anger in relation to the feminine mandate of composure, see Patricia A. Schechter, "'All the Intensity of My Nature': Ida B. Wells, Anger, and Politics," *Radical History Review* 70 (October 1998): 48–77.

112. T. Thomas Fortune wrote in the *New York Age* (August 11, 1888) that Wells is "rather girlish looking in physique, with sharp regular features, penetrating eyes, firm set thin lips and a sweet voice . . . [S]he is as smart as a steel trap." Quoted in *The Memphis Diary of Ida B. Wells*, 51. As Wells's biographer Paula Giddings notes, attitudes toward Wells's beauty altered in the black press as she became more militant. Giddings cites the following article from the *New York Age* in 1889, "'Ida makes the mistake of trying to be pretty as well as smart,' noted one of her colleagues who added that female writers like George Eliot, George Sand, and Harriet Beecher Stowe, while brilliant, 'were not paragons by any means.'" Paula Giddings, *Ida: A Sword Among Lions*, 160–161.

113. Quoted in Paula Giddings, *Ida: A Sword Among Lions*, 129. Giddings cites the *New York Freeman*, who reprinted the story from the *Memphis Watchman* (15 January 1887).

114. Paula Giddings, *Ida: A Sword Among Lions*, 62; Ida B. Wells, *Crusade for Justice: The Autobiography of Ida B. Wells*, ed. Alfreda M. Duster (Chicago: University of Chicago Press, 1970), 18.

115. Ida B. Wells, *Crusade for Justice*, 19; Ta-Nehisi Coates, *Between the World and Me* (New York: Spiegel & Grau, 2015), 10.

116. Malcolm Gladwell, "Talk of the Town: The Politics of Politesse," *The New Yorker*, December 2002. 58.

117. *The Young Lady's Own Book* is quoted in Thomas E. Jenkins, *The Character of God: Recovering the Lost Literary Power of American Protestantism* (New York: Oxford University Press, 1997), 25; Louisa May Alcott, *Little Women*, 79.

118. Elizabeth Cady Stanton, *Elizabeth Cady Stanton as Revealed in Her Letters*, 128; Mary "Mother" Jones, *The Autobiography of Mother Jones* (Chicago: Charles H. Kerr & Co., 1925), 204, quoted in Patricia A. Schechter, "'All the Intensity of My Nature': Ida B. Wells, Anger, and Politics," *Radical History Review* 70 (October 1998): 56. See also Carroll Smith-Rosenberg, "Beauty, the Beast and the Militant Woman," in *Disorderly Conduct: Visions of Gender in Victorian America* (New York: Oxford University Press, 1985), 109–128.

119. Sandra Gustafson, "Choosing a Medium: Margaret Fuller and the Forms of Sentiment," *American Quarterly* 47:1 (March 1995): 41; Karen Sánchez-Eppler, *Touching Liberty: Abolition, Feminism, and the Politics of the Body* (Berkeley: University of California Press, 1993), 149.

120. Lynn Sherr, *Failure Is Impossible: Susan B. Anthony in Her Own Words*, 144.

121. Philip Foner, introduction to *The Voice of Black America: Major Speeches by Negroes in the United States*, ed. Philip S. Foner (New York: Capricorn Books, 1975), 2.

122. Ida B. Wells, *Southern Horrors and Other Writings*, ed. Jacqueline Jones Royster (Boston: Bedford, 1997), 52.

123. Paula Giddings, *Ida: A Sword Among Lions*, 319, 228–229.

124. Ibid., 337.

125. Quoted in Teresa Zackodnik, "Ida B. Wells and 'American Atrocities' in Britain," *Women's Studies International Forum* 28 (2005): 269.

126. Paula Giddings, *Ida: A Sword Among Lions*, 318. The *New York Times* refers to Ida B. Wells as "a slanderous and nasty-minded mulatress" in "British Anti-Lynchers," (August 2, 1894). Gail Bederman, "'Civilization,' the Decline of Middle-Class Manliness, and Ida B. Wells's Anti-lynching Campaign (1892–94)," *Radical History Review* 52 (Winter 1992): 5–30.

127. Paula Giddings, *Ida: A Sword Among Lions*, 306.

128. Ida B. Wells, *Crusade for Justice*, 126.

129. Teresa Zackodnik, *Press, Platform, Pulpit: Black Feminist Publics in the Era of Reform* (Knoxville: University of Tennessee Press, 2011), 150.

130. Ida B. Wells, *Crusade for Justice*, 107.

CHAPTER FIVE

1. David Starr Jordan, *Imperial Democracy* (New York: Appleton, 1899), 6, 25, 14.

2. Ibid., 53. Jordan is referring to the Anglo-Zanzibar War, which lasted only forty minutes on August 27, 1896, making it the shortest war in history. In fact, the British did not kill Sultan Khalid bin Barghash, whom they suspected of poisoning his cousin, the pro-British Sultan Hamad bin Thuwaini,

but they did capture him and eventually allowed him to return to German East Africa.

3. President William McKinley, "Proclamation to the Philippine People," December 21, 1898, http://www.msc.edu.ph/centennial/benevolent.html.

4. Anne Paulet, "To Change the World: The Use of American Indian Education in the Philippines," *History of Education Quarterly* 47:2 (May 2007): 173–202.

5. On the Thomasites, and particularly female teachers as "agents of assimilation," see Meg Wesling, *Empire's Proxy: American Literature and U.S. Imperialism in the Philippines* (New York: New York University Press, 2011), 104–138.

6. John T. Morse, ed., *Life and Letters of Oliver Wendell Holmes,* vol. 1 (Cambridge, MA: Riverside Press, 1896), 304.

7. William Howard Taft, "Testimony before the Senate Hearings," January 31, 1902, 78. On Taft and the water cure, see "Hearings," 75. For a historical overview of waterboarding and the Philippine-American War, see Paul Kramer, "The Water Cure," *The New Yorker*, February 25, 2008, 38–43.

8. According to historian C. Vann Woodward, the post-Reconstruction North looked to "Southern racial policy for national guidance to the new problems of imperialism," *The Origins of the New South, 1877–1913* (1951), revised ed. (Baton Rouge: Louisiana State University Press, 1995), 324. For scholarship on the relationship of the South with U.S. imperialism, see Harilaos Stecopoulos, *Reconstructing the World: Southern Fictions and US Imperialisms, 1898–1976* (Ithaca: Cornell University Press, 2008); Jon Smith and Deborah Cohn, ed. *Look Away! The US South in New World Studies* (Durham: Duke University Press, 2004).

9. Albion Tourgée, "The South as a Field for Fiction," in *Undaunted Radical: The Selected Writings and Speeches of Albion W. Tourgée,* ed. Mark Elliott and John David Smith (Baton Rouge: Louisiana State University Press, 2010), 204.

10. Gerald Horne, *The White Pacific: U.S. Imperialism and Black Slavery in the South Seas after the Civil War* (Honolulu: University of Hawaii Press, 2006), 77–91, esp. 78–80, cited in David Roediger and Elizabeth Esch, *The Production of Difference: Race and the Management of Labor in U.S. History* (New York: Oxford University Press, 2012), 74.

11. W. E. B. Du Bois, *Darkwater: Voices from within the Veil* (1920) in *The Oxford W. E. B. Du Bois Reader,* ed. Eric J. Sundquist (New York: Oxford University Press, 1996), 532.

12. Philippine Information Society, *Facts about the Filipinos* 1:1 (May 1901): 21, 18.

13. *The Times*, April 18, 1899, 9, quoted in Geoffrey Seed, "British Views of American Policy in the Philippines Reflected in Journals of Opinion, 1898–1907," *Journal of American Studies* 2:1 (April 1968): 52.

14. Quoted in Julian Go, *Patterns of Empire: The British and American Empires, 1688 to the Present* (New York: Cambridge University Press, 2011), 19.

15. Louis B. Wright and H. Wayne Morgan are quoted in Louis A. Pérez, Jr., *The War of 1898: The United States & Cuba in History & Historiography* (Chapel Hill, NC: University of North Carolina Press, 1998), 117–119. I

discuss Christopher Bollas's concept of "violent innocence" in the introduction. Christopher Bollas, *Being a Character: Psychoanalysis and Self
Experience* (New York: Hill & Wang, 1992), 165–192.

16. On colonial comparisons between Britain and Spain in the Americas, see
John Elliott, *Empires of the Atlantic World: Britain and Spain in America,
1492–1830* (New Haven: Yale University Press, 2006), 403–405; Edmund
Wilson, *American Slavery, American Freedom: The Ordeal of Colonial
Virginia* (New York: W. W. Norton, 1975), 6–9; 76–77. Commodore Dewey
is cited in Dinah Roma-Sianturi, "'Pedagogic Invasion': The Thomasites in
Occupied Philippines," *Kritika Kultura* 12 (2009): 16.

17. Walter Lippmann, *Public Opinion* (1922) (New York: Free Press, 1997),
63–64; Richard Dyer, "The Role of Stereotypes," in Paul Marris and Sue
Thornham, eds., *Media Studies: A Reader*, 2nd ed. (Edinburgh: Edinburgh
University Press, 1999): 245–251.

18. Gertrude Stein, *The Making of Americans* (1926) (Champaign, IL: Dalkey
Archive Press, 1999), 221; William James, *Psychology: A Briefer Course*
(1892) (Mineola, NY: Dover, 2001), 10.

19. See John Plotz's evocative use of portability in *Portable Property: Victorian
Culture on the Move* (Princeton: Princeton University Press, 2008);
Philippine Investigating Committee, *Senate Document* 333, 57th Congress,
1st Session, vol. 1 (Washington, DC: US Government Printing Office, 1902),
329; Theodore Roosevelt to William Bayard Cutting, April 18, 1899, is
quoted in Walter L. Williams, "United States Indian Policy and the Debate
over Philippine Annexation: Implications for the Origins of American
Imperialism," *Journal of American History* 66:4 (March 1980): 826.

20. Sharon Delmendo, *Star-Entangled Banner: One Hundred Years of America in
the Philippines* (New Brunswick, NJ: Rutgers University Press, 2004), 42, 97.

21. Stuart Creighton Miller, *"Benevolent Assimilation": The American
Conquest of the Philippines, 1899–1903* (New Haven, CT: Yale University
Press, 1982), 179–80.

22. Winthrop L. Marvin, "American and 'Malay' in Hawaii," *The American
Monthly Review of Reviews* 19 (January–June 1899): 457.

23. Quoted in Paul T. McCartney, *Power and Progress: American National
Identity, the War of 1898, and the Rise of American Imperialism* (Baton
Rouge: Louisiana State University Press, 2006), 261.

24. Aziz Rana, *The Two Faces of American Freedom* (Cambridge, MA: Harvard
University Press, 2010), 12–13. Edward Cavanagh and Lorenzo Veracini
argue that colonialism and settler colonialism remain distinct and separate
even when they "interpenetrate and overlap." Cavanaugh and Veracini's
tidy taxonomies, however, break down in the Philippines, where the two
concepts fuse together. For this reason, I prefer Aziz Rana's notions of "set-
tlerism" and "settler empire" as a continuum of expansion. Edward
Cavanagh and Lorenzo Veracini, "Editorial Statement," *Settler Colonial
Studies* 3:1 (2013): 1. Historian Amy Greenberg argues that 1898 did not
mark the beginning of U.S. imperial designs, but their continuation, which
began in the antebellum period when Manifest Destiny expanded to Latin
America. Amy S. Greenberg, *Manifest Manhood and the Antebellum
American Empire* (New York: Cambridge University Press, 2005).

25. Franklin Giddings, *Democracy and Empire* (New York: Macmillan, 1900), 272.

26. Franklin Giddings, *Democracy and Empire*, p. 284, 266, 357; Thorstein Veblen, *The Theory of the Leisure Class*, ed. Martha Banta (New York: Oxford University Press 2009), 18.

27. Moon-Ho Jung, "Seditious Subjects; Race, State Violence and the U.S. Empire," *Journal of Asian American Studies* 14.2 (June 2011): 234.

28. Ibid.

29. Richard Drinnon, *Facing West: The Metaphysics of Indian-Hating & Empire-Building* (1980) (Norman, OK: University of Oklahoma Press, 1997), 324; Stuart Creighton Miller, *Benevolent Assimilation*, 233.

30. Reynaldo Ileto, "The Philippine-American War: Friendship and Forgetting," in *Vestiges of War: The Philippine-American War and the Aftermath of an Imperial Dream, 1899–1999*, ed. Angel Velasco Shaw and Luis H. Francia (New York: NYU Press 2002), 7, 12. See also Sarita Echavez, *The Decolonized Eye: Filipino American Art and Performance* (Minneapolis: University of Minnesota Press 2009), 95.

31. Henry Gannet, "The Philippine Islands and Their People," *National Geographic Magazine*, March 1, 1904, Rpt. U.S. Senate Document No. 175, 58th Congress, 2nd Session, 12.

32. W. W. Marquardt, "Filipino Hospitality," unpublished typescript, undated, 3 pages. Walter W. Marquardt Papers, Box 7, Bentley Historical Library, University of Michigan.

33. Taft is quoted from Jonathan Lurie, *William Howard Taft: The Travails of a Progressive Conservative* (New York: Cambridge University Press, 2012), 39. McKinley is quoted in Henry F. Pringle, *The Life and Times of William Howard Taft, A Biography*, vol. 2 (New York: Farrar & Rinehart, 1939), 160; William Howard Taft, *Four Aspects of Civic Duty* (New York: Scribner's 1908).

34. Finley Peter Dunne is quoted in Stuart Creighton Miller, *"Benevolent Assimilation,"* 13; Helen Herron Taft, *Recollections of Full Years* (New York: Dodd, Mead & Co., 1914), 156.

35. Harry Fowler Woods's photograph of the Taft handshake with the Moro chief was taken on the eve of the Moro Crater Massacre in March 1906. It is likely that the chief featured in this photograph would have been among the murdered.

36. Edward Howe Cotton, *William Howard Taft, A Character Study* (Boston: Beacon Press, 1932), 8–11.

37. Robert B. Westcott, "Taft's Record in the Philippines," *Overland Monthly* 52:3 (September 1908): 26–27.

38. Ibid., 27.

39. John O'Sullivan, "The Great Nation of Futurity," *The United States Magazine and Democratic Review* 6:23 (November 1839): 426–430.

40. Helen Herron Taft, *Recollections of Full Years*, 115; Walter Wellman, "Taft: Trained to Be President," *The American Review of Reviews* 37 (1907): 678–679; Edward Howe Cotton, *William Howard Taft*, 23.

41. J. A. C., "Secretary Taft in the Orient," *Overland Monthly and Out West Magazine* 51 (1908): 8.

42. Jonathan Lurie, *William Howard Taft*, 50; Willard B. Gatewood, Jr. *'Smoked Yankees' and the Struggle for Empire: Letters From Negro Soldiers, 1898–1902* (Urbana: University of Illinois Press, 1971), 257.

43. Willard B. Gatewood, Jr., *'Smoked Yankees,'* 252–257; Paul Kramer, "Race-Making and Colonial Violence in the U.S. Empire: The Philippine-American War as Race War," *Diplomatic History* 30.2 (April 2006): 174.

44. Henry F. Pringle, *The Life and Times of William Howard Taft*, 174–175; Helen Herron Taft, *Recollections of Full Years*, 114.

45. Paul Kramer, *The Blood of Government: Race, Empire, the US and the Philippines* (Chapel Hill: University of North Carolina Press, 2006), 186. For Kramer on "fiesta politics," see *The Blood of Government*, 152–158.

46. Lyman Abbott, "William H. Taft," *The Outlook*, April 4, 1908, 773–774.

47. "Persons in the Foreground: The Ingratiating Mr. Taft," *Current Literature* 45:1 (July 1908): 33.

48. Helen Herron Taft, *Recollections of Full Years*, 166, 148.

49. Elsie Clews Parsons, "American Snobbishness in the Philippines," *The Independent*, February 8, 1906, 332.

50. Ann Laura Stoler, *Haunted By Empire: Geographies of Intimacy in North American History* (Durham: Duke University Press, 2006), 36. Stoler is summarizing Albert Memmi's argument in *The Colonizer and the Colonized*.

51. W. E. B. Du Bois, *Darkwater* in *The W. E. B. Du Bois Reader*, ed. Eric Sundquist (New York: Oxford University Press, 1996), 532.

52. Ernest Crosby, "Why I am opposed to Imperialism," [A Symposium by President George McA. Miller, Prof. Thomas Will of Ruskin College, Trenton, MO, Mr. Bolton Hall and Mr. Ernest Crosby] *The Arena* 28:1 (July 1902): 10.

53. Bolton Hall, "Why I am opposed to Imperialism," *The Arena* 28:1 (July 1902): 7; Senator Fred Dubois from Idaho is quoted in Moorfield Storey, "The Philippine Problem To-Day," *An Address Delivered at the Seventh Annual Meeting of the Anti-Imperialist League* (Boston: The Anti-Imperialist League, 1905?), 28–29.

54. *Spectator* 90 (1903): 686, quoted in Geoffrey Seed, "British Views of American Policy in the Philippines Reflected in Journals of Opinion, 1898–1907," *Journal of American Studies* 2:1 (April 1968): 62.

55. Hugh Clifford, John Foreman, and *The Fortnightly Review* were cited in Geoffrey Seed, "British Views," 62.

56. F. H. Crumbley is quoted in Willard B. Gatewood, Jr., *'Smoked Yankees,'* 271. James Booker is quoted in Gatewood, 284.

57. "Gen. Hughes in Tilt With Senator Patterson," *New York Times*, March 9, 1902, p. 4. The phrase *"negritos Americanos"* appears in Willard B. Gatewood, Jr., *'Smoked Yankees,'* 242.

58. James W. Galloway is quoted in Willard B. Gatewood, Jr., *'Smoked Yankees,'* 253. The *New York Age* is quoted in Gatewood, 280.

59. For a discussion of David Fagen, an African American soldier who defected from the U.S. army to join the *insurrectos*, see Epifanio San Juan, "An African American Soldier in the Philippine Revolution: An Homage to David Fagen," http://clogic.eserver.org/2009/SanJuan.pdf

60. Willard B. Gatewood, Jr., 'Smoked Yankees,' 277.

61. General Wood and the New York Times are quoted in Alejandro R. Roces, "The Moro Crater Massacre," The Philippine Star, March 13, 2010, http://www.philstar.com/opinion/557105/ moro-crater-massacre. Accessed July 18, 2014.

62. Mark Twain [Samuel Clemens], "Comments on the Moro Massacre," March 12, 1906. First published in Mark Twain's Autobiography, ed. Albert Bigelow Paine (New York: Harper and Brothers, 1924), http://www.history-isaweapon.com/defcon1/clemensmoromassacre.html.

63. Ibid.

64. Moorfield Storey, "The Moro Massacre: A Letter" (Boston: Anti-Imperialist League, 1906?). http://www.historyisaweapon.com/defcon1/clemensmoromassacre.html.

65. Moorfield Storey, "The Moro Massacre: A Letter"; Mark Twain, "The United States of Lyncherdom," in Tales, Sketches, Speeches and Essays, 1891–1910 (New York: Library of America 1992), 479–486.

66. W. E. B. Du Bois's letter to Moorfield Storey is quoted in John Bellamy Foster, Harry Magdoff, and Robert W. McChesney, "Kipling, the 'White Man's Burden,' and U.S. Imperialism," in Pox Americana: Exposing the American Empire, ed. John Bellamy Foster and Robert W. McChesney (New York: Monthly Review Press, 2004), 17.

67. W. E. B. Du Bois, Darkwater, 508.

68. Stuart Creighton Miller,, "Benevolent Assimilation," 204.

69. Helen Gougar, Forty Thousand Miles of World Wandering (Chicago: Monarch Book Company, 1905). For more on Helen Gougar, see Robert C. Kriebel, Where the Saints Have Trod: The Life of Helen Gougar (West Lafayette, IN: Purdue University Press, 1985).

70. Helen Gougar, "America in the Philippines: A Conversation with Helen M. Gougar," The Arena 35 (April 1906): 387. For a discussion of how Filipino discontent found expression through Tagalog theater, see Paul Rodell, "Philippine 'Seditious Plays,'" Asian Studies 12–13 (1974): 88–118.

71. Helen Gougar, "America in the Philippines: A Conversation with Helen M. Gougar," 388–389.

72. William Howard Taft, Hearings on Affairs in the Philippine Islands, Senate document 333, 57th Congress, Washington, DC, vol. 1, January 31, 1902, 11–12.

73. Helen Herron Taft, Recollections of Full Years, 151.

74. Willard B. Gatewood, Jr.,'Smoked Yankees,' 251, 237, 243.

75. Kimberly Alidio, "'When I Get Home, I want to Forget,' Memory and Amnesia in The Occupied Philippines, 1901–1904," Social Text 59 (Summer 1999): 109.

76. Richard Slotkin, Gunfighter Nation: The Myth of the Frontier in Twentieth-Century America (Norman, OK: University of Oklahoma Press, 1998), 117–119.

77. General Adna Chaffee is quoted in Stuart Creighton Miller, "Benevolent Assimilation," 205.

78. William W. Marquardt, "The Old and the New: 1901 versus 1914," 4–25. Bureau of Education. Special Articles, vol. 3. William W. Marquardt Papers, Bentley Historical Library, University of Michigan.

79. On colonial ambivalence, see Homi Bhabha, *The Location of Culture* (London: Routledge, 1994). See also Bill Ashcroft, Gareth Griffiths and Helen Tiffin, ed., *Post-Colonial Studies: Key Concepts,* (New York: Routledge, 2000), 10–11. I qualify my claims about the Thomasites through the use of "some," since they varied considerably. Some turned to drink and gambling as Helen Beattie describes, while others were miserable and counted the days until they could return to the United States. (See Harry Cole's letters from the Philippines (1901) at the Bentley Historical Library at the University of Michigan). Others, as James Le Roy admits, were simply unfit for the job.

80. Vicente Rafael, *The Promise of the Foreign: Nationalism and the Technics of Translation in the Spanish Philippines* (Durham: Duke University Press, 2015), viii, 4.

81. James Le Roy, "The American Teacher in the Philippines," *The Outlook,* March 31, 1906, 745–747.

82. Helen P. Beattie, "American Teachers and the Filipinos," *The Outlook,* October 15, 1904, 421–423.

83. Amy Kaplan, "Manifest Domesticity," *American Literature* 70:3 (September 1998): 581–606; Funie Hsu, "Colonial Articulations: English Instruction and the 'Benevolence' of U.S. Overseas Expansion in the Philippines, 1898–1916," (Ph.D. diss., UC Berkeley, 2013), 70–71. For more on maternal colonialism, see Margaret D. Jacobs, "Maternal Colonialism: White Women and Indigenous Child Removal in the American west and Australia, 1880–1940," *The Western Historical Quarterly* (2005): 453–476. On Ida B. Wells on prettiness, see my Chapter 4: Feminine Niceness.

84. Helen P. Beattie, "American Teachers and the Filipinos," 421. On white fathering, see Vicente L. Rafael, *White Love and Other Events in Filipino History* (Durham: Duke University Press, 2000), 23.

85. "Another American Teacher in the Philippines," *Congregationalist and Christian World* (May 31, 1902): 797.

86. Helen P. Beattie, "American Teachers and the Filipinos," 426.

87. A[lbert] L[eslie] Pitcher, "The Need of Good Men in the Philippines," *The Independent* 42 (October 24, 1907): 980. A. L. Pitcher is listed among the original Thomasites in Mary Racelis and Judy Celine Ick, *Bearers of Benevolence: The Thomasites and Public Education in the Philippines* (Pasig City: Anvil, 2001), 286.

88. A. L. Pitcher, "The Need of Good Men in the Philippines," 981. An example of Pitcher's colonial mentality is seen in his article "Living in Hardship: American Housekeeping in the Philippines," *Boston Evening Transcript,* August 20, 1902,16. In this piece, he discusses, in part, the importance of training Filipino boys to be good servants, while discouraging Americans from living for a length of time in the Philippines because of their inability to adapt to a more rugged lifestyle.

89. A. L. Pitcher, "The Need of Good Men in the Philippines," 981.

90. Mary Racelis, introduction to *Bearers of Benevolence: The Thomasites and Public Education in the Philippines* (Pasig City: Anvil, 2001), 6; Julian Encarnacion, "Six Centuries of Teaching and Teachers," *Saturday Mirror Magazine*, August 22,1953, 5, quoted in Mary Racelis, introduction to *Bearers of Benevolence*, 6.

91. Mary Racelis, introduction to *Bearers of Benevolence*, 4.

92. For an example of such a critique of Mary Racelis and Judy Celine Ick's volume *Bearers of Benevolence*, see Dinah Roma-Sianturi, "'Pedagogic Invasion,'" 23–24.

93. Nicholas Thomas writes, "[B]ecause of their confrontations with indigenous interests, alternate civilizing missions and their internal inconsistencies, colonial intentions are frequently deflected, or enacted farcically and incompletely." Nicholas Thomas, *Colonialism's Culture: Anthropology, Travel, Government* (Princeton: Princeton University Press, 1994), 105. See also Julian Go, "Chains of Empire, Projects of State: Political Education and US Colonial Rule in Puerto Rico and the Philippines," *Comparative Studies in Society and History* 42.2 (2000): 335.

94. Albert Leslie Pitcher, "Hunting in Luzon: A Search for Game, Not for Men," *Boston Evening Transcript*, August 6, 1902, 20.

95. W. E. B. Du Bois Papers, University of Massachusetts, Amherst, http://credo.library.umass.edu/view/pageturn/mums312-b001-i346/#page/3/mode/1up. Other black educators in the Philippines include Carter G. Woodson, who would edit the *Journal of Negro History*, Mary E. Dickerson, Frederick Bonner, and his wife Charlotte Bonner of New Haven. See "John Henry Manning Butler," *Journal of Negro History* 30.2 (April 1945): 243–244. Sarah Steinbock-Pratt's blog on the Thomasites has a brief sketch about black Thomasites, https://thomasites.wordpress.com.

96. Ralph Wendell Taylor, letter to his mother Elizabeth Gurney Taylor. August 13, 1907, Box 1, Taylor Family Papers, Bentley Historical Library, University of Michigan.

97. Bess Taylor Thompson and Dr. Gilbert Perez are quoted in Amparo Santamaria Lardizabal, "Pioneer American Teachers and Philippine Education," (Ph.D. diss., Stanford University, 1956), 12.

98. Virgilio Enriquez, "Kapwa: A Core Concept of Filipino Social Psychology," in *Philippine World-View*, ed. Virgilio Enriquez (Singapore: Institute of Southeast Asian Studies, 1986), 12.

99. Virgilio Enriquez, "Kapwa," 16. As Patricia B. Licuanan argued, "*Pakikikpagkapwa-tao* is manifested in a basic sense of justice and fairness, and in concern for others. It is demonstrated in the Filipino's ability to empathize with others, in helpfulness and generosity in time of need *(pakikiramay)*, in the practice of *bayanihan*, or mutual assistance, and in the famous Filipino hospitality." Patricia B. Licuanan, "A Moral Recovery Program: Building a People—Building a Nation," in *Values in Philippine Culture and Education: Philippine Philosophical Studies I*, ed. Manuel B. Dy, Jr., (Washington, D.C.: Office of Research and Publications, 1994), 36.

100. Virgilio Enriquez, "Kapwa," 16

101. "Another American Teacher in the Philippines," *Congregationalist and Christian World*, May 31, 1902, 797.

102. I am referencing Chadwick Allen's evocative concept of trans-indigenous literary studies as a way to imagine a comparative and global method to discuss indigenous-to-indigenous relationships, not delimited by nation-states. Chadwick Allen, *Trans-Indigenous: Methodologies for Global Native Literary Studies* (Minneapolis: University of Minnesota Press, 2012).

103. Mahmood Mamdani, "Settler Colonialism: Then and Now," *Critical Inquiry* 41.3 (Spring 2015): 614.

104. Dylan A. T. Miner, "Makataimeshekiakiak, Settler Colonialism, and the Specter of Indigenous Liberation," *Re-Collecting Black Hawk: Landscape, Memory, and Power in the American Midwest*, ed. Nicholas A. Brown, Sarah E. Kanouse (Pittsburgh: University of Pittsburgh Press, 2015), 218–235.

105. Jane Addams, "The Subjective Necessity of Social Settlements," *The Jane Addams Reader*, 28.

Acknowledgments

T HIS BOOK BEGAN over a decade ago in Alan Sinfield's home in Brighton, England. We were discussing 9/11 and the ubiquitous question one heard at the time, "Why do they hate us?" This question seemed to frame 9/11 as a crisis of American likability, which had the effect of turning a political event into an interpersonal matter of sociability. Alan seemed intrigued by this idea, and I knew then that I had the germ of a book project.

Soon after, I spent a year as a fellow at the Charles Warren Center at Harvard University under the leadership of David Hall and James Kloppenberg, where the project began to develop with the support of Larry Buell, John Stauffer, Ben Reiss, John Plotz, and the Warren Fellows from 2005–2006.

A couple of years later, Leigh Schmidt and Sally Promey invited me to think about niceness in terms of nineteenth-century religion. What emerged from the two symposia on religious liberalism, one at Princeton and the other at Yale, is the "Christology of Niceness" chapter of this book, and I am grateful to both of them, as well as to the interdisciplinary and convivial group of scholars, for giving me the opportunity to develop an important part of my argument. I also want to thank Jennifer Fleissner and Scott Herring at Indiana University, and Robert Levine at the University of Maryland, College Park, for the opportunity to share my work.

This book also benefited from a summer fellowship at the American Antiquarian Society, funded by the New England Modern Language Association. Paul Erickson and the indefatigable archivists and librarians at AAS provided an ideal milieu in which to work. In the final stages of writing, I was awarded the Anne LaBastille Memorial Writer

Residency in Nonfiction at the Adirondack Center for Writing. Thanks to Nathalie Thill, the Executive Director, as well as to the amazing group of writers for our fireside chats. My cousin Lisa Bramen, a senior editor at *Adirondack Life*, kindly suggested that I apply.

I am indebted to my community in Buffalo, New York. My colleagues in the humanities and especially in the English Department at the University at Buffalo have been incredibly supportive in indulging my intellectual obsessions over the years. I want to thank those locally and nationally who have generously read parts of the manuscript at various stages of incubation: David Schmid, Graham Hammill, Robert Levine, Neil Schmitz, and Prentiss Clark. My writing group—Ann Colley, Regina Grol, and Carolyn Korsmeyer—read every chapter, and they have become an ongoing source of support, friendship, and good cheer. Julie Abbruscato and Jamie Currie gave me sound advice about the introduction. Conversations with Ewa Ziarek and Benjamin Soskis helped me decide what not to include. Caroline Levander asked a tough question at the start that significantly shaped this book's form. And toward the finish, David Morgan, Laura Mielke, and Kevin Pelletier helped me tie loose ends. A grant from the UB Gender Institute assisted in the final stages of manuscript preparation. I'm grateful to Kari Winter for her ongoing support. Although I have never taught a seminar on the topic, this work has benefited from my graduate students' curiosity, encouragement, and suggestions. I am grateful for the research assistance of Prentiss Clark, Richard Garner, and Shosuke Kinugawa, as well as Michael Dedek and Tim Postellier. Brian Wells and his wonderful staff continue to provide an ideal room of my own in which to write.

My editor, Lindsay Waters, has supported this project from the very beginning, and I appreciate his loyalty, generosity, and patience. He selected two astute readers, one anonymous and the other Larry Buell, whose suggestions were spot on.

Thanks to the librarians at the Buffalo & Erie County Public Library as well as the dedicated staff at Lockwood Library at the University at Buffalo, especially Laura Taddeo, Stacy Person, Joy Piper, and Susan Dow. I am also grateful to the librarians at the Bentley Historical Library at the University of Michigan, the Houghton Library, and the Schlesinger Library at Harvard.

My friendships in Buffalo and beyond have taught me the meaning of Emerson's insight that "[o]ur intellectual and active powers increase with our affection." While completing this book, my dear friend Kate Ross passed away and although I miss her greatly, I know that her beautiful spirit lives on through her family—Bertrand, Rafael, and Anaïs Juillet.

I want to thank my family, especially my parents, Bruce Bramen and Frances Tirado Bramen, as well as my brother, Gary, whose generosity, encouragement, and kindness have found their way into every one of these pages. To my stepmother Karen Bramen in New Orleans and my extended family in California whose support has always been balanced with a healthy dose of perspective. My expatriate English husband, David Schmid, who has been by my side for over a quarter century, will have to indulge my American proclivity for superlatives when I say that he is simply the most brilliant, generous, wisest, funniest, and kindest person I have ever met.

This book is dedicated to my daughters, Lucia and Liliana, whose love, humor, and intelligence continue to enhance my life beyond words. I apologize now for any mixed maternal advice I have given you about feminine niceness, but I do hope that this book's long journey to completion will inspire your own investments in time, whatever they may be.

Buffalo, New York

The opening sections of Chapter 3 were first published in "The Christology of Niceness: Harriet Beecher Stowe, the Jesus Novel, and Sacred Trivialities," in *American Religious Liberalism*, ed. Leigh Schmidt and Sally Promey (Bloomington and Indianapolis: Indiana University Press, 2012), 39–75. Reprinted with minor modifications by permission of Indiana University Press.

Index

9/11, 7–8, 298n17, 298n18, 299n19

Abate, Michelle Ann, 220–221
Abbott, Lyman, 272
Abolitionism, 3, 24, 25, 37, 65,
  67–68, 73–74, 106, 109–110,
  245, 309n76, 323n64; John
  Brown and, 189, 191–192;
  debate on black character and,
  37, 94–95, 98–100, 102, 118,
  120; Indian hospitality and,
  101; limits of persuasion, 191,
  235; representations of
  Southern slaveholders and, 125;
  testimony and, 117–118; *Uncle
  Tom's Cabin* and, 115–116
Acknowledgment, 9, 15, 43, 61,
  188, 298n18, 299n19. *See also*
  Disavowal
Adams, Henry, 202, 329n16
Adams, John, 22, 28
Addams, Jane, 38, 203, 207, 224,
  295; anti-war activism,
  238–239; Hull House and
  "sympathetic knowledge,"
  233–234; William James and,

213, 232–234, 238, 239; "A
  Modern Lear," 238; Pullman
  Strike and, 235–239; slum-
  ming, 235; Harriet Beecher
  Stowe and, 235; Ida B. Wells
  and, 240–241, 242, 249
Adler, Felix, 195
Adorno, Theodor, 17
Advertisements, 104–105, 196,
  329n21; Aunt Jemima Pancake
  Mix and, 147–149; runaway
  slave advertisements, 118–
  122, 131–132, 145, 317n59;
  J. Walter Thompson, 147
Africans: sociability and, 99;
  faciality and, 104, 112; kind-
  ness and, 100, 113
Agamben, Giorgio, 150
Aguinaldo, Emilio, 266
Alcott, Bronson, 221, 230
Alcott, Louisa May, 38, 203,
  206–207, 234, 241–242, 244,
  249, 333n83. Works: *Jo's Boys*,
  231–232; *Little Men*, 229–232;
  Little Women, 221–229,
  230–232; *Moods*, 220–221

349